151
SERMON
OUTLINES

151
SERMON
OUTLINES

JABEZ BURNS

KREGEL PUBLICATIONS
GRAND RAPIDS, MICHIGAN 49501

151 Sermon Outlines by Jabez Burns. Copyright © 1987 by Kregel Publications, a division of Kregel, Inc. All rights reserved.

Library of Congress Cataloging-in-Publication Data

Burns, Jabez, 1805-1876.
  151 Sermon Outlines.

  Selections from The Pulpit Cyclopaedia, and Christian Minister's Companion, published: New York: Appleton, 1845.
  1. Sermons — Outlines, syllabi, etc. I. Title.
II. Title: One hundred fifty-one sermon outlines.
BV4223.B842   1987   251'.02   86-27520
ISBN 0-8254-2266-3

1 2 3 4 5 Printing/Year 91 90 89 88 87

Printed in the United States of America

CONTENTS

Publisher's Preface 7

1. Future Punishments (Luke 12:5) 9
2. The Unavailing Lamentation (Jer. 8:20) . 11
3. The Terror of the Lord, a Ground for
   Ministerial Persuasion (2 Cor. 5:11) 12
4. On Caring for Others (Gen. 4:9) 13
5. The Sabbath (Isa.58:13,14) 15
6. Union of Personal and Family Religion
   (Josh. 24:15)............................ 16
7. Prejudice, and Its Antidote (John 1:46) .. 17
8. Josiah—a Sermon to the Young (2 Chron.
   34:3) 19
9. Instant Decision Urged (Josh. 24:15) 20
10. Evil Company Prohibited (Exod. 23:2) ... 22
11. Against Profanity (Exod. 20:7) 23
12. Liberality and Selfishness Contrasted
    (Prov. 11:24,25) 24
13. The Satisfaction and Advantages of
    Godliness (1 Tim. 6:6) 26
14. An Ungodly Spirit Rebuked (Luke 9:55) . 28
15. On Vain Thoughts (Jer. 4:14) 29
16. The Right Employment of the Tongue
    (Ps. 34:13) 31
17. Spiritual Apathy Denounced (Amos 6:1) . 33
18. Real Sacrilege (Mal. 3:8) 34
19. Instability (Gen. 49:4) 36
20. Superstition (Acts 17:22) 37
21. The Character and Blessedness of the
    Godly (Ps. 1:1,3) 39
22. The Christian's Original State (Eph.
    2:11,12) 40
23. The Difficulties of Salvation (1 Peter
    4:18) 41
24. The Saint's Prosperity, the Delight of
    Jehovah (Ps.35:27) 42
25. The Way and Manner of Access to God
    (Eph. 3:12) 43
26. Constant Rejoicing (Phil. 4:4) 44
27. The Temptation of Peter (Luke 22:31,32) 45
28. The Temptation of Peter (Luke 22:31,32) 46
29. Preservation From the Destroyer (Ps.
    17:4) 48

30. Saints, the Temple of God (2 Cor. 6:16) .. 49
31. David's Regrets and Consolations
    (2 Sam. 23:5) 50
32. The Law of Liberty (James 1:25) 52
33. The Christian's Regard for an Unseen
    Saviour (1 Peter 1:8) 53
34. Earnestness in Religion, Indispensable
    (Matt. 11:12) 54
35. The Work of Religion Perfected By God
    (Ps. 138:8) 56
36. The Believer's Approach to God (Job
    23:3,4) 57
37. Christian Unity Urged (Eph. 4:3) 59
38. Christ's Prayer for the Unity of the
    Church (John 17:21) 60
39. Thankfulness (Col. 3:15) 61
40. Jehovah's Designs With Respect to His
    People (Isa. 43:21) 62
41. Zion's Future Prosperity (Isa. 62:1) 63
42. Joy in Sorrow (2 Cor. 6:10) 65
43. Heaven Upon Earth (Deut. 11:21) 66
44. Presence of God in the Holy Temple
    (Hab. 2:20) 68
45. The Gracious End of Christ's Mission
    Into Our World (Luke 19:10) 69
46. Christ, the Light of the World (John
    8:12) 71
47. Reverence Claimed for Christ (Mark
    12:6) 72
48. God's Call to the Sleeper (Eph. 5:14) 73
49. On Striving With God (Isa. 45:9) 75
50. Refuge of Lies (Isa. 28:17) 76
51. God's Solicitudes for Mankind (Deut.
    5:29) 77
52. Pride and Obstinacy of the Sinner (Ps.
    10:4) 78
53. God's Gracious Invitation to Sinners (Isa.
    1:18) 79
54. Terms of Discipleship (Matt. 16:24) 81
55. Maintenance of the Christian
    Professional (Heb. 10:23) 82
56. Encouragement to the Tempted (1 Cor.
    10:13) 84

6   **CONTENTS**

57. Believers, Strangers, and Sojourners
    (1 Chron. 29:15) 85
58. Renewal of the Inward Man (2 Cor. 4:16) 86
59. Selfishness (Phil. 2:21) 87
60. The Evil of Spiritual Ignorance (Prov.
    19:2) 88
61. Scriptural Instruction of the Young
    (Deut. 6:6-9) 90
62. Knowledge, Obedience, and Felicity
    (John 13:17) 91
63. On Our Own Mind (Job 34.33) 93
64. The Worship of the Heavenly Host (Neh.
    9:6) 94
65. New Year's Counsels to the Godly (Ps.
    37:1-6) 96
66. Christian Establishment (2 Cor. 1:21) . . . 97
67. The Anointing (2 Cor. 1:21) 98
68. Being Sealed (2 Cor. 1:22) 99
69. The Earnest (2 Cor. 1:22) 99
70. Ssriptural Assurance (2 Tim. 1:12) 100
71. How to Treat Offences (Matt. 18:15-18) . . 101
72. Admonition (2 Thess. 3:15) 102
73. The Weak, Others Comforted (Matt.
    12:20) 102
74. Christian Hope Accounted for (1 Peter
    3:15) 103
75. Penitence and Expected Mercy (Jonah 3:9) 104
76. God's Pardoning Mercy Celebrated (Isa.
    12:1) 106
77. Preaching Christ (Col. 1:28) 107
78. The Help of God for His Own Cause,
    Pleaded (Ps. 74:22) 109
79. On a Revival of Religion (Ps. 85:6) 110
80. Jehovah's Gracious Declaration
    Concerning the Wicked (Ezek. 33:11) 112
81. Adam and Eve (Gen. 1:27) 113
82. Faith and Sacrifice of Abel (Heb. 11:4) . . 114
83. Cain (Gen. 4:1) 116
84. God's Testimony Concerning Enoch (Heb.
    11:5) 117
85. The Fear and Faith of Noah (Heb. 11:17) 119
86. Abraham's Believing Pilgrimage (Heb.
    11:8-10) 120
87. Jacob Wrestling With the Angel (Gen.
    32:24,25) 121
88. Pharaoh and Jacob (Gen. 47:8,9) 122
89. Esau (Heb. 12:16,17) 124
90. The Choice of Moses (Heb. 11:24-26) 125
91. The Burning Bush, an Emblem of the
    Church (Exod. 3:2) 127
92. The Mysterious Pillar (Exod. 13:21) 128
93. Manoah and His Wife (Judg. 13:22,23) . . 130
94. Boaz and Ruth (Ruth 2:11,12) 131
95. Elijah's Sinful Flight (1 Kings 19:4) 132
96. Elisha's Enemies and Guard (2 Kings
    6:15-17) 134
97. David's Distress and Consolation (1 Sam.
    30:6) 135
98. David and His Host in the Cave of
    Adullam (1 Sam. 22:2) 137
99. Mephibosheth (2 Sam. 9:3) 138
100. David and His Family (2 Sam. 6:20) 140
101. David's Address to Solomon (1 Chron.
    28:9) 141
102. Jehovah's Dwelling on Earth (1 Kings
    8:27) 143

103. A Recognition of Pious Vows (Ps.
    56:12,13) 145
104. History of Hezekiah (2 Kings 18:6,7) 146
105. History of Hezekiah (2 Kings 20:1-6) 147
106. History of Hezekiah (2 Kings 20:1-6) 149
107. History of Hezekiah (2 Chron. 32:25) 150
108. The Chaff and Wheat Contrasted (Jer.
    23:28) 151
109. Responsibility (Luke 12:48) 152
110. Obedience to God (Acts 5:29) 154
111. Ezekiel's Vision of the Valley of Dry
    Bones (Ezek. 37:1-10) 155
112. The Saviour's Visit to Our World (Luke
    1:68,69) 157
113. An Epitome of the Gospel (1 Tim. 1:15) . . 158
114. John the Baptist (Matt. 11:11) 159
115. John the Baptist (Matt. 11:11) 161
116. The Poor of the Streets and Lanes
    Invited (Luke 14:21) 162
117. The Wedding Garment (Matt. 22:11-13) . . 164
118. The Woman With the Bloody Issue
    (Mark 5:25) 165
119. Martha's Inordinate Carefulness (Luke
    10:40,41) 167
120. Mary's Happy Choice (Luke 10:42) 168
121. The One Thing Needful (Luke 10:42) 169
122. The Call of Matthew (Matt. 9:9) 170
123. The Syro-Phenician Woman (Matt.
    15:21-28) 171
124. Bethesda (John 5:2) 173
125. The Restored Demoniac (Luke 8:38,39) . . 175
126. The Recovered Leper (Matt. 8:2-4) 176
127. Faith, the Antidote to Fear (Mark 5:36) . 177
128. The Centurion and His Servant (Matt.
    8:5-10) 179
129. The Prodigal Son (Luke 15:11) 180
130. The Prodigal Son (Luke 15:11) 182
131. The Prodigal Son (Luke 15:11) 183
132. Christ Exalted by the Multitude (Luke
    19:37-40) 185
133. The Ten Virgins (Matt. 25:1) 186
134. The Ten Virgins (Matt. 25:1) 187
135. The Good Samaritan (Luke 10:36,37) 189
136. The Pharisee and Publican (Luke
    18:10-14) 190
137. The Penitent Malefactor (Luke 23:42,43) . 192
138. Satan's Palace (Luke 11:21,22) 194
139. Vessels of Wrath (Rom. 9:22) 195
140. Vessels of Mercy (Rom. 9:23) 197
141. The Conquering Redeemer (Rev. 6:2) . 198
142. All Things for the Christian's Good
    (Rom. 8:28) 200
143. The Death of the Righteous (Num. 23:10) 202
144. Messiah's Final Triumph (Ezek. 21:27) . . 203
145. The Enemies and Friends of Jehovah
    (Judg. 5:31) 205
146. Perpetuity of Christ's Name and Praise
    (Ps. 45:7) 206
147. The Six Mornings (Isa. 21:12) 209
148. The Gospel Standard (Isa. 62:10) 210
149. Light and Darkness, or the Church and
    the World (Exod. 10:22,23) 212
150. The Christian Ministry (Ezek. 10:14) 214
151. A Ministerial Charge (Col. 4:17) 215

Scripture Text Index 219

PUBLISHER'S PREFACE

As *a* preacher, you must keep in mind the spiritual needs of your congregation. As a *busy* preacher, you do not always have the time that is needed to adequately prepare for the next message. As a *concerned* preacher, you want to have the help that will benefit your church family.

Jabez Burns was one of the most well-known English preachers of the 19th century whose sermon outlines have become standard resources for many preachers. In a day of shallow sermons, the Jabez Burns' *Sermon Outline Series* provides original, spiritual, and meaty outlines for dynamic preaching. The messages are biblically sound and cover a great variety of subjects. The content is timeless, substantial, and satisfying.

These interesting, appealing outlines present both familiar and obscure biblical texts. They are presented to "prime the pump" for preachers; to achieve a more efficient and effective ministry. Preachers and teachers will find their ministries enriched with the use of these sermon starters and seed thoughts.

NOTE TO THE READER

Because of the unfamiliarity of most of us today with the Roman numeral system, used throughout this book for chapter numbers, the following conversion table may offer welcome assistance to many readers:

I	1	XXII	22
II	2	XXIII	23
III	3	XXIV	24
IV	4	XXV	25
V	5	XXVI	26
VI	6	XXVII	27
VII	7	XXVIII	28
VIII	8	XXIX	29
IX	9	XXX	30
X	10	XL	40
XI	11	L	50
XII	12	LX	60
XIII	13	LXX	70
XIV	14	LXXX	80
XV	15	XC	90
XVI	16	C	100
XVII	17	CX	110
XVIII	18	CXX	120
XIX	19	CXXX	130
XX	20	CXL	140
XXI	21	CL	150

151 SERMON OUTLINES

1

FUTURE PUNISHMENTS

" **Fear** him which, after he hath killed, hath **power to cast into hell.**"—LUKE xii. 5.

OUR subject is replete with that which is truly solemn, awful, and momentous ; yet it is one of those topics which evidently come within the proper sphere of ministe rial duty ; it is a part of the counsel of God. The great apostle said, " Knowing the terrors of the Lord, we persuade men." Before entering, however, immediately on the discussion of the subject, a few prefatory observations may be necessary, perhaps essential.

(1.) That the great and blessed God has a right to make laws for the government of his intelligent creatures.

(2.) That these laws may justly be connected with rewards to the obedient, and with punishment to the disobedient.

(3.) That in the present life it is evident men are not punished and rewarded according to their moral character and doings.

(4.) That there must be therefore another world where the guilty will be punished, and the righteous rewarded.

(5.) That if men are not punished or rewarded in a future state, then the administrations of God are not equitable and just.

(6.) That the scriptures, however, do most clearly and fully reveal such rewards and punishments in the world to come.

(7.) That we can know nothing with certainty on this subject. except what is contained in the word of God.

(8.) Then the word of God only must be our guide and oracle on the fearful subject to which your attention is now invited. Our subject embraces two leading points.

I. WHY THERE IS A HELL, &c. But a word or two as to the signification of the term. In scripture, the word does not always mean a state of punishment, but occasionally the grave, and the unseen world, Acts ii. 31 ; but in most passages it distinctly points to a place of future punishment. Let the following suffice :—" The wicked shall be turned into hell,"&c. " And in hell he lifted up," &c. Now there are three reasons why there should be a hell :—

The first respects Deity. He is a holy being ; he cannot behold iniquity with allowance. Is it reasonable that his enemies should dwell in his sight—share his palace — mingle with his holy hosts ? Think of vile, polluted, malevolent spirits, hating God and holiness, and say if it is not necessary that they should have a world to themselves, and dwell in a state of exilation from God.

Our second reason respects holy beings. There are angels—-holy beings—glorified saints. Are these to bear the society of the vile and wicked? If so, the next world, to the righteous, would be vastly worse than this. Now, the godly can retire to their closets, &c.; to the house of God, &c.

Our third reason respects the wicked themselves. Is it not meet and righteous that they should be in a state of restraint, and not allowed to wage eternal war and rebellion against God and his holy government? These reasons will all be illustrated, if we look at our prisons. Who will deny that such places are necessary? Of what avail would be our laws? We say, the honor of the king, and the majesty of his government, require a prison for the lawless and the vile. We say, it is necessary for the safety and welfare of the community at large, or else neither property nor life would be secure. Who would wish to live in society where the most vicious and cruel of mankind range abroad at pleasure? &c. Therefore, that the power of evil may be restrained, the laws regarded, and the rights of the community respected, the prison is necessary. Equally so, and for the same reasons, hell. The honor of Jehovah, the justice of the divine government, the well-being of the righteous, and the restraint of the vile, all demand that there should be a hell. Let us now,

II. CONSIDER THE SCRIPTURAL ACCOUNT OF IT. It is obvious, that some of the descriptions of the Bible are figurative. "Lake of fire." "Lake that burneth with fire and brimstone;" "where the worm dieth not," &c. I know some have contended for the literal existence of the fire and the worm; but we conceive there are insurmountable objections to those opinions. Among the revealed representations of hell, we have,

1. *The nature of the place affirmed.* It is a prison—a place of confinement into which all the rebellious and unholy are to be thrust. As such, it is stated that it was originally intended for the devil and his angels, Matt. xxv. 41. Men, by uniting with the devil in sin, become his companions, and sharers of the hell prepared for him and his angels. This prison is one of darkness—outer darkness—the darkness of death, &c.

2. *The nature of the misery is also revealed.* It is represented as being extreme—absolute—unmitigated; as horrible as the burning of the flesh with fire—yea, with fire and brimstone. It is described as producing weeping, wailing, and gnashing of teeth. It is represented as a state of utter torment, "I am tormented in this flame." Lost spirits are delivered to the tormentors.

3. *The sources of their misery are also revealed.* The misery of hell will arise,

(1.) From the loss of all enjoyment. There will be no peace, no joy, no happiness for the lost. Not one instant's cessation of horror and wo; not one bright interval; not one cheering moment. The wretched in this life are sometimes cheered by the visits and sympathies of friendship; but the lost will never enjoy that—by the intervention of sleep; but the eye of the lost will never be closed in sleep. All sources of enjoyment and happiness will have fled forever, &c.

(2.) From the infliction of the divine wrath; a sense of God's displeasure; his just and righteous indignation, Psalm xi. 6. "Upon the wicked," &c.

(3.) Earnest and unallayed desires. The representation given of hell in the parable of the rich man; he saw Lazarus afar off. It is highly probable that the lost will see the bright and joyous scenes of heaven—hear their songs—behold their triumph—see the oceans of pleasure. Oh! how they will long to enjoy them! But the desire even for a drop of water will be absolutely refused. Then, too, these wicked desires will remain in all their unsubdued force. The miser seeking gold—the sensualist pleasure—the drunkard his cup. But now they have the burning, feverish desires, but no means of realization.

(4.) From remorse of conscience. Sin will now be seen in all its blackness; seen in the light of the flames of perdition. How, then, will the lost curse themselves! Look at Esau, crying with many prayers for his birthright; but he had sold it—it was gone forever. Now the sinner will see the infatuation of his course. To sell the soul, and heaven, and eternal salvation, for the bubbles of time—for a title—for show, pomp, &c.—an hour's mirth, &c. Every recollection will produce remorse—excite horror. Wealth prostituted; health and strength spent in toiling the way to ruin; talents perverted; pious parents and friends;

but now the gulf between. Bible—but it was neglected; sabbaths wiled away, and gospel mercies not improved; conscience drowned, stupified, &c.; Christ and his cross, &c., despised.

(5.) From the companions of their misery. In hell will be all the vile of the universe, hateful and haters of one another. All the black, debased spirits, that ever cursed the world, with all their propensities and crimes. Think upon them; think of being shut up with fifty of the vilest assassins; but here will be all who ever lived and died in sin, besides the devil and his angels, for whom hell was originally prepared.

(6.) From a sense of settled and eternal despair. For the misery of the lost will endure forever; despair of relief will be the bitterest ingredient in their cup. But many dispute the eternity of the future punishment of the lost. Revelation is explicit.

1. The same words were employed to describe both the one and the other—both heaven and hell. "These," says Christ, "shall go away into everlasting," &c. Again, "where the worm dieth not," &c. The smoke of their torment ascendeth forever and ever.

2. We remark, there is no proof that the punishment will in the least purify the wicked; and if they remain eternally unholy, they will eternally be fit only for hell.

3. God's mercy is pleaded; but we never read of any exercise of it towards the lost, or those of any world but this. Besides, have not fallen angels as much hope on this ground as lost sinners?

4. Here we see the necessity of imprisoning some for life—so long as they live in this world; and this is just and wise. Why not so then in Deity, with respect to the next life? The word of God gives no hope for the lost. How, then, must they feel the pressure of eternal despair! an eternal night; an eternal ocean of waves of sorrow; eternal pain and anguish.

APPLICATION

1. *We warn all of you against this hell of misery and endless wo.* Oh! flee from it.

2. *A way of escape is opened in the gospel.* You need not one perish. It is the will of God, your salvation, &c.

3. *Deceive not yourselves by forming false ideas of a future state.* Even exclu-

sion from heaven is enough; or by its duration, a thousand years of agony—even that, sufficient to deter.

4. *Let the Christian rejoice, and bless God, who has delivered him from the wrath to come.*

2

THE UNAVAILING LAMENTATION
"The harvest is past, the summer is ended, and we are not saved."—JEREMIAH viii. 20.

I SHALL not dwell on the literal application of the text to the distressed and despairing condition of the Jews, to whom it refers, but give it a personal and spiritual bearing on the eternal interests of your soul's salvation; and in doing so, shall particularly dwell on the following propositions.

I. THAT GOD HAS GIVEN YOU THE GRACIOUS SEASONS OF SUMMER AND HARVEST.

II. THAT THESE MAY PASS AWAY UNIMPROVED.

III. THAT THE REGRETS OF SUCH WILL BE AWFUL AND OVERWHELMING.

I. THAT GOD HAS GIVEN YOU THE GRACIOUS SEASONS OF SUMMER AND HARVEST. Summer is the season of opportunity for laboring. Harvest, of plenty for gathering; these are the working and gathering seasons God has given you.

1. *The gracious season of summer.*

(1.) The summer of life; preceded by the spring of childhood. We consider the summer of life to begin with that period when we clearly see and discern between good and evil; much earlier in some than others; now this summer is of diversified length; some of you have had ten, twenty, thirty, forty years of this summer season; some have only a very limited and evanescent summer.

(2.) The summer of reason; thus man is distinguished from the brute beast. He is distinguished for reflection; he can survey, take a retrospect, look on the boundless future; he should be wise, &c.

(3.) The summer of opportunities. To gain knowledge—to receive holy impressions,—to prepare for death—to be meet for eternity.

2. *The gracious season of harvest.* Season of abundant blessings.

(1.) Harvest of knowledge; if ignorant,

it is wilful. The light of the gospel shines; the word of God is possessed; the voice of instruction crieth; the means of improvement provided.

(2.) Harvest of privileges. Sabbaths; sermons; means of grace, &c. How these crowd our years, and months, and weeks; scarcely a day when we might not enjoy and benefit by these.

(3.) Harvest of blessings. The tidings of the gospel, the provisions of mercy in Christ, pardon, acceptance, the prayers of the pious; the Holy Spirit; eternal life, &c. But these seasons,

II. MAY PASS AWAY UNIMPROVED. It was so with the antediluvians; with the inhabitants of Jerusalem; with thousands of others; with myriads in our day, around our doors. Was so with many of you for years; it is so now, we fear, with many present; this will be fearfully exhibited at the last day; then they will cry to the rocks and the hills, &c.; but can we account for it?

1. *Many do not think.* "The ox knoweth its owner," &c. His gross, stupid apathy and indifference; eat and drink, and toil, but never consider either their present state, or future destiny.

2. *They will not forsake their sins.* They love to do evil, it has become their habit. They roll the pleasures of sense &c., under their tongues as a sweet morsel; held fast in Satan's bonds; not convicted, not sorry, not anxious.

3. *They will not believe.* Do not hear as they ought; forget, &c. Do not believe the threats, nor the promises; in sin's hatefulness, and hell's terrors; in God's love, and heaven's glories. Unbelief hardens the heart, blinds the eyes.

4. *They will procrastinate.* Defer the most important concerns, year after year, season after season; from youth to maturity; from maturity to old age; old age to death.

III. THE REGRETS OF SUCH WILL BE AWFUL AND OVERWHELMING.

1. *Sometimes their regrets are expressed in this world.* On the bed of languishing, on the approach of death; often heard it; occasionally persons die in a state of apathy, but often awake just to see the precipice, &c.

2. *They will surely be uttered in eternity.* How fearful the contrast, no light, no probation, no blessings, no means, no ray of hope! These regrets will,

(1.) Be the regrets of intense agony "I am tormented," &c. Agony of recollection; agony of seeing heaven in the distance, agony of self-condemnation.

(2.) Regrets will be unavailing; no space for repentance, no ear for prayer, no fountain, no cross, &c.

(3.) Of black despair. The billows of the ocean rolling in all the fearful raging foam of endlessness. No sound heard, but the wailings of fellow kindred spirits damned, &c., and the terrific exclamations, "Who can dwell in endless fire?" "Who can endure everlasting burning?" &c. "The harvest is passed," &c.

APPLICATION

1. None would choose this portion.
2. Who would risk it?
3. Who will flee from it? Now is the summer, now is the harvest, &c. Oh! I would call, and urge, and invite, &c.

3

THE TERROR OF THE LORD, A GROUND FOR MINISTERIAL PERSUASION

"Knowing therefore the terror of the Lord, we persuade men."—2 COR. v. 11.

THE apostle refers, in the verse before the text, to the solemnities of the judgment day, the judgment seat, the judge, the appearance of every man, and the destinies of each and all. What an awful subject! How solemn and momentous! Now the object of the Christian ministry is to impress these scenes on the minds of men, that holy fear may be produced, and a change of life adopted. Hence he says, "Knowing therefore the terror of the Lord," &c. Consider,

I. THE TERRORS OF THE LORD AS REVEALED TO US.

II. THE INFLUENCE THIS PRODUCES ON THE CHRISTIAN MINISTER.

I. THE TERRORS OF THE LORD, &c. Now by the terrors of the Lord we understand the exhibition of the justice of God, in the trial of his probationary creatures at the last day.

1. *The day is spoken of as terrible.* "The great day of his wrath," &c. Doom's-day; the day to which all other days now have reference; the day uniting time and eternity; a day often spoken of in the holy

scriptures; the day of God, that great and terrible day,

2. *The appearance of the Judge will be terrible.* Arrayed in all the infinite grandeur of his perfections, "Behold he cometh," &c. "The Lord Jesus shall be revealed from heaven in flames of fire," &c.

3. *The solemnities of the day are terrible.* The erection of the great white throne, the sound of the trumpet's blast, the opening of the graves, the sea giving up its dead, the heavens wrapped together as a scroll, the earth reeling as a drunken man, the sun black as sackcloth, the moon red as blood, the globe experiencing all the throes of dissolution, time ready to expire, the heavens and the earth passing away. Then the universal convocation. All the generations, and tribes, and individuals of mankind, before the eternal tribunal; the opening of the books, the public declaration of every man's sins, the sentence of eternal death, &c. How fearful will be that awful hour! Then shall they cry to the rocks and to the mountains, &c., shall seek annihilation, &c., but the officers of divine vengeance shall bind them hand and foot, &c.

4. *The terrors of the infliction of wrath which shall endure for ever.* Think of the wondrous devouring fire, everlasting burnings, the abiding tempest, the unending storm, the bottomless pit, whence ascendeth the smoke of the torments of the lost forever and ever. Now these terrors are revealed to us; these are the truths of this book. They are just, the holiness of God demands them, conscience attests this. They are certain, God cannot change, &c. We have had some presages of them in the judgments of God on the old word, Sodom, &c.

II. THE INFLUENCE A KNOWLEDGE OF THE TERRORS OF THE LORD PRODUCES ON THE CHRISTIAN MINISTER. "We persuade men."

1. *To hear what God has spoken.* Hear the word of the Lord.

2. *To consider and reflect on these things.* Is it not wise and reasonable?

3. *To believe the declarations of the divine word.* To receive them as truth.

4. *To prepare for this great and terrible day.* Sin invests that day with all its horrors. Then it must be forgiven, forsaken.

(1.) *The Judge must become our friend.* He desires and seeks this.

(2.) *We must give ourselves to his cause and people, and honor him in the world.*

The saints will not only escape, but be openly justified, confessed, exalted, crowned, and glorified. Oh, then,

1. We would *persuade,* because you are reasonable beings.

2. We persuade *each,* as it is a personal concern.

3. *All,* as there is a way of escape for every one.

4. *Now,* because this is the accepted time, &c.

4

ON CARING FOR OTHERS

" Am I my brother's keeper ?"—GENESIS iv. 9

OUR text was the language of the fratricide of Cain, the first human murderer, the murderer of his brother. God was now holding inquisition for blood. He is in the presence of his Maker and his Judge. A question is proposed as to his knowledge of his brother Abel; to which, in the language of heartlessness, he replies by the interrogatory of the text, " Am I my brother's keeper ?" Who can read it without being shocked at the monstrous indifference it evinced ? You all stand aghast from such selfish isolation, and Cain is condemned in the court of your consciences. But if Cain was wrong, he was so in principle as well as in expression ; and if Cain was wrong, so are all who possess the same spirit, though not extended to the same degree of indifference. We affirm, that every man is bound to feel and care for his fellowman ; and to a certain extent, every man is his brother's keeper. We will consider,

I. SOME CASES WHERE IT IS INVARIABLY CONCEDED THAT WE OUGHT TO CARE AND FEEL FOR OTHERS. Now this is admitted,

1. *In reference to parents and children.* How weak, helpless, and dependent, are children! Uncared for, they must perish. A mother's love and attention to her infant child, ever form a subject for the illustration of the tenderest passions of the heart. A father is expected to toil for their subsistence ; to pity, to protect, to watch over, &c. And Christianity demands, that parents should train them up in God's fear, labor for their spiritual welfare.

2. *In reference to relatives and friends.* Brethren and sisters are supposed, by their identity of interests, to feel and care for each other. Hence, a brother's neglect

and indifference are justly branded as unnatural. So also when persons are bound in the bonds of mutual regard, connected with the true spirit of friendship. How Jonathan cared for David, &c.

3. *In reference to pastors and flocks.* Here especial affection and regard are properly expected; here love and diligent care are to be evinced. As the shepherd cares for and watches his flock, so the Christian shepherd is to care and watch for souls. How was this exhibited in Paul! how faithful, how tender, how devoted! and this is to be reciprocated. " Brethren, pray for us." " May the Lord have mercy on the house of Onesiphorus," &c. Now these are instances universally allowed. Let us now consider,

II. THE LEGITIMATE EXTENT TO WHICH THIS PRINCIPLE SHOULD BE CARRIED.

1. *Should we not care for our neighbors?* Those at our doors; where we are located together. " Thou shalt love thy neighbor," &c. In this way all who compose our families, servants, &c., who work in our shops, &c., those whom we see daily.

2. *Should we not care for our country?* Love of country, or patriotism, has ever been held a distinguished virtue. Desire its freedom, its prosperity, its intellectual elevation, its moral well-being: our fatherland, the country of our ancestors, of our birth, &c.

3. *Should we not care for the suffering?* The poor, fatherless, orphans, widows, the afflicted, &c. We do violence to our nature if we do not compassionate these; humanity demands it. I advance one step beyond.

4. *I ask, should we not care for the world?* This is philanthropy; love to our species everywhere, and a desire to bless our race. All other limits are too contracted; the true circle of goodness is the world; every man of every clime, &c., especially those needing my compassion, requiring my help. If such a one dwell in the sterile frigid regions of Greenland, or in the burning torrid zone, if he cry for my help, I must not ask, " Am I my brother's keeper?" I am bound to care for his bodily weal, I am bound to care for his mental state, for his condition as a man, and a citizen of the world ; as an immortal being, accountable with myself to God, &c. My care must be affectionate, sincere, self-denying, &c.

Indifference is criminality, neglect is sin, &c. I notice,

III. THE GRAND CONSIDERATIONS WHICH SHOULD LEAD TO THIS AFFECTIONATE REGARD.

1. *The oneness of our nature.* " God hath made of one blood," &c. ; no alien blood, no captive blood, no ignoble blood, &c. I see in Adam and Eve the original parents of us all ; I see an identity enlinking the whole together ; I assail my own nature if I inquire, " Am I my brother's keeper ?"

2. *We are all dependent on the same Providence.* Whatever is the color, the station, or the class, all hang on God's beneficent care ; he gave being to the whole, cares for the whole, gives his sun to shine, &c., his air, his rain, his benefits, &c. Oh yes! in one grand sense they may all kneel and say, " Our Father !"

3. *We are exposed to the same perils.* Perils of adversity, perils of sickness, perils of bereavements, perils of sin, perils of Satan, perils of death ; all equally sojourners in the world, all mariners on life's stormy sea, all hastening to the same home of dust, all destined to the same solemn, boundless eternity. I trample on these ties if I inquire, " Am I my brother's," &c.

4. *We are interested in one common redemption.* I delight in that truth of the gospel, " God so loved the world," &c. " He is the propitiation," &c. I would not monopolize the light, the air, the stream, but much less the Redeemer's grace ; " Christ by the grace of God," &c. Then by that one precious Saviour, that one great sacrifice, one universal gospel, I cannot disregard one immortal spirit of any country or condition ; I insult my Saviour, I trample on the gospel, if I inquire, " Am I my brother's keeper ?"

5. *We shall stand before one final tribunal at the last day.*

APPLICATION

Our text should lead us,

1. *To lay the axe at the root of selfishness,—self-ease,—self-care.*

2. *Let the spirit we have recommended be universally cherished, and we hasten on the jubilee of the world.*

3. *By this we test our true character.*

5
THE SABBATH

" If thou turn away thy foot from the sabbath, from doing thy pleasure on my holy day : and call the sabbath a delight, the holy of the Lord, honorable ; and shalt honor him, not doing thine own ways, nor finding thine own pleasure, nor speaking thine own words : then shalt thou delight thyself in the Lord ; and I will cause thee to ride upon the high places of the earth, and feed thee with the heritage of Jacob thy father ; for the mouth of the Lord hath spoken it."—ISAIAH lviii. 13, 14.

THE subject of the sanctification of the sabbath has, of late, extensively engaged the attention of the disciples of Christ. Many persons have professed to doubt the divine obligation of Christians to it ; they say, it was only binding upon the Jews under an inferior dispensation. Now to this subject let us direct our attention for a few moments. The sabbath was instituted during man's innocency in Eden ; afterwards it was placed in the moral code of the ten commandments ; it was associated with the most blessed promises, and its violation with the most terrible threatenings. Its repeal is never hinted at. It is said expressly, "The sabbath was made for man." Not for the Jew or the Gentile, but for the species, for all mankind, even to the end of the world. Now Christ being Lord of all, was Lord of the sabbath. It is clear, that after his resurrection he assembled with his disciples on the first day of the week, and it is absolutely certain, that the apostles and primitive Christians did the same, and have done so through every age to the present time. We fear, then, that all disputes on this subject have arisen more from the heart than the head ; and, on the ground of the divine word, we call upon all who love the Lord Jesus Christ, to remember his sabbath, to keep it holy. Listen, then, to the beautiful statements of the evangelical prophet. Observe,

I. THE THINGS WHICH THE TEXT PROHIBITS. We are,

1. *Not to do our own ways.* That is, not to attend to our own lawful concerns ; not to buy or to sell ; not to work or employ others, except in case of evident necessity and mercy, see Exod. xx. 8, &c. How criminal are those masters and mistresses who forget the spiritual concerns of their servants on this day !

2. *We are not to seek our own pleasure.* It is not to be a day of worldly recreation ; amusements, innocent on other days, are criminal on this : all pleasure-trips, and journeys, and parties, are equally unlawful ; so also all reading of a mere entertaining description.

3. *We are not to engage in worldly conversation,*—" Nor speaking," &c. ; foolish jestings are never seasonable, but conversation about trade, and commerce, and science ; conversation about news, politics, &c., are all unprofitable and improper on this day. We see then the extent of the prohibition ; it includes actions, feelings, and conversation. Observe,

II. WHAT IS ENJOINED.

1. *We are to call the sabbath a delight.* To look upon it as such ; to reckon it not a toil, and not so much a duty and a load as a delight, a privilege, a blessing. Now if we feel and call it so,

(1.) We shall *hail* its approach.

" Welcome, sweet day of rest
That saw the Lord arise,
Welcome to this reviving breast
And these rejoicing eyes."

(2.) We shall *enjoy its exercises ;* we shall feel it to be a day of freedom, of holy pleasure, and enjoyment.

(3.) We shall *reflect* upon it with delight ; recall its scenes, revive its events meditate upon its services, &c.

2. *We must esteem it the holy of the Lord.* The Lord's day ; his holy or sacred day ; hence we shall labor to spend it in a *holy manner,* not negatively, merely avoiding sin, but earnestly seeking holy *influences* and blessings. The reading will be holy, conversation, meditation, songs, praying, &c. Thus we shall labor to keep the sabbath day.

3. *We must call it honorable.* The day God has honored, Christ has honored, saints of old, apostles, and confessors ; and the day the great church of Christ honors : the soul's chief day, day for spiritual things, the sabbath, which is typical of the heavenly rest. God honors it with special promises, &c. Now, if we honor it, it will not be the shortest day ; it cannot be spent in trifling ; we shall give it fully to God and divine things ; we shall labor to exalt God and to extend his glory ; to imitate God, and do good to our fellow-men.

III. THE MOTIVES BY WHICH IT IS ENFORCED. We shall have,

1. *The enjoyment of God.* God will give us real satisfaction and abiding delight ; God will be the portion of the soul, the joy, and the life of the soul. Now is it pos-

sible for the soul to enjoy God without we honor his sabbath? &c.   Think of the smile of God, and the light of his countenance.

2. *God will greatly dignify and exalt us.* "I will cause thee to ride," &c., see chap. xxxiii. 18 ; Deut. xxxii. 13, " Him that honoreth," &c.

3. *He will give us a rich and satisfying portion.* "Feed thee," &c., with all the blessings of the covenant.   Now this is included in one promise, " I will be thy God." All will follow this ; this includes both temporal and spiritual blessings ; all for time and eternity.   All this is ratified by the solemn word of the unchangeable Jehovah, who hath spoken it.

APPLICATION

1. Let me press this subject upon the solemn attention of the professors of religion ; they must make a stand against sabbath profanation ; their principles require it, their comfort and usefulness.   Be careful in small matters, consider all connected with you ; think of the glory of the Saviour, the purity of the church ; think of the holy sabbath.

2. Let me entreat sabbath profaners to turn to God ; you must displease God, you must be under condemnation, you cannot enjoy religion, you cannot be fit for heaven, your bodies will fare better, your minds, your souls, &c.

3. Let us all improve our sabbaths as they pass along ; every one bears its report to the Judge of all ; every one will do us good, or render our account more awful. Thousands are now having their last one. " Oh that they were wise," &c.

6

UNION OF PERSONAL AND FAMILY RELIGION

" But as for me and my house, we will serve the Lord."—JOSHUA xxiv. 15.

How striking the scenes to which this portion of the word of God introduces us. Joshua, the faithful servant of God, who had been the unswerving professor and worshipper of Jehovah during a protracted life, and now mellowed by holy influences, ready for the enjoyment of the blissful reward, ere he gives up his office, and lays down his life, assembles the Israelitish tribes at Shechem, reiterates the goodness of God to them as a people, and urges upon them, in a most earnest manner, the fear and service of the Lord.   He appeals to their judgments in this matter, and reminds them that God's service must be voluntary, exhorting them to choose whom they would serve.   He then appeals to his own resolution, whatever course others might adopt ; he says, " As for me, and my house, we will serve the Lord."   We observe,

I.   THAT TRUE RELIGION CONSISTS IN SERVING THE LORD.   This service implies,

1. *A knowledge of his character and will.* This must precede every other department of God's service.   To know God, as revealed in his word ; to know his will concerning his creatures.

2. *A right state of heart towards God.* This is not natural to man.   Men are at enmity with God—do not love or approve of God—therefore are not disposed to serve him.   An entire change of heart is essential ; the carnal principle must be slain ; a spirit of love and delight imparted ; this takes place in regeneration.

⋅ 3. *A constant waiting upon God.*   To learn his mind ; to know his designs concerning us ; to hear his commands ; to be counselled by him.

4. *Sincere obedience to God's authority.* Keeping his statutes from the heart, and walking in his ordinances, &c., to do them. Having his law in our heart, and exemplifying it in our conversation and life.   Thus we must personally serve God.

II.   THAT PERSONAL RELIGION MUST FORM THE BASIS OF THE RELATIVE SERVICE OF GOD.

1. *This alone will enable persons rightly to understand relative religion.*   How can they instruct, direct, counsel their families, unless they know and serve God themselves ?   Besides, example is equally essential with religious authority and precept.

2. *This alone will ensure the divine approbation.*   God will not be pleased with mere forms of piety, or the externals of worship.   There must be the entire consecration of the heart to the Lord.   God will bestow his blessing, and cause his smile to rest, where there is the true exemplification of his Holy Spirit and word.

III.   THAT RELATIVE RELIGION SHOULD EVER ACCOMPANY THE PERSONAL ENJOYMENT OF IT.   Here all religious heads of families should feel, and resolve, and act as Joshua.

1. *Where there is true personal piety, there will be the faithful discharge of relative duties.* There will be an eye towards God's authority in all the stations we occupy, whether conjugal, parental, fraternal, or filial. Piety will show itself in the adornments of all the relative spheres in which Providence may place us.

2. *Where there is personal piety, there will be a deep solicitude for the spiritual welfare of our families.* How can it be otherwise? Shall we not value their souls, and hence seek their spiritual well-being? We shall not only desire their present temporal happiness, but their present eternal salvation. Our love is singularly defective if it does not include this.

3. *Where there is personal piety, there will be the means of family religion.* The word of God will be read—family prayer presented—family praises offered—and a family standard of piety maintained.

4. *Where there is personal piety, there will be earnest efforts made to promote family religion.* Family worship, &c., will be followed; serious counsel—affectionate entreaty—scriptural discipline—and fervent private prayer. We shall labor to enlighten the mind, to incite desires after holiness, and thus win them to Christ.

IV. THAT FAMILY RELIGION MAY BE URGED BY A VARIETY OF SOLEMN CONSIDERATIONS.

1. *From the family idolatry of pagans.* If there is family idolatry, surely there should be family religion.

2. *From the family wickedness of sinners.* Families unite to sin against God—to live in vanity—in religious negligence—in dissipation—in worldliness—and sometimes in avowed skepticism. How, then, should Christian families be devoted to the service of God, and the interests of religion.

3. *From the influence of families on churches.* All the active members of Christian churches are mortal. The fathers are going the way of all flesh. Where shall we look but to the families of Christians for the pastors, and teachers, and deacons of the next generation?

4. *From the happy family influence religion exerts.* It irradiates—humanizes; produces peace, comfort, and holy harmony. It is a type of the heavenly state.

APPLICATION

1. *This subject is especially adapted to Christian heads of families.* To you it particularly belongs. Sincerely consider it, and examine yourselves by it.

2. *In the families of the wicked abideth the displeasure of God.* Let such be warned, &c.

7

PREJUDICE, AND ITS ANTIDOTE

" And Nathanael said unto him, Can any good thing come out of Nazareth? Philip saith unto him, Come and see."—JOHN i. 46.

OUR text contains an interrogation and an answer. Both the question and the reply were from good men. Nathanael, a stern, devotional Jew—Philip, a sincere disciple of Jesus Christ. But Nathanael was under the influence of a very common, yet pernicious evil; he was the victim of prejudice. Philip, full of love and joy in having found Christ and meeting with Nathanael, exclaimed, " We have found him of whom," &c., verse 45. Now, when Nazareth was mentioned, Nathanael said, " Can there any good thing come out of Nazareth?" If it had been Rome, or especially Jerusalem, without examination the tidings would have been hailed; but a small, insignificant place like Nazareth, brought out the latent weakness of Nathanael, and hence the exclamation of the text. Philip treated the prejudice of Nathanael most properly. He invited investigation, " Come and see." Our subject, therefore, is prejudice, and its antidote. Let us notice,

I. SOME OF THE PREJUDICES MEN FORM IN RESPECT OF RELIGION. And consider,

II. CANDID INVESTIGATION AS THE ONLY ANTIDOTE.

I. SOME OF THE PREJUDICES MEN FORM AGAINST RELIGION. Prejudice is prejudging, or concluding on any subject, without previous examination. In looking at some instances of its manifestation, we may notice,

1. *The prejudices of skeptical minds against the Christian religion.* In many instances disbelief arises from depravity of heart; but there may be doubts entertained by men who may honestly seek the truth. These doubts respect,

(1.) The necessity of revealed religion.

They say reason is sufficient, as enlightened and guided by the works of nature ; but if so, why have not some of the most profound students of nature found out the Supreme Good, and the way of holiness ? If 4000 years had passed over before the dawn of Christianity, had not the world been fairly tried ? Plato and Socrates had propounded their schemes of philosophy five hundred years before Christ ; Seneca was cotemporary with Christ ; Solon, the illustrious Grecian sage, lived nearly six hundred years before Christ ; these had all exerted their talents and influence, and, so far as morals, and purity, and goodness are concerned, in vain. The great themes of religion are guessed at ; they were wandering to seek abodes of pleasure with feeble tapers, surrounded by palpable darkness. Their glimmering rays of reason only made the darkness more visible, and confusion more confounded.

(2.) The prejudices of skeptics also regard the mysteries of revelation. They find heights they cannot reach—depths they cannot fathom — comprehensive subjects they cannot grasp, and hence they reject revelation ; but is it otherwise with nature ? Look at *that* volume. The geologist knows a little—the astronomer a little—the chemist a little—the mineralogist a little—and the zoologist ; but what do they all know together ? Why, scarcely the first elements. Even their most profound professors will confess this. Why, therefore, is it strange that the great and marvellous should extend to the Bible ? If it had been otherwise, they would have said, it cannot be God's book ; it is not great, and grand, and sublime enough. But it is with the Bible as with nature ; light—air—bread—water—all abound, all are accessible ; so the privileges and blessings of Christianity are all clear and simple, so that " a wayfaring man, though a fool, may not err therein."

(3.) The prejudices of skeptics have extended also to the enjoyments of experimental religion. They consider Christian experience as fanaticism, the result of a diseased or fanciful imagination ; they treat it as monomania, and generally connect it with mental imbecility. Surely this is quite prejudging the case. A little reflection would cause them to reason thus : The number of those who experience the joys of religion is very great ; myriads of testimonies ; the various classes of persons ; rich and poor—wise and ignorant—learned and illiterate ; persons of all ages and countries ; persons who had no object to serve, &c. ; persons for many years together ; persons in the article of death, &c.

2. *Let us advert to the prejudices of the formal against spiritual religion.* Many admire religion, as far as attending church and chapel ; a form ; going through the routine of duties and ceremonies ; but all else they call cant, fanaticism, or hypocrisy. Now surely religion, if real, must be internal. Should it not be ardent and sincere ? should it not be precise, and strikingly rigid ?

3. *There are the prejudices of one class and section of Christians against others.* Many are so prejudiced that they see nothing excellent out of the pale of their own sect. Roman Catholics unchristianize all Protestants ; the English church does the same with all Dissenters ; Dissenters often do the same with one another. This spirit has produced intolerance, envy, hatred, persecution, and death. The inquisition, the star chamber, the ecclesiastical courts, are all the offspring of this prejudice. Why can we not distinguish between men and opinions ? Who can doubt the piety of such men as Fenelon, Massillon, and thousands of others of the papal community ? The most rigid dissenter must think of such men as Bishop Hall, and Archbishop Leighton, and Tillotson, and Barrow, and many others, with delight. Where is there a sect but has had its ornaments, and noble, and pious-minded advocates and friends ? We should hate error—have fixed principles—hold fast every grace of truth—but yield to all and every sect credit for the excellencies they may embody, or the truths they may hold. Can we at all account for the existence of prejudice ? It is not always a low, illiterate thing. We find it beneath crowns, and in communion with mitres, and learning, and talents, and even piety. We may, notwithstanding, attribute prejudice,

(1.) *Often to ignorance.* That is, of the subject, person, or thing in question.

(2.) *To education.* Taught certain principles ; imbued with certain predilections.

(3.) *To pride.* We esteem ourselves, and our opinions, more highly than others.

(4.) *To the influence of our reading, and friends.* Consult only, or at least generally, authors and friends who are of our views, &c.

(5.) *To indolent rashness.* Want of diligent examination; precipitancy in decision. Notice some of the evils of prejudice :

1. It is a mental and moral evil.
2. It is an injury to our fellow-creatures.
3. It is an impediment to improvement.
4. It is grievous to God. We ask,

II. WHAT IS THE GREAT REMEDY FOR PREJUDICES AGAINST RELIGION ? " Philip said, Come and see." Investigate for yourselves ; judge from minute observation. Sometimes there is only one step from prejudice to credulity, i. e. from one evil to another. We remark,

1. *That a fair and candid examination of the scriptures, in most cases will produce conviction as to their divinity.* Sir W. Jones, Lord Lyttleton, Soame Jennings, Hon. Robert Boyle, and hundreds of others, have thus emerged from infidel darkness into the light of gospel day.

2. *A candid examination of the subject of the supreme importance of religion, will lead to the conviction of the great necessity for spiritual and internal piety.*

3. *A candid examination into the excellencies and good of other sects, will lead to the abandonment of sectarian bigotry and hatred.* We shall exercise forbearance—admire the good, &c. We say to all who ask, " Can any good ?" &c. " Come and see"—Nazareth, and its great prophet—yea more, &c. See him in the synagogue ; see him going forth to work miracles of mercy, &c. Observe him establishing the new dispensation of grace and salvation ; opening the gates of paradise to an exiled world ; breaking down all national and sectarian barriers ; inviting all to be happy ; dying to redeem every soul of man. Behold him, despisers ! Behold him, ye bigoted Jews ! Behold him, ye Gentiles ! Sit a his feet ; drink the streams of knowledge ; obey his commands ; be imbued with his spirit ; and then reply to the question, " Can any good ?" &c.

8

JOSIAH—A SERMON TO THE YOUNG

" For in the eighth year of his reign, while he was yet young, he began to seek after the God of David his father."—2 CHRON. xxxiv. 3.

It is very profitable to listen to wise proverbs and maxims ; to hear the counsels of the wise and good ; and it should be the study of the young to grow in knowledge and wisdom ; but it is still more instructive to observe the personal excellencies of those around us. To see the precepts of the wise, speaking and living in the conduct of the good and pious. Now to this our text calls the attention of the young people present. It refers to Josiah, one of the kings of Judah, and relates, not what he said, but what he did, and what is worthy of your attention and imitation. " While he was yet young," &c. Observe,

I. THE BLESSED BEING REFERRED TO. " The God of David." David was not Josiah's immediate father, but was his predecessor, just as Abraham was the father or predecessor of the Jewish nation. Three hundred and seventy-four years intervened between the death of David and the reign of Josiah ; but there are several things worthy of notice in this appellation. " The God of David."

1. *The God who so distinguished and exalted David.* Who found him a ruddy youthful shepherd, and gave him courage and might to slay the vaunting Goliath—who led him through the perils of Saul's court, up to the throne of Israel. Surely promotion cometh neither from the east nor the west, but from the Lord.

2. *The God who was David's portion and joy.* God loved David, and proclaimed him a man after his own heart, and how David exulted and delighted to commune with him and to bless him, of whom he exclaimed, " Whom have I in heaven but thee," &c. "O Lord, thou art my God !" &c.

3. *The God whom David served and celebrated.* He delighted in his law, walked in his statutes, loved his commandments, both privately and publicly sought to exalt God. Died in the enjoyment of the divine favor, &c. The true God of Israel was David's God, and this God was the object of Josiah's pious solicitude.

II. THE COURSE JOSIAH ADOPTED. He sought God. It is said, " he began to seek after God." Now, this supposes,

1. *That he felt his need of God.* Men naturally live without God, disregard him, neglect his laws, &c. Far from him by wicked works ; what is worse, most are satisfied with this, do not seek after God.

But Josiah felt his need of God, doubtless felt his sin, his misery, his helplessness without God. Man was not only formed by God, but for him. He is the centre of felicity and blessedness.

2. *That his soul desired God.* As his portion, Saviour, and friend. However rich, we are poor without God. However imaginarily excellent, yet miserable. However surrounded by acquaintance, yet friendless. Now these desires are likened to the feelings of hunger and thirst, like the desire of the tempest-tost mariner for the light of the morning.

3. *That he employed suitable means to find God.* By perusing God's word, for here God is to be found. By worshipping with his people, for here God has engaged to be present. By fervent secret prayer, for to such the Lord is graciously near. Whosoever shall call upon the name of the Lord, &c. Now, doubtless Josiah sought God,

(1.) Earnestly, with all his heart. The promise is to such.

(2.) Humbly, prostrated before God. In sackcloth and ashes.

(3.) With perseverance, urging his suit, pressing his plea, &c.

(4.) Through the promised Messiah. For the pious Jews had reference to the predicted Saviour in their worship and services; now just so must you seek God if you desire sincerely to find him.

4. *Josiah found God, obtained his favor, and lived in his service.* He was successful, he obtained mercy, God loved him, and he loved God. He reformed the manners of the people; put down idolatry, &c., ver. 3 to 7. So that his religion was personal, sincere, and public; it was real, practical, manifest. Now I would,

III. PRESS THE EXAMPLE OF JOSIAH UPON YOUR IMMEDIATE IMITATION. Now, my dear young friends, is it not worth your while to do as Josiah did? Do you not admire his character and conduct? But perhaps you say,

1. *That you are too young.* Not to know good from evil—not to be wise and happy—not to die and be lost forever; besides, Josiah was only sixteen years of age. A time the most critical, often thoughtless. Thousands have begun to serve God as early as your age. Or you object,

2. *My parents are irreligious.* Their example must be bad, &c. Much to be regretted, &c. But Josiah's father was one of the worst of men, read chap. xxxiii. 21, &c. Religion is a personal thing. Or you say,

3. *I am unfavorably situated for religion.* The family, or shop, &c., quite irreligious, they would laugh or jeer, &c. But think of Josiah's difficulties; a complete idolatrous nation, yet he faced the whole, and was religious and good when the multitude were vile; but you say he was a king, then the greater danger, and more were the snares and temptations; or probably you object,

4. *I fear I should not hold out.* With that you have nothing at present to do. You must first begin; but Josiah held out, see chap. xxxvi. 25. God is sufficient for your preservation, &c. He has engaged to keep and sustain you. Thousands began early and held out. John Wesley, Dr. Watts, Whitfield, Doddridge, Matthew Henry, &c., &c. Myriads more. It is more likely that you will hold out if you do begin early. Habits of piety formed, &c. God honored, &c. Now in conclusion, let me urge your immediate seeking of the Lord.

1. *On the ground of your dignity.* It will adorn, be a crown of glory, &c. Elevate the mind, &c. May exalt you even in this life. On the ground,

2. *Of your happiness.* "Her ways are ways of pleasantness," &c. "Happy art thou, O Israel."

3. *On the ground of safety.* Then all will be right. Prepared for all events, ready for life or death.

4. *The miseries avoided.* Sin disgraces, often destroys health, &c. Makes bitter work for after repentance. Urge, exhort, direct.

9

INSTANT DECISION URGED

"Choose you this day whom ye will serve."— JOSHUA xxiv. 15.

JOSHUA was an eminent Old Testament saint, the devoted coadjutor of Moses, and afterwards his faithful successor. He survived Moses twenty-four years; but now his course is finished; he has lived a hundred and ten years; he is ripe for the heavenly garner; he has only to deliver his last dying counsel and then enter upon his reward. He calls for an interesting assembly, verse 1. He recapitulates the events of their history,—he urges personal piety,—avers his own resolution,—refers the matter to their free determination, and calls for their decision. How interesting! How affecting must have been the scene! Let us make it our own, it equally belongs to us. The text clearly contains the following propositions.

I. That true religion consists in serving God.

II. That man is responsible for that service.

III. That God demands decision as to this service. And,

IV. That to-day is the best season for concluding on this service.

I. That true religion consists in serving the Lord. We do not by this exclude knowledge, conviction, repentance, faith, &c., but these have essentially to do with our entrance on the divine service. Thus David exhorted Solomon to serve him with a perfect heart, &c. "This is the whole duty of man, to fear God and keep his commandments." Paul says, "I serve God with my spirit in the gospel of his Son." "The blood of Christ shall purge your conscience from dead works to serve the living God." "Let us have grace, whereby we may serve God," &c. "I beseech you, brethren," &c. Now this service includes,

1. *The worship of God.* To bless—adore—praise and extol the Lord. To give him homage, reverence, and thanksgiving.

2. *It includes obedience to his ordinances.* "To walk in his ordinances to do them." To regard with serious attention all the institutions of the gospel. Thus the first church continued steadfast in the apostles' doctrine, &c. It includes,

3. *Practical regard for his moral laws.* These respect God, mankind, and ourselves. To love him, &c. Our neighbor, &c. To devote our souls and spirits to glorify him. The exercise of faith—patience—humility, and self-denial, is of course a portion of the divine service. His word contains the rules by which our conduct, words, and spirit, are to be ordered. The poet sings,

> " Teach me to walk in thy commands,
> 'Tis a delightful road ;
> Nor let my head, nor heart, nor hands,
> Offend against my God."

II. Man is responsible for this service. God never coerces men into it. Will not have the service of constraint. The material part of the universe obey him of necessity. He gives them laws, &c. But man is rational, intelligent, and free. God will only have the cheerful service of the heart. What more clear than the text? "Choose ye." Here are two courses—two ways—God and idols, &c. ; God and sin ; God and the world ; God and self ; God and Satan. God calls on man to decide and act. Now man surely can do this ; if not, he is not free ; if not, he is not responsible. Let us ascertain this from other portions of scripture. See the case of Cain, Gen. iv. 7. Moses and the Israelites, Deut. xxx. 19. So to the Jews, God said, " Turn ye, turn ye," &c. So Christ invited and exhorted, and said, " Ye will not come," &c. " O that thou in this thy day," &c. These passages clearly urge this doctrine on our consciences. If you say that though you may determine yet you have not power to act, forget not that God will give his Spirit to them who ask him, and that if you seek, and knock, and ask, the promises of grace and mercy are full, explicit, and direct. Reject this doctrine, and you are compelled to admit that of fatal necessity, which turns all men into mere machines, and takes the possibility both of virtue and vice out of the world. But every one of us must give an account of himself to God. This responsibility,

1. *Is personal.* For ourselves only. We cannot be so for any other absolutely ; yet there is relative responsibility ; as to the duties of life, &c.

2. *It is universal.* All persons of sane mind ; young and old—rich and poor—every soul now present before God. We remark,

III. God demands decision as to this service. "Choose ye." To decide,

1. *Is our duty.* God calls us to it. He demands it. He will not allow compromise.

2. *This decision is possible.* Not out of your power. Not impossible.

3. *This decision always precedes a religious course.* This is the turning point. Look at the prodigal, " I will arise," &c. Look at Saul, " Lord, what wilt thou have me to do ?" The three thousand on the day of Pentecost. So in all who are converted.

IV. To-day is the best season for

CONCLUDING AS TO THIS SERVICE. "This day."

1. *This day is given us by God for this purpose.* He says, "Now is the accepted time," &c. "To-day," &c.

2. *No other period so adapted.* Distance is widening,—impediments increasing,—difficulties growing,—opportunities wasting. Now God invites—heaven smiles—Jesus beseeches—ministers entreat—the Spirit waits and hovers over your souls—angels attend, &c.

3. *This may probably be the only season.* How many have been ruined by to-morrow! An hour's delay has sometimes brought destruction. "Choose ye this day," &c. O yes, *this* day.

APPLICATION

1. *Who will respond to the text?* See verse 16, 21. Do you say so? In your hearts—earnestly—humbly—prayerfully?

2. *What will you do if you refuse?* What service? What master? What reward?

10

EVIL COMPANY PROHIBITED

"Thou shalt not follow a multitude to do evil."
—EXODUS xxiii. 2.

NOTHING is more evident than that evil is in the world—moral evil—sin. How it originated in the universe is a matter which has greatly perplexed the wisest of mankind. It is one of the secret things, &c. How it was introduced into this world is specifically detailed; the agent—the temptation—the disastrous effects are all very minutely related. Evil is not only in the world, but has spread over its entire surface, and polluted all its inhabitants. To guard us against one of the most fatal sources of its pestiferous effects is the design of the important counsel of our text, "Thou shalt not," &c. Observe,

I. WE HAVE A FEARFUL TRUTH IMPLIED. "The multitude do evil;" that is, the great majority of mankind live in the practice of evil—are transgressing the laws of the Most High God.

1. *Let us substantiate this.* Sacred history attests it, see the condemnation of the old world, Genesis vi. 5 and 6. Only eight persons living in the fear and service of God. Afterwards the nations of the earth walked in the vanity of their darkened minds. Only the Jews had the knowledge and worship of the true God; of them the majority were Israelites only in name. How fearful the state of the world at the advent of the Saviour—the true religion corrupted, and the world lying in the hands of the wicked one. This darkness was partially removed during the first centuries of the Christian era; but afterwards even the Christian system became corrupted, aggrandized with worldly pomp, and then sunk extensively into forms and ceremonies. How melancholy the state of the world at the reformation! How extensively it is so yet; the multitude of nations are yet pagans, and Mahommedans, or savage. Multitudes of persons even of Christian countries are unconverted. The multitude even of our congregations are yet strangers to spiritual religion. Multitudes of all ranks and degrees, of the rich and of the poor, of the learned, of the illiterate, of the young, and of the aged.

2. *Let us account for it.* We do this by referring,

(1.) To the indwelling of evil in the human mind. This is its natural state; to this it is prone; here its feelings, and desires, and actions, are at home. The fountain being corrupt, the streams are necessarily so. The tree being bad, the fruit is such. The soul being depraved, the life is naturally wicked.

(2.) We account for it on the ground of Satanic influence. Men by nature are under his power—his vassals; his influence is exerted therefore within them; he leads them in the way of evil.

(3.) On the ground of human example; children, so soon as they can think or act, have evil placed before them—often neglected—brought up in ignorance and sin.

(4.) On the ground of the sacrifices religion demands; strait is the gate, narrow the way. There is the yoke of obedience, the cross of self-denial, the life of mortification, the crucifying of the flesh—all must be left if Christ be followed.

II. WE HAVE A LAMENTABLE TRUTH SUPPOSED. That men are liable to be influenced by the multitude. This, in some measure, arises from the constitution of human nature. In some persons this tendency is very powerful.

1. *Persons generally act by impulse rather than judgment*—and thus follow the multitude to do evil.

2. *Most persons look up to others*, and are influenced by their actions. The rich are thus, &c., by the poor ; the learned by the ignorant ; servants observe and imitate their masters and mistresses ; children their parents, &c. Friends one another.

3. *To forsake the multitude requires moral resolution and fortitude.* Men are not willing to risk the approbation of those around. Thus it has ever been that men are greatly influenced in their conduct by the multitude. When the people cried Hosanna, the multitude united, and when the priests said, Crucify him, the people cried, " Away with him, his blood be upon us," &c.

III. WE HAVE IMPORTANT COUNSEL GIVEN. " Thou shalt not," &c.

1. *It is irrational.* Carry this out, and in heathen lands you would worship stocks and stones. In uncivilized regions be wild, and devourers of each other. Reason demands reflection—enforces consideration, &c.

2. *It is unscriptural.* God, in every age, and under every dispensation, has demanded the opposite. This distinguished Noah, Abraham, the prophets, the apostles, and the pious in all periods and countries of the world. To follow the multitude is to disobey God—to be the vassals of Satan, and to travel in the dark path of guilt and wo.

3. *It is unsafe.* All evil doers will perish. The wages of sin is death to each and all its servants—broad way, and its crowd of travellers are united to death, even eternal death. A multitude of evil doers cannot avert God's wrath, cannot mitigate each other's misery, and cannot escape everlasting torments—however numerous, each must die alone, and each appear for himself before the judgment seat of Christ, and each hear and bear his own inevitable doom.

IV. THAT SINNERS MAY DESIST FROM THIS COURSE, AMPLE FACILITIES ARE GIVEN.

1. *The right and good way is clearly revealed.* " Thus saith the Lord, Stand in the way and see," &c. Christ announced the narrow way, the way of holiness and salvation. It is a plain path, so that the wayfaring man need not err therein.

2. *Holy examples are placed before us.* " Be followers of those who through faith and patience," &c. Abel, Enoch, Noah, David, Daniel, and the apostles, especially the bright example of Jesus.

3. *Divine grace is promised.* Grace to save from sin, " Whosoever shall call on the name of the Lord," &c. Grace to resist evil—grace to persevere, &c.

4. *The most momentous motives are presented.* Present peace and happiness—joy in death—eternal glory.

APPLICATION

1. To whom is the text applicable especially ?

2. Who have obeyed its wise counsels ?

3. Who will do so this day ?

11

AGAINST PROFANITY

" Thou shalt not take the name of the Lord thy God in vain ; for the Lord will not hold him guiltless who taketh his name in vain."—EXOD. xx. 7.

OUR text is one of the commandments given with such solemnity by Jehovah to Moses on Sinai. It is a commandment often referred to in other parts of the sacred writings as one part of the moral code. It is one of universal and everlasting obligation. God addresses it to all his intellectual creatures, and its violation is an act of guilt, that will assuredly involve the delinquent in the displeasure of God. Let us therefore consider,

I. HOW THIS COMMANDMENT IS VIOLATED.
II. THE REASONS BY WHICH OBEDIENCE TO IT MAY BE URGED.

I. HOW THIS COMMANDMENT IS VIOLATED.

1. *By heinous acts of perjury.* Calling on God, or appealing to his name for the confirmation of a lie. This is a flagrant act of infamy, and which is justly punishable by the statutes of the land. Often have the guilty been screened, and often have the innocent been ruined, by this kind of perjury. Common lying is generally the precursor to false swearing.

2. *By calling upon God's name to curse ourselves or others.* Imprecations and curses are the most awful instances of profanity. How frequently do we hear men using language of the most profligate character, and associating the name of God with woes of the most horrible description !

3. *All light and irreverent uses of the name of God.* How many well-meaning persons err in this way, and sometimes

Christians interlard the name of God with trifling or worldly converse, who appeal to God on trivial occasions—who talk about God without serious or reverent reflection! We almost fear to illustrate this, yet it ought to be clearly understood. "God knows." "By the help of God." "As sure as God's in heaven." "God help you." "God bless you;" are the usual expressions in the mouths of the most wicked in this great city. How common is this sin! In all its characteristics; among nearly all classes. It is one of our national vices. How God's people should lay it to heart!

II. THE REASONS BY WHICH OBEDIENCE TO THIS COMMAND MAY BE URGED.

1. *It is solemnly forbidden in the text.* Therefore it is clear and binding in its authority. No reader therefore of the Bible can plead ignorance as an excuse for profanity. That law which was given under circumstances of such unparalleled sublimity, says, "Thou shalt not take," &c. Jesus showed the importance of this command by presenting it as the first petition in his divine prayer. "Hallowed be thy name."

2. *Profane swearing strikes at the root of all reverence for religion.* How can God be esteemed, and adored, and venerated, if men use his name profanely? There can be no fear of God—no deprecation of his wrath—no awe of his majesty—no regard to his authority. An irreligious state of heart must be the result; pious feeling, a spirit of devotion, or true seriousness cannot exist with profaneness.

3. *It is a sin extremely unnatural.* We can account for many evidences of depravity. We can understand how men may be gay, or sensual, or worldly, or angry, or even revengeful. May account for almost every sin, however vile and awful; but for profanity, no reason can be assigned. It does not gratify any passion—it does not obtain any enjoyment—it does not procure any advantage—it does not advance its votary to any glory. It is a superfluity of sin. A causeless, stupid, senseless crime against God, even the true and blessed God.

4. *It is a sin that greatly corrupts society.* A spirit of reverence for God, recommends religion. It must tell on society. Its influence will be seen and felt. It will check vice and keep in certain bounds glaring impiety. But profanity curses so-ciety, it blights every lovely thing, it is fearful in its effects on the young, who soon catch the spirit, and imitate what they hear. I add also, it is as indecent as it is vile. An insult to every educated and right-principled member of society.

5. *It is a sin that will fearfully harden the heart.* Hence how common for this class of persons to associate profanity with serious and affecting things! Men have been known to do this in sickness, in pain, when undergoing operations. Soldiers in the field of battle; sailors at sea; persons even in the struggles of death. I believe there is no vice which so excludes all excellency, and opens the flood-gates to all vileness and hardness of heart.

6. *It has often procured the signal wrath of God.* "Because of swearing the land mourneth." To blaspheme God's name was a capital offence under the law, Levit. xxiv. 10, &c. How often has instant judgment fallen upon perjurers, upon wicked persons who have imprecated God's wrath! A man in a village in Scotland, competed with others which could use the most horrid oaths, and was smitten with swelling of the tongue so that he could not draw it into his mouth, and died in three days. Heaven cannot be inhabited by the profane; hell must be their portion, and even there I doubt if the swearer will find a fallen angel so vile as himself.

APPLICATION

1. *The remedy.* Solemn consideration of the grandeur and glory of God. Consider how angels act, &c. Guard your lips, watch against the rising of your heart; pray for God's Holy Spirit to change your soul: you must be new creatures. Dwell upon the senselessness of the crime, &c.

2. *Let Christians set a striking example in reverencing God's name.* And let their example and influence check bold transgressors, instruct our children, &c.

12

LIBERALITY AND SELFISHNESS CONTRASTED

"There is that scattereth and yet increaseth; and there is that withholdeth more than is meet, but it tendeth to poverty. The liberal soul shall be made fat; and he that watereth shall be watered also himself."—PROVERBS xi. 24, 25.

OUR subject directs us to two very opposite courses, and the general consequences of each. The truths of the text are of a very important character; they include the reactive influences which benevolence and selfishness produce, and are followed by a most cheering and delightful promise to the generous and liberal soul. When we remember that the second great command respects our fellow-creatures, an apology will not be necessary for calling your attention to an entire discourse on these topics; yet, lest any should conclude, that religion is constituted of those actions which have respect to mankind only, allow me to remind you, that all acceptable piety commences with repentance towards God, and faith in our Lord Jesus Christ; these, connected with regeneration, form a basis for the structure of personal piety. Personal piety includes supreme love to God, and unfeigned love to our fellow-men. Our text specifies one branch of our love to mankind, and it is beneficence; observe, then, the contrast instituted, and the promise made.

I. THE CONTRAST INSTITUTED. Observe this contrast,

1. *In reference to the characters introduced.* One is described as a scatterer, that is, one who distributes, a person of feeling mind and generous enlarged heart; one whose soul is expanded and warm. This character refers to the *habit*, to the prevailing disposition and conduct, not to an occasional act, &c. It includes also *purity* of motive, not an ostentatious giver, who makes it the subject of parade and show. Jesus describes the truly generous as not allowing the left hand to know, &c. This character also implies *perseverance* in well-doing. Abounding and continuing, &c. Now the other is described as a *withholder*, that is, a selfish man. One niggardly, of contracted spirit; one afraid to distribute of his substance. Who hoards it up, and thus monopolizes what God confers; views himself as the end, and not the channel of God's bounty; not like the ocean yielding freely to the water-spout; not like the clouds which give their plenteous rain; nor like the earth yielding its increase, &c.

2. *The contrast of the text respects the results arising from the conduct specified.* He who scatters increaseth.

(1.) Now this is often the case, even as it respects temporal blessings. Beneficence often obtains a reward in kind; God has a thousand ways of securing this. The wi-dow who dared to share her meal and oil with the prophet, had it miraculously continued to her. It is not often that really benevolent persons sink into want. David's experience was, that he never saw the righteous forsaken, &c.

(2.) It is ever the case in reference to internal enjoyment; and what is the end of all we have but enjoyment? Now the good man enjoys what he has. There is God's blessing on it, and with it, and in it; he has the satisfaction which a truly good and sanctified conscience confers. If spiritual blessings are given in exchange for our temporal benefactions, surely the recompense is ample and sufficient.

(3.) This will surely be the case in reference to an eternal reward. The day is coming when every one shall receive a reward for every deed of goodness and mercy; when every kind word, and action, and visit, and gift, shall be noticed, acknowledged, and recompensed. We are instructed in this, where Christ says, though the poor cannot recompense, yet ye " shall be recompensed at the resurrection of the just." He that withholdeth tendeth to poverty. There are claims which must have a preference. Our own wants and those of our families, prudent arrangement for the contingencies of life. These things " are meet." But he who withholdeth, &c., more than this, it often tendeth to poverty. Some withhold, because they fear *want*, dare not trust divine providence; some withhold, because the demands of pride and fashion drain all their resources; some of a *sordid avaricious spirit*, they are earthworms; like the horseleech, or the grave, or the sea, they are ever craving; some withhold on the ground of the *ingratitude* of the poor. All these are so many evidences of a selfish nature. This often defeats its end.

(1.) Such cannot guard against contingencies. Failure of banks, fires, bankruptcies, &c. God can blight every movement; accidents, afflictions, can drain all dry; this is not unfrequently the case.

(2.) Then there is always poverty of enjoyment; however much, it is not enjoyed. Mental sterility, spiritual barrenness, nothing bright or cheering within; it is the frigid zone, winter, ice, darkness.

(3.) Then such shall be poor indeed at death; not a title to a better world; not a jot or tittle can they take with them; they brought nothing into the world, &c. And when the Master demands an account, how fearfully appalling and eternally terrific; such is the contrast instituted. Observe,

II. THE PROMISE MADE. "The liberal soul," &c. That is, he shall flourish, &c.

(1.) God's blessing shall rest on his affairs; see Psalm xxvii. 3, xli. 1.

(2.) God's blessing shall rest on his soul; he shall be happy. He that hath mercy on the poor, "happy is he." God will answer his prayer, Isaiah lviii. 6, 7. His soul shall be very fruitful, Isaiah lviii. 10, 11. Such shall be established in divine things. "The liberal deviseth liberal things, and by liberal things he shall be established." Now we may ascertain some grounds why the liberal soul, &c.

1. *This is the design of our being invested with these blessings.* All things have reference to some end; nothing made for itself. Look at the sun, the moon, the stars, the sea, &c. And God never gave wealth to be locked up in banks or cabinets, but to be diffused, &c. Every thing else is perversion, to scatter is the great design, &c.

2. *There is the benevolent character of God placed for our imitation.* "Be ye merciful as your Father," &c. "Be ye followers of God as dear children," &c. "He is good to all," &c. "With such sacrifices he is well pleased."

3. *There is the divine connection between means and end.* I have spoken of the end of our means. Let us look at the philosophy of using our gifts.

(1.) Take the golden grain, and hoard it up, it will moulder and rot; sow it, and it will yield thirty, sixty, &c.

(2.) Take the power and disposition to communicate knowledge, and your teaching will enlarge, and improve, and enrich your own minds.

(3.) Take Christian instrumentality to do good and employ it, and your ability will increase, and your own souls be abundantly blessed, you cannot fail to get good; just so those who scatter abroad, shall increase. The bread cast upon the waters shall not perish, &c. It is but little we can do; but a short period allotted us; let us then not be weary, &c. And let us, in the midst of all, seek enlarged communications of the divine favor. Let us not trust in our benevolence for acceptance with God. Let humility always clothe us, remembering that at best we are unprofitable servants.

13

THE SATISFACTION AND ADVANTAGES OF GODLINESS

"But godliness with contentment is great gain."
—1 TIM. vi. 6.

THERE is a very current maxim, of great value and importance, that a contented mind is a continual feast. Without a great degree of this, happiness is utterly impossible. Neither wealth, nor honor, nor the gay scenes of pleasure, can confer real solid enjoyment on the soul of man. To these we may add learning, knowledge, power, and influence; the whole of which may be possessed; and yet as it regards solid bliss, vanity may be written upon the whole, and vexation of spirit. In a thousand points we are vulnerable; to a thousand diseases we are exposed; a thousand events may arise to distract and distress us. Our very breath is in our nostrils, and however earthly good may surround us, we are liable every moment to be exiled by the stroke of death from the whole. We would invite all searchers after true happiness to seek that real blessing in another path. It may assuredly be found and enjoyed; and our text gives us the direction—the infallible recipe. "Godliness with contentment," says the apostle, "is great gain." Let us consider,

I. THE SCRIPTURAL DEFINITION OF GODLINESS.

II. THE TRUE NATURE OF CONTENTMENT.

III. THE ADVANTAGES ARISING FROM THE UNION OF THE TWO. Let us endeavor to give you,

I. A SCRIPTURAL DEFINITION OF GODLINESS. And to a mere definition we must confine ourselves. It necessarily involves,

1. *A saving knowledge of God.* "This is life eternal," to know God in his natural attributes and moral perfections; in his works and government, especially as the Redeemer of the world—as the great source of love and mercy to our fallen race. To know this for ourselves—not because the Bible records it—the preacher declares it, but because we have experienced his power

and truth, and love in our own souls ; because he is our God, and we are his children. Not a learned, metaphysical knowledge of God, but a personal, inward, experimental sense of his grace and mercy. To know him in Christ ; God manifest in the flesh ; Immanuel, God with us, and for us, and in us. Godliness includes,

2. *The indwelling of the Holy Spirit.* "Because ye are sons, or children, God hath sent forth," &c. "The Spirit of God beareth witness," &c. Hence the new covenant promise runs thus :—" I will put my Spirit," &c. "As many as are led by the Spirit of God," &c. "Know ye not that ye are the temples," &c. It includes,

3. *Conformity to the will of God.* The mind conformed—the heart conformed—the life conformed. The mind agreeing—the heart delighting—the life obeying. In this state the thoughts, desires, purposes, expressions, and actions, will be under divine authority and control. To please God will be the great end of life. Enoch had this testimony before his translation, that he pleased God. The apostle said he exercised himself to maintain a conscience, &c.

4. *Devotedness to his service and glory.* The godly desire to make God known ; to show forth his praise ; to extol him and exalt him before men ; to labor with God and for God ; by the entire surrender of all we are and have to his cause and glory. " Glorify God in all things." " Whether ye eat," &c. " No man liveth to himself."

> " Were the whole realm of nature mine,
> That were a present far too small."

" The love of Christ constraineth us," &c. This is godliness—the godliness of the New Testament ; that which is saving, &c. We now pass on to consider,

II. THE TRUE NATURE OF CONTENTMENT. Now, this implies a state of mind acquiescing in the arrangements of God respecting us, and our lot and portion in the world. It is the opposite of ambition, anxiety, and avarice ; it is equanimity of spirit, arising from an internal approbation of God's government and ways. Of course, there are special seasons when contentment is to be exhibited and proved. We need not wonder that persons should be contented when they have health, prosperity, friends, &c. ; but contentment shines in the fiery furnace of affliction—in the night of adversity,

when friends forsake us, or when by death we are bereaved of them. It flourisheth in persecution, in reproaches, in suffering, and in death. In one word, it reconciles the mind to the various circumstances in which God may choose to place us. Now, contentment is not a sullen, mechanical principle ; not a stoical state of mind ; not mere affectation. It is in harmony with the greatest possible sensitiveness ; it can feel and discriminate ; it would prefer ease, and enjoyment, and prosperity ; but it can bend to the burden, bow to the correcting hand, drink the afflictive cup, submit to the severe stroke, or even resign itself to death. Now, a godly contentment is grounded,

1. *On the perfect excellency of the divine character.* God is the sum of all perfection ; pure light, pure goodness. All that is great, and glorious, and wise, and merciful, and righteous, form his divine character. Contentment says, " His wisdom cannot err ; his powerful arm cannot weary ; his plans cannot be frustrated ; his goodness cannot be exhausted ; his love cannot change ; his promises cannot fail ; his righteousness cannot do wrong ; and his tender mercy is over all his works, and it endures through all generations." Godly contentment rests,

2. *On the equity and benignancy of his government.* That government extends to all creatures, and all worlds ; it combines all events. God cannot but reign righteously, for there is no iniquity in him. He must reign bountifully, for he is good to all. Just as the sun cannot shine without diffusing heat and light, so God in all his government must act righteously and benignantly. That righteous and good government, or providence, encircles me and you always, every instant, and in every place. That trial—that cross—that sorrow—that bereavement, was a part of it. " The Lord reigneth," &c., is the song of the Christian. Godly contentment rests,

3. *On the richness of the divine gifts.* What has he not given us ? The earth, the heavens, the sea, the sky, the valley, and the mountain—the vital atmosphere—the light of day. What more ? Life, powers, sensibilities, &c. ; many sources of enjoyment. His revealed will as the guide to immortality ; exceeding great promises ; his own Son—his ever blessed co-equal Son, the Prince of life, and the

Lord of glory. Here the apostle will assist us, " If God spared not his own Son," &c. Oh! read it with emphasis. With this Son, the Holy Spirit, and eternal life, shall we not be content ? What higher, what richer, what greater, what more enduring blessings could he have imparted ? Godly contentment arises,

4. *From humbling views of ourselves.* As creatures, how unworthy, guilty, polluted, profitless, rebellious, wayward children ! What have we merited ? What is our desert ? If God were to take all he might justly take, what should we have left ? Oh! ask and reply to that question.

5. *From a sense of the infinite superiority of spiritual over earthly things.* That spiritual gifts are the perfect gifts ; more precious and durable ; more excellent, as adapted to the mind and heart ; and if these be healthy, and happy, and prosperous, it must be well with us, and if not, it cannot be well with us. Whatever we may possess, we must be wretched and miserable indeed.

6. *From the evanescence and uncertainty of the present state of existence.* Look at the past, like the stream ever flowing—the present, fleeting—the future approaching. We are travelling to the sepulchre, to the divine tribunal, to eternity. The soul will then be all—the favor of God all—its salvation all.

III. The advantages arising from godliness and contentment. " Great gain." Satisfaction of soul is the result ; solid, internal enjoyment ; comfort, which sets circumstances at defiance—which is within, a source of blessedness ; what the world cannot give or take away ; a perpetual feast ; an invulnerable defence ; an unchanging, radiant prospect ; a certainty of blessedness. How great, how superlative, how everlasting this gain !

APPLICATION

1. Examine yourselves on these two points—godliness and contentment.

2. They exercise a mutual influence on each other.

3. Admonish those who have neither.

14

AN UNGODLY SPIRIT REBUKED

" Ye know not what manner of spirit ye are of."
—Luke ix. 55.

Our text presents us with a striking instance of the weakness and sinful infirmities of two of the eminent disciples of the Saviour. One of these was the beloved John, who afterwards became so distinguished for meekness and love. Between the Samaritans and the Jews the most deadly animosities prevailed ; they even refused to each other the common civilities and courtesies of life. Hence the exclamation of the woman to Jesus, " How is it that thou, who art a Jew, askest water ?" &c. Jesus had now set his face to go up to Jerusalem, and on his way had to pass through a Samaritan village, and he sent messengers that they would prepare for him. It is written that they would not receive him, because he was on his way to Jerusalem. They probably hoped that Christ would tarry with them, and decide the protracted controversy about the right place of worship in their favor. When James and John saw this, they indignantly exclaimed, " Wilt thou that we command fire ?" &c. Their desire was that they should at once be consumed. They quote scripture in support of it ; but wisely they refer it to Christ. The only good thing in it was the interrogation in reference to it, " Wilt thou ?" The answer of our Redeemer is the text of this occasion, " But he turned and rebuked them," &c. From this striking and instructive portion of the divine word, we notice,

I. That the professed disciples of Christ may be greatly influenced by a wrong spirit. Let us,

1. *Notice some instances wherein this is exhibited.*

(1.) In maintaining bitterness of mind to those who have different views of divine truth. How rare it is to see exhibited a spirit of affectionate candor with regard to other sects and parties ! Our own opinions are the right, the orthodox ones. To differ from us is to go from the way of truth. A very small variation is sufficient to set them down as heterodox, and perhaps to unchristianize them altogether. If we are compelled to speak well, it is in a cool tone, or with several deductions, which nullify all that has been said. This is sometimes the case in reference to doctrines, or forms of worship ; to ordinances, to discipline, &c. Thus the state church treats dissenters, and thus dissenters treat the state church ; Roman Catholics, Protestants; and Protestants, Roman Catholics. Now, if Christ were present in this arena of disputation and strife, do you think he would agree either with the churchman or the dissenter in their unhallowed strifes? No! he would say to each, and to the whole, " Ye know not," &c.

2. *It is seen in carrying our dislike of men's sins into dislike of their persons.* We are to hate all evil, both in ourselves and others. We cannot detest too much the pollution which may be manifest in those around us ; but this indignation and hatred must not include the person of the sinner. I must hate profligacy, but have compassion on the profligate ; hate drunkenness, but feel for the drunkard ; hate avarice, but love the souls of the avaricious ; hate hypocrisy, but yearn over the hypocrite," &c. When our wrath goes beyond this, we tread unhallowed ground ; we become transgressors ; and Christ says to us, " Ye know not," &c.

3. *It is seen in cherishing an unmerciful and unforgiving spirit towards our enemies.* Nothing is so pre-eminently exhibited in the divine word as the indispensable importance of love, even to our enemies. We are commanded to put away all malice, and anger, and wrath. Our own forgiveness is even suspended on that of forgiving others ; yet, how Christians err in this! How often they are implacable ; how often feel and speak evil of their supposed enemies! Sometimes this is done on the most trivial ground—often arising from mere spleen and envy. I ask, is it so with any of you ? Do you know of any one towards whom you thus feel ? If so, the rebuke of Christ is addressed to you, " Ye know not," &c.

II. Let us account for the existence of this spirit. We marvel not at this in unconverted persons, who are strangers to the love of God, and the power of the Holy Spirit ; but we expect the image and spirit of Jesus in the regenerated, converted follower of Christ.

1. *It arises from the very partially sanctified state of the heart.* Much of original corruption remains within ; much spiritual territory to be possessed ; attainments of grace low ; the soul frigid and sterile.

2. *It arises from the influence of unhallowed prejudices in the mind.* In some cases imperfect education, or ministerial instruction ; trained in an atmosphere of bigotry and strife ; indoctrinated into sectarian principles instead of the principles of the gospel. Hence some ministers and churches are celebrated for bitterness of spirit, exclusiveness of feeling, and party animosity. Often our reading has much to do with it ; the word of God a very secondary book ; only read authors of our own party and creed, &c.

3. *From self-ignorance and self-deception.* " Ye know not," &c. Know our name, and creed, and peculiarities, but not our spirit. Know the spirit of others, and can condemn it, yet know it not in ourselves. Live without self-examination, with little self-communion, or fellowship with God ; thus err and deceive our own souls. We come,

III. To specify the divine remedy for this wrong spirit.

1. *The cultivation of an humble and lowly spirit.* To see and feel our own unworthiness—our own defects, and failings, and sins. A sense of these will abase, occupy our reflections, confessions, &c. We shall neither have time nor disposition to unchristianize or excommunicate others.

2. *A diligent perusal of the divine word.* Here are admonitions, exhortations, counsels, &c. ; here are beacons, as in the text ; here our models, &c. Deeply imbued with the spirit of the word will greatly preserve us.

3. *A careful imitation of the example and spirit of Jesus.* His nature—his mission—his life, &c. ; all breathe pure, infinite love, &c. His Spirit dwelling in us is religion. How did he feel, and act, and speak ? What the design of his mission ? What the influence of his love, &c. ?

APPLICATION

1. Attention to our spirit is of the utmost importance.

2. Our own happiness and improvement identified with it.

3. A right spirit only will recommend religion.

15

ON VAIN THOUGHTS

" How long shall thy vain thoughts lodge within thee ?"—Jer. iv. 14.

The religion which is acceptable to God must be of the heart, it must have its dwelling in the heart, it must sanctify the heart ; and from a heart devoted to God, will issue works of righteousness to the divine glory. Hence great stress is laid upon this in the sacred volume, " My son, give me thine heart," &c. " A new heart will I give you," &c. And in the verse of the text, " O Jerusalem, wash thine heart," &c. But our text limits us to one subject or branch of the heart, that is, the thoughts—" How long," &c. By thoughts we mean the exercise of the faculties of the mind confined within itself, in distinction to those operations of the mind, which are embodied in words or actions ; therefore thoughts involve the cognizances or perceptions of the understanding, the conclusions of the judgment, the decisions and purposes of the will, and the ideas of the imagination, and the conclusions of the mind in general : but imaginations, desires, and purposes, will comprehend chiefly what we mean by thoughts. Let us consider the thoughts the text refers to, show their vanity, urge their exclusion from the heart, with some directions for securing that object.

I. THE THOUGHTS REFERRED TO. It is obvious that the thoughts must often be engaged in reference to the things of this life. Business, and the lawful concerns of our families, must employ our thoughts. Excess here is only sinful ; to have the thoughts wholly absorbed. Now this is the case with many. But of the thoughts which are referred to I notice,

1. *Proud and high-minded thoughts.* When persons think more highly of themselves, &c. ; when their defects, &c., are lessened, and supposed excellencies magnified. The human heart is naturally disposed to pride ; proud thoughts will lead to a proud countenance and to pride of life.

2. *Thoughts which refer to human applause.* Thinking how we can obtain the goo word and favor of the world ; to have the good opinion, especially of those around us, and to bask in the beams of honor. Now these thoughts will also lead persons to a course of action degrading to themselves, and with which hypocrisy will be a main and leading ingredient ; such will adopt soft and oily words, and an apparent condescension of gait and conduct.

3. *Worldly thoughts.* Anxiety concerning earthly good, " Why take ye thought," &c. ? what shall I eat, &c. ? Thus the soul will be chained down to the earth ; only contemplate the material good of this

life. Those thoughts lead to covetousness, which is idolatry.

4. *Envious and malignant thoughts.* Looking with pain and dislike on the good of others, feeling uneasy at their prosperity, anxious to depreciate their reputation, secretly preparing arrows of enmity to injure them.

5. *Thoughts of speculative wickedness.* When sin is acted in the mind, when evils are lodged in the soul and presented to the imagination, and then fostered in the prolific soil of the human heart. These thoughts are peculiarly prevalent in persons of corrupt imaginations ; polluted conversation, and sensual books, greatly tend to this evil. I refer,

6. *To the general dissipation of thoughts.* When there is no mental order or self-government ; when the mind is open to every intruding thought, and when the soul is like the channel of a muddy stream, ever receiving, and ever communicating that which is foolish, and trifling, and sinful. I connect with these, those whose thoughts are ever occupied with the mere ideal, always living in a world of fancy ; the theatre, and works of fiction, greatly tend to produce and foster such thoughts. Let us,

II. SHOW THEIR VANITY. They are vain,

1. *As they are foolish.* Contrary to a sound understanding and real wisdom. No man can improve, either mentally or morally, under their influence ; even as it regards the attainment of real knowledge and enjoyment as rational beings in this life, they are foolish. There are so many sources of mental enjoyment in the works of nature, in wholesome reading, in the discoveries of science, and wonders of art ; but how foolish when we reflect that we are candidates for eternity !

2. *As they are empty.* Nothing substantial in them ; they afford no real enjoyment, no true pleasure ; as well might a man attempt to live on the wind, or in viewing pictures of food and drink.

3. *They are evil in the sight of God.* Our accountability extends to the thoughts— " God searcheth the heart," &c. Every thought is to be brought into judgment ; evil thoughts must be forsaken and pardoned, or they will condemn us forever ; and evil thoughts are generally the precursors of evil actions ; they are often the seeds or germ, &c. We,

III. URGE THEIR EXCLUSION FROM THE

HEART, WITH SOME DIRECTIONS FOR SECURING THAT OBJECT. "How long," &c. ; surely long enough already ; our happiness, safety, and spiritual improvement, are sufficient reasons for the exclusion of these vain thoughts. But how is this great object to be secured ? There must be,

1. *A deep conviction of the evil of these thoughts.* Feel them to be the plague of our souls ; feel them to be our burden, our misery, &c. Nothing can be effectually done without this.

2. *We must be humbled before God on account of them.* They must be loathed, confessed with sincerity and abasement of heart before the Lord ; the soul contrite before the Lord, covered as with sackcloth, &c.

3. *We must seek purification through the blood of Christ.* Christ's blood cleanseth from all sin, even sinful thoughts. It purifieth the conscience.

4. *We must daily supplicate the sanctifying power of the Spirit.* He is the sanctifier ; he gives us spiritual power to resist evil ; he will impart to the soul the things of Christ, and impart his holy mind ; he will enable us to war with these thoughts, &c.

5. *Recognise God's omniscience and cultivate his fear.* Be in that fear all the day long. Remember he is conversant with our thoughts. Pray daily, "Cleanse thou me from secret faults," &c.

6. *Store the heart with the divine thoughts of his holy word.* "I hate vain thoughts, but thy law do I love." "Thy word have I hid in mine heart," &c.

APPLICATION

1. *Learn the exclusive spiritual claims God has upon us.*

2. *Labor after inward purity of heart.*

3. *Thoughts are only evil when cherished, &c.,*—When they "lodge within us." Reject them if possible on their approach, at any rate by prayer and faith exclude them if they have taken possession.

16

THE RIGHT EMPLOYMENT OF THE TONGUE

"Keep thy tongue from evil, and thy lips from speaking guile."—PSALM xxxiv. 13.

WE have considered, on previous occasions, the spirit and the thoughts ; our present subject is the tongue : a subject to which the scriptures often invite our attention. Unless the tongue be under the sanctifying influences of the grace of God, we are told by the apostle that our religion is vain, and that whoso offendeth not in word, that man is a perfect man. A good man, out of the good treasure of his heart, will bring forth wise and useful conversation. But an evil man, out of the bad treasure of his heart, will bring forth only a stream of pollution and death. A wholesome tongue, says Solomon, is a tree of life. Our subject then is the religious use of the tongue. Let us notice, then, what we should avoid ; what use we should make of it ; how we may do it ; and the motives for so doing. In the use of the tongue,

I. WHAT SHOULD WE AVOID ? The text specifies evil in the general—"from evil."

1. *From the evil of impiety and blasphemy.* All expressions against God's character, and glory, and works, and will. All witty citations and perversions of scripture. All jocular uses of the divine word. All rash and speculative speaking on the solemn concerns of the soul, religion, and eternity.

2. *From the evil of profaneness.* All cursing, swearing, and imprecations, taking God's name in vain. "Thou shalt not take the name," &c. All exclamations in which God's name is irreverently used. Many sincere Christians err here. Never use any of the divine titles but with awe and godly fear.

3. *From the evil of falsehood.* Now this is a monster evil—it assumes an almost endless variety of shapes and hues.

(1.) One of its forms is that of slander—when we declare that which is false to injure another.

(2.) Another is that of detraction, when we may not assert any positive evil, but withhold from the real merits of those of whom we speak, or endeavor to fritter away their excellencies, and rob them of their true reputation.

(3.) Evil speaking—when we become the conveyers of evil concerning others without good evidences of its truth ; and also when we needlessly dwell on the infirmities or sins of others—this is severely reprehended in scripture. The backbiter is an odious character. Among other modes of falsehood there is,

(4.) That of false jesting, where persons

invent the ridiculous and the ludicrous, and palm it upon people as truth.

(5.) Falsehood used in trading and business, when an untrue impression is made upon a seller or buyer. Persons are guilty of this in extolling their articles, and others in cheapening them. What a world of iniquity is exhibited to the eye of Deity in the transactions of trade; how few even of professors have clean hands! I refer,

(6.) To flattery, when we desire to gratify persons, by stating excellencies which we do not believe them to possess. Some persons court this, are ever eagerly seeking the company of such, but it lessens not the guilt of the flatterer. We should not only keep ourselves from the evil of falsehood of all kinds, but also from the evil,

4. *Of talkativeness.* The tongue was never designed to be in perpetual motion as the muscles of the heart, or the blood in the veins. Talkativeness is an evil in itself, and also leadeth to much evil. " In a multitude of words there wanteth not sin." Few perpetual talkers have good consciences. There are times when it would be cruel to be silent, but there are surely seasons when it is cruel not to be so.

5. *From the evil of anger and contention.* Wrathful words—words spoken hastily—words designed to irritate, and incense, and provoke. How James refers to this, chapter iii. verse 5, &c. But we ask,

II. WHAT USE SHALL WE MAKE OF THE TONGUE?

1. *Let it be placed under the influences of wisdom.* Let it give utterance to that which is wise, and be the instrument of conveying knowledge. Have something to say when we speak, and something worth saying.

2. *Let it always be identified with truth.* Abhor falsehood as mean and contemptible, but especially as grievous to God, and ruinous to the soul. " Speak the truth one to another," &c.

3. *Let it be the instrument of peace.* Avoid all wrangling, and strife, and contentions. This be your motto, " I am for peace." Let the tongue not be dipped in gall, nor in the oil of dissimulation, but the holy oil of amity and love; " speaking the truth in love."

4. *Let it be the minister of edification.* Use the tongue for the good of mankind,

Col. iv. 6. Speak to instruct—to comfort —to encourage and warn, &c. We ask,

III. How WE MAKE THIS USE OF THE TONGUE?

1. *By seeking the sanctification of the heart.* The mouth is the channel for the stream from the inward fountain of the soul. From the state and fulness of the heart the mouth speaketh. If the fountain be pure, then will the streams be so. A heart filled with heavenly wisdom and holy love will ever produce a pious and edifying conversation. As the heart is, so will be the tongue.

2. *By having it under strict government and control.* If allowed to run riot, or left to itself, evil must be the result. A wise man will place under restriction this difficult member. He will discipline it. " Keep it as with bit and bridle," &c.

3. *Exercise Christian vigilance in reference to it.* Have watch as well as guard. Keep a sentinel at the door of thy lips. Be slow also to speak. Exercise caution and circumspection, &c.

4. *Employ it in holy services.* Reading the divine word, prayer, praise, Christian conversation, &c. And let the prayer have especial respect to this difficult member. Now let us glance,

IV. AT SOME MOTIVES FOR THE RIGHT APPLICATION OF THE TONGUE. Because of the connection,

1. *Between the tongue and the conscience.* Is not conscience oftener grieved and defiled by the tongue than any thing else? Who does not know this? If a good conscience is worth having, then " Keep thy tongue," &c. Because of the connection,

2. *Between the tongue and our real prosperity.* " A wholesome tongue is a tree of life," &c. It will exert a favorable influence on the whole soul. On account of the connection,

3. *Between the tongue and our usefulness.* Our influence will greatly depend on this. If this member is extensively wrong we shall do little good in the world. If it be seasoned with the salt of grace we shall extensively be blessings to others. On account of the connection,

4. *Between the tongue and the judgment day.* Words as well as actions will be judged. All that we have said as well as done—every idle word. A falsehood will then cover with shame, and exclude from the heavenly state.

APPLICATION

1. *Let the subject be the test of personal examination.*

2. *Let it be duly pondered in its momentous bearings on our highest and best interests.*

3. *Let those who are the slaves of an evil tongue seek deliverance by the power of divine truth and grace.* A new heart is essentially necessary.

17

SPIRITUAL APATHY DENOUNCED

" Wo to them that are at ease in Zion."— AMOS vi. 1.

SOME men are at ease in their sins, though heinous and aggravated, through their consciences being seared and insensible ; some are at ease in their indifference to religion, through the absorbing power of worldliness, or through the fascinating pleasures of life ; some are at ease through carnal presumption, resting on the exercise of the final mercy of God ; some are at ease by the delusions of self-righteousness, depending for acceptance and salvation through the deeds of the law ; but to none of these classes does our text refer. It distinctly points to the professors of religion —the visible servants of God—the members of his church. " Wo to them that are at ease," not in the world, but " in Zion"—in the church. Let us define the characteristics ; ascertain the causes ; and show the evil of this state of mind. Let us,

I. DEFINE THE CHARACTERISTICS. And in this definition we shall more especially accompany the description, by showing the evidences of this state of heart and mind. In the church it is delightful to observe the spiritually-minded, the active, the liberal, the zealous followers of Christ. Now those at ease in Zion form the contrast of each of these classes. The apathy supposed in the text is,

1. *Opposed to spiritual-mindedness.* The mind is greatly under the power of the carnal principle ; secular and earthly things have the ascendency ; communion with God is rare and feeble ; devotion at a low ebb ; the thoughts, desires, feelings, &c., are of the earth, earthy ; the rays of celestial light are but dim in the chamber of the understanding ; and the fire of hal-lowed emotion is almost extinguished on the altar of the heart.

2. *It is opposed to holy activity.* Activity is one of the essential laws of the universe ; it is especially so in relation to mind. The powers of the soul were destined for activity. Without this there can be neither health nor vigor. Activity is essential to the welfare of our own souls—essential to the discharge of the duties of the Christian life— essential to the prosperity of the church and kingdom of Christ in the world. Heaven is the scene of holy activity ; hell is the theatre of wicked and malignant activity ; the world is one field of varied yet incessant activity ; and is the church of Christ the only sphere for unconcern and apathy ? Is it not painfully evident, that not more than one in twenty are actively employed in honoring the Redeemer, and seeking the extension of his cause ?

3. *It is opposed to generous liberality.* We cannot expect persons to be generous and self-denying for that which has no hold upon the heart. Most people will support what they greatly esteem and love ; but if the heart is not influenced, there will be no generous liberality. What is given to the cause of God will be doled out on the principle of duty, or propriety, or respectability. Now, such a state of feeling will never provide the means for converting the world. How different this to the first Christian churches ! Let me read a passage or two : Acts ii. 44, iv. 3, &c. ; 2 Cor. viii. 1, &c. Men cannot be profuse in the family and in the world, in pleasure and luxuries, and calculating in the church, unless they are at ease in Zion.

4. *It is opposed to fervid zeal.* The concerns of personal religion are so great and lofty, that they demand the most intense devotedness of our powers to God. " Fervent in spirit." But besides these, there are the great interests of the cause of Jesus, none of which can be effectually promoted without fervid Christian zeal. All that is great, and glowing, and good in the visible kingdom of Christ, has been produced by the zeal of its loyal subjects, followed by the blessing of God. It was zeal that made our confessors and martyrs ; zeal that raised and sustained the Reformers and the Puritans ; zeal that gives men the missionary spirit, and supports them in their spheres of self-denial and suffering. We cannot dispense with this spirit, unless

Satan is to overcome, and the world have the ascendency. How criminal, then, is the apathy of that spirit of slumber which rests on many of the professors of religion ! Let us, then,

II. ASCERTAIN THE CAUSE OF THIS EVIL. It may arise from,

1. *Mistakes as to the true nature of religion.* Religion is not only enjoyment and privilege, but duty, labor, and activity. Religion makes a man better and happier, but it also makes him the servant of the Saviour; a laborer in Christ's vineyard; a soldier in Christ's army. "I beseech you, brethren, by the mercies of God," &c.

2. *From the feeble influence which the doctrines of the cross produce within us.* These doctrines are calculated to constrain the soul to entire devotedness. "God forbid," &c. "Yea, doubtless," &c. The love of Christ should constrain us, &c. Who does not admire these lines ?

> "Were the whole realm of nature mine,
>   That were a present far too small:
> Love so amazing, so divine,
>   Demands my life, my soul, my all."

But do we seriously believe them ? do we feel them ? If not, it is only sentiment—only poetry. Now, the apathy of the formal must greatly arise from the feeble influence of these doctrines on our hearts; and the cause of this must be, the great distance we live from Calvary. We do not cling to it, look up to the Sufferer, hear his dying groans, feel his love, or we could not be at ease in Zion.

3. *Unnecessary intercourse with the men and things of the world.* The most devout and holy know how chilling this is; even with the utmost watchfulness it is so. But if this atmosphere is often breathed—if this society is preferred—if much of our leisure time is thus occupied, how can it be otherwise that we should not be at ease in Zion ?

4. *Forgetfulness of our responsibility.* We must every one give an account of himself, &c.; we are stewards, and must render an account of our stewardship; we are accountable for our talents, time, influence, property. &c.; we are accountable for all the good we possess ability to do, in the world and in the church. The day of reckoning will come, and how desirable that we be found faithful—that Christ may say, "Well done," &c. Let us, then,

III. SHOW THE EVIL OF THIS STATE OF MIND. "Wo to them," &c.

1. *It is evil in itself.* Displeasing to God; grieves his Spirit; perverts his mercies, &c.

2. *It is evil in its influence.*

(1.) On the persons who are at ease. It renders the soul barren; it robs it of peace; it often leads to apathy.

(2.) It is evil in its influence on the brethren; it is withering in its effects; it will infect others; lull others into that state of lethargy.

(3.) It is evil to the church; takes away its beauty and vigor; renders its influence almost powerless; throws it into the shade, and rejoices its adversaries.

(4.) Its influence is bad on the world. Men must see that it is not the religion of the New Testament, of Christ, and the apostles. It hinders the conversion of souls; hardens skeptics, &c.

APPLICATION

1. *Let the text be the test of our present condition.* Are we condemned by it ? or do we pass through the ordeal with triumph ? I fear most of us are condemned.

2. *Let it lead to greater devotedness.* All have need of this. Let us aim at this for our own sakes—for the sake of the church —especially for Christ's sake.

18

REAL SACRILEGE

"Will a man rob God ?"—MALACHI iii. 8.

ROBBERY—robbery ! Why, you say, the very term has only meaning when used in connection with the most profligate and abandoned portion of society. How insulted any man would feel to be denounced as a robber; lost to all correct notions of righteousness; to be desperate, daring, and reckless; not to regard the rights and feelings of others. How low are such sunk in the scale of society ! Surely, I have not one such person here. But our text seems to charge men with the highest kind of robbery—robbery of God. It has been observed, "To rob the poorest individual is felony; to usurp the prerogatives or riches of a monarch is treason; but to rob God is sacrilege." I fear that not only the Jews were guilty of this, but also that many here are not clear in this matter. "Will a man rob God ?" What is it to rob God ? The heinousness of doing so, and its consequences, be now therefore considered.

I. WHAT IS IT TO ROB GOD ? To rob God is to deprive him of any of his just rights. God has a just and equitable claim,

1. *On our homage and reverence.* If his name is profaned, or used with levity, or interlards our conversation, it is robbery of God. Jesus has shown us the importance of this, in making it the first petition of the prayer he taught his disciples, " Hallowed be thy name." Many persons do this through thoughtlessness, &c. God is greatly to be feared, and his venerable name held most sacred.

2. *God has a claim on our grateful love.* We ought to love supreme excellence—the most perfect good. God is such. Infinite love ; eternal goodness and mercy. But see his goodness to us. How striking— bountiful — pitiful — constant — never-failing ! Ought he not to be praised ? Is he not worthy to be praised, &c. But if he is not extolled and blessed, then do we rob God. This is his right and due. Silence and indifference is guilt.

3. *God has a claim upon our obedience.* He is to be served ; with lip and life ; from the heart ; with diligence, earnestness, &c. He is to be served before men. Every omission of duty robs him—every transgression robs him. Who, then, is not guilty ? &c.

4. *God has a claim upon our time.* It is all his gift. Every year—month—day. He requires a portion of it to be devoted to him. He demands the youth of life ; ought he not to have it ? The flower of our days, &c. " Wilt thou not from this time ?" &c. He demands a portion of every day in religious worship, morning and evening ; prayer—thanksgiving—reading—meditation. He demands the day of holy rest ; he did this from the creation ; he did this by Moses in the law ; he received this from the disciples. Who has not robbed God of youth—of daily time—of the sabbath ?

5. *He has a claim upon our means and talents.* I refer to our ability of doing good. Honoring him ; teaching the knowledge of him ; glorifying him ; supporting his cause ; regarding his poor, &c. His interests are to have a high, extensive, and deep place in our affections and esteem. Who has not robbed God of these ? How little he has had ; how unfair a proportion, &c. Reply ye, who is free from guilt ? &c. Consider,

II. THE HEINOUSNESS OF ROBBING GOD.

Now, it is not a light thing ; it is a great sin ; very grievous to him. Measure it,

1. *By the Being we rob.* God ; not only the greatest, most exalted, and blessed Being, but our heavenly Father—our Preserver—our Saviour.

2. *By the persons guilty of it.* Recipients of his bounty—objects of his care — for whom he has given his own Son. Let Satan and unredeemed spirits be so infatuated ; but can ransomed creatures—souls for whom the Saviour died ?

3. *By its glaring rashness and presumption.* Men rob privately in the dark—in hope of escape ; but we rob God when his eye is upon us ; when he is surrounding us ; while he is recording the deed— writing it down against us. What daring —what effrontery—what hardness and infatuation ! Consider,

III. ITS FINAL RESULTS. It has present evil results ; it is unwise ; it is self-injurious. We rob ourselves ; we rob ourselves of his favor, his approval, his love, his blessing, his peace ; but its final results must be calamitous. There will,

1. *Be the arrestment.* He will send his officers, &c. ; bring us before his bar, &c. " We shall all stand before," &c.

2. *There will be the conviction.* We cannot clear ourselves. His own gaze will light up every conscience, and all our guilt will flash before our eyes. This conviction will be public.

3. *There will be the sentence.* Separation from the holy, the elevated, the happy. Doomed to the abode of the devil and his angels ; everlasting blackness and fire. " The wicked shall be turned into hell," &c. I apply the subject by asking, what shall we do to avert the doom stated ?

1. *There must be confession.* Go, and acknowledge your sin. He requires this. Do it humbly—ingenuously—sincerely.

2. *Restitution.* As far as possible. Cannot give him back youth and time ; but now surrender yourselves, body, soul, and spirit.

3. *There must be amendment.* Repent ye, or reform ye. " Cease to do evil," &c. " Turn ye," &c. " If the wicked man,' &c.

4. *There must be trust in Jesus Christ.* Christ is our Mediator ; the way—the fountain—the sacrifice, &c. Who will surrender himself thus to God ? Seek mercy and obtain everlasting life.

19
INSTABILITY

" Unstable as water, thou shalt not excel."—
GENESIS xlix. 4.

OUR text was one of the predictive declarations of the dying Jacob. It related to
his first-born Reuben, who on account of
an early flagrant transgression was disrobed
of the dignity and privileges of the first-
born ; but we select the text as containing
a great truth, or maxim, equally true
whether we consider it in reference to mere
mind, or to morals in general. Instability
is the great impediment to pre-eminent
excellence. The unstable scholar shall
not excel in learning ; the unstable trades-
man shall not generally excel in worldly
prosperity ; the unstable philosopher shall
not generally excel in intellectual attainments ; decision, constancy, perseverance,
are essential to success. It is just so in
religion.

I. LET US SEEK OUT A FEW SIMPLE ILLUS-
TRATIONS OF THE TEXT.

II. ACCOUNT FOR ITS EXISTENCE.

III. PRESCRIBE A REMEDY.

I. LET US SEEK OUT A FEW ILLUSTRATIONS
OF THE TEXT.

1. *We often see this instability in inquirers after religion, and they do not excel in the
formation of their moral character.* How
many hear the word of God from principle,
and often with pleasure, and are not rejecters of the truth ? The word commends itself to their minds, they hear and they feel
it ; it produces conviction, emotion, and
they resolve to yield themselves to God.
How often these feelings are combined with
prayer, with deep anxieties, and mental
conflict ; but they defer, they allow the
internal disquietude to be allayed, they enter on the scenes of domestic duty or business, and then, alas, their averments and
resolves all pass away. This is often repeated, week after week, year after year,
and the heart still is unchanged and the
character not formed. Never far from the
banquet, but they do not enter ; always
under the sound of the gospel, but they
do not obey it. " Unstable as water,"
&c.

2. *We often see this in professed Christians in reference to a variety of particulars.*

(1.) In reference to knowledge. Instability in scripture reading. There is one
hallowed fountain of knowledge, the holy
scriptures ; it is our duty, our privilege, to
be familiar and mighty here, but the reading of many is distinguished by inequality
and instability, and therefore they remain
children in understanding ; babes in wisdom ; when they ought to be approaching
perfection, they are only acquainted with
the first elements of divine truth.

(2.) Christians often do not excel in self-
government, through instability in moral
discipline. The evil of our nature is only
partially removed in regeneration ; then the
old man is crucified, but lingering he requires the continual application of mortify-
ing means. The divine direction is, " Work
out your own salvation, for it is God," &c.
" Mortify your members," &c. " Crucify
the flesh," &c. We are to bring ourselves
under restraint, &c. Bit and bridle to the
tongue, &c. Yet how often is our moral
feebleness displayed ; almost as churlish,
or morose, or passionate, or frivolous, as
when we set out in religion. How is it ?
Our discipline has been unstable. By fits
and starts ; the rein has now been held
tight, and then thrown loose over the necks
of our passions, and thus unstable, we could
not excel.

(3.) Christians often do not excel in
fruitfulness through instability in the means
of grace. Our conflicts and trials weaken
us. The world is barren ; earthly scenes
make us spiritually lean and frigid ; God
has appointed the means of grace for our
refreshment ; these are the green pastures,
the banqueting house, &c. " They that
wait upon the Lord," &c. Instability in
regard to these necessary and gracious appointments, always causes sterility and barrenness. God is dishonored, and his rich
goodness undervalued.

(4.) Christians often do not excel in usefulness through instability in the exercise
or cultivation of their talents. An active,
persevering employment of our talents is
essential to usefulness ; we cannot do much
good without this ; we must seek a sphere
of labor suited to our talents and time, &c.
Enter on it heartily, and perseveringly follow it ; thus we cannot fail to do some
good, our power to do good will increase ;
additional talents will be given to him that
hath. How many act like the man with
one talent !

(5.) Christians often do not excel in the
enjoyments of religion through instability

in the exercise of devotion. A devotional spirit brings immediately into close fellowship with God; this is especially connected with God's favor and loving-kindness; then he will cause his face to shine, &c. Thus we shall be lifted above the petty difficulties of this world. "Our path resemble the morning light, shining brighter," &c. Deserted, or neglected closets, formal prayers, &c., eat out the enjoyment of piety to the core; thus unstable as water, &c. In reference to instability,

II. LET US ACCOUNT FOR ITS EXISTENCE.

1. *It is sometimes constitutional.* This is often the peculiar failing, the besetting sin, the most vulnerable part. Vacillation is often owing to the temperament, and the peculiar development of the individual; it is not however thus beyond remedy, but it will need greater determination, skill, and labor, to master it.

2. *It is often the result of inconsideration.* We do not duly ponder, fully examine, and then lay down those rules which under God's blessing would preserve us from it. A greater regard to a contemplative habit of mind, &c.

3. *Often occasioned by unwatchfulness.* We are too little on our watch-tower. Thus open to the wiles of the adversary, &c. For this evil, let us,

III. PRESCRIBE A REMEDY. In one word, this is the grace of God; by the grace of God we can do all things, and, of course, overcome this evil. Grace will enlighten, restrain, govern, sanctify, make fruitful, useful, happy, &c.

1. *But its need must be felt.* Not labor in our own power, &c. Be conscious of our weakness, &c. Desire it, &c.

2. *But this grace must be sought.* We must ask for it, for this end, fervently, &c.

3. *This grace must influence us.* Not resisted, not neglected &c. But we must co-operate.

APPLICATION.

May our subject,

1. Lead us all to strict examination. Most, I fear, are chargeable in some way, or to some extent, with instability.

2. May we resolve this morning to give ourselves to God with purpose of heart, and to cleave to the Lord with all our souls.

3. To excel should be the desire of all the children of God.

20

SUPERSTITION

" I perceive in all things ye are too superstitious."—ACTS xvii. 22

THE truth of the apostle's charge, in reference to the Athenians, is at hand, for to propitiate imaginary deities, they had filled their city with innumerable altars; idolatry had attained a kind of perfection in the city of Athens. Wealth, and genius, and authority, had all been presented at her shrine. In addition to the gods known and famed in their mythology, they had erected one altar to the unknown God. This had particularly struck the mind of the great apostle, and this he made the subject of his discourse. "Whom, therefore, ye ignorantly worship," &c. Superstition is defined, unnecessary fear, and is generally associated with reverence for imaginary beings. Let us glance,

I. AT THE ORIGIN AND CAUSES OF SUPERSTITION. The first superstitious act on record is presented to us in the holy scriptures, in the case of our first parents immediately after the fall, Gen. iii. 7, 8. Here guilt was the cause, ignorance or blindness was the result, and superstitious means of safety the scheme they adopted. How foolish and futile to cover themselves from the eye of omniscience, or to flee from an omnipresent God! We present this as the general basis of all superstition, ignorance of the word and works of Deity. As men are in darkness, and are strangers to these, they will be superstitious; as they emerge into the light of revelation and true knowledge of the works of God, they are freed from this baneful and distressing curse. Notice

II. THE UNIVERSALITY OF SUPERSTITION.

1. *It has darkened by its dreary mists all countries and ages.* The ancient Jews, though favored with the light of a partial revelation, were not free from its idolatrous apostacies. Egypt may be termed its nursery; here it was cherished in ten thousand forms. At one period, they had 30,000 imaginary deities. Their two leading gods were Osiris and Isis,—thought to be the sun and moon. They also worshipped the ox, the dog, the wolf, the hawk, the crocodile, and the cat; they likewise adored trees, plants, and roots; the country was full of temples and priests; they taught the doctrine of the transmigration of souls, &c., and their lives were one round of ab-

surd usages, rites, and customs. The ancient Carthaginians worshipped a variety of deities, especially Celestis, likewise called Urania, or the moon ; and Saturn, known in scripture by the name Moloch. It was this monster idol, in whose burning arms the children were sacrificed, while their dying agonies and shrieks were drowned by the noise of drums and trumpets. Two hundred children were at one time sacrificed to this sanguinary deity. The Persians worshipped the sun, and paid divine honors to fire ; but all ages and all countries, whether civilized or savage, have had their absurdities and superstitious customs. Neither war nor peace—ignorance nor learning—philosophy nor art—poetry nor music, could remove the baneful curse of superstition from the world.

2. *In the modern history of the world, superstition has held the empire of mind in its debasing and cruel grasp.* Let us look at this in three or four aspects. In reference,

(1.) To witchcraft. James the First wrote a learned work on witchcraft, and our English parliaments legislated for the punishment of this crime with death. Witchfinders were appointed in every district. A variety of ignorant and wicked modes of testifying the accused were adopted. Three thousand were put to death during the long parliament ; in various parts of Germany not fewer than a hundred thousand—in England altogether not fewer than thirty thousand in two hundred years. Sir M. Hale, that upright and pious judge, condemned two to be burned in 1664, and two were executed in Northumberland so late as 1722.

(2.) To soothsaying and astrology. That is, the belief that the destiny of persons is influenced by the planets under which they are born. Gross superstition ! The Romans, Chaldeans, Assyrians, Egyptians, Greeks, Arabs, and the Brahmins of India, have all been devoted to this supposed art. In Europe astrology has been patronised by crowned heads, and by whole bodies of the learned. Dr. Dee, the author of the prophecies of the destruction of the metropolis, was a distinguished man in the time of Queen Elizabeth, and richly patronised by her majesty. In our own times we see the influence of this in our astrological almanacks, and the eager avidity with which every predictive pamphlet is bought and read. Allied to this, and built on it, is the whole mischievous fabric of fortune-telling, and yet thousands of otherwise intelligent persons give this their countenance, even in our own enlightened day and times.

(3.) The superstitious application of the unknown laws of nature. Eclipses of the sun or moon were viewed with horror, and there are recorded instances of learned persons, who, on such occasions, have fainted with fear ; comets were judged to be omens of wars, earthquakes, famine, or pestilence. The northern light at one time filled beholders with alarm, and their imaginations often fancied they beheld horsemen, and chariots, and armies. The flitting lights on waste and damp lands were considered presages of peril ; so also a variety of easily accounted for events ; the ticking noise of a little insect, by many is called the death-watch ; the screech owls screaming at the window—the dog howling in the night—the curling of the melting tallow in the candle—the falling of salt, &c. ; so also the whole round of lucky or unfortunate days.

(4.) The superstitious rites associated with religion. It is the belief of some, even of the Protestant community, that at the baptism of a child the devil is cast out. Is it much better to imagine that the application of a little water to the face changes its nature, regenerates it, &c., as now taught by many in the church of England ? Look also at the consecration of burial grounds—the tolling of church bells at the death of parishioners who desire it : in one word, look at every rite, and custom, and ceremony mixed up with religious worship, which is not clearly taught in the Bible, and no other term can be appropriately given to them than that of superstition.

III. THE EVILS OF SUPERSTITION. These are manifold.

1. *It prostrates and degrades the exalted powers of the mind.* Mental slavery, night and darkness of the soul.

2. *It never leads to holiness.* Indeed superstition steps forth to take the place of genuine piety, and dispenses with repentance and obedience, &c., and gives shadows, and thus it cheats and deceives the mind.

3. *It is destructive to real peace and enjoyment.* Superstition has nothing bright or radiant to cheer. No, its temple is darkness—its spirit cruelty—its influence is terrifying.

4. *It keeps men from the one true way of*

salvation. One of Satan's chief instruments. Conscience, &c., demands religious interposition for its relief; Satan therefore gives it vanity, and lies, and superstition.

IV. THE REMEDY. We present it in one word—"knowledge."

1. *Knowledge of the divine works.* The light of natural philosophy, and the discoveries of science, have done much to lessen the superstition of our country; no one now faints at an eclipse, or dies of fright at the appearance of a comet. But,

2. *A knowledge of God's word. Here is pure truth.* All, every word simple truth—appropriate truth; it is sent for our deliverance. Oh, abide by it; seek its enlightening influences; let it dwell in you; obey it; believe, and worship, and live according to this book. One great truth. The Son of God was manifested that he might destroy the works of the devil; of these superstition is one. It will teach you what to fear, and how to exemplify it. God, death, judgment, wrath to come. Let me urge this upon you. To you is the word of this salvation sent. God now commands all men everywhere to repent, &c.

21

THE CHARACTER AND BLESSEDNESS OF THE GODLY

" Blessed is the man that walketh not in the counsel of the ungodly, nor standeth in the way of sinners, nor sitteth in the seat of the scornful. But his delight is in the law of the Lord; and in his law doth he meditate day and night. And he shall be like a tree planted by the rivers of water, that bringeth forth his fruit in his season; his leaf also shall not wither; and whatsoever he doeth shall prosper."—PSALM i. 1–3.

THIS delightful portion of the Old Testament, denominated the Psalms, contains an inexpressibly rich mine of precious treasure. And these treasures are of the most diversified character. It contains a portion of almost every variety the Bible presents to our view. It is descriptive and preceptive. It contains odes and sacred songs. It has both its praises and its prayers. It directs to duty, and exhibits the goodness and mercy of God in the promises he has given to them that love him. It exhibits the terrors of divine wrath to the wicked, and opens to the child of God a bright and glorious passage to eternal glory. This delightful book opens upon us with the language of blessing, and to this we now direct your prayerful attention. In this description of the godly man, notice,

I. THE EVILS WHICH HE AVOIDS. Here three terms and three representations are placed before us.

1. *He walketh not in the counsel of the ungodly.* Now by the ungodly, we are to understand those who are more especially negatively wicked. That is, who may be free from notorious vices, but who are not the recipients of the grace and Spirit of God. Now there may be great external decency, and yet the heart in an ungodly state. The child of God does not walk in the counsel of these. He is not governed by their suggestions. Does not unite in their associations. He cannot do this, for two must be agreed, if they walk together.

2. *He standeth not in the way of sinners.* Now life is often represented as a course or way. Every act is a step in this way. —Now the way of the sinner is evil, a way of transgression. It is a broad way,—a way that declineth,—a way of darkness, and which terminates in the gulf beneath. Now the godly man does not stand in this way. His course is the narrow up-hill track, a way of light and comfort, and which leads to Zion's hill.

3. *He sitteth not in the seat of the scorner.* This is a most flagrantly wicked and presumptuous condition of mind. It is one expressive of deep depravity, reckless madness, and desperation. The scorner laughs at piety, treats religion with contempt, and ridicules the people of God. This is the most awful state of wickedness, and is generally the prelude to the just judgments of God. Now observe the degrees which the text presents to us, and their connection with each other.

(1.) Men listen to the counsel of the ungodly, and walk in their fellowship.

(2.) They go on until they can take up their position in the way of the practically evil.

(3.) Then they become hardened and infatuated, until they can mock at sin, and treat with scorn the condition of the pious.

II. THE COURSE WHICH HE PURSUES. And here we have,

1. *His delights.* That which is the highest source of enjoyment to him. And this is the sure index to the character, " He delights in the law of the Lord," in the holy scriptures; which contain the

revealed will of God to man. The word of God is precious to all his people. Job said, " I have esteemed the words of his mouth," &c., Job xxiii. 12. David said, " The words of thy mouth are better to me than thousands of gold and silver." See Psalm cxix., which is full of the thoughts of the Psalmist on this subject.

2. *His practice.* He meditates in it day and night. Now to meditate, is to consider its meaning ; to weigh it ; to revolve it over in the mind. Now this is necessary to rightly understanding it, and benefiting by it. This is his constant practice. Day and night, morning and evening, when engaged in the affairs of the day, or perhaps when retired to his bed, his heart would silently dwell on the wonders of the divine law.

III. The happiness he enjoys. He is described as " blessed ;" that is, he is made happy in the favor of God. Now this blessedness is described in several respects.

1. *In its spiritual fruitfulness.* " Like a tree," &c. " He shall neither be barren," &c. " He shall be strong and flourishing, in the courts," &c. He shall have his fruit in " season." Grace and strength according to his state, &c., of affliction—prosperity, &c.

2. *In the constancy of his profession.* " His leaf shall not wither," &c. He shall hold on his way,—stand fast in the faith of the gospel,—hold fast his profession, —not go back.

3. *Divine success shall attend all his engagements.* That is, all his spiritual engagements shall be blessed ; and all his temporal affairs shall be connected with the benign influence of the providence of God. " All things shall work together for good," &c. See this beautifully illustrated, Psalm xxxvii. 3–6, and xxiii. and xxiv. 37. Such is the happiness of the godly man.

APPLICATION

1. *See the connection between holiness and devoted attention to the divine word.* Verse 1, you see what evils he avoids ; and verse 2, you see how this is done. Christ thus prayed, " Sanctify them by thy truth," &c.

2. *See the connection between daily meditation in the law of God, and spiritual prosperity.*

3. *Learn one great cause of spiritual*

weakness and barrenness. Neglect of the law of the Lord. How often do you read it ? How frequently meditate ? &c. entreat you to find time for this. Be Bible Christians. How rich the revelation we possess compared with David's portion ! We have the prophecies, gospels, the Acts of the apostles, epistles, &c.

22

THE CHRISTIAN'S ORIGINAL STATE

" Wherefore remember . . . . that at that time ye were without Christ."—Ephesians ii. 11, 12.

The apostle is calling the attention of the Ephesians to the consideration of their former condition previous to their salvation by Jesus Christ. He refers to several particulars—Gentiles, aliens, strangers, hopeless, and without God in the world. He introduces this list of their miseries by the language of the text. At that time " without Christ." Our text refers to the believer's original condition, and calls his remembrance to it.

I. The believer's original condition. " Without Christ." This description applies to all mankind, however diversified their natural state in other respects.

1. *Without the saving knowledge of Christ.* Do not know him in his dignity—graciousness—merits—value, &c.

2. *Without an experimental interest in Christ.* Not stones built upon him ; not members of his body ; not branches of Christ the living vine ; not living by faith in him, and by him.

3. *Without love to Christ.* Not prizing him as the pearl of great price ; not esteeming him " the fairest among ten thousand," &c. ; not acquainted with Peter's feelings, " Lord, thou knowest," &c.

4. *Without regard to his authority.* Not recognising his lordship ; not owning his authority, sceptre, laws, &c. ; living as if there were no Christ, &c. Now let me remind you that such a state is one,

(1.) Of extreme evil. It is a sin against the infinite love of God ; against the unceasing mercy of the Redeemer. Base ingratitude, &c.

(2.) Of great misery. Slaves, diseased, wretched.

(3.) Of imminent peril. Out of Christ ; no hope ; heirs of wrath and hell. Exposed to eternal death. The text calls the believer,

II. To REMEMBER HIS ORIGINAL STATE.

1. *To remember it, and be humble before the Lord.* No room for spiritual pride. O think of the rock, and the hole of the pit, &c.

2. *To remember it, and celebrate it with thanksgiving.* The Christian should rejoice in Christ always, and in every thing give thanks.

3. *Remember it, and compassionate those who are still in that miserable condition.*

4. *Remember it, and consecrate ourselves to the service of the Lord.*

23

THE DIFFICULTIES OF SALVATION

" And if the righteous scarcely be saved, where shall the ungodly and the sinner appear?"—1 PETER iv. 18.

THE scriptures often present truth to us by way of contrast. This is a powerful way of impressing the mind. Truth and error, holiness and iniquity, heaven and hell, are often thus placed before us. In this way characters, and their necessary destinies, are often drawn in the inspired records of revelation. " Say ye to the righteous it shall be well," &c. " The wicked shall be driven away," &c. " These shall go away into everlasting punishment, but the righteous," &c. Such is the spirit of the text. " If the righteous scarcely," &c.

I. NOTICE THE CHARACTER. " The righteous." Now those who are represented in the New Testament as being evangelically righteous, are such,

1. *As are justified by the grace of God.* Not now guilty transgressors, but forgiven and considered righteous, and treated as such through faith in Christ. Until thus justified we are guilty, unrighteous, condemned before God. " For Christ is the end of the law for righteousness to every one that believeth," Rom. x. 4. " Wherefore the law was our schoolmaster to bring us unto Christ, that we might be justified by faith," Gal. iii. 24. Such,

2. *As are renewed in righteousness by the Spirit of God.* This is effected in regeneration, when God takes away the stony heart, &c.; when we are born of the incorruptible seed of the word of God, born of the Spirit; when all old things pass away, &c.; when, as the workmanship of God, we are created anew unto good works. Such,

3. *As are righteous by conformity of heart and life to the law of God.* When sanctification is begun, and carried on in the soul, and where the life yields the fruit of righteousness to the glory of God; when we know, and love, and do the will of our Father who is in heaven. Now this is the character. Notice,

II. THE IMPORTANT TRUTH IMPLIED. " That the righteous scarcely are saved." Not saved without difficulty. Before we enter upon this, observe,

1. *There is a cheering truth expressed.* That the righteous *are* saved. Now they are delivered from the reigning power, and from the guilt and condemnation of sin, and they have a title to eternal salvation; their names are written in heaven; they are children and heirs of God and eternal life; they have the earnest of glory in the grace dawning within them; they have the first fruits, &c.

2. *There is amplitude of provision, and sufficiency of means for their salvation.* The grace of God is abundant; the love of Christ passeth knowledge; the influences of the Spirit possess almighty energy; and as to means, there is the light of revelation, ordinances, promises, a throne of grace, intercession of Christ, &c. Yet mark, the salvation of the righteous is,

3. *Connected with great difficulty.*

(1.) The reception of salvation is so. The kingdom is likened to a pearl, and all must be sold to possess it. To a feast, and all must be forsaken to come to it. The gate is strait; the kingdom of heaven suffereth violence, &c.

(2.) To retain present, and obtain eternal salvation is difficult. Look at the enemies of the Christian, the spirits of darkness, Satan and his host, the darts and the wiles of the devil; look at the situation of the Christian, in a world hostile to God; in arms against heaven; the seat of Satan; to the Christian it is a field of warfare, and how many are slain! a restless sea, and how many are wrecked! enchanted ground, and how many are bewitched with its fascinations; a race-course, and he must agonize to the goal of death. Look at the Christian's weakness, how infirm, how imperfect, what little strength! Need you wonder then that he is saved with difficulty ?

Not one Christian that ever entered heaven had an overplus of grace; not one, too much holiness.

III. THE SOLEMN QUESTION PRESENTED. "Where shall the wicked and ungodly appear?" I need not stay to define who are signified by the wicked; and the ungodly means all who are strangers to the saving grace of God, who have not the Spirit of God, the image of God, who do not love and obey God. Now if the *pardoned* and *regenerated* are scarcely saved, where shall the *guilty* and *depraved* appear? if those who *fear* and obey God are, &c., where shall the *impious* and *profane* appear? if those who *deny* themselves are, &c., where shall the *profligate?* &c.; if those who make religion their *business* are scarcely saved, where shall the *neglecters* and *despisers* appear? if those who *believe* and *pray* are scarcely saved, where shall the *unbelieving* and *prayerless* appear? Finally, if those who *do good*, and labor to follow Christ are scarcely saved, where shall the *servants* of the *devil*, who do evil, appear? I leave these observations to your solemn and deliberate consideration; let reason reply, let conscience reply, let scripture reply. They will appear at the left hand of God. The end of the wicked and ungodly must be despair and eternal wo; none can escape who neglect this great salvation.

APPLICATION

1. *Let the subject deeply impress you with the momentous meaning of the term* SAVED. Delivered from the wrath and misery of hell, and lifted up to heaven and eternal glory.

2. *Let the subject command all your energies and powers.* You cannot do too much, or sacrifice too much, in order to your salvation. See what men do for earthly glory, and for the riches of this world.

3. *Let the sinner and the ungodly now yield themselves to God.* There is mercy with God, &c. He invites, he promises. "Let the wicked forsake his way and the unrighteous man his thoughts, and let him return unto the Lord, and he will have mercy upon him," &c.

24
THE SAINT'S PROSPERITY, THE DELIGHT OF JEHOVAH
"Let the Lord be magnified, which hath pleasure in the prosperity of his servant."—PSALM xxxv. 27.

OUR text contains several words which may properly form topics for our present meditation.

I. THE CHARACTER TO WHOM THE TEXT REFERS. "His servant." Angels are the servants of the Lord. Jesus, the Mediator, became the servant of the Lord. All saints are such. "Being made free from sin, ye became the servants of God," &c. Jehovah, and the prince of darkness, divide the world. Only two classes; servants of sin, and of holiness. God's servants,

1. *Know his will.* Have ascertained wherein his pleasure consists.

2. *Wait upon him.* Appear before him to inquire—to ascertain his pleasure, &c. Their eyes are directed to the Lord.

3. *Obey his word.* His word is law; they have respect to all his commandments; delight in the law of the Lord.

4. *Depend upon him.* He gives them sustenance. He feeds, clothes, protects, rewards, &c.

II. THE PROSPERITY SPOKEN OF. This is not worldly prosperity; that is often the bane and ruin of the individual. But it is,

1. *Advancement in divine life.* Growing in conformity to God; rising higher in spiritual attainments, &c.; from the child to the man, &c.

2. *Vigor of the divine graces.* Faith strong—hope bright—love increasing—humility deepening, &c.

3. *Increase of divine peace.* "Peace flows as a river," &c.

4. *Usefulness in the divine cause.* Honoring God; establishing his kingdom, &c.

5. *Satisfaction with the divine portion.* Real enjoyment. "Godliness with contentment," &c. "Happy art thou," &c.

6. *Expectation of the divine glory.* "Looking for that blessed hope," &c.; waiting for the appearing of the Lamb.

III. THE DECLARATION MADE. "The Lord taketh pleasure," &c. He delighteth in the prosperity of his servants.

1. *He takes pleasure in making provision for it.* Our prosperity is of the Lord. All fruitfulness from him, &c. Now he has made ample provision.

2. *He takes pleasure in imparting the blessings.* He waits to supply; he expostulates. "Hitherto ye have asked nothing," &c.

3. *He takes pleasure in observing their prosperity.* This is his delight, to see the

results of grace ; the fruits of the Spirit ; his own likeness, &c.

APPLICATION

1. Let his servants magnify and bless his name.
2. Be faithful and persevering.
3. Who will become servants to God ?

25

THE WAY AND MANNER OF ACCESS TO GOD

" In whom we have boldness and access with confidence by the faith of him."—EPHESIANS iii. 12.

By the fall man has become darkened, and his heart alienated and estranged from God. Sin keeps man separated from God, and exposes him to his severe displeasure. In redemption we are brought near to God. By the death of Jesus we have a new and living way opened into the holiest of all ; now God can descend to the sinner, and the sinner ascend to God. Jesus is the ladder, or the way of access, between man and God—between heaven and earth. Now, this is the subject of the text. Notice,

I. OUR ACCESS TO GOD. It is only applicable to the believer. " Without faith," &c. We have especial access to God in three exercises :—

1. *Prayer.* Prayer is speaking to God, telling God our need, making known our requests, seeking his favor, &c.

2. *Praise.* Is celebrating the divine goodness ; thanking God for his mercy and grace ; speaking to him, and extolling his name ; the overflowing of the grateful soul in the divine presence.

3. *Meditation.* This is the soul's silent intercourse with God ; the mind contemplating, reflecting, and thinking upon God. Now, these may be separate or united exercises of the soul ; they may be public, domestic, or private. Our access to God should be frequent, so as to recognise God always, and in all things. Notice,

II. THE MEDIUM OF OUR ACCESS TO GOD. " In whom," &c. That is, in Christ, see verse 11. Now, Christ is the medium and depositary of all spiritual blessings.

1. *God only holds intercourse with men through Christ.* " I am the way," &c. " One God, and one Mediator," &c. Of old, God would only be approached through the medium of sacrifices. " Without shed-

ding of blood," &c. All these typified the Lord Jesus, the true and perfect sacrifice for the guilt of the world. There is but one way to the holiest of all—whether we come there to praise, or pray, or meditate— and that is the way consecrated for us by the blood of Christ.

2. *Sinners must be in Christ, to have comfortable access to God, and be accepted of him.* " In whom." We must be personally accepted in the Beloved before our services can please God. God does not demand any spiritual services from men until they are spiritually in Christ. The first great demand of God is, that we believe in the name of the Son of God. This brings us into a vital union with Christ. " There is no condemnation," &c. And then we are privileged to have access to God, by our union to his Son.

3. *Faith in Christ's person and work must distinguish each act of access to God.* The life of a Christian is a life of faith. Faith is not to be an occasional act of the soul, but the soul's constant exercise. When we approach God we should ever feel our personal *unworthiness*, and this should lead us to exercise faith in the *dignity* of Christ's person. We should feel our constant *guilt*, and this should lead us to trust in Christ's *death*. We should feel our *unfitness* to come before God, and this should lead us to depend on Christ's intercession at the right hand of God. Thus faith must always be exercised in our access to God.

III. THE SPIRIT IN WHICH GOD DESIRES US TO APPROACH HIM. With " boldness." This is enjoined, " Let us, therefore, come boldly," &c., see Heb. x. 19. Now, this is not to be irreverent, unhallowed boldness—not self-righteous, self-complacent boldness—not presumptuous boldness ; but it must be with the boldness of confidence— with holy freedom and liberty of speech— with the boldness of expectation that our suit will be heard and received. Now, this boldness of the believer in his access to God may be grounded,

1. *On the nature of the Deity.* The Being we approach is not a despot—not a malevolent Being ; his nature and his name is love. He is only terrible to incorrigible sinners. " He is the Lord merciful," &c. We may have boldness,

2. *From his divine relationship to us.* He is our Father—our spiritual Father. " As a Father," &c. " If we being evil." &c.

The child fears not—doubts not ; so, when we go to God, let us remember it is our privilege to address him as " Our Father," &c.

3. *From the delight he expresses in his people having access to him.* God is displeased if we have not frequent access. He invites us to live to him, and in him—the fellowship cannot be too close. He invites us to draw near—He allures, &c. The great end of all blessings is to draw us closer to God.

4. *From the presence of Christ in the holiest on our behalf.* Jesus is the officiating High Priest ; his incense is ever ascending ; all power is in Christ's hands ; the Father always heareth him, &c. " We have an advocate with the Father."

5. *From the remembrance of past instances of success.* Never did the Lord falsify his word, forget his promise, or turn away the seeking seed of Jacob empty. He has been better to us not only than our fears, but has done for us better than we ever asked or thought.

APPLICATION

1. *Urge the ungodly to immediate reconciliation.*

2. *Let the believer exult in his privilege of access to God.*

3. *Let holy, fervent boldness and confidence characterize our approaches to him.*

26

CONSTANT REJOICING

" Rejoice in the Lord alway : and again I say, Rejoice."—PHIL. iv. 4.

IT has ever been one of the most common and powerful objections to Christianity, that it is opposed to the present happiness and enjoyment of mankind. Now this has been of immense injury to the Christian cause, especially in preventing young and lively persons giving it their attentive consideration. Dr. Watts had respect to this objection in those admirable lines—

> " The sorrows of the mind
> Be banish'd from this place ;
> Religion never was design'd
> To make our pleasures less."

Now, this objection is truly fallacious. It originates in two misapprehensions.

(1.) As to the nature of rea joy. The silly mirth of the tavern or of the inebriated party, is mere noise, mere chaff ; such joy reason itself cannot commend.

(2.) As to the gloom of the religious ; now that is not always gloom which appears so. There may be seriousness of countenance, and a solemn state of mind, yet no gloom. Who can think of God, of death, and of eternity, and not be serious ? The gloom of the pious, when real, does not arise from religion, but often from a deficiency of it, and the sufferings arising therefrom, &c. See that parent, he appears gloomy, he feels for his children. That woman, her countenance is sad, her husband is a mocker. No ! true religion enforces and produces real, solid, abiding joy. The Christian has many causes of rejoicing ; works of nature—of providence —of redemption ; his own state, privileges, &c. ; but there is one pre-eminent, the text supplies it, " Rejoice," &c. Notice,

I. THE OBJECT OF THE CHRISTIAN'S REJOICING. " Rejoice in the Lord." All Christian duties and privileges have respect to the Lord Jesus Christ. He is to be preached ; we are to believe in him ; to be baptized into him ; found in him ; here in the text, to rejoice in him. " Rejoice,"

1. *In the perfection and glory of his person.* Our Redeemer is the Lord of Hosts ; the mighty God of Jacob. Immanuel, God with us. " Unto us a child," &c. He is the Lord of angels ; object of eternal worship and praise ; the king of glory ; the fairest among ten thousand, &c.

2. *In the completeness of his work.* He has wrought out a perfect righteousness— he has overcome our foes—he has redeemed us to God—he has finished his saving arrangements.

3. *In the offices he fulfils.—He is our prophet.* A teacher from God. The great apostle and prophet of whom Moses, &c. Of the last and most perfect dispensation. *Our priest,* he has offered an acceptable sacrifice unto God. Ever intercedes, &c. *Our king.* Oh think of his goodness, graciousness, potency, glory. " Grace is poured into his lips," &c.

4. *In the tenderness of his sympathies.* " He is touched," &c. He does not break the bruised reed, &c. " As the head." &c. ; never forgets, nor neglects, &c.

5. *In his inexhaustible fulness.* The believer entirely depends upon him. Out of his fulness, &c. ; if it failed, what would

become of his church ? We read of the unsearchable riches of his grace.

6. *In the immutable perpetuity of his regards.* "Having loved his own," &c. Whatever, or whoever fails, he will not. Our own condition will alter, but not his grace, &c. "The same yesterday," &c. This is the rock of triumph to the godly.

II. THE CONSTANCY OF THE CHRISTIAN'S REJOICING. "Alway : and again I say," &c. We doubt not that we should rejoice in prosperity, when we are happy, &c. ; but this is not alway. We are to rejoice,

(1.) Under persecution. See Matthew v. 11, 12.

(2.) In temptations. See James i. 2, 4.

(3.) In keen afflictions and fiery trials. 1 Peter iv. 12. Hence some were tortured, &c. Not accepting deliverance. "Alway." "For all things work together," &c. Let us notice,

III. SOME OF THE REASONS FOR THE CHRISTIAN'S CONSTANT REJOICING.

1. *It is a duty which we owe to God.* Not left to our own will, &c. He says, "Rejoice," &c. "Rejoice evermore." He says, "Arise, shine," &c. ; besides, his Spirit produces this, "The fruit of the Spirit is joy," &c., Gal. v. 22.

2. *It is an exercise most profitable to ourselves.* Hear what the wise man says, "A merry heart maketh a cheerful countenance ; a merry heart doeth good like a medicine." "And the joy of the Lord is our strength."

3. *It will do honor to our profession and recommend religion.* It is said of some that " every one had the countenance of a king ;" of the disciples, "they took knowledge," &c. Moses bore the radiance of the divine beauty on his countenance. Spiritual rejoicing will recommend religion to those who are without. Seeing this, they will say, "We will go with you," &c.

4. *It will be preparatory to the enjoyments of heaven.* Heaven is the region of felicity. "In thy presence is fulness," &c.

> "The hill of Zion yields
> A thousand sacred sweets," &c.

APPLICATION

1. *Learn the superiority of the joys of religion to all other joys.* Divine—spiritual —real.

2. *Invite the inquirer after bliss, to Jesus.*

Are you weary ? Are you thirsty ? Are you saying, "Who will show us any good ?"

3. *How joyless the state of the condemned sinner !*

27

THE TEMPTATION OF PETER
PART 1

" And the Lord said, Simon, Simon, behold, Satan hath desired to have you, that he may sift you as wheat ; but I have prayed for thee, that thy faith fail not ; and when thou art converted, strengthen thy brethren."—LUKE xxii. 31, 32.

IT is said that " whatsoever things were written aforetime were for our learning, that we through patience and comfort of the scriptures, might have hope." Our text is one of those portions of the divine word, replete with useful instruction, and is well adapted to promote our spiritual security and well-being. Among the disciples of Christ, Peter occupies a very prominent and distinguished place. He was a bold, ardent, and devoted follower of the Saviour. He was one of the most distinguished of the apostles, and had the honor of opening the kingdom of Christ, both to the Jews and the Gentiles. By the characteristics of his mind he was exposed however to danger. Hence by his very spirit and temperament, he was in danger of impetuosity and rashness ; an evidence of this immediately follows the text. " And he said unto him, Lord, I am ready," &c. His want of humble fear and his lamentable fall are beacons to us, and address us in the language of the apostle, "Let him that thinketh he standeth, take heed lest he fall." Observe in the text. A dangerous enemy referred to ; the design of that enemy specified ; the gracious intercession of Christ affirmed ; and a subsequent duty enforced.

I. A DANGEROUS ENEMY REFERRED TO. That enemy is " Satan," who is justly described as our adversary, accuser, murderer, destroyer, &c. The character of Satan is fearfully exhibited in the history of our world. He was the tempter, who by the serpent seduced our first parents ; he was the instigator of Cain to slay his brother Abel ; he has been exerting his spiritual power to ruin and destroy human beings from that period to this. We see his hatred of the holy and the happy in the case of Job, chap. i. ver. 6, 7 ; see Zech.

iii. 1, &c. We have also recorded his vile and impious attack on the Messiah, the Son of God, Matt. iv. 1, &c. Against this enemy we are incessantly warned. "Your adversary, the devil, goeth about," &c. "Resist the devil," &c. "Above all, take the shield of faith, by which ye may quench,' &c. Now this enemy,

1. *Is insidious in his attacks.* He is a spirit, and therefore, without notice, can have access—be in our dwellings—near our persons—inflaming our spirits, &c. Hence his subtlety is often the subject of scripture remark.

2. *Malevolent in his designs.* To blight, curse, destroy; to becloud the understanding, pervert the judgment, inflame the passions with evil, and pollute the conscience. He hates purity and happiness, and therefore labors to efface them.

3. *Persevering in his attacks.* It would appear, that for thousands of years, he has been pursuing his cruel avocation, and he is still going about, &c. He assails the young convert—harasses the aged Christian—and often only ceases his temptations on the dismissal of the soul to the regions of light.

4. *Fearfully successful in his efforts.* He keeps the mass of mankind in his hellish thraldom. God of this world—prince of the power of the air, &c. His temptations keep myriads from godly decision, and unnumbered hosts of the followers of Christ have apostatized through his hellish devices. Such is the enemy presented to us in the text. We have,

II. THE DESIGNS OF THIS ENEMY SPECI-FIED. "Desired to have you," that is, desired to have the people of God under his power—directly exposed to his fiery darts—in his cruel grasp—that he may sift, &c.—exercise them with the most trying and harassing temptations. If possible, that they may utterly fail, and faint under the process, and thus be regained to the standard of sin and death. In tempting and sifting the people of God, he endeavors often to suggest,

1. *That they have no interest in the divine mercy.* That their faith and hope are counterfeit; that their joys are merely animal excitement; that theirs is false security; that they are yet in the gall of bitterness, &c. Thus he labors, that they may cast off their confidence in which they have great recompense of reward. He suggests,

2. *The hardness of God in his providence towards them.* He refers to the prosperity of the wicked; how they flourish as the green bay-tree, &c. No sorrow, no bands in their death, &c. Asaph was severely sifted on this subject, Psalm lxxiii. 1–17. He urges,

3. *That God has withdrawn his consolations.* That our deadness, formality, hypocrisy, &c., have provoked the Lord, and therefore that he has abandoned us. Often the pious thus sifted, have cried, "Hath the Lord forgotten to be gracious," &c. "Is his mercy clean gone," &c. Or he excites,

4. *To indifference on the ground of divine mercy.* That the Lord will not be rigid with his people. That the divine partiality will overlook their infirmities. That they may sin, because grace doth abound; and perhaps he exhibits the failings of Abraham, of Moses, of David, of Peter, &c., and says, it is presumption to expect to be more holy than these. Let me just refer to certain circumstances, under which we give Satan great advantage in his temptations, and which are presented in that part of the history of Peter to which our text refers.

(1.) Great self-confidence, trusting to our experience—courage—wisdom, &c. &c.

(2.) Unwatchfulness. Being at ease. Spiritually indolent. Not on our guard.

(3.) Unnecessary admixture with the world. Sinful society. Worldly, trifling intercourse—Satan's ground. All these in Peter's case. I conclude by reminding you,

1. *That Satan desires to have you.* Each and all.

2. *That you are not ignorant of his devices.*

3. *To put on the whole armor of God.*

28

THE TEMPTATION OF PETER
PART 2

" And the Lord said, Simon, Simon, behold Satan hath desired to have you that he might sift you as wheat ; but I have prayed for thee, that thy faith fail not ; and when thou art converted, strengthen thy brethren."—LUKE xxii. 31, 32.

THE admonition of Christ to Peter, we should have supposed would have effectually preserved him from the perils to which he was exposed—an admonition so plain, so earnest, so emphatic—but alas ! the sequel of his history proves the contrary. With the warning fresh in his mind—with the courageous avowal yet hanging on his lips, the Saviour's hour of arrest arrives. He is seized by the violent band, and, at first, Peter magnanimously draws his sword, &c., forgetting that moral and not physical courage was demanded on the occasion. Christ is hurried away to the Jewish tribunal, and now Peter's defalcation commences, but Peter followed afar off; he then rashly ventures into the society of Christ's enemies, and afterwards falls into the snare Satan had laid for him, denying with oaths and curses that he knew the Messiah! Alas! how frail is man! How brittle his resolutions! How evanescent his goodness! "Like the morning cloud," &c. Let us now consider,

III. THE GRACIOUS INTERCESSION OF CHRIST. "But I have prayed for thee," &c. Here Christ stands before us in his character as the great High Priest of our profession. To pray for his people,

1. *Was necessarily connected with his office.* He has left us a rich instance in his prayer for the disciples, &c. John xvii. Doubtless he often prayed for his disciples when he spent whole nights in solitude, and secret devotion. And now "exalted to the right hand of the Majesty on high, he ever lives to make intercession," &c. In this exercise Christ delighted, and therefore his prayer would be earnest, tender, and faithful. His prayer,

2. *Was that Peter might not apostatize from the faith.* Peter evidently had faith in Christ—was a true and real believer, and Christ desired that he might not utterly cast off his trust and adherence to him. But how does this agree with the result? Peter's faith was suspended—ceased to exercise its sustaining influence—did not repel the dart of the enemy, nor preserve him from sin. But Peter did not entirely and fully apostatize. He did not yield himself up to evil; desert Christ's standard, and go over to the enemies cause. Sudden as was his sin, equally so was his contrition. Deep as was his guilt, still deeper his sorrow. Though cast down he was not destroyed; hence there is an immense difference between one gross sin, and entire apostacy. The best of men have been overcome by the former, without yielding to the latter. Observe,

3. *Christ's prayer was successful.* He obtained for Peter grace that held him even

when over the gulf; that rescued him from the lion's mouth, from the very grasp of the destroyer. Peter became penitent, believing, and was restored to God's favor and mercy. He was reconverted. Lifted out of the mire and clay, &c. "Restore unto me the joys," &c. "If any man sin," &c. Notice,

IV. THE SUBSEQUENT DUTY ENFORCED. "When thou art converted, strengthen thy brethren." Now let us ask,

1. *How he was to do this?*

(1.) By the exhibition of his own example. He would be a living trophy of the efficacy of the grace of God—its power to raise and restore. His own spirit would be inspired by the experience he had previously known; his love and gratitude would correspond in some degree with the mercies he had enjoyed. Thus his humility, his gratitude, and his zeal would have a favorable influence on his brethren.

(2.) By his instructions and counsels. He who had felt the severe, trying power of the enemy—who had reaped the grief and anguish of his own sin in departing from God—who had been arrested by the gracious look of the Saviour, surely would be best fitted to enlighten, admonish, and counsel others. Such would be most earnest in warning others.

(3.) By directing them to the only source of restoration. His fall and misery had brought him to know the power of Christ in saving, healing, and comforting. How he could speak of this! how enlarge and expatiate on it! how urge it! and in this way he could strengthen his brethren. He could do it,

(4.) By personal exertion on behalf of the fallen. If our sins and falls do not make us compassionate and pitiful, and solicitous for our fellow-erring Christians, it is strange indeed. Who that had fallen like Peter, could be harsh, and censorious, and indifferent to the brethren who had been overcome by temptation. "Brethren, if a man be overtaken in a fault," &c. "They that are strong should bear the infirmities of the weak," &c.

(5.) By fervent prayer to the Father of mercies on their behalf; as Christ did for Peter, Christians are to do for each other. See James v. 16; 1 John v. 15, 16, &c. We inquire,

2. *Why he was to do it?*

(1.) Gratitude to the Saviour. This is

the best expression of it, to " strengthen the brethren." To exhibit his mind to them. Feel and pray, &c., as he did.

(2.) Love to the brethren. Feeling for them, knowing the misery of a fallen state, grief and distress of sinning against Christ.

(3.) Zeal for the cause of Christ. Would we have Satan to triumph—the church to be injured—the wicked to conquer ? Surely not. It is lamentable when they fall, but worse when they remain in the pollution of their sin. Restored, they often are most valiant for Christ, &c. So Peter.

APPLICATION

1. *Learn the mutability of the best of saints.* All frail, weak, &c.

2. *Learn the solace and security of the righteous.* The love and intercession of Christ.

3. *The necessity of repentance and reconversion.* Tears—confession—supplication —change of conduct, &c.

4. *How the church should treat the fallen.*

29

PRESERVATION FROM THE DESTROYER

" By the word of thy lips I have kept me from the paths of the destroyer."—PSALM xvii. 4.

MAN's present state is one of probation. Here he is on trial for eternity ; here his principles will be tested by circumstances, and by the temptations of the evil one. But for his salvation and preservation God has made ample, available provision. Of their own ability no one could avoid and escape the influence of Satan's temptations. This terrific enemy by his subtlety, his untiring perseverance, would involve in ruin the most devoted, &c. Now the Psalmist tells how he kept himself, &c. " By the word of thy lips," &c. Let us make some observations,

I. ON THE DESTROYER.

II. HIS PATHS.

III. OUR MEANS OF PRESERVATION.

I. ON THE DESTROYER. The destroyer is Satan. His name is peculiarly appropriate. A murderer from the beginning. He destroyed himself, and his compeers in the first sin. He destroyed our first parents, and brought death, &c. His work is to destroy. He is a most successful destroyer ; myriads, &c., of all ages, and countries, and classes.

1. *He destroys man's moral dignity.* Debases—brings from his lofty original state. Casts down—dims the fine gold. Transforms the sovereign into a slave ; heir of glory, into an outcast. Removes the halo of glory, and covers with shame and ignominy.

2. *He has destroyed our portion.* Our original Eden with its plenitude of blessedness. Beggared our race ; involved in treason ; then proscription, and confiscation, and poverty followed. Portion of health, also gave sickness and pain, &c.

3. *He destroys the body.* Introduced death, made a sepulchre of the world. Smote that beautiful temple of God ; caused it to decay and fall, and moulder in the dust. Go to the beds of the dying, &c. Go to the grave-yard, &c.

4. *He destroys the soul.* Makes it morally wretched here. Appals it with guilt ; exposes it to wrath ; deludes, poisons it ; entices it into the black pathway of wo ; and finally triumphs in its everlasting condemnation and misery. Draws it down to the everlasting abodes prepared for himself and his angels.

II. HIS PATHS. Only one way, broad, dark, downhill, delusive, &c., way of sin. But in this way are many paths.

1. *There is the path of skepticism.* Rejection of truth—of divine revelation—of God's existence—of providence—of the divine claims, &c.

2. *The path of the scorner.* Who sneer and treat with ridicule serious and eternal things. Fools who mock at sin.

3. *The path of the pleasure-taker.* Lovers of pleasure more than God ; who run into excess and riot, &c. Those who are found in the scenes of mirth, in the ball-room, &c.

4. *The path of the worldly.* Who love the present evil world ; who seek its treasures only ; live on it and in it. Children of this world, creatures of time and the present.

5. *The path of the trifler.* Who understands and feels, &c., but still treats God and the soul as inferior objects. Who is not duly affected, not decided, &c., wile away means, opportunities, and life itself.

6. *The path of the self-righteous.* Who turn from the gospel and the cross of Christ, and lean to their own righteousness, &c. Trust in themselves, like the Pharisees of

old, &c. All these, with many others, are the paths of the destroyer.

III. OUR MEANS OF PRESERVATION. "By the word of thy lips," &c. The word of God is the grand instrument of our safety, &c. Let us see this established from other portions of the scriptures, Psalm cxix. 9 and 11 ; Psalm xxxvii. 31. I observe,

1. *The word of God is the means of our deliverance from these paths.* God's word proclaims liberty, &c. "Ye shall know the truth," &c. Christ's words deliver from the power of Satan, &c. The preaching of the gospel is the power of God, &c. The destroyer cannot resist the almighty word, &c.

2. *It also guides those whom it delivers.* "Thou shalt guide me," &c. It reveals the way of life, shines upon it, &c. Makes our duty plain, exposes the snares, &c. Preserves from Satan's devices.

3. *It preserves those also whom it guides.* "Kept by the power of God," &c. Commend you to God and the word of his grace. It sanctifies, &c. ; thus Christ employed it as the sword, defensive and offensive, "Thus it is written," John xvii. 14, 19. Now in addition to the instrument of safety, there is its use, its application ; " by the word ;" by its perusal ; by meditating on it ; by applying it in faith ; by it being prayerfully employed.

APPLICATION

1. *Let us not forget our peril.* Watch, &c. Be vigilant, &c.

2. *Remember our remedy.* Be familiar with it, &c.

3. *Urge all to escape, &c.* The way is open, you are invited, warned, entreated, &c.

30

SAINTS, THE TEMPLE OF GOD

"For ye are the temple of the living God."—2 CORINTHIANS vi 16.

THE term temple is one which peculiarly designates the habitation of the Godhead. Hence the heaven of heavens is in glorious reality the most holy place, and is the proper, essential temple of the universe. But the word, as you are aware, was applied to that magnificent structure erected by Solomon, and which is so often referred to in the Old Testament scriptures. To the first there was added the second temple, to which the prophet Haggai referred, " The glory of the latter house," &c. To this temple Christ went up in his youth— and this he purified by the expulsion of the buyers and sellers—and the destruction of this he clearly foretold. The word temple may, by a spiritual application of the term, be applied to the whole New Testament church ; but our text applies it to individual Christians, and so it is used in several parallel passages ; 1 Cor. iii. 16, and vi. 19 ; Eph. ii. 21 ; and 1 Pet. ii. 5. Now, let us on this occasion,

I. CONSIDER THE RESPLENDENT SIMILITUDE.

II. THE PRIVILEGES INVOLVED IN IT. And,

III. THE DUTIES ARISING FROM IT.

I. CONSIDER THE RESPLENDENT SIMILITUDE. Now, when we say the Christian is the temple of God, we observe the appropriateness,

1. *In its construction.* It was of divine devisal ; its form, its plans, &c., were all of God. He was the architect and artificer ; the emanation of his own good, wise, and holy mind. Now, the salvation of the soul, involving its restoration from sin, and misery, and death, was entirely of God ; his own infinite skill devised the whole scheme. It was the bright emanation of his holy and compassionate mind, not the production of human knowledge and power, &c.

2. *In its erection.* The materials,

(1.) Originally unfit, distant. So in reference to human beings—carnal, defiled, far off. These materials were,

(2.) Prepared and rendered suitable ; so the soul enlightened, purified, and converted, &c. ; brought nigh.

(3.) In this a suitable instrumentality was appointed ; not miracles, but means. God could have done it by either ; so he employs his servants, his word, his ordinances ; men of rare gifts and powers, &c.

3. *In its dedication.* When finished, the temple was dedicated, publicly, devotionally, entirely. Just so the Christian. To this we are repeatedly called. " I beseech you, brethren, by the mercies of God," &c. This is called putting on the Lord Jesus ; confessing Christ before men ; making a good profession. Now, this must be done publicly before men ; devoutly ; with

fervent prayer ; entirely ; consecrating our whole selves, &c.   The similitude is seen,

4. *In its moral magnificence.*   The grandeur of the temple filled with wonder and amazement ; overawed, when completed, &c.   Now, there is a moral magnificence in the Christian character.   How changed. What a transformation ; were we to say from a brute to an angel, it would not do justice to it.   A rebel, now a friend ; an alien, now a child ; a curse, now a blessing ; the palace of demons, now the dwelling of God ; truth in the place of error ; knowledge instead of darkness ; wisdom in the place of folly ; purity instead of defilement ; righteousness instead of sin ; heaven instead of hell.   Now, let us consider,

II. THE PRIVILEGES INVOLVED.

1. *The divine recognition.*   He owned the temple—called it his—put his name on it ; thus it was hallowed and glorious Now, so does God treat his servants ; he calls them his own—gives them his name. " My sons and my daughters," &c. ; my people ; my jewels.

2. *Divine residence.*   God dwelt in the temple ; his glory filled it.   He was there addressed in prayer and praise ; he was consulted, worshipped, &c.   Now, all this is the privilege of the saint.   " Dwell in you," &c.   " We will come unto you," &c.   We may commune, speak his praise, seek his mind, &c.

3. *Divine benediction.*   God's blessing was eminently in it, and on it, and for it. Prophecies and promises.   " My heart and mine eyes," &c.   " Whereby are given to us great and precious promises," &c. God's blessing is upon his people.   Now consider,

III. THE DUTIES ARISING FROM IT.   Now, the following, selected from many, must suffice :—

1. *Purity.*   The temple was to be holy ; not for profane use—not for carnal purposes.   Now, God cannot delight in us except as we are pure.   The conscience, affections, &c., must be holy to the Lord. Now, we must seek after this, labor for it, &c.

2. *Constant service.*   The fire was not to go out ; the worship was to be incessant ; the offerings regular.   Now, he requires this from us.   " Pray without ceasing ; rejoice evermore," &c.   Our offerings, too, must be constant ; the offering of a broken spirit, &c. ; our liberality to his cause, &c.

3. *Reverential awe and hallowed tranquillity.*   The worship was to be with fear and reverence.   God is greatly to be feared, &c.   Fear before him, all his saints, &c. ; peace, &c., is indispensable ; God is not the author of confusion ; we must put away all wrath, &c. ; the spirit of the dove and the lamb.

4. *Reflection of God's glory.*   The Jew went up and beheld the symbol of Deity ; he shone forth there.   Now, we are thus to be reflections of God's likeness ; the world should see God in us.   " Take knowledge of us that we have been with Jesus," &c. " Epistles read and known," &c.   " Show forth his praise," &c.   Now, these are the duties.

APPLICATION

1. *What reason for humiliation and shame !*   Are there not idols in this temple —impurities—disorder ? &c.   Let us bow down before the Lord ; seek a fresh consecration, &c.

2. *Subject full of God's condescension.* " Will God dwell ?" &c.   " To that man will I look," &c.

3. *The soul of the sinner is Satan's seat.*

4. *Who will now become the temples of the Lord ?*

31

DAVID'S REGRETS AND CONSOLATIONS

" Although my house be not so with God, yet he hath made with me an everlasting covenant, ordered in all things, and sure," &c.—2 SAMUEL xxiii. 5.

THE whole history of David is fraught with instruction.   It was a most astonishing series of sunshine and cloud, of darkness and light, of prosperity and adversity, of sorrow and joy ; but in the great providence of God he had now reached the margin of life.   He had crossed the desert, and the goodly land was before him ; he had weathered the storm, and the haven was in view ; he had fought the good fight, and the crown glittered in prospect ; he was uttering now his last words—his dying sayings, and they were worthy of the illustrious prophet, the royal monarch, and the highly-favored servant of the Lord.   Let us consider the regrets, the experience, and the happiness of David, as expressed in our text.

I. OBSERVE HIS REGRETS. "Although my house," &c. The expressions of the text are elliptical : something is implied more than we read. He evidently meant that his house was not so,

1. *As it ought to be.* The family should resemble the celestial abodes of the blessed ; full of God's light—the residence of the divine favor—the scene of divine obedience —the circle of divine love ; in one word, what Joshua resolved, " As for me and my house, we will serve the Lord." But in David's family there were jealousies, envyings, bickerings, disobedience to parents, rebellion, and almost every foul thing that could reflect the perdition beneath.

2. *It was not as David had desired it to be.* He had, doubtless, longed for the highest well-being of his family. His example had reflected the earnest piety of his own soul ; his influence, his prayers, &c., doubtless had been incessantly offered ; but instead of spiritual fertility, there was barrenness ; instead of order, confusion ; instead of holiness, sin.

3. *Yet it was as many of the families of the righteous have unhappily been.* Who can reflect on this without grief ? The first family had within it Cain, a fratricide ; Noah's family had within it Ham, the father of the Canaanites ; Abraham's family had a mocking Ishmael ; Isaac's, a profane Esau, &c. Then look at the sons of Aaron and Eli, and so of many others of the servants of God ; but still the grief and regret was not the less. To how many does it apply here ? How few the exceptions—how exceedingly rare ! Can we account for it ? We would refer,

(1.) To the truth that piety is not hereditary. The Jews erred in this, " We are the children of Abraham," &c. No ! religion ever was, and ever will be, personal.

(2.) It often arises from the glaring imperfections and weaknesses of pious parents. Children often reason that religious persons should be faultless ; they expect perfection, and the contrast is so striking. Our religion is so scanty, so feeble, light so glimmering, example so irregular, that children stumble, are prejudiced against religion, and perhaps rush into the world. We are not sure that one glaring inconsistency will not do more to harden them, than a year's propriety of conduct to do them

good. Let this admonish every parent present who professes religion. There may be many things in your families to pity, but perhaps much more to blame. But observe,

II. DAVID'S PERSONAL EXPERIENCE. "Yet God hath made with me an everlasting," &c. He, doubtless, referred to the covenant of redeeming mercy, with which he was experimentally acquainted. Now this covenant, or agreement, is the great act of God in offering mercy to mankind, through the person and work of Christ, who is the Mediator of the new covenant. Now, this covenant is the subject of revelation, especially of New Testament revelation. To this covenant David had given his believing assent. He had applied it with all its blessings to his own soul, so that it became experimentally his. God allows all who believe to have the same interest in it, and happiness from it, that David had. Now, of this covenant he affirms,

1. *That it is everlasting.* Not only everlasting with regard to time, but in God's own mind and purpose before all time. This redeeming thought was part of his gracious design from all eternity. So is it everlasting in its duration. It was parallel with all time, and extends to all eternity ; it is a covenant never to be annulled ; it elevates its participants to everlasting dignity and joy ; its grand promise is eternal life.

2. *It is ordered in all things.* As such, its mediation, its promises, its dispensations, its conditions, are all arranged and settled ; nothing confused, &c. ; like all God's works, reflecting his own order and harmony. The whole plan reflects God's infallible wisdom, and is certain to accomplish what he designed ; for, observe,

3. *It is secure.* Men may violate covenants—God cannot ; they may fail for want of ability, &c. Adverse circumstances may thwart ; but this is sure—on a rock. It has been assailed, forsaken, &c. ; but it is still sure. Hell and devils are in league, &c. ; but it is sure,

(1.) To glorify its Author.

(2.) Reward the Mediator.

(3.) Save all believers.

(4.) And overthrow all its foes. Now, though David's house was not so, &c., yet from this experience observe,

III. THE HAPPINESS HE ENJOYED. This happiness arose,

1. *From the salvation he realized.* In the

covenant was " all his salvation." Salvation from past guilt and wrath, from pollution, from condemnation ; salvation into God's favor and kingdom ; salvation even in death ; salvation, including the opening grave and eternal glory. So is all our salvation in this covenant ; and so also from this all true and genuine happiness flows. No substitute for this ; this is the one thing.

2. *From the satisfaction he expressed.* " All my desire." It was the pre-eminent thing, the absorbing, &c. ; that which made up for every deficiency ; that reconciled to every lot ; that which was the end of life itself. Other things might be subordinately desired and valued ; but this chiefly, this always, &c. " The Lord is the portion of my soul," &c. Nothing but an interest in God's covenant can or ought to be all our desire. " Whom have I in heaven but thee ?" &c.

APPLICATION

1. *Learn to expect relative and domestic disappointments.* Here are our sweetest joys, or our keenest sorrows. Every home is not a sanctuary from toil, and trouble, and guilt ; our houses are infected with the plague of sin.

2. *The responsibility of the parental office.* Tears and lamentations are worse, if possible, than hypocrisy, if we do not seek the salvation of our children. If you do not instruct, how can you mourn their ignorance ? If you do not impress, and influence, and pray ? &c. Do think of these things, &c. We shall all be constrained to do so before we leave our families. Let that hour often be anticipated ; it will benefit us, &c.

3. *Think and feel for the children of the irreligious.* This one end of sabbath school tuition, to care for the children of the poor.

4. *Are you interested in this covenant ?*

5. *Death-bed hopes must rest on this covenant alone.* Not on creeds, works, usefulness, &c.

32
THE LAW OF LIBERTY

" But whoso looketh into the perfect law of liberty, and continueth therein, he being not a forgetful hearer, but a doer of the work, this man shall be blessed in his deed."—JAMES i. 25.

OUR text, and the preceding verse, refer to the manner of hearing the divine word—

and this is, indeed, a subject of great importance. It is important to take heed what we hear, and also how we hear, and likewise as to the results of our hearing. Some only hear with the external ear; they know what words we speak, but do not labor to comprehend the sense and signification. Others hear for the time, and try to understand ; but when the benediction is pronounced they conceive all is over, and pay no further attention. Others hear, and retain a general knowledge and remembrance, but do not apply it to their own hearts and consciences, nor practise what they hear ; but the good hearer " looketh into the perfect law," &c. Our text contains,

I. A STRIKING REPRESENTATION OF THE DIVINE WORD.

II. A TRUE PORTRAITURE OF THE CHRISTIAN HEARER.

I. A STRIKING REPRESENTATION OF THE DIVINE WORD. A threefold description.

1. *A law.* Law of God ; the legislative enactments of King Messiah ; the revealed will of God ; the moral rule of action, given by one who had authority—Jehovah ; binding upon those to whom it is addressed ; promulged for their instruction and benefit ; sanctioned by rewards and punishments Now this law,

2. *Is perfect.* As it is,

(1.) The law of a perfect Lawgiver.

(2.) A perfect rule of life. It ensures all that relates to the mind, lip, and life.

(3.) As it is perfectly equitable. Pure ; free from all error ; no weakness or imperfection ; nothing overlooked, &c.

(4.) Perfect, as it relates to all states and circumstances in which men are placed. The monarch, the subject, the prince, and the beggar ; all civil and social relationships are embodied.

(5.) It is absolutely sufficient ; it needs no addition ; cannot be improved.

(6.) Because it is the standard of all perfection. All other laws are good or bad as they resemble this.

3. *It is a perfect law of liberty.* Now three ideas here :

(1.) As a law of truth and equity, it frees the mind from the bondage of ignorance and error. " Ye shall know the truth," &c.

(2.) As a law of love and mercy, it brings us into the liberty of God's forgiving grace.

(3.) As a law of holiness, it frees the soul from the dominion of sin. "The law of the Lord," &c., see Psalm xix. 7. Our subject gives us,

II. A TRUE PORTRAITURE OF THE CHRISTIAN HEARER.

1. *He gives intense regard to the divine word.* Looketh, as the cherubim did, into the ark which contained the divine law. He does not give it casual or superficial attention, but intense and earnest ; see this set forth, 1 Peter i. 10, &c. This is his spiritual habit, his Christian course. "He looketh" into it.

2. *He extensively retains what he hears.* "Not a forgetful hearer." The memory of persons differs exceedingly ; liable to infirmities and decay. Not necessary to retain the words, but the sense and meaning. How many are forgetful hearers ! Is it not because they are not sufficiently interested ? because they do not labor to remember ? because they are not judicious in reference to hearing ? Three simple rules :

(1.) Prepare for hearing by prayer, &c.

(2.) Be wakeful and intent in hearing.

(3.) Be deliberate and silent after hearing ; avoid unnecessary talking for at least a few minutes, that it may sink into the mind.

3. *He exemplifies the word in his life and conduct.* "A doer of the work." Conforms to the law ; obeys what is spoken ; endeavors to live the truths of the divine word ; walks in the good way, &c. ; and in this he perseveres, for he "continueth therein." He follows on to hear, and learn, and to know, and do the will of God. The Christian hearer,

4. *Is a blessed, or happy character.* "Blessed in his deed." In this course he enjoys God's favor and blessing ; the end of hearing is answered ; his soul delights in the word ; it is the joy of his heart ; he is truly blessed ; this has a good influence on him in the various eventful scenes of life.

APPLICATION

1. Let us try ourselves by the text.

2. What reason for improvement.

33

THE CHRISTIAN'S REGARD FOR AN UNSEEN SAVIOUR

" Whom having not seen, ye love; in whom, though now ye see him not, yet believing, ye re-joice with joy unspeakable and full of glory."— 1 PETER i. 8.

THERE is, in real religion, a mutual reciprocated feeling between God and his people. Religion is said to consist in knowing God, and God is said to know his people. To be known of God is to be approved and accepted of him. Religion is represented as essentially including love and delight in God ; and God has stated, in the most affectionate forms of expression, his love and delight in his people. The Christian dwells in God, and God dwells by his Holy Spirit in the hearts of his children. The Christian honors God, and whoso honoreth God, doth he also honor. Our text refers to three of the leading features of genuine spiritual piety.

I. FAITH IN AN UNSEEN SAVIOUR.

II. LOVE TO AN UNSEEN SAVIOUR.

III. JOY IN AN UNSEEN SAVIOUR.

I. FAITH IN AN UNSEEN SAVIOUR. Faith is contradistinguished from sight. Thomas believed only upon palpable evidence, when to doubt were impossible. The apostles and first disciples saw Christ ; he tabernacled among them ; they beheld and heard, &c. ; yet, as regarded his divinity, his true Messiahship, they had to believe as his life and miracles testified of him. The saints, before his advent, had to believe on the ground of promises, prophecies, and types. These pointed to Christ, and giving full credit to these, they saw the day of Christ, and rejoiced and were glad. The followers of Jesus now have the record of the gospel, the testimony of the various evangelists and apostles ; he is no longer in our world, living a life of spotlessness, teaching and performing miracles of grace and mercy. Faith believes the record which God hath given of his Son, receives it as a truth worthy of all acceptation, exclaims with Peter, "I believe that thou art Christ ;" with the woman of Samaria, "This is indeed the Christ ;" with the centurion, "Surely this is the Son of God ;" with Thomas, "My Lord and my God." Believing is realizing Christ in all his offices, work, and grace ; accepting him as God's gift, looking to him as the Lamb, building on him as the foundation, fleeing to him as the refuge, trusting in him as the only hope, &c. Now believing on such evidence, is what we do every day in other matters. In books of voyages, &c., in works on history, &c., in ancient biography, &c., lives of Alfred the Great, Socrates, Alexander, &c. Now on the record of the New Testament writers we thus believe in the Lord Jesus Christ. The next principle recognised is,

II. LOVE TO AN UNSEEN SAVIOUR. "Whom having not seen ye love." Now love to this unseen Saviour is grounded on a belief,

1. *Of his character as revealed in the divine word.* In him is every thing lovely and excellent; purity, truth, meekness, goodness, patience, grace. Desire of all nations; fairest among ten thousand, &c. This love is grounded,

2. *On a belief of what he has done for us.* Pitied us, &c. He hath redeemed us, &c., given himself for us, lived, sorrowed, died for us. Oh, who can have such claims as Christ?

"Were the whole realm of nature mine," &c.

3. *On a belief of the relationship and offices he sustains towards us.* He is our elder brother by choice, &c. He is our unfailing friend; he proved himself a friend in need, &c. He is our surety, took our place; our advocate, he ever liveth, &c. "We have an advocate with the Father." He is our life, the life of our souls, &c.

4. *We love him on the ground of faith in what he has engaged to do for his people.* What has he done already? Who can recite it? What is he doing? Oh, draw aside the veil, and look into the holiest of all, &c. But we now ask, what has he engaged to do? to keep, to guard, to sanctify, to support in death, to crown with glory, to confess us, &c., to give eternal life, &c. Believing all this, surely we may exclaim, "Whom having not seen we love." But,

III. WE REJOICE IN AN UNSEEN SAVIOUR Faith works by love, and both are productive of joy.

1. *We rejoice.* This is the spiritual habit of the soul, to joy in God, to rejoice in Christ Jesus. It is said the disciples were glad when they saw the Lord. To find Christ and know him is matter of great joy. The woman and silver penny, &c. The disciples going to Emmaus. Now this is joy peculiarly spiritual; joy of heart, really felt and experienced. It brightens the countenance, nerves the soul, fills the mouth with holy praise.

2. *This joy is beyond expression.* Can-not be told; words not to be found; speech too poor; requires another language, a seraph's tongue, &c.

3. *This joy is full of glory.* Joy from God's glorious mind, the joy of God; joy of the glorious gospel, joy full of the impress of Christ's glory, joy anticipating endless glory, a ray from the noontide light, a draught from the celestial fountain, a bunch of Canaan's grapes; the earnest, the first-fruits of that glory which shall be revealed, &c.; not full of anxiety, distress, or fear, but full of glory.

APPLICATION

1. *Do you believe in Christ?* Have you received Christ, ventured all upon him? &c.

2. *Do you love Christ?* Do your thoughts, lives, &c., attest it?

3. *Do you rejoice?*

34

EARNESTNESS IN RELIGION, INDISPENSABLE

"And from the days of John the Baptist until now, the kingdom of heaven suffereth violence, and the violent take it by force."—MATT. xi. 12.

THE Saviour had just passed a high eulogium on John the Baptist, but had also stated that the least in the kingdom of heaven, &c. John was greater than any of the prophets in the dispensation in which he lived, and the office which he discharged; but he only heralded the Lord's anointed. He saw the dawn of the day, but the least of the Saviour's disciples was greater, more ennobled and favored by being in the kingdom, enjoying Christ, and sharing in the blessings of his reign. The Saviour then refers to the excitement which had been produced by the preaching of the Baptist. From his day the kingdom of heaven suffered violence. He went forth and called men to repentance, great multitudes heard and obeyed, and were baptized; and this eagerness still continued, for while the Jewish priests, and scribes, and Pharisees rejected the Saviour, the people, especially publicans, and harlots, and outcasts, pressed into the kingdom of God. The kingdom of heaven, or the New Testament dispensation, is still upon the earth, it reveals the same privileges, and offers the same blessings now to us, &c.; and it must be accepted in the same way. Let us then consider,

I. THE NATURE OF THE VIOLENCE WHICH MUST BE EMPLOYED.

II. THE MOTIVES WHICH SHOULD IMPEL US TO EXERCISE IT.

I. THE NATURE OF THE VIOLENCE WHICH MUST BE EMPLOYED. By violence, we understand moral energy and fire. The idea is that of a person pressing through a crowd, or an army storming a citadel. Now the violence necessary to securing the blessings of salvation includes,

1. *A violence of resolution in opposition to vacillating inconstancy.* Many resolve and re-resolve, and yet do not advance. Their resolves are like the morning cloud and early dew. They say, they will go into the vineyard, but do not. Now this procrastination is the ruin of thousands. To attain the blessings of the gospel, there must be determinate violence; a vehement decision; a making up of the mind. Set your heart and soul, &c.

2. *This violence includes thorough self-denial, in opposition to ease, and self-indulgence.* Nature loves ease, apathy, self-indulgence. Christ demands mortification, self-denial, and cross-bearing. No man would enter the list of wrestlers with folded arms; no one compete for the wreath, and give way to luxury and enjoyment. We are to strive to enter in; literally, agonize. Self must be chased out of all its retreats and fastnesses. The old man must be crucified if Christ is to benefit us.

3. *This violence includes the effort of the whole soul in opposition to a divided heart.* God will be found of us when we seek him with the whole heart. Often the understanding, judgment, and conscience, agree, but the affections and will are opposed; now thus success cannot be realized. A double-minded man, or a man of two minds, is unstable, &c. There must be resolution, self-denial, and concentrated effort. Every faculty and feeling must enter on the work, &c.

4. *There must be the violence of ardent prayer in opposition to listlessness of desire.* The desires suited to those who would enter the kingdom, are described by hungering and thirsting, panting, fainting, &c. " My soul followeth hard," &c. There must be importunity. Knock, seek, appeal, cry out, plead, persevere. Languor can do nothing, the throne must be stormed. " I will not let thee go." This importunity is urged by Christ in the parable of the importunate widow, &c. Exemplified in the Syrophenician woman; need I add, that this ardent prayer must fasten itself by faith on the divine word. Rely on the testimony God has given, &c. Hold by the horns of the altar, &c.

II. CONSIDER THE MOTIVES WHICH SHOULD IMPEL US TO EXERCISE THIS VIOLENCE.

1. *The resistance with which our spirits have to contend.* Our own hearts will resist—unbelief, reigning sin, indolence of spirit, &c., enmity to God. The world will resist us by ridicule perhaps, or by interposing its spirit, and maxims, and enjoyments; especially its honors, pleasures, &c. Satan will resist us. When the father brought his afflicted child, who was possessed, Satan threw him down, &c. He will not tamely resign his palace and throne; now it is only by violence that we can succeed in overcoming the resistance.

2. *From the pre-eminent value of the object to be attained.* " A kingdom." The Persian monarch promised Esther to the extent of half his kingdom, but this is a whole kingdom, and a heavenly one; kingdom of grace here, and kingdom of glory forever. In this kingdom there is dignity, and riches, and enjoyments. An inheritance, a crown, dominion, and pleasures for evermore, a kingdom of eternal glory, everlasting felicity; is it not worth striving for? See how men strive for a morsel of bread, few riches, few honors; and what are all these but toys and bubbles, &c.

3. *On account of the limited period of effort which is afforded.* There might be some show of reason for indifference and ease, if we had a thousand years, or even a century. But our probation is most absolutely short, and exceedingly uncertain. We cannot boast of the morrow, cannot tell what a day may bring forth, &c. The poet has very solemnly said,

" Lo, on a narrow neck of land,
'Twixt two unbounded seas I stand,
 Secure, insensible ;
A point of time, a moment's space,
Removes me to that heavenly place,
 Or shuts me up in hell."

To-day, then, how earnest and violent ought we to be !

4. *On account of the awful loss we shall*

sustain if we do not gain it. But two states of existence hereafter; kingdom of glory, and kingdom of darkness—heaven and hell—paradise and perdition; and there is no way of gaining the one and shunning the other, but that specified in the text. Oh, then, is it not all-important, &c. This is a reason high as heaven, deep as the abyss of wo, and long as eternity. "The kingdom of heaven," &c.

APPLICATION

1. To those who possess it, and are of it. This termination must be carried out. Show the same diligence to the end, &c.

2. Who will enter the lists for the kingdom of heaven, and now? We invite and urge all.

3. The thoughtless and indifferent must perish.

35

THE WORK OF RELIGION, PERFECTED BY GOD

"The Lord will perfect that which concerneth me: thy mercy, O Lord, endureth for ever: forsake not the work of thine own hands."—PSALM cxxxviii. 8.

PIETY is not the exhibition of any separate virtue or grace, but the union and harmony of all the graces in their due proportions, and well-regulated influence on the character and life of the possessor. For instance, it is not mere magnanimity, but holy heroism, mingled with circumspection and godly fear; it is not merely resolute confidence, but implicit trust, associated with vigilance and solicitude; it is not faith alone, but faith which produces good works, fruit of righteousness; it does not so look up to God as to forget the use of means, and unites these with fervent prayer for the divine blessing. We are led to this train of thought from the spirit of the text. See the confidence of the Psalmist, "The Lord will," &c. But that confidence is followed with earnest supplication. "Forsake not," &c. But let us consider the general tenor of the text. And we notice,

I. TRUE RELIGION IS THAT WHICH CONCERNETH US. It is emphatically the one great and supreme concern and end of life; it is the one thing needful. Not a vain thing, for "it is our life." Whether we consider the nature of the soul, our responsible condition, the uncertainty of life, the probable nearness of death, the solemnities of judgment, and the awful realities of eternity—religion is that which especially concerneth us. If so, then,

1. *It ought to be our first concern.* "Seek ye first the kingdom of God." This is the basis of all happiness and security, ought to be laid first; first in life, first every day, first in preference to all other things.

2. *It ought to be our chief concern.* Not only first, but most prominent. Exercising our chief thoughts, meeting our chief desires, influencing our chief actions, &c. It must have the ascendency if it is to prosper. Religion, if at all secondary, will decline. As the heart is one of the chief vital organs of the body, so the affections surrendered to God, must be chiefly swayed by his Spirit and grace.

3. *It must be our personal concern.* Friends may do much for our religious comfort and welfare, but only when our own personal exertions are put forth; none can repent for us, pray instead of us, meditate for us, enjoy or serve God for us. Religion is essentially personal, and every one must give an account for himself to God.

4. *It must be our constant concern.* Religion is not to be impulsive, but habitual. The healthy exercise of the mind; the daily rising of the emotions to God. Persevering obedience to the divine laws. "Rejoice evermore, pray without ceasing," &c. Daily walking in the path of duty; growing in the divine likeness; warring the good warfare; faithful unto death; "always abounding in the work of the Lord," &c. Stability and perseverance essential to our salvation. We notice,

II. THAT TRUE RELIGION IS THE WORK OF GOD'S HANDS. Our concern, and God's work.

1. *God made all the arrangements necessary to our being religious.* Exercised his compassion—sent forth his Son to redeem us—given the Holy Spirit—commanded the heralds of truth— pened a way in his providence for our hearing the gospel, &c., &c.

2. *Religion in the soul is the direct production of divine influence.* Are we enlightened? "God who commanded the light out of darkness," &c. Are we converted? "He turned us from darkness," &c. Are we regenerated? "He hath begotten us again," &c. Are we justified?

We are "justified freely by his grace." "His workmanship, created anew to good works."

3. *Religion depends on the communications of his grace.* Jesus said, "Without me ye can do nothing." "He that hath begun the good work will carry it on," &c. He laid the foundation, and will bring on the head stone. All our comfort and strength, &c., are from God. But notice,

III. TRUE RELIGION IN THE BEST SAINTS IS YET IMPERFECT. "The Lord will perfect that," &c. Supposing all the graces of religion in the soul, they are only in a progressive state ; none perfect. Who is perfect in knowledge ? In faith ? In patience ? In obedience both as to matter and manner ? In love ? In resemblance to Jesus ? How true of each and all, " There is yet very much land to be possessed," see Philippians iii. 12, &c. We observe,

IV. FOR A CONSUMMATION OF RELIGION EVERY TRUE CHRISTIAN IS SOLICITOUS. They know and feel their imperfections ; they mourn and grieve ; they long and desire. Now this solicitude is accompanied with consolation and hope ; and this consolation and hope rest,

1. *On the divine engagements.* "The Lord will perfect," &c. He has engaged to do it. Given many promises. He will never leave nor forsake his people. He will be with them in the waters, and in the fire. "In six troubles," &c. This consolation and hope rest,

2. *On the unchanging mercy of God.* "Thy mercy, O Lord, endureth," &c. God's engagements are all founded on his mercy, and not our worthiness. The mercy of the Lord is from everlasting to everlasting, &c., &c. Now his tender mercies are especially exercised towards his saints. This consolation and hope rest,

3. *On the unfailing efficacy of prayer.* Hence the prayer, " Forsake not the work," &c. " God will be inquired of." All the saints of God have been sustained, &c., but none without prayer. Prayer is God's ordinance, and he has ever honored it. " The fervent effectual prayer of the righteous availeth much." All the saints of the Most High have been eminent for prayer ; Abraham, Jacob, Moses, David, the apostles, &c. All the glorified in heaven can attest, that praying breath was never spent in vain. Let our subject,

1. *Lead to individual examination.* Are we concerned about true personal religion ?

2. *Let the subject cheer the servant of God.* "He will perfect," &c. Then throw away your fears. " His mercy endureth," &c. Then exercise hope and confidence in him.

3. *Let the subject incite to devotional diligence.* The use of God's appointed means in the spirit of humble, continuous prayer.

36

THE BELIEVER'S APPROACH TO GOD

"Oh that I knew where I might find him ! that I might come even to his seat : I would order my cause before him, and fill my mouth with arguments."—JOB xxiii. 3, 4.

OBSERVE from these words,

I. THE PLACE OF APPROACH SPECIFIED. " His seat."

II. THE MANNER OF APPLICATION ADOPTED. " I would order my cause," &c.

III. THE MODE OF PLEADING DETERMINED. " I would fill my mouth," &c.

I. THE PLACE OF APPROACH SPECIFIED. " That I might come even to his seat." The seat or throne of Jehovah is in the heaven of heavens, infinitely above the seats of cherubim and seraphim. We should ever have three views of the seat of Jehovah.

1. *Its grandeur.* See Isaiah vi. 1–3. " I saw also the Lord sitting upon a throne, high and lifted up, and his train filled the temple. Above it stood the seraphim ; each one had six wings ; with twain he covered his face, and with twain he covered his feet, and with twain he did fly. And one cried to another, and said, Holy, holy, holy, is the Lord of hosts ; the whole earth is full of his glory." See also Ezekiel i. 26–28. " And above the firmament that was over their heads was the likeness of a throne, as the appearance of a sapphire stone ; and upon the likeness of the throne was the likeness as the appearance of a man above upon it. And I saw as the color of amber, as the appearance of fire round about within it, from the appearance of his loins even upward, and from the appearance of his loins even downward, I saw as it were the appearance of fire, and it had brightness round about. As the appearance of the bow that is in the cloud in the day of rain, so was the appearance of the brightness round about. This was the

appearance of the likeness of the glory of the Lord. And when I saw it, I fell upon my face, and I heard a voice of one that spake."

2. *Its purity.* God dwells in the holiest of all ; the purity is such, that the heavens appear as if unclean before him. He sits upon the throne of his holiness. Justice and judgment are the habitation of his throne. The seraphim and cherubim continually cry, "Holy, holy, holy," &c. Now the grandeur of his seat might overwhelm us, and the purity of it fill us with terror as guilty sinners before him. Considering the throne or seat as such we might exclaim,

> "Lord, what shall earth and ashes do ?
> We would adore our Maker too ;
> From sin and dust to thee we cry,
> The Great, the Holy, and the High."

But there is another feature connected with the seat of Jehovah, and that is,

3. *Its graciousness.* "It is a throne of grace." Now here we come to God through Jesus Christ the propitiatory. Through the person and work of Christ, God can be just, and yet the justifier of the ungodly. This should never be forgotten in prayer. "There is one God," &c. "We have an advocate," &c. Now as a throne of grace the sinner may approach, the unworthy may draw near, obtain mercy, and find grace to help, &c. Observe,

II. THE MANNER OF APPROACH ADOPTED. "I would order my cause," &c. In presenting our cause before God, we must ever keep in view,

1. *Our utter unworthiness.* Job in one place confessed that he was vile. Should we not all feel thus. See the example of David, "Hear my prayer, O Lord, give ear to my supplications, in thy faithfulness answer me, and in thy righteousness, and enter not into judgment with thy servant ; for in thy sight shall no man living be justified." Psalm cxliii. 1, 2. We cannot be too conscious of our nothingness and sinfulness before God. In ordering our cause we must have respect,

2. *To the spirit of true sincerity.* "God is a spirit," &c. Lord, search me and try me, and "see if there be any way of wickedness in me, and lead me in the way everlasting," Psalm cxxxix. 24. Then in ordering our cause before God, there must be,

3. *Submission and obedience to his will.* We may express our darkness, helplessness, and misery ; we may call upon God to hear, and help, and deliver. but after all we must lie in his hand, wait his time, and be satisfied that what he doth shall be best. Notice,

III. THE MODE OF PLEADING DETERMINED. "I would fill my mouth with arguments." Now God leaves his people to plead before him. A fervent wrestling spirit, he will not, he cannot despise. Now there are many arguments which we may plead before God.

1. *There is the argument of his universal goodness.* He is good to all, and his tender mercies, &c. He blesses all his creatures. He clothes the grass, and feeds the ravens, causes his showers to fall upon the ground of the wicked, &c. If so, how much will he bless his own children, the objects of his love !

2. *There is the argument of his engagements and promises.* Now the engagements of God, relate to the *keeping* of his saints ; to their preservation. To *giving* them all needful good. That he will *hear* all their cries, *deliver* them from all their enemies, *supply* all their wants, and never, never *leave* or forsake them. Such are powerful arguments. "Hath the Lord spoken, and shall he not perform ? Hath he said it, and will he not bring it to pass ?"

3. *There is the argument of his past loving-kindness.* Shall we not plead what he has done ? He has been our *help* from our birth. He was our *benefactor* in youth, &c. What has he not done for us ? How richly, freely hath he blessed us ! Now we ought not to forget his past loving-kindness. We should plead it with gratitude, and infer, believing from it, his power and willingness to help us.

4. *There is the argument of his work within us.* Our desires for his presence and favor arise from the motions of his Spirit in our hearts. These longings are his own implanting. He has sent the Spirit of his Son into our hearts, and this Spirit excites our longings after him. "For we should know not what to pray," &c.

5. *There is the argument of the advocacy of his Son.* Christ has died and risen from the dead, yea, he hath ascended, and ever lives to make intercession for us. "We have an advocate," &c. "Him the Father heareth always."

APPLICATION

1. *Let me urge all anxious seekers of Christ to go to the seat of God.* He waits to save. He is ready to pardon.

2. *Here is the Christian's true resource in time of trouble.* Imitate Job. Say, " O that I knew where I might find him !" Then go to his seat, " Cast your burden upon him," &c.

3. *How truly wretched is a prayerless state !*

37

CHRISTIAN UNITY URGED

" Endeavoring to keep the unity of the Spirit, in the bond of peace."—EPHESIANS iv. 3.

SIN has not only made man hostile to God, but has set one man in battle array against another. Shortly after Adam sinned against God, did his first-born slay his brother ; and from that period of his foul deed of hatred and blood to the present, strife, and war, and revenge, have thrown their deep shade over the history of our world. Sin in its chief essential element is discord. It divides, separates, confuses, and distresses. Now those who are converted are not perfectly freed from all the remains of the carnal mind, and therefore in them are roots of bitterness which distract the hearts of the pious, and produce division and disunion among the friends of Jesus. In apostolical times, we see an instance of this between the holy Paul and Barnabas, who were greatly imbued with the Holy Ghost. This existing spirit in the visible church has led to various schemes for the promotion of greater affection among Christians. Yet up to this day divisions and distractions of the church continue. The only sure balm for the healing of these rancorous wounds is found in the text. " Endeavoring to keep," &c. Our text refers to the true principle of unity, and to the right method of maintaining it. The text refers,

I. To THE TRUE PRINCIPLE OF UNITY. " Unity of spirit," not,

(1.) Denominational unity ; where the members of a sect are allied by a certain name, creed, form of worship, &c. Which of the hundreds of sects, like Aaron's rod, shall swallow up all the rest ? Not,

(2.) By an attempted uniformity. Before this can be effected, all minds must be uniform ; all modes of education ; all books, and reading, and study. Variety is the law of the universe, and is quite accorda it with general unity. As the rays of light are formed of every color of the rainbow. As the various stars all present the splendor of the firmament. As the various gases combine in the atmosphere of life. As the various objects are all necessary to form the picturesque of the landscape. As the several features are essential to the beauty of the countenance. A tame and general uniformity in the church would be an anomaly in the universe. Not,

(3.) By extra liberal concessions. When persons are willing to forego any view of truth, &c., for the sake of visible harmony. Unity, even of the right kind, is too dearly paid for if purchased by the sacrifice of one grain of truth. No, the principle of the text is unity of spirit. And this spirit is the Spirit of the Lord Jesus Christ. " If any man have not the Spirit of Christ," &c. Now supposing all Christians to have this, then there must be unity of spirit. Color language, creed, mode of worship, will not, cannot prevent it. Now this unity of spirit involves,

✓1. *True spiritual affection.* Love one to another—love to all saints—love unfeigned —love that will produce sympathizing care, beneficence, tenderness, pity, and mutual prayer. Love in deed, and not merely in word.

2. *This spirit is essentially a spirit of humility.* Pride is the great cause of contention. Men never can be united, while they stand on the stilts of their own preconceived superior excellency. The man who says, " I am more righteous than thou," will always say to his brother, with the same breath, " Stand off !" But if we think of ourselves in the spirit of Christian humility, we shall be prostrated together in the dust ; and thus before the footstool of God's mercy, the spirit of unity will be felt, and cherished.

3. *This spirit must ever be a spirit of kindly forbearance.* See verse 2. How often this is urged on our careful attention, Col. iii. 12, &c. ; Rom. xiii. 1, &c. Thus only can the spirit of Christian unity be really promoted. But notice,

II. THE RIGHT METHOD OF MAINTAINING IT. Now this method is

1. *Personal.* We are to " keep the unity of the Spirit," &c. Every man for

himself. Not legislators to do it, or synods, or sects, but each Christian must keep his own spirit, and maintain that unity of feeling, that true catholicity of heart, which will abhor distraction and division. This method is associated with,

2. *Decided effort.* "Endeavoring." It will not come as a matter of course, but rather the opposite ; therefore we must endeavor ; strive for it ; labor for it ; read for it ; pray for it ; exhibit it whenever and wherever we can do so. This method is identified in the text,

3. *With a pacific compact.* " In the bond of peace." We are to consider ourselves and all true Christians, united in holy bonds of fraternal amity. We are to keep that bond inviolate. Use all methods for the bond being more close, and dear, and strong. Our motto must be, " I am for peace." Our spirit must be that of peace. We must seek the wisdom that is peaceable. We must especially pray that the heart may be engarrisoned, or kept by the peace of God, &c.

APPLICATION

1. A firm and persevering regard to divine truth is compatible with this spirit.

2. A decided maintenance of the principles of true Christian liberty alone can lay a broad foundation for this peaceful unity.

3. Legitimate exertions for the removal of the corruptions and abuses of Christianity, will not break the Christian unity, however it may affect the unity of the denominations of the universal church. Luther—the puritans—Wesley—the Free Church of Scotland—dissenters in their present efforts, therefore, are not condemned by this subject.

38

CHRIST'S PRAYER FOR THE UNITY OF THE CHURCH

" That they all may be one, as thou, Father, art in me, and I in thee ; that they also may be one in us, that the world may believe that thou hast sent me."—JOHN xvii. 21.

NOTHING is oftener repeated than this, " There is only one church." The Roman Catholics loudly utter this ; the church of England ; and the various bodies of dissenters. It seems to be a settled principle amongst most Christians ; but then, each sect arrogates to itself the exclusive title of the one church, and some do this to the exclusion of all other Christians. There never was a period when it became Christians to understand this subject more than at the present. Our subject leads us directly to it. It was the solemn prayer of the blessed Saviour, and reiterated three times in the course of his intercessory address to the Father, verses 11, 21, 22.

What is the church of Christ ? The great body of believers scattered over the face of the world.

Is the church one ? In one respect, indeed, it is. All converted, renewed persons are members of Christ's spiritual body ; but in its visible aspect it is divided and torn—church against church, sect against sect, &c. This cannot be pleasing to God ; it is explicitly opposed to Christ's prayer ; it weakens the influence of Christianity ; it must ultimately cease, and the text will eventually be accomplished. Before we enter upon our subject, we ask,

(1.) When and where did divisions commence ? At Corinth ; see 1 Cor. i. 12.

(2.) The cause of divisions ; 1 Cor. iii. 3.

(3.) From that day the church of God has been the seat of disputation and variance.

I. To WHAT EXTENT IS UNION IN THE CHURCH OF CHRIST POSSIBLE ?

II. How MAY WE CONTRIBUTE TO IT ? And,

III. WHY WE SHOULD DO SO.

I. To WHAT EXTENT IS UNION IN THE CHURCH OF CHRIST POSSIBLE ? Absolute, minute, and universal oneness is, perhaps, impossible with imperfect and erring beings ; but true Christians may be united,

1. *In spiritual affections.* Love is the very essence of religion ; one main feature in the child of God ; an essential principle in the mind renewed by divine grace. Surely it is not indispensable that persons should in all particulars hold all our sentiments to entitle them to our affection. The good Samaritan displayed kindness and generosity to the poor Jew. Love to the whole family of God is necessary to the existence of true religion, " By this shall all men know," &c. We should be united,

2. *In mutual supplications.* " Pray one for another," &c. This we are to do for all men, but especially for the family of Christ. If in error, we should seek for

their spiritual enlightenment; if weak, for their being strengthened. Now, fervent intercession for the whole church is calculated to beget greatness of soul, and catholicity of spirit.

3. *In ardent efforts for the extension of Christ's cause.* If Christians would forego their jealousies and bigoted animosities until the great common foe were conquered, they would have little to do in the end but join in the song of triumph. There is ample for all to do. The field is the world —dark, besotted, dreary, perishing. Should not all unite for its salvation? Ignorance, skepticism, profligacy, stupor, worldliness, &c.

4. *In holy emulation to glorify God.* Persons lose sight of this in seeking their own sectarian purposes. Few ask, " How does God view it?" Will he be pleased? Will it honor his word—please the blessed Spirit—exalt Christ? Self, alas! has the place of God—our opinions—our modes of worship, &c.—our denominations. If God were constantly before us, we should not be able to see these in a light of such magnitude. The sun would render the stars invisible; the sea would render the little rivulet perfectly insignificant. All Christians may unite to glorify God to this extent. Without sacrifice of truth, or compromise of principle, all thus may be one. We ask,

II. How MAY WE CONTRIBUTE TO THIS UNITY OF THE CHRISTIAN CHURCH?

1. *By cherishing the Spirit's holy influence.* His motions tend to unity. He heals; he binds up; he harmonizes. We cannot drink deeply of this stream without there springing up the same spirit of love and unity.

2. *By setting the example of Christ before us.* Of him it is said, " He pleased not himself." How we should remember his numerous exhortations to humility and condescension, " Whoso will be greatest must be as a little child," see also John xiii. 14.

3. *By using always purity of speech.* Not using sectarian language; not the garbled expressions of this or that denomination. Many may be known by their prayers—by their modes of conversation. In Christ's kingdom there is only one language—the language of pure revelation; and this ought to be so spoken, that none should know what meeting we attend, or what sectarian name we bear; and in the latter

days there will not be three hundred religious dialects as there are now. Human phraseology has done much to make divisions, and more to keep them up. To this, I add,

4. *Let us treat all Christians with candor and respect.* Let us excel in courtesy. While we honor all men, let us especially honor the friends of Jesus everywhere, and on every occasion. We ask,

III. WHY WE SHOULD LABOR FOR THE UNITY OF THE CHRISTIAN CHURCH?

1. *Because it is the will of God.* This ought to suffice. What parent does not love this in his family? God much more in his church.

2. *Christ prays for it.* It is one of the desires of the soul of the Saviour. He travails for this, and without it will not be satisfied.

3. *It will tend to our strength and comfort.* " Union is strength." It is more, it is comfort; it is the luxury of enjoyment.

4. *The world's condition demands it.* " That they all," &c. A divided church cannot convert the world. We must be united before we conquer; then, and then only, we shall prevail. We shall not silence the infidel, or assist the doubter, until we are united ourselves.

APPLICATION

1. *The condition of the church is calculated to fill us with grief.* Weeping and sorrow might well fill our souls. The church of Rome—Puseyism, &c.

2. *This unity must be personal.* Associations, &c., can do little.

3. *Let us think of the unity of heaven.* No discord there; there all are one, &c.

39

THANKFULNESS

" And be ye thankful."—COLOSSIANS iii. 15.

WE ask,

I. WHAT IS INCLUDED IN THANKFULNESS?

1. *A right appreciation of the benefits God confers.* Think of his dignity, and of our unworthiness.

2. *A sincere value of the blessings bestowed.* Every gift of God should be prized.

3. *Fervent acknowledgment to God for his goodness to us.* The heart must move the tongue, " Open thou my lips," &c.

The tongue never so truly well employed as in blessing God.

4. *Affectionate obedience to God for his benefits.* "What shall I render?" &c. He asks our hearts and lives.

II. ON WHAT GROUNDS SHOULD WE BE THANKFUL?

1. *Our relation to Deity.* His creatures —his dependents—his children.

2. *The mercies bestowed.* Temporal and spiritual. Life—preservation—privileges —redemption, &c. What are,

III. THE CONSIDERATIONS THAT SHOULD EXCITE TO THIS DUTY?

1. *Its reasonableness.* All creatures have some mode of expressing their delight. Harmony of the spheres; birds of the air, &c.; fields, rivers, winds, &c.; especially superior beings—seraphim, &c.

2. *Its pleasurableness.* Some duties painful; self-denial, &c. This luxurious; essence of joy—light of the soul, &c.

3. *Its profitableness.* Health of the soul. It gives vigor—pleases God, &c.

4. *Its durableness.* The very atmosphere of heaven. Will endure forever and ever.

40

JEHOVAH'S DESIGNS WITH RESPECT TO HIS PEOPLE

"This people have I formed for myself; they shall show forth my praise."—ISAIAH xliii. 21.

THE text refers to the seed of Jacob, the literal house of Israel. You are well aware how obviously it is true in reference to that nation. God resolved to deposite his truth and worship with one special people. Accordingly, he called Abraham to be the father of this nation, and he gave him many great and glorious promises, and formed his seed into a people for himself, that they might show forth, &c.; and as a nation, they did show forth, &c. In their laws, in their worship, in their deliverances, &c., they did show forth the praises of God. But on account of their apostacy God excluded them from their distinctive place as his elect, and diffused his goodness to the nations of the Gentiles. Thus the apostle speaks, Rom. xi. 17, 20; the church of Christ now enjoys the appellation of "The people of God." Whether Jews or Gentiles, or both, to them the text will appropriately apply, "This people," &c.

I. THE PEOPLE REFERRED TO. That is, the people of God, sometimes called saints, the righteous, the servants of God, the children of God, &c. Now of this people we notice,

1. *They are a saved people.* Not only redeemed, but saved. Christ is the "Saviour of all men, but especially of them," &c. The apostle says, "By grace are ye saved," &c. Not shall be, &c., but are, &c., see Titus iii. 5; 1 Cor. i. 18. They have felt the efficacy of divine grace; tasted and handled the things, &c.; have been delivered from the wrath to come; justified, renewed, adopted, and sanctified, &c.; saved from sin to righteousness, from darkness and sin into the knowledge, favor, love, and image of God.

2. *They are a peculiar people.* So they are described by the apostle. Not like others, they are not of the world, unlike the world, they are only pilgrims and sojourners. Hence their manners and customs, their costume and speech, their spirit and temper, their conduct and pursuits, are all peculiar to themselves; it must be so, it ought to be so, the opposite would be evil, &c. Now in addition to this,

3. *They are a distinct people.* There are many peculiar people in the world, who are yet of the world. But this people are distinct and separate. A people in the world, but unconnected in heart, in life, in conversation, in profession. Christ's army in a world which is in arms against him; Christ's vineyard in the waste-howling desert, &c.; Christ's disciples following his steps, &c.; crucified to the world, &c. Notice,

II. THE FORMATION SPECIFIED. "This people have I formed," &c. Consider,

1. *The nature of this formation.* Formed into a "people." God did not intend believers to be isolated beings, he designed they should be collected, united, a people. Hence they are likened to a family, flock, company of travellers, congregation or church, city, nation. Only in this way can they exercise their graces, &c.; exhibit Christianity in its social influences, and extend it in the world. Beautifully likened to the human body; 1 Cor. xii. 14, 20. Observe,

2. *The Author of this formation.* "I have formed," &c. It is divine, it is of God. The church is God's husbandry, God's building; he gives the same Spirit

to all, but a diversity of operation, that each may add to the comfort and prosperity of the whole. Hence the term, " The church of God." God's collecting, calling, saving, uniting, keeping, &c. Notice,

III. THE END CONTEMPLATED IN THIS FORMATION. "For myself," &c. God is the first cause, and the great end of all things. He could have existed alone, but it pleased him to form the universe, &c., he made all things for himself, &c. Now he has formed the church especially for himself. It is called his rest—his dwelling—his delight ; and he designs that they "should show forth," &c. They do this,

1. *By exhibiting the effects of his gracious operations.* They are internally different, but this cannot be seen except by God, but its effects are seen, the fruit is different. "What fruit ?" &c. " But now being made free," &c. " Took knowledge," &c. The sick whole, the lepers are now cleansed, curse a blessing, the dead alive, &c.— " They show forth," &c.

2. *By laboring to diffuse his glory.* They live and act for this, pray for it, &c. " Let the whole earth," &c. They seek the glory of God, in heart and life identified with it, &c.

3. *By pious resignation to the divine appointments.* Happy in affliction, calm in peril, peaceful in death. See how Job glorified God ; see the apostles and first Christians ; see every poor, and sorrowful, and dying Christian.

APPLICATION

1. *Of what people are you personally a part ? of the world or the church ?*

2. *Let the people of God think of their high vocation, and the end of religion, " To show forth," &c.*

3. *God will be glorified in the punishment of the finally impenitent.*

41

ZION'S FUTURE PROSPERITY

" For Zion's sake will I not hold my peace, and for Jerusalem's sake I will not rest, until the righteousness thereof go forth as brightness, and the salvation thereof as a lamp that burneth."—ISAIAH lxii. 1.

IT is not quite clear whether the prophet is speaking in the text in his own name, or in the name of Jesus, the true Messiah and Head of his church. We rather view tne text, however, as that of Isaiah, whose heart burned with holy zeal for the enlargement of the church, and the diffusion of the divine glory. But the sentiments uttered are truly worthy of all the servants of Jehovah, in every age of the world. Every faithful minister of Christ will earnestly appropriate the language of the prophet as his own, and exclaim, " For Zion's sake," &c. We would further ask, why should not the text be expressive of the feelings of every Christian ? All who have tasted that the Lord is gracious—all who are identified with the progress of divine truth, and feel compassion for deathless souls, may well utter, with deepest emotion, the sentiment of the text, " For Zion's sake," &c. In this last and most extensive sense, we shall view this beautiful passage on this occasion. Observe,

I. THE LIMITED AND OBSCURE CONDITION OF THE CHURCH IMPLIED. By Zion and Jerusalem, we understand the spiritual church and kingdom of God. The figures of the text involve the idea, that this church requires extension and additional glory. Now, what is the true state of the church of God, even in this late era of the world's history ? We fear that the true church of Christ in all lands, including the professors of all Christian denominations, would not be more than twenty millions, and probably not so many. Of course, I do not reckon all the nominal Christians of the world. Of Mahommedans, there are about 160 millions ; of Jews, nine or ten millions ; and 700 or 800 millions of benighted, perishing pagans ; while regions of the earth are yet dreary, sterile, and the very regions of death. Even in Europe, there are vast masses with only the flickering light of papal superstition, or the equally dim and sickly rays of the Greek church. Two thousand five hundred years have transpired since Isaiah penned the text, and yet what extensive domains of darkness and wo are still lying in the hands of the wicked one. Satan is yet the prince of this world. How circumscribed the church of God ! How little is yet known of her spiritual power and glory ! Even in the countries. of her greatest prosperity, the majority of the people are at variance with her holy principles, and strangers to the felicity and blessings she confers. Observe,

II. The truly noble spirit averred. " I will not hold my peace," &c. " I will not rest." Here silence, and indolent inactivity are disavowed. How, then, can we speak and act for the extension of the righteousness and salvation of the gospel economy ?

1. *The Christian minister can speak in the exercise of his public duties.* One part of our public work is to present to you the prophecies which relate to the travail of Christ's soul, and the subjugation of the world to his cross. His office is included in that commission which commanded the preaching of the gospel to every creature. It devolves upon him, therefore, to keep this subject in view ; to dwell upon it in his ministrations ; to unite the friends of Jesus in this great work. While he preaches and teaches Christ to those at home, he must ever remember the perishing millions abroad.

2. *Sabbath school teachers should impress this on the children of their charge.* The minister must act upon the generation that now is ; the Sunday school teacher on the generation rising up—on those who are to be the pastors, deacons, and members of the church in the succeeding generation. The Sabbath school must be the nursery of the missionary spirit. It has already sent scores into the missionary field ; and if well indoctrinated in the truths of universal philanthropy, it will be the army of reserve for extending the hallowed crusade of mercy and grace through the world.

3. *Parents should also train up their families in the missionary spirit.* It should form a part of household conversation ; the condition, misery, and claims of the heathen should be early instilled into the mind of the young and rising generation ; information from time to time should be imparted ; their pity elicited, their compassion drawn forth, their generosity excited. Thus every Christian family, in its social character, should be enlisted on the side of missions.

4. *All Christians should speak with God in prayer.* In the short epitome of prayer left us by Christ, two petitions directly bear upon it : " Thy kingdom come," &c. It was predicted that the Redeemer's glory should engage the petitions of his pious followers. " Prayer shall be made for him continually." Now, our prayers should often embrace this great subject. We should plead, and supplicate, and wrestle with God ; we should press our suit, urge our requests, &c. ; be intent, and earnest, and believing. We should remember what promises we have to plead—what reasons to incite us—what instances of success to cheer us ; especially we should remember, how in our prayers we are one with God. His covenant, his engagement, both to Christ and his church, are most specific on this subject. Therefore he will hear and approve of our intercessions. But earnest prayer to God,

5. *Must be followed with corresponding activity.* " I will not rest." God will not convert the world by miracle, nor by the abstract influences of the Holy Spirit, but by the means which he connected with his kingdom at the beginning. " This gospel of the kingdom," &c. By the diffusion of the truth, &c. Did all the followers of Christ speak and pray only, it would necessarily be inefficient. Besides, without corresponding effort, it would be hypocrisy towards God, and a mockery of the heathen. Men must go into these dreary regions of the world ; then they must be sent and supported ; they must have Bibles, and tracts, and schools ; then the church at home must be active and liberal. " If they descend into the mine," as Carey said, " those at home must hold the rope." If they go forth in the war, we must provide the ammunition ; and those who do not this ought never to speak or pray about Christian missions—of course I mean if they have the least ability to help. Notice,

III. The reasons on which the magnanimous resolve of the text is grounded. " For Zion's sake." " For Jerusalem's sake." There are several reasons implied in the one avowed.

1. *For the sake of the God of Zion.* That his glory may fill the whole earth ; his name be everywhere adored, his laws obeyed, and a revenue of praise from all his creatures be presented.

2. *For the sake of the King of Zion.* He has given Christ to be " Head over all things to his church." Christ is set as God's holy king in Zion. Now, the sorrows and sufferings of Christ were to be rewarded by universal empire ; see Isaiah liii. 10, 11, " And I, if I be lifted up." Love to Christ, and sympathy with him, should excite us to say, " For Zion's sake," &c.

3. *For the sake of the church itself.* When the visions of prophecy are realized, then will be the jubilee of the church—her consummated glory—her final triumph. Do we not desire this? long for it? Has not the church been a peculiar blessing to us and our families? Should not gratitude, therefore, influence us? If not, let love of self do it; for the prosperity of Christ's kingdom involves in it our prosperity. We cannot speak, and labor, and give to the cause, without deriving incalculable blessings to our own souls.

APPLICATION

Address,

1. *Those whose spirits harmonize with the prophet of old.* Who feel the emotions, and express their desires and resolutions as he did.

2. *Those who are not acting in concert with the text are so far at variance with the Redeemer.*

3. *The claims of missions are loud and comprehensive at the present period.* We live in the last times; our facilities are numerous; the openings of providence signally striking and wide. Let us not slumber, then, when the day is breaking, when the momentous triumphs of the cross must be close at hand, &c.

4. I might refer largely, and last of all —*To the truly miserable and pitiable condition of the heathen.*

42

JOY IN SORROW

"As sorrowful, yet always rejoicing."—2 Corinthians vi. 10.

THE text, and the whole paragraph, refer to the apostles, and the first preachers of the gospel. In it we see the toil, and suffering, and peril to which the ambassadors of Jesus were first exposed. Several portions of the passage are presented in the way of paradox, &c., see verse 9, &c. The text is equally applicable to all the disciples of Christ, in every age of the world. Of all such it may be said, "As sorrowful," &c. Let us look at several particulars in which the text is especially exemplified. It is true,

I. IN RESPECT TO THE ADVERSE AND AFFLICTIVE SCENES OF LIFE. This world to the Christian is a valley of tears—a howling wilderness—a stormy ocean; many things to disappoint and try the Christian. The ordinary troubles of life, in which they share with their fellow-men; peculiar afflictions to which they are liable as Christians. Now these are *many.* "Many are the afflictions of the righteous." "It is through much tribulation," &c. These often involve the friends of Jesus in sorrow —often cast down and dispirited on account of the way; but in these there is cause for constant rejoicing.

(1.) Their afflictions are limited and light.

(2.) Their enjoyments numberless.

(3.) Their support constant and efficient.

(4.) Their trials salutary and useful.

(5.) Prospect of a world where they shall be for ever unknown.

"When I can read my title clear," &c.

II. OFTEN SORROWFUL ON ACCOUNT OF THEIR OWN IMPERFECTIONS AND INFIRMITIES AS CHRISTIANS. So little light; so little confidence; such a wavering hope; so little strength; so often turned aside from the path of duty; so listless in devotion; so unfruitful, &c. Now these are real causes of sorrow to the sincere Christian. But even here there are *reasons for always rejoicing.*

(1.) That there is the least genuine grace.

(2.) That God is so condescending and tender. "As a Father," &c. "He knoweth," &c.

(3.) That Christ sympathizes and intercedes for us.

"He knows what sore temptations mean,
    For he has felt the same."

(4.) That there are provisions of grace to meet all our need.

(5.) That there is a fountain always opened, and the promise, "If we confess," &c.

III. OFTEN SORROWFUL, WHEN ANTICIPATING THE SOLEMNITIES OF DEATH AND JUDGMENT. The Christian recognises his stewardship, &c. He knows he must die, and give an account. When his Lord calleth, he will have to surrender it up. There is, too, the act of dying, and the reality of judgment. Feeling his unprofitableness he dreads, and perhaps almost despairs; fears the ordeal and the issue. But we should always rejoice, for,

(1.) Dying grace is pledged; and never

has the pledge been broken, and the soul deserted.

(2.) Death is a conquered servant, not a reigning tyrant.

(3.) The Judge is our brother and our friend. Reverse the text. Sinners rejoice, and yet are really sorrowful.

IV. OFTEN SORROWFUL ON ACCOUNT OF OUR CONNECTIONS IN LIFE. Those who have tasted of the grace of God cannot be indifferent to their relatives and friends. So far from this, they long and pray for their salvation. How often they see no hope of their desires being granted! Perhaps enemies, mockers, or careless, &c. ; entirely indifferent. Now this is a cause of sorrow. Yet there are some grounds of rejoicing :—

(1.) We are only responsible for the use of means.

(2.) While mercies and privileges are continued there is hope.

(3.) All our friends and kindred are not in this state.

V. OFTEN SORROWFUL IN REFERENCE TO THE CHURCH OF CHRIST. So little real, abiding good effected ; so many only have a name ; so many very occasional in regard to the means, &c. ; so many not using their energies for the weal of sinners ; so many who go back ; so few full of hope, and faith, and zeal, and good works. Yet here we may also rejoice that,

(1.) There are some who do honor to religion ; who love the ordinances ; who are full of love and the Holy Ghost ; who are ripening for a better world.

(2.) Some who are useful, and consistent, and persevering.

(3.) That the Lord is very good to his people, and fills his poor unworthy servants with all needful good, &c. ; and that he will not cast them off, nor forsake, for his name's sake.

VI. OFTEN SORROWING ON ACCOUNT OF THE WORLD—THOSE WHO ARE WITHOUT. Whose eyes are grieved for the transgressors ; whose eyes weep, because men keep not God's law. " Oh ! that the wickedness of the wicked," &c. Yet, we rejoice to see so many blessed institutions for the young, for the poor, for the ignorant, for benighted neighborhoods, for the intemperate, &c. ; and that some good is done, some are converted, &c. One such instance is precious *beyond the value of the world.*

APPLICATION

1. *Learn the mixed state of the present world.* Light and darkness, joy and fear, &c.

2. *Seek supremely a better world.*

3. *Look for the mercy of God.* " Be diligent," &c.

43

HEAVEN UPON EARTH

" As the days of heaven upon earth."—DEUT. xi. 21.

WE often speak of heaven ; the way to it is by evangelical obedience to God's word. Often we desire heaven : we need not wait till we die to enjoy it, we may have heaven now, heaven in our hearts.

> " The men of grace have found,
> Glory begun below ;
> Celestial fruit on earthly ground,
> From faith and hope may grow."

Let me call your attention,

I. To THE LITERAL REALIZATION OF THE TEXT. " The days of heaven upon earth" were enjoyed by our first parents in Eden. Paradise was a striking type of heaven. So heaven is called, and we read of its streams, and of its tree of life.

1. *Paradise was the region of purity, and so is heaven.* It is the holy city. Nothing that defileth can enter into it.

2. *Paradise was the abode of honor and dignity, and such is heaven.* All there are ennobled, dignified. Possess dominion, glory, and honor.

3. *Paradise was the scene of happy communion, and such is heaven.* Angels, and God himself conversed and held intercourse with our first parents, and saints and angels have one blest and endless communion in heaven.

4. *Paradise was the seat of delightful pleasures, and such is heaven.* There are the rivers of pleasure. Oceans of delight. Fulness of joys, and pleasures for evermore. Paradise indeed was strikingly typical of the heavenly world. Let me now call your attention,

II. To THE SPIRITUAL REALIZATION OF THE TEXT. Now this is enjoyed by the members of Christ's mystical and spiritual church. Observe,

(1.) The gospel dispensation is called the kingdom, or reign of heaven. " Repent ye," &c. Thus he says the kingdom of heaven suffereth violence, and the violent take it by force. To Peter he said, " I will give to thee the keys of the kingdom of heaven." Observe,

(2.) The description given of the gospel church, as contrasted with the old dispensation, is exceedingly interesting and appropriate, Heb. xii. 18–24. Now it is in the true spiritual church of Christ, that we have the days of heaven upon earth.

1. *We have a heavenly king.* He came down from heaven. He is Lord of heaven. The light and glory of heaven. Is worshipped and adored by all the hosts, &c.

2. *We have heavenly blessings.* The calling is called a heavenly calling, Heb. iii. 1. "Heavenly gifts," Heb. vi. 4. " Blessed be the God and Father of our Lord Jesus Christ, who hath blessed us with all spiritual blessings in heavenly places in Christ," Eph. i. 3.

(1.) Divine peace is the peace of heaven ; and this peace Christ gives to all his disciples. " My peace I give," &c. " The peace of God," &c.

(2.) Our joys are heavenly. " Whom having not seen, ye love ; in whom, though now ye see him not, yet believing, ye rejoice with joy unspeakable and full of glory." 1 Peter i. 8.

(3.) All our supplies are heavenly. " Every good gift, and every perfect gift is from above, and cometh down from the Father of lights, with whom is no variableness, neither shadow of turning," James i. 17. All the holy influences of the Spirit descend from heaven. Our bread is from heaven, and the streams of which we drink flow from between the throne of God and the Lamb.

3. *We have heavenly communion.* Every exercise connected with Christian fellowship is heavenly.

(1.) Prayer is the united flame of devotion ascending to heaven.

(2.) Praise is the grateful incense arising and mingling with the ascriptions of the heavenly hosts.

(3.) At Christ's table we feed upon the bread of heaven, and eat together of the true manna which descends from heaven. How appropriate the lines of the poet.

> " Happy the souls to Jesus join'd,
> And saved by grace alone ;
> Walking in all his ways, they find
> Their heaven on earth begun."

4. *We have heavenly delights and anticipations.* How often have we enjoyed the Spirit as an earnest or first-fruits of the heavenly inheritance ! How often experienced the rapture of Peter, " Lord, it is good to be here." How often had some of the kindred feelings of Paul's ecstasy, " Whether in the body, or out of the body," &c. How often felt raised almost up to heaven, until the imagination has seemed to behold the gates and the scenery of the new Jerusalem ! We have exclaimed, " This is none other than the house of God," &c. How often would we have given the preference to be absent from the body, and to be present with the Lord ! Surely these are as the days of heaven upon earth. Observe,

III. THE FUTURE GLORIOUS REALIZATION OF THE TEXT. This earth is not to be Satan's seat forever. Not the scene of sin and wo and the curse forever ; not to be the grave-yard of the redeemed forever ; it is destined to a glorious renovation. To be lifted up from the degradation of the curse. To be the seat of moral loveliness, and become the garden of the Lord. To cease being the walk of prowling beasts of prey, and become the abode of the innocent and the happy ; to cease to be the field of blood, and become the land of peace, when the nations shall not learn war any more, and when nothing shall hurt or destroy in all God's holy mountain. " The wolf also shall dwell with the lamb, and the leopard shall lie down with the kid ; and the calf and the young lion, and the fatling together ; and a little child shall lead them ; and the cow and the bear shall feed ; their young ones shall lie down together : and the lion shall eat straw like the ox. And the sucking child shall play on the hole of the asp, and the weaned child shall put his hand on the cockatrice's den. They shall not hurt nor destroy in all my holy mountain : for the earth shall be full of the knowledge of the Lord, as the waters cover the sea," Isaiah xi. 6–9. " Violence shall no more be heard in the land, wasting nor destruction within thy borders ; but thou shalt call thy walls salvation, and thy gates praise. The sun shall be thy light no more by day ; neither for brightness," &c.

(1.) Now, all this is certain, because it hath been pledged in the solemn covenant of the Father with the Son.

(2.) It is certain, for it is written in the

unalterable volume of truth, that " the whole earth shall be filled," &c.

(3.) It is certain, for the beginning of the conquests have been achieved, and now, " He who hath many crowns upon his head, is going forth from victory to victory." Now by way of application, we ask, How may we contribute to bring about the blissful consummation ?

1. *We must become the subjects of heavenly grace.* Every converted soul is one restored to the heavenly reign of Jesus. So much sin and misery blotted out ; a source of evil stopped, and a source of good opened. The image and spirit of the wicked one are erased, and the image and spirit of God exhibited. Now this is the first step, then,

2. *We must exhibit heavenly graces and dispositions.* Where we move we must try to produce a heavenly atmosphere, heavenly influence, the holiness of heaven. We must reflect the goodness of heaven, we must diffuse the kindness and mercy of heaven.

3. *We must devote all our energies and means to promote heavenly institutions.* There are two mighty interests contending for the supremacy, for the universal triumph. It is not difficult to see on what side the various institutions are allied. We know the tree by its fruits. There is the preaching of the gospel ; there are meetings for prayer ; there are tract and visiting societies ; there are Bible and missionary societies. Now are we giving all the weight of our influence to these institutions ? Are we supporting and praying for them ? All can do the latter. " Thy kingdom come." Do we internally long for it ? By the employment of means, shall there be as the days of heaven upon earth.

4. *You are all contributing to, or hindering the coming of Christ's kingdom.* Which is your position ? How are you acting ? Let us see how we really stand before God.

44

PRESENCE OF GOD IN THE HOLY TEMPLE

" But the Lord is in his holy temple : let all the earth keep silence before him."—HABAKKUK ii. 20.

THE feelings of the mind are necessarily differently impressed by the circumstances in which we are placed, and the scenery by which we are surrounded. Go to the house of social festivity, and there joy and gladness are the only elements which will appear appropriate or be excited by it. Go to the house of mourning, and how very apposite the sentiments, and the emotions felt ! Go to the house of legislature, there the interests of the nation, the efficiency of statesmen, and the principles of politics, necessarily engross the mind. Go to the hall of science, and there the wonders of nature, and the productions of art, lead us to the heights of admiration, or into the depths of profound inquiry. Go to the court of justice, and see human nature degraded in fetters, exiled, or doomed to death ; and another class of feelings differing from all the preceding are produced. Go to the palace of royalty, enter the throne-room, see the splendid equipage and dazzling trappings of earthly greatness, &c. Envy or ambition, and thoughts of human grandeur, will have the ascendency. I desire to introduce you into an assembly, more deeply interesting, instructive, and solemn, and yet more elevating than any of these ; it is the temple of Jehovah—the house of the living God. That to which the text refers, " But the Lord is in his," &c. There is a threefold temple inhabited by Jehovah. The heaven of heavens ; the temple seen by Isaiah and John, &c. ; the temple of the sanctified heart. " With that man," &c. " Know ye not that ye are the temple," &c. The assembly of his saints. " Wherever two or three," &c. To the last our attention will be confined.

I. WHAT THE DECLARATION IMPLIES.

II. THE DESIGNS OF HIS PRESENCE.

III. THE IMPRESSION IT SHOULD PRODUCE.

I. WHAT THE DECLARATION IMPLIES. It does not limit the divine presence. The heaven of heavens cannot contain him. He fills immensity. " Whither," &c. His spirit pervades all creation ; but it refers to the especial presence of God in the rich condescensions of his grace. God is there by the ubiquity of his nature ; but he is there especially,

1. *By the revelations of his mind.* The assembly of saints is to be the pillar and ground of truth. Here the word of God is deposited. Anciently in the ark were the two tables of the law. Now the law and the prophets, and the gospels, and the letters of the apostles—the completed

canon of truth. Now here is God's mind, and will, and purpose. His statutes and blessings, &c. Just as the sovereign is often said to be, where his will is proclaimed, &c.

2. *God is present by his ordinances.* The ordinance of praise respects him, and recognises him as near. So adoration and prayer, so baptism and the supper. These have his impress upon them.

3. *God is present by the power of his Spirit.* The Spirit is the gift of Christ to the church. " I will send the Spirit of truth," &c. " He shall abide," &c. " God is a spirit," and must be worshipped as such, &c.

II. THE DESIGNS OF HIS PRESENCE.

1. *The design of inspection.* He tries the heart and the reins ; he examines the motives, &c. ; he observes the conduct, the expressions, the thoughts ; he sees who sincerely bows the knee, &c. His eyes see all, and all perfectly.

2. *The design of gracious assistance.* He is present to help his people—to calm—to enlighten—to incite—to open the heart and lips, &c. To impart the hallowed fire to our souls, &c. To open the ear, and loosen the tongue, &c.

3. *The design of seasonable consolation.* God has engaged to comfort his people " in Jerusalem." " Even as a mother," &c. " Comfort ye, comfort ye," &c. A sense of sin is felt, &c. The mind depressed, &c. Trouble encountered, &c. God listens to their plaints and moans ; he hears the cry of his people, and imparts seasonable consolation.

4. *The design of effectual co-operation.* God allows us to be considered co-workers with himself: but our labors will effect nothing without his blessing. He gives efficacy to all means—to prayer, to preaching, &c. As the means involve the conversion of souls, the establishment of saints, and the furtherance of the gospel, the Lord is present to secure, by his Holy Spirit, these great and momentous ends. Then in reference to the divine presence, we ask :

III. WHAT IMPRESSIONS SHOULD IT PRODUCE ?

1. *Reverential awe.* " Let all the earth keep silence." Can divine worship be too reverently regarded and conducted ? Is it reverent to come in late ; to rush in so as to disturb ; to gaze about—to be listless—to sleep—to cover the head before you get out

—to talk about worldly things at the door &c., &c. We forget that " the Lord is in his holy temple," &c. It should produce,

2. *Devout preparation.* We go to meet the Deity, to see him by faith—to hear him speak—to speak to him—to be blessed, &c. Then we should prepare, so as to be collected, quiet, thoughtful, &c. " Take off thy shoes," &c.

3. *Deep spiritual humility.* If God is in his temple, then he alone should be exalted. As all the stars disappear from our vision before the rising sun, so God is the great Sun of righteousness, &c. The people are as nothing, but dust, &c. The minister, &c. God all in all. How abased and lowly we should be ! We should bow down and worship. Body and mind should be prostrated before him.

4. *Great encouragement.* We cannot fail in our object. Every good can be obtained, every evil avoided. God possesses an infinite fulness of blessedness for his people. Other things may fail—friends absent—minister not equal to his usual state, &c., but God is in his holy temple, &c.

APPLICATION

1. *Learn the dignity of Christian worship.* To come immediately before God, &c.

2. *The value of a mediator.* We need a days-man, an intercessor, &c.

3. *The importance of revelation.* To know how to come, &c.

4. *The value of the Spirit.* To assist our infirmities, and help in every time of need.

45

THE GRACIOUS END OF CHRIST'S MISSION INTO OUR WORLD

" For the Son of Man is come to seek and to save that which was lost."—LUKE xix. 10.

THE mission of Jesus to our world was associated with astounding wonders and inexplicable mysteries. Never in any respect was there any thing like it. Warriors have visited countries, but their footsteps have been marked with blood, and their career with misery and death ; travellers have explored distant regions, but their object has been to discover the wonders of nature, or monuments of art ; philanthropists have occasionally gone forth on errands of humanity and mercy, and have given of their profusion to the sons and daughters of misery; but Jesus, the blessed Messiah, came into our world to bear the fetters, to submit to the shame, and to endure death for a race of guilty rebels, and by suffering, concentrated in his own person, what they deserved, to seek and to save that which was lost. Let us briefly advert,

I. To the DISTINGUISHED PERSONAGE REFERRED TO. "The Son of Man." And here we are led to consider the incarnation of the Son of God. Jesus is often described as the Son of God, Lord of Glory, &c. But as Mediator, it behooved him to assume the nature of man; and thus it is written, "God sent forth his Son," not in his essential and glorious form, but "made of a woman," &c. Hence he took upon himself not the nature of angels, but was of the seed of Abraham. Several reasons why Jesus became the Son of man :—

1. *As Mediator, he must be interested in both parties.* Hence he was God with God, and man with man.

2. *That he might suffer and die for man.* The divine nature could not suffer.

3. *That as kinsman, he might have right to present himself a ransom, &c.* Here the same nature suffers that had sinned, and was condemned.

4. *That he might be an example to his people.* Enduring their infirmities; living, &c., with the same nature, in the same world.

5. *That he might sympathize with them as their great and tender High Priest, &c., in heaven.*

II. Notice the EMBASSY OF THE SON OF MAN. "The Son of Man came." Three questions will elucidate this :—

1. *From whence did he come?* He came from heaven, the palace-royal of Jehovah; from the throne of the Father; the glory of the celestial state. He had ever been with the Father; was as one brought up with him; by him had all things been created, &c. He was the first-begotten of God—the first-born of every creature—the delight and fellow of the Father—the righteous Lord, and heir of all things; he came from the heaven of heavens.

2. *Where did the Son of Man come to?* He came to this fallen, benighted, and miserable world; a world in a state of sinful revolt, misery, and death. What condescension! What grace! How he abased

himself, &c. He made his footstool his dwelling-place; he came not on a transitory visit, but to be a citizen of it; to live in it for more than thirty years.

3. *In what manner did he come?* Not with regal pomp; not with a train of celestial attendants; not in grandeur; not to dwell in its palaces, &c. A poor village was his birth-place; a poor virgin his mother; a stable his first residence. He took upon him the form of a servant; he came not to be waited upon, and ministered unto, but to be the servant of servants.

III. The GREAT END OF THE SAVIOUR'S ADVENT. "He came to seek," &c. Now, here is a distinct reference to the state of the human family. "Lost." Not in the absolute sense; not irrevocably. Some emblems may assist us here.

1. *Look at that sheep which has left the fold.* It is straying on the dark and distant mountains, exposed to every beast of prey. Such was our state. "All we like sheep," &c. We never should have returned; we should have wandered on, in endless mazes lost.

2. *Look at the mariner.* His vessel has driven against the hidden shoal—has become a total wreck; he has escaped to the summit of a barren rock. Is he not lost? He cannot long survive—cannot recross the trackless deep. Such the state of man.

3. *Look at that sickly, wretched being.* The leprosy has spread its desolating foulness through the whole system; no remedy, &c.; the disease is deepening and spreading. Is he not lost? So man became defiled. "From the crown of the head," &c.

4. *Look at that malefactor.* He has committed some capital offence—has been tried, convicted, condemned. Is he not lost? He is in the eye of the law a dead man. So sin had involved us in guilt, and brought us under condemnation; the black curse of eternal death hovered over our miserable world. Thus, brethren, we were lost. Now, the end of Christ's mission was to seek and to save that which was lost. As the kind shepherd, he followed the straying sheep, &c.; he traversed the dreary mountains, &c., and prepared a fold for his straying flock; he visited the desolate mariner on the rock, and brought close to him the life-boat of salvation, and freely offered to conduct him to the regions of bliss, and shores of immortality; he came to our hos-

pital world, and brought a balm—the balm of health and life—to heal the leper, &c. ; he came to the condemned prisoner —took his place—bore his doom—died in his stead—suffered the just for the unjust, &c.

APPLICATION

1. *Herein we see the condition of all men by nature.* A condition from which the grace of God hath provided deliverance.

2. *Are you found of Christ ?* Restored —saved.

3. *The incorrigible wanderer will be lost forever.*

4. *Now urge the acceptance of Christ upon all present.*

46

CHRIST, THE LIGHT OF THE WORLD

" I am the light of the world."—JOHN viii. 12.

OF all the material creatures which God has made, light is the fairest and most striking emblem of himself. God is light —the Father of lights, and in him is no darkness at all. Light is also one of the metaphorical titles of the Redeemer, and with John it was a favorite comparison. In him " as the Word," or Logos, " was life, and the life was the light of men." Jesus also adopts the same expression in reference to himself, " I am the light of the world." The emblem is exceedingly appropriate on account of the purity of light, on account of the joy which it diffuses, but chiefly as it is the source of manifestation. By it all things are discerned ; without it, yet having the organs of sight, we perceive nothing. Jesus is the great Sun of the universe—the fountain of light and life. We observe, then, that light is the emblem of life ; and,

I. HE IS THE LIGHT OF BEING TO ALL HIS CREATURES. Light is the symbol of life— darkness of death. The state of things before his creative power was exerted was dark and void, and light was the first creature he spake into being. It is probable that the light of existence is as extensive as the universe—that everywhere living beings exist. Throughout all his animated works, he is the light. He gave life to every thing, and he holds the life of every creature in his hands. In him all things live and move, &c. ; the glow-worm and the man, the insect and the angel, the un perceptible animalcule and the seraph. Light is the emblem of knowledge, and,

II. HE IS THE LIGHT OF INTELLIGENCE TO ALL RATIONAL BEINGS. He has given each the instinct or reason best fitted to its nature, &c. He has endowed the mind of man with all its lofty powers ; with understanding, judgment, memory, and all the capacities with which it is ennobled. The still greater, clearer, and more elevated powers of angels are all conferred by him. Light is the emblem of joy and gladness, and,

III. HE IS THE LIGHT OF THE GOSPEL. As a revelation of God's mind ; it is called the glorious gospel of the blessed God, because it is irradiated by the beams of the Son of God. He brought life and immortality to light. Take Christ away, and we have no gospel. What was the condition of the world when Christ was not known ? Dark ! dark ! Darkness covered the earth, and gross darkness the minds of the people ; so dark that neither philosophy, nor science, nor literature could remove it. In this benighted condition, man could obtain no certain knowledge,

1. *As to the true God.* Hence the whole scene of idolatry ; hence the unnumbered deities. Every thing was appealed to, and worshipped by some as God ; sun—moon —stars—the sea—rivers—the wind—fowls of the air—beasts—fishes—creeping things. Hence, too, idols formed of wood, and stone, and clay, &c. Christ revealed the true and living God. " No man hath seen God," &c. As the Father of mercies, and the fountain of compassion, tenderness, and love. The world was dark,

2. *As to human sin and misery.* And Christ made this manifest ; and he presented himself in contrast to the world, a perfectly holy being ; but, most of all, he showed how they could be pardoned and removed—how the guilty could be forgiven and delivered from it. So dark were mankind, that they had adopted cruel rites to obtain this. He presented the Father, and the returning prodigal ; the publican, &c. ; himself as a sacrifice for sin. The world was dark,

3. *As to the supreme good.* Some had looked for this in pleasure, some in knowledge, &c. Christ showed that it consisted in the enjoyment of the love of God ; a right state of heart towards God and towards

men ; in one word, " Love." Dwelling in love, &c. The world was dark,

4. *As to futurity.* The state of departed spirits he revealed. Heaven of bliss—hell of wo ; eternal life, and eternal death ; also as to the body, its resurrection by the mighty power of God. We observe, light is the emblem of hope, and,

IV. CHRIST IS THE LIGHT OF THE CHRISTIAN'S CHARACTER AND EXPECTATIONS. "God who commanded," &c. He has opened their eyes, and now they see ; he has given them day—the day of salvation ; he is in them as their light. " The day star hath arisen in their hearts." Once darkness, now light, &c.

> " He is our soul's bright morning star,
> And he our rising sun."

Light is the medium of beauty, and,

V. HE IS THE LIGHT OF THE CHURCH. The language of Isaiah may be applied to the church, " Arise! shine," &c. The church is not in darkness, but in light. The church is a city set upon a hill ; all her light is from Christ. He is the sun—the centre of all her light and glory: he reflects his glory upon her ; he bespangles her firmament with the stars of his right hand, &c. ; he causes the spirit of light and comfort to dwell within her ; and the course of his church is to be increasingly radiant and glorious, until the light of the moon be as the light of the sun, &c., and the whole earth be filled with her glory. Light is the emblem of glory, and,

VI. HE IS THE LIGHT OF HEAVEN. Rev. xxi. 23. On Tabor, the apostles were overwhelmed with his effulgent rays, &c. ; but in heaven he shines forth infinitely brighter than the sun ; illumines the celestial temple, so that there is no night there.

APPLICATION

1. *How many are in darkness!* Of ignorance—sin—unbelief. Christ is the light of the world. Why tarry far off? Why remain children of night and darkness ? &c. Awake, &c.

2. *According to our fellowship with Christ will be the Christian's light.* Nearness to Christ. and we have light, hope, joy, &c. Labor,

3. *To bring others to the light.* Every Christian should feel that,

> " 'Tis all his business here below
> To cry, Behold the Lamb !"

47
REVERENCE CLAIMED FOR CHRIST

" Having yet therefore one son, his well-beloved, he sent him also last unto them, saying, They will reverence my son."—MARK xii. 6.

OUR subject relates immediately to the Jews, and their rejection and murder of the Messiah. It also directs our attention to God's judicial dealings with them as a nation, and the election of the Gentiles to their privileges and blessings. The Saviour also here predicts, or rather applies an ancient prediction to himself; see verse 10, " And have ye not read ?" &c. Our present design is the consideration of the words of our text as they will properly apply to us. Observe, then,

I. THE DIGNIFIED CHARACTER OF CHRIST. " God's well-beloved Son." This representation presents Jesus to us,

1. *In his divine nature.* God's one Son. Angels are called sons of God ; saints are the sons of God ; but Jesus is God's one Son—a Son in a very different sense to angels or saints ; for to which of the angels did he ever say, " Thou art my Son," &c. For when he bringeth in the first-begotten into the world, &c., Heb. i. 5, &c. Christ, as the Son of God, possesses a oneness of nature with the Father, " I and the Father are one." " Whoso hath seen me hath seen the Father," &c. He also possesses an equality of glory, &c. He thought it not robbery to be equal with God, &c. He is over all, God blessed for evermore. His name, his power, his dignity, &c., are supremely pre-eminent. Observe, Christ is placed before us,

2. *As the object of the Father's delight.* " His well-beloved." It is written, " The Father loveth the Son," &c. Thus did Isaiah prophesy, xlii. 1. At his baptism, God proclaimed his love when the heavens were opened, &c. " This is my beloved Son," &c. This was repeated at his transfiguration ; see also in Christ's sacerdotal prayer, John xvii. 24. Notice,

II. THE MISSION OF CHRIST. " He sent him also." God had sent his prophets and ministering servants to teach, to warn, and reveal his will to his people ; but, last of all, he sent his Son.

1. *From whence ?* From his own bosom. " No man hath seen God at any time ; the only begotten Son, who is in the bosom of the Father, he hath declared him." He enjoyed inexpressible glory and joy with the Father before the world was ; but from

heaven's dignity and bliss he was sent forth, and came down to us.

2. *To whom was he sent?* To a world of sinners. First of all, to his own; to the Jews, the seed of Abraham; to the house of Israel; but also with an express design for the benefit of the world.

3. *For what was he sent?* To be the Saviour of the world; to restore men to the favor, image, and enjoyment of God.

(1.) He came to destroy the works of the devil, and set up the kingdom of heaven on earth.

(2.) He was sent to illumine a dark world by the doctrines of the gospel.

(3.) To recover an alienated world by his power and grace.

(4.) To redeem an accursed world by his death upon the cross.

(5.) And to purify a polluted world by his spirit and blood. It was an embassy of pure, infinite, inconceivable love and grace.

III. THE REVERENCE GOD DEMANDS ON BEHALF OF HIS SON. He said, they will reverence my Son, i. e. treat him with deference, with supreme respect; give him their obedience. Let us ascertain,

1. *The manner in which this reverence should be evinced.*

(1.) By adoring love of his person. This is what angels give him. "Worthy the Lamb," &c. How rapturously David wrote and sang, Psalm xlv. 1, 2.

(2.) By cheerful obedience to his authority. Christ must be regarded in his princely authority. No reverence without obedience—the cheerful obedience of the heart. When one said, "Thy mother and thy brethren are without," he said, "Whoso doeth the will," &c.

(3.) By studious imitation of his example. He hath left us an example, "My sheep hear my voice." If we say that we have received him, we should walk as he also walked.

(4.) By ardent zeal for his glory; making Christ's interest our own; living to spread his name and praise; seeking the prosperity of his kingdom and cause in the world; having one heart with Christ in all his spiritual designs.

2. *The grounds of this reverence.* They are very many.

(1.) Think of the glory of his person. The supreme God; the King of kings; Jehovah of hosts; the ruler of the universe.

(2.) Contemplate the purity of his character. The source of perfect holiness; light, and beauty, and perfection of Christ; not one spot or frailty; the Holy One of Israel.

(3.) The riches of his grace. Not only purity, but purity embodied in love, in goodness. Mercy is the radiant bow of his throne; mercy, that has astonished heaven; mercy, infinite, boundless, eternal. Herein is love, that he laid down his life, &c.

(4.) The preciousness of his benefits. By reverencing him we enjoy his favor, love, communion, spirit, grace, and glory.

(5.) The terribleness of his wrath; see it in the history of the Jews, and read Psalm ii. 11, &c. Rev. vi. 12.

APPLICATION

1. *Address sinners.* Rejection of Christ will involve you in endless wrath and ruin.

2. *Saints.* Aver your reverence for Christ. Not only cherish it, but exhibit it. Fearlessly profess him before men, and ever live to the glory of his name.

48

GOD'S CALL TO THE SLEEPER

"Awake, thou that sleepest, and arise from the dead, and Christ shall give thee light."—EPHE-SIANS v. 14.

VARIOUS are the similitudes employed in scripture to describe the state of the sinner. He is represented as an alien, a rebel, an outcast, a captive; as diseased, blind, wretched, and lost. He is spoken of as deceived and perishing. Our text describes him as asleep, and also dead. Let us consider,

I. THE SINNER'S AWFUL STATE.

II. GOD'S GRACIOUS CALL.

III. THE GREAT PROMISE.

I. THE SINNER'S AWFUL STATE. Asleep and dead, or perhaps the Spirit designs the sleep as the sleep of death, a deadly sleep, a sleep tending to death. Now this deadly sleep is characterized by the following striking symptoms.

1. *It is a state of darkness.* In sleep the organs of vision are closed; there may be the rays of light, the beauties of nature, &c., but they are not seen. Such is the condition of the soul, in a state of darkness; without true and saving knowledge; ignorant of himself, of God, and of the

things that belong to his peace. He has the capacity, and there is the revelation, the light of the gospel shining, but he sits in darkness, and in the shadow of death.

2. *It is a state of insensibility.* Asleep, the person hears not, enjoys not; he is temporarily dead to all around him. Such is the state of the sinner; he hearkens not to God; he enjoys him not; a thousand blessings are near him, but he has no taste nor desire for them.

3. *A state of inactivity.* In sleep all the limbs are at ease; no desires formed; no plans laid out; no work effected. Such is the state of the sinner as to all moral and spiritual labor. He labors not for the bread, &c.; he agonizes not for the crown; he strives not for the goal; he works not out his salvation; he flees not from the wrath, &c.; he walks not in the way of holiness; he prepares not to meet his God.

4. *A state of illusion.* Sleep is the season of dreams, of vain and vapid imaginations. How striking these dreams often are! how vivid! how like reality, truth, yet all illusive. A state of sin is one of illusive dreams. Afflicted with the plague of sin, yet they dream of health; poor, dream of riches; debased, of dignities; wretched, yet dream of bliss and joy; condemned and in the way of ruin, yet dream of heaven and eternal life; life ebbing, they dream of years to come. Who can describe the dreams of sin and sinners?

5. *A state of peril.* Asleep, they are no longer able to watch and defend themselves. Now the horrid assassin and murderer wend their cruel way to shed blood. How many have slept only to awake in eternity; so also from accidents, fire, storms, &c.; also from disease and sudden death. So exposed is the sinner; exposed every moment to the just displeasure of God; thus while Belshazzar was feasting; thus while the rich fool was planning; thus while Herod was deified.

6. *This sleep is a state of disease.* Not natural and healthy sleep, but the result of disease, the effect of moral depravity. Hence it becomes more profound, more universal, more unexcitable, till it terminates in eternal death. Sleep of death, ending in death everlasting. From this state men never awake themselves. Observe,

II. GOD'S GRACIOUS CALL. It is God speaking in the text, and he is speaking in mercy with a view to our salvation. Not as he will speak at the last day, when his voice will awake the dead, and shake the universe. God thus calls,

1. *By the various circumstances and events of life.* Often by adversity—by affliction—by bereavements—by the example and advice of friends—by instances of his displeasure, sudden deaths, &c.

2. *By his blessed word.* By the word written and preached. Most read or hear it read, and how it describes our state, &c.; how it calls to repentance, &c.; how it urges salvation. But especially by the preaching of the word. The minister goes forth expressly to warn, arouse, and exhort. Have you not been called hundreds, yea, thousands of times? " If any man have ears," &c.

3. *God calls by the admonitions of conscience.* Who has not felt the inward conviction, the inward rebuke, the inward warning? &c. Now thus God calls men, but to what?

(1.) To awake; to shake off the lethargy; to arouse themselves; to exercise their powers; "Consider your ways," &c. To reflect, &c.

(2.) To arise from the dead; to forsake the position of sleep and death; the company and state of the dead, &c. Illustrate it by a person who has taken some powerful opiate; or some one who has been overcome by intense cold, and where sleep would be death. Now power is ever given to obey.

III. THE GREAT PROMISE. "Christ shall give thee light."

1. *The blessing promised is light.*

(1.) The light of saving knowledge.

(2.) Of true peace and joy by the forgiveness of sin.

(3.) Of holiness. " A new heart," &c. Become a child of light, &c.

2. *The source of the blessing is Christ.* Christ is appointed to this. It is his work, &c. In the days of his flesh, &c. To many here. Whosoever cometh, &c.

3. *The manner of its bestowment.* "Shall give." All his blessings are gifts. Free, rich, meritless, suit all cases, &c.

APPLICATION

1. *We call upon the sinner to awake.* Now; in earnest.

2. *Warn the Christian against lethargy.* " Let us not sleep as do others," &c

49
ON STRIVING WITH GOD

"Wo unto him that striveth with his Maker."
—Isaiah xlv. 9.

The sinner is variously represented in the writings of this holy book. The idea of rebellion is one of frequent recurrence. A sinner rebels against God's authority and dominion. The sinner is frequently styled an enemy, and this is evident both from his heart, and tongue, and life. The heart is in a state of enmity, &c.—the tongue impiously exclaiming, "Depart from us, for we desire not," &c., and wicked works distinguish the ungodly man. Very frequently the sinner is described as fighting against God, or contending with him, and this is the idea of the text, "Wo unto him," &c. Let us notice,

I. The manifestation of this strife.
II. The evils of such a course.
III. The final results.

I. The manifestation of this strife. To strive is to oppose, and in a variety of ways sinners exhibit opposition to God. There is,

1. *The unblushing opposition of infidelity.* Nothing can exhibit more daring wickedness than infidelity—denying God. Excluding his existence or government from his own world. To say there is no God! or to affect to say so, or to reduce him to an indifferent spectator of his works and creatures. In connection with infidelity there is the rejection of the scriptures, and boasting of the sufficiency of nature to teach us virtue and religion. What part of nature? Or what can we know of moral right, &c.—of evil? &c. Apply this to truth, to honesty—to prayer, &c. It is all mockery, you might as soon expect a child to learn to speak by hearing the winds. No! the rejecter of the Bible will not find another oracle of truth in the universe. How devoted this class of individuals are in prosecuting their work! How eager to dissuade others from their adherence to the Christian religion!

2. *The fearless transgressions of the bold and daring in iniquity.* Those who drink in iniquity as an ox, &c. Who lay aside all the restrictions of conscience and the respect of the virtuous around them. Who give themselves up to every evil way and work. Whose language is filthy and brutal. Who have no fear, nor shame, nor sense of their responsibility, and who are in fact demonized by habitual sins.

3. *Those who resist the providential dealings and interpositions of God for their salvation.* Providence subserves the designs of grace. The movements of the divine government are often full of instruction—often act as warnings and beacons. Adversity, sickness, and bereavements are often employed to lead to thought and consideration, to reflection, repentance, and personal religion. The resistance of these is striving against God. If these do not soften they harden. Some metals melt while others harden in the furnace. God hedges up the way of some, that in their afflictions they may seek him; if they do not, they must break through and fight against him.

4. *Those who will not yield to the overtures of the gospel.* The gospel proclaims men enemies, and seeks their return to friendship; traitors, &c.; wanderers, &c.; and urges, "Be ye reconciled to God." "Agree," &c. "Be at peace," &c. The gospel proclaims an amnesty; but of course it is on the principle of throwing down their weapons and ceasing to strive and rebel. Whoso persists in unbelief strives against God—yea, against the riches of his grace.

II. The evils of such a course.

1. *It is full of infatuation.* It cannot be vindicated upon the principle of reason or propriety. It is evidently a sign of the mind being blinded by the wicked one. Either the faculties of the understanding and judgment are in entire darkness, or they are wofully perverted. There cannot be greater madness or more complete folly than to strive against God.

2. *It is fraught with evils to our own souls.* It acts negatively in excluding the greatest blessings God has to bestow. "Your sins have withholden good things," &c. It excludes the divine favor, peace of conscience, and a hope of immortality. It deprives us of all the rich communications of heaven. Besides, it acts positively to our injury. It degrades the mind, it hardens the heart, it sears the conscience, it fills with fear. "The wicked flee," &c. It converts conscience into a gnawing worm. It often makes life insupportable, and drives to delirium or to despair.

3. *It is full of ingratitude.* Look at the child that despises and treats irreverently his parent. How you feel indignation to

rise, &c. That child is the sinner who strives against his Maker. Look at that befriended individual who calumniates and seeks the ruin of his patron and benefactor —conspires against his property and life. Look at that ransomed slave who unites with the bloodthirsty enemies of his benefactor, &c. But all figures must fail in the illustration. But in reference to striving against God, notice,

III. ITS FINAL RESULTS.

1. *We cannot injure Deity.* We might injure a potsherd like ourselves. Even a weak man may injure a powerful one. But God is too high for the arrows of the sinner's rebellion. We cannot baffle, or confuse, or disturb his felicity. Neither,

2. *Can we benefit ourselves.* Who hath hardened himself against the Lord and prospered? Who indeed? Is there any case on record? The man who strives against God converts the pure stream into a deadly current, the wholesome air into a pestilent atmosphere, and all the enjoyments of life into sources of wretchedness and misery. It blights all the soul's prospects of felicity forever. Nor can we,

3. *Escape the triumphs of the divine judgments over us.* One must prevail. We cannot; then God will; and his prevailing will be our wo. " Wo unto him," &c. The vengeance of God is the direst wo, and it must be endured; the wo of his displeased and incensed countenance; the wo of his righteous sentence; wo of his fiery indignation which shall consume the adversaries; wo of everlasting misery as the desert of iniquity; wo unto him—to each and all such. To the beggar and the monarch; to the great and the small; to the learned and the ignorant; to the young and the old; to all and every one.

APPLICATION

Probably there are four descriptions of character here.

1. *The strivers against God, who are indifferent, perhaps reckless.* Oh think and stop in your career, &c.

2. *Those who occasionally relent and hesitate.* Allow those good emotions to prevail. They are heaven's distilling dews. " Grieve not the Spirit of God," &c.

3. *Those who are suing for mercy.* Oh now exclaim, " I yield, I yield, I can hold out no more," &c.

4. *To the children of God.* Rejoice in your religious experience, and labor for the weal of others. Feel for others,

" Oh tell to all the world around
What a dear Saviour you have found."

50

REFUGE OF LIES

" And the hail shall sweep away the refuge of lies."—ISAIAH xxviii. 17.

NUMEROUS are the stratagems of Satan to ruin souls. In some he effects this by hurrying them on in the broad way of open transgression; in others by rendering them the victims of some peculiar constitutional sin; as pride, cruelty, oppression, avarice, &c.; in others by inciting a spirit of disbelief to the truth. " The fool hath said in his heart, There is no God." In others by inducing inattention to the things of the soul. But our text leads us to contemplate the false refuges to which he causes others to betake themselves. Observe, sinners often feel the necessity of a refuge; they frequently betake themselves to refuges of lies; such refuges will be ultimately swept away.

I. SINNERS OFTEN FEEL THE NECESSITY OF A REFUGE. This arises sometimes from,

1. *An internal sense of guilt.* Unless in cases of utter obduracy, transgression and remorse are ever wedded together. Even Pagans have felt these workings of conscience, these pangs of guilty torture. Under these, men sigh for peace, long for rest, and earnestly desire a refuge.

2. *From the calamitous events of life.* Sudden adversity, domestic bereavements, visiting the open grave of some friend; bodily indisposition, mental disquietude, &c.

3. *From the supposed nearness of death.* How men, who mock at religion in health, quail at the approach of death! How Voltaire trembled in a storm, how anxious then to have deliverance, to obtain a refuge!

4. *Under the alarming influences of the preached word.* When the truth has flashed across the mind and startled the conscience. Thus Felix, and thus thousands. How lamentable that these impressions and convictions are often so fleeting, so evanescent; but still more so when they flee to sources of false security. Notice then,

II. SINNERS FREQUENTLY BETAKE THEMSELVES TO REFUGES OF LIES. Of these notice,

1. *Partial reformation of life.* Giving up the grosser sins of which they have been guilty : intemperance, avarice, profanity, wrath, injustice, fraud, &c. Now the amputation of a member, when the whole body is diseased, is fruitless.

2. *A general regard to Christian morality.* To the outward acts of obedience. If parents, parental regard to their children ; if children, filial obedience ; discharge of the social duties, general uprightness, external decorum, propriety of speech, a rigid regard to truth, all of which are good in their legitimate sphere and extent.

3. *An outward profession of religion.* Punctual regard to public worship, a proper regard to ordinances, a name among the people of God, zeal against infidelity and rreligion. Then we may notice,

4. *A prominent and public sectarian spirit.* Rigid adherence to party, and sect, and creed ; violent anathematizing all others ; great ardor in the public events of the church to which they belong. " Come, see my zeal," &c.

5. *Distinguished generosity and charity.* Liberality to the poor, works of beneficence, enrolled among the compassionate and benevolent. " Give their goods to feed the poor," &c. Now all these are often only refuges of lies ; all these may engage a man's anxious attention, and the root of the matter have no place in his heart. We may add,

6. *A general reliance on the mercy of God.* A kind of self-confident persuasion that God is good, that he will not punish, an indefinite resting on his clemency, forgetting his righteousness, purity, truth, &c.

III. SUCH REFUGES WILL BE ULTIMATELY SWEPT AWAY. They will be so,

1. *In a dying hour.* Then the mental vision often becomes peculiarly acute, the moral sense keen and distinct, and the honesty of the Spirit throws off the tinsel mask, which is now manifestly worse than useless. How poor and worthless is self-righteousness, in all its possible extent, to a spirit just stepping into the presence of the holy God ! A queen of England, although professing to be " defender of the faith," and having bishops at her control, felt this, and died in circumstances of unutterable alarm.

2. *In the morning of the resurrection.* Then all classes and distinctions will be reduced to two. None but the righteous will have a part in the first resurrection.

Others will rise with shame, confusion, and horror, to everlasting contempt.

3. *In the decisions of judgment.* God will judge all men in righteousness. The wicked and the righteous will be separated, as a man separateth the sheep from the goats ; no pretence will avail, no disguise, no plea, no stratagem, no importunity, no effort to flee, &c. All refuges of lies will be swept away.

APPLICATION

1. Warn against these destructive schemes and wiles of Satan.

2. Exhibit the one only refuge, Jesus Christ, who delivers from the wrath to come.

3. Urge instant faith in him ; " Count all things but loss," &c. All who believe in him are secure for both worlds ; to this refuge repair every one, earnestly, and now.

51

GOD'S SOLICITUDES FOR MANKIND

" Oh that there were such an heart in them, that they would fear me, and keep all my commandments always, that it might be well with them, and with their children forever."—DEUTERONOMY v. 29.

OUR text refers to God, and his ancient people Israel. At the time of the giving of the law, under the influence of fear, and no doubt in the full sincerity of their hearts, they had said to Moses, " Speak thou unto us all the words that the Lord our God shall speak unto thee, and we will hear it and do it." God approved of their holy determination, but knowing the deceitfulness of the heart, he says, " Oh that there were such an heart in them," &c. Jehovah had the concern for Israel he has for you, he desires you to possess sincere and unfeigned piety, that religion, which will benefit you forever, and be a blessing to your posterity after you. We shall ground several propositions upon the text.

I. TRUE RELIGION IS INSEPARABLY CONNECTED WITH A PECULIAR STATE OF HEART. " Oh that there were such an heart," &c. The state of the heart naturally is evil ; an evil root, an evil fountain. It is described as a heart of stone ; cold, hard, unyielding, deceitful, &c. ; it is described as proud, self-willed, and carnal. Now, with this state of heart there can be no piety. This heart, therefore, must be renovated, so as to become a new heart, flesh instead of stone, spiritual instead of carnal, contrite instead of callous, lowly instead of proud; in one word, it must be renewed and made spiritual, cleansed, &c. " Old things," &c. This is a very important consideration, the basis of acceptable religion. " My son, give me thy heart," &c.

II. A RIGHT STATE OF HEART WILL BE CONNECTED WITH THE FEAR OF GOD. Many dare God, insult, blaspheme, &c.; many never think of God, &c.; many regard him with horrific dread. All these states of mind are equally contrary to religion. A right state of heart will produce fear, reverential fear, holy fear, filial fear. " The fear of God" is often used for the whole of religion. His perfections, works, glory, judgments, should all inspire this fear.

III. A RENEWED HEART WILL BE EVINCED BY EVANGELICAL OBEDIENCE. Not will-service, not self-righteousness, not meritorious obedience, but evangelical obedience, as the fruit of a right state of mind, the effect of faith, the obedience of love. Now this evangelical obedience should be evinced in two ways.

1. *By its universality.* " All my commandments." They are all right, wise, good; all of them are important and necessary; ye cannot be right-minded and wish to choose, &c. " Ye are my friends if ye do whatsoever," &c.

2. *By its perpetuity.* " Always." Most men do what is right occasionally, but our obedience must be constant. " Always,— in season and out of season, in prosperity and adversity, under reproach, persecution," &c.; at all rates and hazards, " Be faithful unto death," &c.

IV. TRUE RELIGION IS ESSENTIALLY CONNECTED WITH OUR WELL-BEING. "That it might," &c. Now this is true,

1. *As to our present well-being.* It is well for the body and the soul, for the mind and the heart. It exalts—improves— blesses—comforts—saves, &c.

2. *As to our future well-being.* It shall be well with the righteous, " They shall be mine," &c. They are heirs of glory. " Shall see the King in his beauty," &c.; they shall die in peace, and dwell with God forever. " When flesh and heart fail," &c.

V. JEHOVAH IS SINCERELY CONCERNED THAT THIS RELIGION SHOULD BE OUR INDIVIDUAL PORTION. Hence his declarations— provisions—invitations—forbearance, &c. His nature disposes him to this, his glory also.

APPLICATION

1. *Learn the true characteristics of acceptable religion.* Renewed heart, fear, and evangelical obedience.

2. *Learn the desirableness of true piety.* Our welfare, &c.

3. *The influence of true piety on our posterity, &c.*

4. *The inexcusableness of those who are irreligious, &c.* " Oh that," &c.

52

PRIDE AND OBSTINACY OF THE SINNER

" The wicked, through the pride of his countenance, will not seek after God."—PSALM x. 4.

Two points in theology we deem of essential importance; they cannot be too highly estimated, too seriously pondered, or too frequently considered. The first is this, all good is from God; he is the one source of light, and purity, and bliss. Whatever excellency or enjoyment pertains to men, God is the author, and the whole glory belongs to his name. The second is, that the evil and misery of man are of himself, and that all the blame of his wretchedness and ruin is his own. This is often exhibited to us in the scriptures, &c. Two or three passages shall suffice. " I have called," &c. " Ye will not," &c. " Whatsoever a man soweth," &c. And also the text. The text contains a character to be defined—a line of conduct to be explained—and the cause which is assigned for that conduct. The text contains,

I. A CHARACTER TO BE DEFINED. " The wicked." We are too apt to apply the term to the notorious—to the profligate, &c. There is one view I wish to impress upon you, that the absence of real piety involves the charge of wickedness. We are not to judge by the opinions of men, by human laws, but by the scriptures of divine truth. I ask not the magistrate of the district—I ask not the persons you travel with—I ask not your neighbors, or friends, or family; but I inquire of the oracles of eternal truth. Do you believe in the Lord Jesus Christ? Do you enjoy and obey the influences of the Spirit? Do you love God supremely?

Are you spiritually minded ? Do you seek first and chiefly the kingdom of God, &c. ? Are you actuated by the holy principles of the gospel ? If not, however intellectual, you do not know God ; or moral, you do not serve him ; or amiable, you have not his mind ; or religious, yet you have not the Spirit of Christ Jesus ; unless the heart has been renewed, and the mind of the Saviour imparted, we belong to the class described in the scripture as being wicked. How many then of this character are now before God in this assembly ? Do I belong to it, or have I been saved from it ? Observe in the text,

II. A LINE OF CONDUCT WHICH MUST BE EXPLAINED. "Will not seek after God." Let some truths premise our remarks here. Men are alienated from God by sin. All men have forsaken him. God is willing to be sought by his wandering children. He desires their return ; he employs means for it ; many by these means have returned and sought God, and obtained mercy. But the wicked will not seek, &c.

1. *They will not seek after the knowledge of God.* "Some men," &c. All other knowledge they admire, extol, &c. They would be ashamed to be ignorant of letters —of general science—of literature, &c. But they know not God, &c. ; neither will they seek in the volume of eternal truth to attain this knowledge. No time, or talent, or opportunity, given to this. Created things, but not the Creator. Sublunary, but not the immortal. Often frivolous, &c., but not the supreme good.

2. *They will not seek after reconciliation with God.* They have rebelled, transgressed, &c. God is displeased with their conduct—they are under sentence of wrath, yet they act and live as though they were secure. No sincere anxiety to enjoy the favor of God.

3. *They will not seek conformity to God's likeness.* Most men desire to resemble some one or some class. The ambitious, the rich, the influential ; but they care not to resemble the divine holiness ; aim not at attaining the image of God. They do not love or admire spiritual purity, therefore will not seek to possess it.

4. *They do not seek after fellowship with God.* "God is not in all their thoughts." They desire not communion with God either in public or private ; they say, " Depart from us, we desire not the knowledge of thy ways." They seek this in reference to kindred spirits ; they commune with nature and art, but not with God. Let us notice,

III. THE CAUSE OF THIS PROCEDURE WHICH THE TEXT ASSIGNS. " Pride." Undue esteem of self. Arrogant estimation of their own powers, &c.

1. *Pride hates the view which the scriptures give of human nature.* It will not have man dethroned. Will not allow his total depravity—his helplessness—misery, desert, &c.

2. *Pride approves not of the divine supremacy.* Each carnal heart would rule —hold the reins—sway the sceptre. Likes not God's control. Approves not being subordinate in every thing to Deity.

3. *Pride often rejects the way of salvation.* As a free gift, all of grace. It says, Let me do something—excel and win it— strive and conquer for it—suffer and earn it—work and pray for it.

4. *Pride objects to the means connected with salvation.* Contrition, confession, abasement, restitution, lowliness, &c., of heart, confession of Christ before men.

5. *Pride dislikes the universality of salvation.* Murmurs that the vilest, &c., should be equally welcome ; or the poorest—or the most illiterate. It would have a dispensation to itself—a respectable religion, a peculiar kind of service, not vulgar, &c.

APPLICATION

1. *Have you sought after God ?* In truth. Earnestly and prayerfully.

2. *Or are you indifferent ?* What is the cause, &c. Is it pride ? Examine, be particular, faithful, minute, &c.

3. *The threats to the proud are fearful.* Publicly disgraced, brought low, &c. ; covered with shame, &c. No distinction in the great day, either of rank, or talent, &c.

4. *All are now invited to seek after God.* " Let the wicked forsake his way," &c.

53

GOD'S GRACIOUS INVITATION TO SINNERS

"Come now, and let us reason together, saith the Lord : though your sins be as scarlet, they shall be as white as snow ; though they be red like crimson, they shall be as wool."—ISAIAH i. 18.

IT is scarcely possible to conceive of a more interesting and delightful exhibition of the love and mercy of God, than is presented to us in these words ; unless they had been found in the volume of eternal truth, we might justly have doubted their veracity. For the speaker in the text is Jehovah, a Being infinitely happy and glorious in himself, whose felicity and dignity cannot be enlarged or diminished. He needs not, on his own account, the return of the sinner to himself ; besides, he is the offended party. It is his authority which nas been slighted. His laws violated—his goodness abused—his holy image effaced. How marvellous, then, that he should stoop to ask reconciliation with poor wretched man, the rebel and traitor against heaven ! Yet so it is. " Come now, and let us reason together," &c. Notice,

I. THE CHARACTERS ADDRESSED. Now the characters are not such as excel in moral excellency, but the reverse, the debased, the vilest and most degraded of sinners, represented, in their iniquities, as being like unto scarlet or crimson. How apt we are to think that such are too low to be raised up, too defiled to be made clean, too far alienated to be reclaimed ! Whatever we may think, these are the invited in our text, and these are the characters we are now to contemplate. Who then are included in the description ; their sins being as scarlet, &c. Now it includes,

1. *Those whose sins are glaring and manifest.* There is much invisible evil in existence. Much hidden in the deep recesses of the soul. Much that the eye of man or angel never sees. There may be hidden thoughts of impiety, and blasphemy, and infidelity, and anger, and malice. But externa circumstances act in the moral world as the shore to the ocean, limiting and bounding its waters. Now a great many of the ungodly are thus restrained, and it is well for society and the church of Christ that it is so. But we find numbers who have gone beyond this boundary, who are not ashamed of their iniquities. Who countenance wickedness in public places and bear the mark of the beast in their foreheads. Many revel in iniquity. Drink it in as the ox drinketh water. Loudly blaspheme. Openly debase themselves, and glory in their shame. The sins of such are as scarlet or as crimson.

2. *It will apply to those whose iniquities are especially productive of much evil and misery.* To those who are ring-leaders in sin ; those who constrain others to do wickedly ;

those who are champions of vice ; ridiculers of piety, and who labor to throng the road to hell with their fellow-sinners ; and here let me refer to those who are heads of families. Your children and domestics look up to you ; they will extensively be, what you appear to be. You create the deadly atmosphere they breathe, you poison the waters they drink. What cruelty such display to their families ! You swearing, you drunken heads of families, you who have ruined your children.

3. *It will apply to those who have sinned against great privileges and mercies.* Now it cannot be doubted that many who are in a condition of darkness would have been otherwise, had they possessed the privileges which others have enjoyed. Thus Christ said, " Wo unto thee, Chorazin ! Wo unto thee, Bethsaida," &c. As it is with nations and cities, so it is with individuals. How many have had privileges and mercies of a high character ! I place among these pious parents. You had their example, their prayers, their best counsels, their dying entreaties. I place religious society. You have moved in a circle favorable to piety ; you have seen religion embodied, &c. A faithful ministry. You have had the gospel in purity, plainness, and affection. I place also striking providences. God has met you in affliction, in bereavements, &c. What did you say, resolve, and vow before God ? And what have you done ? Are you not ingrates, promise-breakers, mockers of God ?

4. *It will apply to backsliders.* Such as have once been enrolled in Christ's army, but who have deserted and gone over to the camp of the devil. Who once prayed, but now have refrained, &c. What an awful state ! What grief you have caused to the church ! How you have dishonored Christianity, and wounded the Saviour in the house of his friends ! How infidels have scoffed ! How the world has been hardened ! Poor miserable apostate ! are not thy sins " as scarlet, yea, as crimson," &c.

5. *It will apply to aged transgressors.* Those who have grown gray-headed in the service of sin. Old age is unnerving that arm, which has ever been lifted up against God. Oh think of the course you have pursued ! Think how countless your sins ! Think how unnumbered your provocations ; and yet you are adding to the dye and making it deeper and deeper. What hard-

ness of heart ! What callousness of spirit ! What thoughtlessness of soul ! " Your sins are as scarlet," &c. Observe then,

II. THE INVITATION JEHOVAH PRESENTS. " Come and let us reason," &c. He wishes to have your state and condition tested by reason. He gives you the opportunity of self-defence ; he is willing to hear all your motives, and arguments, &c. Now will you come to God, and reason with him ? What will you say ?

1. *You cannot plead ignorance.* You have been conscious of the evil of your ways. Reason, conscience, scripture, condemn you. You have known better ; your eyes have been open. You have seen the evil, and yet have chosen it.

2. *You cannot plead necessity.* The Jews of old said, they were sold to do evil ; that is, they could not avoid it. Now, if any of you imagine this, it is the grossest self-deception ; it cannot be the will of God that you should do evil. This is horrid and impious indeed. You have sinned freely, it has been your own act and choice.

3. *You must plead guilty.* And in doing so you must cast yourselves upon the mercy of God. If guilty, and if all the evil and blame is with you, then God must be clear, and you condemned. What then must be the result, must sentence go forth ? Not if you will,

4. *Plead the merits of Christ.* Here is the sacrifice for sin. Here your hope, your plea.

> " 'Tis just the sentence should take place—
> 'Tis just, but oh ! thy Son has died."

Now in availing yourself of this plea, all that God requires is repentance and faith. Confess and forsake sin, and believe on the Lord Jesus Christ. If you do this, then notice,

III. THE GRACIOUS PROMISE GIVEN. " Though your sins be as scarlet," &c.

1. *All your sins shall be blotted out.* Every one both of omission and commission. All your sins of heart, lip, and life ; from the first to the last. Blotted out as a cloud.

2. *You shall stand accepted in Christ.* He shall behold you in Christ as righteous. Look at the hue and the dye of the guilty sinner ; when accepted look again. Not one mark, not one spot, not one charge.

3. *By sanctifyng grace you shall be made fit for glory.* He will give you a new na-

ture, and make you really and perfectly holy. " Without spot or wrinkle," &c. And this shall be followed,

4. *By the gift of eternal life.* Rom. vi. 23 ; 1 John v. 11.

APPLICATION

1. *Let me urge you all to come and reason with God, and do it now.* There is salvation for every one.

2. *If you will not come, you will be without excuse.*

3. *You must come to him in death and judgment.*

54

TERMS OF DISCIPLESHIP

" Then said Jesus unto his disciples, If any man will come after me, let him deny himself, and take up his cross, and follow me."—MATTHEW xvi. 24.

To perfectly holy beings it must be a source of indescribable pleasure to obey God. The faculties and powers of such intelligences only find a proper sphere of exercise in the divine service. To hearken to God, to do with the most fervent zeal his will, is the highest enjoyment of which they are capable. Now, the very reverse of this is true when applied to depraved, polluted creatures. Sin, then, is the end of their actions, and in that they have carnal delight and pleasure. Sin in such cases is natural, even as the stream must be foul where the fountain is corrupt— the fruit worthless, when the tree is evil. Religion, therefore, does violence to the carnal mind ; self must be crucified ; and, from the necessity of the case, no man can be a disciple of Jesus unless he deny himself, &c. Observe the course prescribed ; the advantage with which it is connected ; and the means of its exemplification. Notice,

I. THE COURSE PRESCRIBED. Three things are noted by the Redeemer :—

1. *Self-denial.* " Let him deny himself." Self is often ignorant, presumptuous, confident, wayward, &c. Self seeks gratification, ease, and exaltation. Now, all these are the fruit of sin, and contrary to God and holiness. There cannot be religion with self-satisfaction—with self-righteousness—with self-pleasing. Just as in taking the nauseating draught, violence is done to the taste—or in the painful am-

putation of a member, violence is done to the feelings; so, in serving God, the old man, the flesh must be crucified; self must be subverted; and the will of God become the supreme law of the mind.

2. *Reproach and suffering.* "Let him take up his cross." The cross is the symbol of ignominy and pain, and there can be no genuine evidence of piety without bearing the cross. This cross is often composed of the envy and reproaches of the wicked —the false accusations and persecutions of those who hate the Redeemer and his holy cause; and so long as the world is under the power of Satan, it will harass, defame, and, if possible, injure the followers of Jesus. This Christ expressly stated to his disciples; and the experience of all true Christians establishes that scriptural statement, "That it is through much tribulation," &c.

3. *Imitation of the Saviour.* "And follow me." Jesus is the example of his people. "He hath left us an example," &c. "My sheep hear my voice." We must follow him in a conscientious regard to the ordinances and commandments of God; in a public avowal of holiness to the world; in the hallowed exercises of pure devotion; in the discharge of the practical duties of the Christian life; in a life of continued activity and benevolence; in patient resignation under suffering. Christ must be set before us. "Looking unto Jesus," &c. Notice,

II. THE ADVANTAGES WITH WHICH THIS COURSE IS CONNECTED.

1. *A dignified union to Christ and his people.* By coming out from the world, Christ will receive us. He will admit us to enjoy union and fellowship with him; have a place in his spiritual family; be numbered among his disciples; have a relationship to Christ more exalted than that of the highest angel in heaven.

2. *A saving interest in his favor and love.* He will grant us the full and free remission of all sin; impart the spirit of adoption; give us internal tokens of his approbation; "Manifest himself," &c.; see John xiv. 23, xv. 1, &c.

3. *A constant supply of his all-sufficient grace.* Without this the Christian's life could not be sustained. His grace alone is sufficient for us; this he will freely and abundantly pour out. His love to us, his engagements, the experience of all saints,

confirm this. He desires to bestow it in all its refreshing plenitude.

4. *A participation of his glory forever.* "If we suffer with him, we shall also be glorified with him." Observe Christ's express declaration, "Whosoever, therefore, shall confess me," &c., Matt. x. 32. Hear his sacerdotal prayer, "Father, I will that they also whom thou hast given," &c. John xvii. 24; Rev. iii. 5, 21. Now, a faithful regard to the course prescribed will eventually terminate in glory, immortality, and eternal life. We inquire, then, in reference to this course,

III. THE MEANS OF ITS EXEMPLIFICATION. How shall we deny ourselves?

1. *By obtaining a nature suited to the work.* The heart must be renewed; new spirit imparted, &c. By faith in Christ Jesus we become the sons of God, and partakers of the divine and holy nature.

2. *By seeking the aids of the Holy Spirit.* The Spirit will enable us to crucify the flesh, to forsake evil, to imitate Christ. He will guide, sanctify, establish, keep.

3. *By the continued exercise of faith.* "The just shall live by faith," &c. I am crucified with Christ, &c. By faith the Old Testament heroes conflicted and overcame.

4. *By having a single eye to the divine glory.* God will then honor, and support, and bless us; fulfil all his word, &c., guide by his counsel, &c.

APPLICATION.

1. Here is encouragement for the Christian.

2. Hope for the penitential inquirer.

3. And admonitory warning for the formal.

55

MAINTENANCE OF THE CHRISTIAN PROFESSIONAL

"Let us hold fast the profession of our faith."— HEBREWS x. 23.

THE apostle, in the previous verses, has been exhibiting Jesus Christ in his sacerdotal character. He represents the church as the house of God, over which Jesus is the great High Priest. He exhorts believers to an experimental acquaintance with his saving benefits, "Let us draw near," &c. He then enforces the importance of

Christian stability, " Let us hold fast," &c. Consider,

I. WHAT THE CHRISTIAN PROFESSION INVOLVES. It involves,

1. *A saving knowledge of Christ.* Ignorance of Christ unfits for a profession. The gospel was written, and is preached, that men may know Jesus Christ. " This is life eternal," &c. " I count all things but loss for the excellency of the knowledge of Christ Jesus our Lord." We would see Jesus, is the inquiry ; and then it should be, We have found him, &c. Jesus Christ in you, the hope of glory.

2. *It involves trust and confidence in Christ.* " Profession of our faith." Faith receives Christ—builds on Christ—unites us to Christ—and makes Christ all our own. Faith is the vital act of the soul, by which we commit all our concerns into his hands ; expect from him and through him every blessing here ; and finally, eternal life.

3. *It involves a public attestation of our approbation of Christ.* To profess, is to show forth—to exhibit—to let others see and know that we are the Lord's. It is to take his name as our badge—belong avowedly to his cause ; to wear the livery of Christ ; to speak the words of Christ ; to show the spirit of Christ ; to seek the glory of Christ ; to be his witnesses—his confessors ; to go forth without the camp ; an opposite course to his enemies, and quite distinct from the formal and indifferent.

4. *It involves obedience to his ordinances and commands.* " My sheep hear my voice, and follow me." " If ye love me, keep my commandments." The promise is, that he will put his law into our hearts, and that we shall walk in his statutes and ordinances to do them. This is not the obedience of fear, or of toil, but of love and a willing mind. "The love of Christ constraineth us." Now this profession Christ demands, if a man will be his disciple, that he should take up his cross and follow him. He said, " Whosoever is ashamed of me, I will be ashamed of him," &c.

II. BY WHAT IS A CHRISTIAN PROFESSION OPPOSED ? This opposition is implied, not expressed ; but the exhortation is pointless without this. Now, this profession,

1. *Will be opposed by our adversary, Satan.* " Simon, Simon, Satan desires to have thee," &c. " Your adversary, the devil, goeth about seeking whom he may devour." His wiles—darts, &c.

2. *An ungodly world will oppose this profession.* " Marvel not that I said unto you, that the world will hate you." Christians have been hated, and persecuted, and reviled, and mocked, and put to death in all ages. If ye were of the world it would love you, but it now hates you ; often worldly friends and relatives ; a man's foes are often those of his own household.

3. *The remains of evil within us will oppose this profession.* An indolent heart ; self-love ; pride ; ease ; the flesh will war against the spirit ; spirit of discontent, &c. But,

III. HOW IS THE CHRISTIAN PROFESSION TO BE MAINTAINED ?

1. *By holding fast to the sanctifying word of truth.* " I have no greater joy than that my children walk in the truth." "Sell it not." " Let the word of Christ dwell in you."

2. *Let us hold fast to the means of grace ;* see verse 25. God has appointed the church to be a social compact—to form a united bulwark to the enemy. In the means of grace, we meet with God and take courage. Here we are refreshed for our journey ; here we brighten our armor ; here we stand on the mountain-top, and get a glimpse of the land which is afar off ; here we drink of the brook by the way, and lift up our head.

3. *Let us hold fast to the person and work of the Saviour.* " He exhorted them all that with purpose of heart they would cleave unto the Lord"—adhere to him. " Except ye abide in me, and I in you," &c. Christ is our life. We walk in him, and derive all our grace, &c., from him. We must be nothing, and Christ Jesus every thing. Christ the Alpha, and the all in all ; Christ our foundation—way—dress—food—pearl —joy—song—glory, &c. In salvation it must ever be, " None but Christ ; none but Christ !"

4. *Let us hold fast to believing prayer.* Be instant in prayer, praying with all prayer. " Pray in faith, nothing doubting." Pray in secret. " Pray always," &c. Notice,

IV. THE IMPORTANCE OF CARRYING OUT BOTH THE LETTER AND THE SPIRIT OF THE TEXT.

1. *It is very important to those who are without.* " The world." If we give up our profession infidels and blasphemers will rejoice, worldlings will be hardened, form-

alists satisfied, inquirers discouraged. The mischief may be everlasting.

2. *It is important to our fellow-Christians.* How distressing to see those who walked with Christ turn aside—to see the soldiers of Christ desert! It tends to damp the zeal of the friends of Zion. How painful for the apostle to say, " Demas has forsaken me," &c.; how distressing to Moses to see the thousands of Israel sinning and perishing in the desert! But,

3. *It is all-important to ourselves.* If we go back, Christ's soul will have no pleasure in us. If, after we have put our hands to the gospel plough, we look back, we become unfit for the kingdom. Give up the profession of faith, and hope goes, peace goes, Christ goes, and heaven goes; for only he who endures to the end shall be saved.

APPLICATION

1. *For the maintenance of this profession there is ample provision made.* Jesus says, " My grace is sufficient for thee."

2. *Remember your state before you professed the Saviour.* At that time when you were without Christ, and without hope, &c.

3. *Think of your enjoyments in religion.* Of the pleasures you now possess, &c.

4. *Look to the end.* The goal—the crown—the kingdom. Life is fast ebbing, time is receding, eternity approaching. Oh! then, hold fast.

5. *Who will resolve to profess Jesus now?* You half-hearted, you undecided, you seekers after bliss, now determine.

56
ENCOURAGEMENT TO THE TEMPTED

" There hath no temptation taken you but such as is common to man; but God is faithful, who will not suffer you to be tempted above that ye are able: but will with the temptation also make a way to escape, that ye may be able to bear it."
—1 CORINTHIANS x. 13.

IN this chapter the apostle is referring to several events in the history of the Israelites; and especially to the evils into which they fell. He then notes that these things were written for our admonition, &c., see verse 11. He then draws this important practical inference, " Wherefore," &c., ver. 12. Then he speaks of the temptations to which they might be liable, and assures them, " There hath no temptation," &c. Observe,

I. WHAT IS SAID CONCERNING THE TEMPTATIONS OF THE BELIEVER. It is clearly intimated,

1. *That believers must have temptations.* Now the term signifies to try, and often refers to the assaults of our enemy, the devil. The snares by which he endeavors to destroy the soul. It signifies also the opposition or enticements of evil men, and it includes the trials into which God may bring his people. In the text it must be confined to the first two of these, viz. the evils to which we may be exposed from Satan, and an evil world. Now these will ever be opposed to the happiness and holiness of the people of God. It is Satan's nature to deceive and destroy. " In the world," &c. " Marvel not," &c. Exemption is not to be expected, indeed, is not desirable. " Count it all joy," &c. James i. 2, &c. Indeed, without these we cannot be conformed to Christ. We must share in his sufferings, if we would participate in his glory. " Whosoever overcometh," &c. Now this implies temptation and opposition.

2. *It is affirmed that our temptations shall not be uncommon.* " There hath no temptation," &c. Now this is a great mercy. We shall only drink of the common cup. Have to do with the common evils, &c. We are apt to imagine our condition worse than that of others. There never was but one who could truly say, " There is no sorrow like unto my sorrow." Let me hear your complaints, in reference to your trials and temptations, which of them is uncommon.

(1.) Are you tempted to horrid and gross evils? Think of Job, who was tempted to curse God and die; think of Jesus, who was tempted to idolatry—to the worship of the devil.

(2.) Are you tempted to despond through a sense of your unworthiness,—see Abraham, the friend of God, yet he calls himself dust and ashes. Job exclaims, " Behold I am vile," &c. Isaiah, " Wo is me." Peter said, " Depart from me," &c.

(3.) Are you tempted that your trials are severe and greater than others? Look at Jacob, Aaron, David, Job, the first Christians.

(4.) Are you tempted to doubt the efficiency of prayer? Think of Paul, who prayed thrice, &c. Remember the importunate widow. Perhaps you merely wished. God desired to excite you to holy ardor, &c.

(5.) Are you tempted that God will forsake and leave you? See the case of Job, xxiii. 1–10. See Asaph, Psalm lxxvii. 7, &c. Observe,

II. WHAT IS SAID CONCERNING THE FAITHFULNESS OF GOD TO HIS TEMPTED PEOPLE. "God is faithful." His truth and will are not affected. "I am the Lord, and change not." He is of one mind, &c. All the saints of past generations exclaim, "O Lord God, faithful and true!" One act of unfaithfulness would shake the confidence of all the saints and angels in heaven. He cannot be otherwise. Now the faithfulness of God will be seen in his goodness to his tempted people, and that in three respects.

1. *Temptation shall always be proportionate to your strength.* "Who will not suffer you to be," &c. He knows your frame, &c. He remembers your state. He watches the fire and the floods. He apportions the medicine, &c. What consolation there is in this!

2. *He will ever provide a door of deliverance.* "Also make a way of escape," he did so to Abraham, in the ram caught. Never allow us to be shut up in temptation. See the case of the Israelites on their way to the Red Sea, when he divided the waters. When there is no other, there is always a way upwards. "Call upon me," &c. Psalm cvii. 11.

3. *Until his people are delivered, they shall have strength to be able to bear it.* He will uphold and strengthen, as he did Paul. "My grace is sufficient," &c.

APPLICATION

Let the Christian remember,

1. *Life is a state of trial, and we shall have grace sufficient for it.*

2. *Eternity a state of reward, and glory will amply compensate for the sorrows of life.*

3. *Let not temptations drive you from Christ, or produce apathy and carelessness as to your spiritual state.*

57

BELIEVERS, STRANGERS, AND SOJOURNERS

"For we are strangers before thee, and sojourners, as were all our fathers; our days on the earth are as a shadow, and there is none abiding." –1 CHRONICLES xxix. 15.

OUR text is the declaration of David, and is found among his last words. He lived to a good old age, therefore his testimony is the language of experience; he was a man both of knowledge and wisdom, therefore this saying should be treasured up. Besides, he had reigned forty years over the nation of Israel, so that this is a royal saying. But he was a holy man, one in whom dwelt the spirit of inspiration; he wrote as he was moved, &c., so that this is God's saying to us through David. The truth expressed in the text is a general one; it has been realized in every age of the world; so that we cannot err in applying it to the present time and occasion. We remark, however true,

I. THAT THE TEXT IS NOT THE LANGUAGE OF MANY OF OUR FELLOW-MEN. They are the children of this world—the creatures of time; all their actions and arrangements, maxims, plans, spirit, &c., have to do with this world. They read and think, they buy and sell, &c., build, &c., only in reference to time. Absorbed in the things of time, they are strangers to heavenly and eternal things. Yet, whether they will or not, they must sojourn only for a season; the stream of time is bearing them onward, &c. "The place that knows them now," &c.

II. THE TEXT HAS BEEN THE LANGUAGE OF THE GODLY IN ALL AGES. Abraham, when treating for a burying-place, said, "I am a stranger and sojourner," &c.; the patriarchs, who died in faith, are represented as confessing that they were strangers, &c.; Peter exhorts the scattered Christians of his time to pass the time of their sojourning here in fear, &c.; the Christian recognises this truth.

1. *He feels that he is a stranger.* His affections, &c., are not here; he uses the world, but does not love it. As a traveller, his heart is fixed on his home; as a mariner, on the haven above.

2. *He acts as a stranger.* He conducts his affairs as such; he buys, &c.; he rejoices, &c.; he does not entangle and absorb his mind, &c.; he sits loose, &c. Then he has to do constantly with his intended residence; his prayers go there, his hopes, his desires; he receives intellectuality from them; he is preparing himself for that world; he has a title; he has the nature of the inhabitants; he is meetening for it.

3. *He speaks as a stranger.* His lan-

guage is that of Zion ; he speaks of Christ and spiritual things ; his language shows that he is a stranger, &c.

4. *His dress is that of a stranger.* Garment of righteousness. He is seen and known by the works which men behold ; his dress is not that of worldly vanity and show, but the righteousness of his Lord and Master.

III. As a sojourner the Christian's state is deserving of peculiar attention.

1. *It is exceedingly uncertain.* " It is as a shadow." It may be a flitting, transient one, or more lengthy, but it is not to be reckoned upon, or trusted to. At best it is but a shadow.

2. *The Christian's time here is short.* As a swift post ; as a weaver's shuttle ; as an eagle ; as a vapor ; as a thing of naught.

3. *The Christian's removal hence is certain.* No one's time is abiding. God dwells in one endless duration without change ; but man must quit this state of being. " I know that thou wilt," &c. " The living know," &c. Nothing can reverse that solemn, stern decree, &c.

4. *But we add, the Christian's sojourn is ever under the divine direction and care.* He does not wander at random ; he is not the creature of chance ; he is not without a guide and guard. The providence of God is all these, and infinitely more to him. God illumines his way, directs his steps, supplies his wants, chases away his fears ; he conducts by his counsel, and afterwards receives into glory. We notice, finally, the Christian sojourner's removal hence is always his advantage. On earth he is distant from his inheritance, friends, and complete dignity. " To live is Christ, but to die is gain." " Mark the perfect man," &c. An abundant entrance is administered, &c.

APPLICATION

1. *To the man who does not feel the text.* Let me entreat you to pause, and think, and weigh its truths ; let the year pass in review. How many of your friends and acquaintance have died ? Do not shut your eyes and ears ; this will not avail. Love the world as you may, you must leave it ; you cannot stay, nor take it with you. Seek a better ; from this hour do so ; your lease may almost have expired.

2. *To the Christian stranger.*

(1.) Be vigilant, that you do not imbibe the spirit of the world.

(2.) Exhibit the joys of Christianity in your experience. " Thy statutes shall be my song," &c. " Return to Zion singing," &c. " The joy of the Lord," &c. This will recommend your Saviour and his religion.

3. *Let us do all we can for the improvement of the world.* There is very much to be done. What ignorance, wretchedness, sin, &c. Shine ; do good ; diffuse the graces of religion ; exert Christian influence.

4. *Especially let us labor to take others with us to heaven.* " Come with us," &c. Let our present meditation embrace God's blessings, that we may be thankful ; God's grace and sufficiency, that we may trust in him ; our sins, that we may be contrite, &c. ; the great remedy, that we may come to it, &c.

58

RENEWAL OF THE INWARD MAN

" For which cause we faint not ; but though our outward man perish, yet the inward man is renewed day by day."—2 Corinthians iv. 16.

The text refers to the sufferings of the apostles, and their being overruled for the good of the churches, and the glory of God. He then refers to their preservation and continuance in their holy calling. " For which cause we faint not," &c. Observe,

I. Of what the apostle speaks. " The inward man," signifies the mind or soul, that living, intellectual being which thinks, and wills, and desires, &c. All moral qualities and responsibilities have to do with the soul. The body—the outward man— is the mansion of the inward man. The senses and members of the body obey the supreme dictations of the soul. Now, the inward man has its desires and necessities. It is capable of exhaustion and weakness ; it is vulnerable, and may be injured ; or it may be diseased, and it is exposed to spiritual death. Notice,

II. What the apostle declares concerning it. He says, it is renewed. The word signifies to restore, to invigorate, &c. Now, the Christian's toils, conflicts, sufferings, and temptations, produce weakness, fatigue, &c. ; therefore the soul of the Christian requires to be renewed, or he would faint and be overcome. Now, we require,

1. *The renewing of our desires.* The hungering and thirsting to be kept up; desires after God and holiness, &c.

2. *Our affections.* Our love to God, and his word, and ordinances; love to his holy precepts.

3. *Our ability and spiritual strength.* Power to resist evil, to walk in the way of the Lord, to go onward in the Christian conflict. Now, this renewal of the inward man must be *constant,* " Day by day." Thus the body is renewed day by day; thus, by dews and showers, the earth is renewed day by day. We ask,

III. How GOD RENEWS THE INWARD MAN DAY BY DAY.

1. *By the communications of his word.* God's word is spiritual food, milk, honey, water, &c.

2. *By the visitations of his Spirit.* His Holy Spirit revives, quickens, strengthens, &c.

3. *By blessings on the ordinances.* "They that wait," &c. How necessary,

(1.) That we feel our need of this. And,

(2.) That we humbly, yet believingly, seek it by daily prayer.

59

SELFISHNESS

" For all seek their own, not the things which are Jesus Christ's."—PHILIPPIANS ii. 21.

OUR text is to be understood as involving a very general censure, but not in reality a universal one. Most persons act very extensively under the influence of selfishness. Very few, compared with the multitude, crucify self, or rigidly practise the true spirit of self-denial. Now, there is a principle of self-love which is lawful, and which is planted in our nature for the very wisest of purposes. Every man has an innate love of life, of happiness, &c. We are not to be indifferent to these things; but love to these things may become so inordinate, and so absorb our feelings and thoughts, as to transform us into the characters condemned in the text, or as described by the apostle, when writing to Timothy, " Lovers of their own selves." Let us consider some exhibitions of this spirit—trace it to its source—notice its evils—and recommend the means of deliverance from it.

I. LET US CONSIDER SOME EXHIBITIONS OF THIS SPIRIT. It is seen,

1. *In a desire to obtain self-gratification.* This gratification may consist in the pleasures of sense—in amusements of the world —or in mental recreations; but, whatever may be the choice, if the spirit is occupied in arranging, and contriving, and carrying out expedients to meet its own absorbing desires, then is it evident that selfishness is predominant.

2. *In seeking to assume self-dominion.* Love of power is not confined to legislators and men of rank; it is often seen in the tyranny of the village schoolmaster; in the arrogance of heads of families; in masters and mistresses; in ministers and officers of the church. Now, let this be the ruling passion, and selfishness is evidently predominant.

3. *In intense eagerness for popular applause.* Some would be monopolizers of the good-will and praises of mankind; constantly panting after the approbation of their fellow-creatures; seek with deep solicitude the honor that cometh from men. The most vain and censurable methods are often adopted to obtain this end. The joy of such is suspended on the verdict of popular opinion.

4. *In a craving after the possessions of the world.* This is a very common passion, and one of the worst; to seek their own temporal prosperity in preference to every other object. This spirit of covetousness has been known to trample upon all rights, dissolve the dearest ties, and adopt the most odious measures for the sake of gain. A thirst for gold is one of the most debasing passions that can pollute and pervert the soul. Now, these are the most common exhibitions of the spirit of selfishness. Let us,

II. TRACE THIS SPIRIT TO ITS SOURCE. This is expressed in one word—depravity. It arises from the moral derangement of the powers—from the undue elevation of one of the feelings of the heart over the higher and more noble faculties of the soul. We see it as the master-spirit in the first transgression. Was it not this that prompted the desire to take and eat of the fruit of the tree of knowledge of good and evil? and this perverted, diseased nature, has been handed down to all the posterity of the first guilty pair. Hence it is the natural bent of the fallen nature—the necessary tendency of the corrupt mind; and hence the universality of its manifestation in all ages, classes, and countries; the mass seek their own; all grades of human beings are distinguished for it. It is the plague-spot of our world, and the bane of the family of man. There may be customs, and usages, habits, &c., all favorable to it; but the spring of this stream is man's depravity, the evil state of the heart. Let us note,

III. ITS EVILS. These are legion. Look at it,

1. *In its influence on the mind and heart of its victims.* Its very tendency is to deface the image of God; to dry up the fountain of goodness in the soul; to demoralize the man; to wither its moral beauty and loveliness; to spread o'er it the foul plague spot. It robs it of its enjoyment, prevents its growth and expansion, and eclipses its glory.

2. *Observe its influence on society.* It either isolates, or binds men together in clannish bands, or in base and unprincipled confederacies. Let it be carried out to its full length, and it would leave weakness unaided, misery unpitied, wretchedness unregarded, ignorance unlamented, and all the sorrow and grief of our world uncared for. A man of this kind is often the curse of the domestic sphere, the bane of the neighborhood, the iceberg of the church, and the barren fig-tree of the world.

3. *It is one of the anomalies of the universe.* God has created all creatures and things to have a mutual influence for good on one another. The angels live not for themselves; the sun shines for the benefit of the solar system; the wind blows, the rivers run, the ocean moves, the earth feeds, all nature exercises her functions for relative principles and ends; there is not one isolated, self-destined operation in the universe.

4. *It is totally unlike God.* "The Father of lights, from whom proceedeth every," &c. God exists to diffuse blessedness; he reigns for this; all his attributes have respect to this; all his works, and ways, and word, &c. Especially, how unlike God manifest in the flesh, &c.; how unlike the anthem of the angels at his birth; his life, his death, &c. Observe,

IV. THE MEANS OF DELIVERANCE FROM IT. The renewal of the mind and soul; the entire sanctification of body, soul, and spirit; the indwelling of the Holy Spirit in all his guiding and controlling influences. Thus the fountain will be made pure, the tree good, &c.

APPLICATION

1. The existence of this spirit in the church is owing to the low spiritual state of believers.

2. Against it all Christians should prayerfully strive.

3. It can have no existence in the heavenly world.

60

THE EVIL OF SPIRITUAL IGNORANCE

" That the soul be without knowledge is not good."—PROVERBS xix. 2.

OUR text is one of the concise proverbs of Solomon. Most of these brief sentences contain a great fund of thought, and they have this especial recommendation, they are easily committed to memory, and the impression they make is often long and vividly retained. The ancients were famous for conveying their doctrines and principles in this condensed form. The Proverbs of Solomon, as they are unrivalled in beauty and excellency, so they stand forth as being indited under the inspiring influences of God. They are divine, therefore they are true. And they are generally as important as they are true. Of all these proverbs there is not one of greater moment than that of our text. "That the soul," &c.

I. LET US ILLUSTRATE AND ESTABLISH THE TRUTH OF THE TEXT. Before we enter on the chief point, we offer a few preliminary remarks. By the soul we mean the intellectual, thinking part of man. That spiritual, reflecting, undying, and dignified inhabitant of our frail and perishing bodies. Knowledge signifies perception, illumination. The opposite of ignorance and darkness of mind. Now knowledge may either be associated with that which is temporal, or metaphysical, or moral. It may either be speculative or practical. Knowledge of nature, or science, or art, is good, and desirable, and important. But that knowledge which is pre-eminent is religious knowledge. Knowledge of God and his will; knowledge of ourselves, our condition, our duty, our privileges and blessings, our destiny ; knowledge of Jesus Christ and his great salvation. This is the excellency, the essence, the perfection of knowledge. This is all necessary and necessary to all ; it is so always, and will be so forever. A man may be wise, and good, and happy, without other kinds of knowledge, but none can be so without this. Then it is to spiritual and divine knowledge that we shall limit our subject on the present occasion. Now for the soul to be without knowledge is not good, because,

1. *It frustrates the end of our being.* The soul was formed for knowledge just as the sun for the communication of light. And as the bed of the ocean for the reception of the water, so the soul to be the depository of knowledge. Thus did Adam appear when formed in the image of his Creator. One grand and chief resemblance was in the intellectual faculties with which he was endowed, and the knowledge with which God invested him. The senses of the body are designed to be the inlets of knowledge as to the things around us. The eye, the hand, the taste, the smell, the hearing ; the soul has its powers too ; the understanding, by which we perceive and know ; the judgment, by which we conclude as to the properties, &c., of the things we contemplate ; the imagination, which colors and presents objects before us in their ideal forms. Memory, by which we retain and keep fast the things perceived and known. Now these powers avail not, they are perverted, if the soul be without knowledge, &c. " That the soul," &c.

2. *Because it is its degradation and debasement.* Knowledge is one of the glories of the divine nature ; so it is also the dignity of man. In the fall, man lost much of this ; darkness spread its fell mists over the soul ; darkness pertains to the world beneath and exposes to its shame and contempt. Knowledge pertains to God and heaven, and makes us partakers of the glory of God. Without knowledge, man the monarch becomes the slave, the savage, the degraded creature of the material earth, and the companion of animals and beasts that prowl upon its surface. Not to know God and his will and works is the deep prostration of the creature of his image and his favor. For the soul, &c.

3. *Because it is its misery.* How pleasant, how cheering is its light ! How sweet to behold the works of God, to look abroad on the fair face of nature, &c. Now to be without knowledge is to be blind, for knowledge is the sight of the soul ; knowledge is the food of the soul, and without it, it must starve and die ; knowledge is the health of the soul ; ignorance is the disease and leprosy of the soul. View that being enslaved, blind, starving, diseased, and then you have a faint representation of the soul without knowledge.

4. *Because it is the guilt and condemnation of the soul.* Ignorance, especially to those under the privileges we possess, is sinful : it is criminal. We have the means, the facilities of knowledge. God requires us to possess it. If we are without divine knowledge, it is because we have disliked it, neglected it, and wiled away our opportunities and mercies. In the night none can see or discern the beauties which surround them ; but ours is the day ; the day is the period of light. Jesus proclaims himself the light of the world. We blame men not for being strangers to languages, to philosophy, to science, or art, without the facilities ; but men may have moral intellectuality, spiritual knowledge. It is in the scriptures ; it is published from day to day, and it is highly criminal not to know God and Jesus Christ whom he hath sent. Not to know ourselves and our destiny ; not to know the day of our visitation. It is not good,

5. *Because it will be the death, the total ruin of the soul.* For the children of ignorance and darkness walk in the way of darkness, and their end will be blackness and darkness forever. " My people perish for lack of knowledge." The soul without knowledge is unfit for the enjoyment of God, and incapable of participating in the bliss of heaven. A person may have a volume of superior merit before him, but of what avail is it if he cannot read it ? He may be surrounded with the most splendid scenery, but what avails it if he is blind ? An essential prerequisite for heaven is the saving knowledge of God ; this is life eternal. Heaven is the region of knowledge ; the world of eternal light and day. Let me, then,

II. Ask what are the principles which our subject involves.

1. *The lamentable condition of those who are spiritually ignorant.* How many of these dwell around us ! Are there not such in this assembly ? The state of such

is truly pitiable, dark, condemned, perishing.

2. *The high estimation in which we should hold the privileges we possess.* We have the book, emphatically the key of knowledge; the whole mind of God to man; the guide to happiness and heaven. We have the messengers of knowledge; the preachers of the gospel are sent forth, that their lips may dispense knowledge. All the ordinances of religion are adapted to this end. We have many especial facilities which no age of the world ever had; abundant streams flowing from the press; means of instruction, especially schools. How different to our forefathers!

3. *The responsibility of the church of Christ to diffuse the knowledge of God abroad.* Believers are to shine, &c. We are to labor, holding forth the word of life, &c. We are to train up the rising age, &c. We are to pray, "O Lord, send out," &c.

APPLICATION

1. *Have you this knowledge?* If so, grow in it, &c.

2. *If not, seek till you possess it.*

61

SCRIPTURAL INSTRUCTION OF THE YOUNG

" And these words which I command thee this day, shall be in thine heart: and thou shalt teach them diligently unto thy children, and shalt talk of them when thou sittest in thine house, and when thou walkest by the way," &c.—DEUTERONOMY vi. 6–9.

OUR text is found in connection with a paragraph of peculiar weight and sublimity. Moses, that distinguished servant of Jehovah, is rehearsing to the people of Israel the high commandments of the Lord; he introduces the subject in the following striking and powerful manner; " Now these are the commandments," &c. Here you will perceive duty and privilege, obedience and reward, are united together. He then calls for their special attention. " Hear therefore," &c., verse 3. This exclamation he repeats, when referring to the unity of the Godhead, verse 4; he then lays the basis of his exhortations in the especial religion of the heart, verse 5; and then immediately builds upon it the duties prescribed in the text. " And these words," &c. Let us consider the subject to which

the text refers; the duties the text enjoins; the mode of performance the text recommends. Now we have to notice,

I. THE SUBJECT TO WHICH THE TEXT REFERS. " And these words." Now the text may mean the entire law and will God had made known to Moses, and then revealed to the people, or to the immediate paragraph which precedes the text; but we may justly apply the text to the sacred scriptures in general. To the lively oracles both of the Old and New Testaments; the Bible in its comprehensive and complete character, including Moses and Christ, the prophets and the apostles. Now the scriptures contain a revelation of all essential truths; a summary of all Christian duties; a charter of all desirable blessings; it is the true guide to the knowledge of God, salvation, immortality, and eternal life. Emphatically the book of books, and to all who desire it, the record of salvation. It gives light to the ignorant, wisdom to the simple, and peace to the unhappy; it converts the soul, guides the feet, and sanctifies the heart; it is the pilgrim's staff, and the warrior's sword; the mine of wealth, and passport to glory! What a subject! A book, which has God for its author—truth for its matter—and salvation for its end. We pass from the subject,

II. TO THE DUTIES THE TEXT ENJOINS. It is the scriptural instruction of their children; to teach them the words of God and salvation. Now look at this in several lights.

1. *Our children are naturally ignorant of these things.* None, by mere dint of natural effort, ever found out the true knowledge of God; uninstructed, therefore, they will grow up in mental and moral darkness.

2. *In these things our children have a deep interest.* They have minds capable of instruction, the capacity for knowledge. There seems to be an inherent desire for knowledge; it is the very atmosphere of the soul's health and well-being. The true wealth of our children depends greatly on their acquisition of divine knowledge; their happiness essentially depends upon it; their usefulness in this life; and what is most of all, their eternal salvation. " My people perish for lack of knowledge."

3. *For the instruction of our children we are responsible.* I deny that this responsibility rests anywhere to the exclusion of

the parent ; on him it rests. " Thy children," and as much as it rests upon them to provide food, and raiment, and medicine, &c. The care of the mind as well as of the body is committed to them, and the one is infinitely more weighty than the other. Parents may not in every case be able to teach their children, but then they must see that it is done. In our sabbath-schools, the church of Christ provides for those who cannot have Christian instruction at home, and also to aid those parents who are thus laudably engaged. Now we proceed to consider,

III. THE MODE OF PERFORMING THIS DUTY THE TEXT RECOMMENDS. The text enjoins,

1. *The possession of experimental religion in the teacher.* " These words, &c., shall be in thine heart." A mere mechanical teacher must have mechanical skill—a mental teacher, intelligence—a moral teacher, the principles of true morality in his own soul. The Christian teacher aims not only at informing the mind, and storing the memory, but amending the heart. A knowledge therefore of true religion only, can qualify the instructor for his work. The heart is the moral lever, to give weight and efficiency to the counsels of the lip ; the heart only can make us earnest, and intent, and solicitous. Now this applies to all moral instructions. Parents, guardians, sabbath-school teachers, &c. The text enjoins,

2. *Diligence in the execution of this work.* It is not to be done cursorily, or with indifference ; not by spasmodic throes, but by continued efforts ; the difficulty of the task renders diligence indispensable. The variety of the instructions to be conveyed to the mind, and the short period allotted for the execution of the task. Only the diligent will extensively succeed. We have enjoined,

3. *Frequency of effort.* Observe the detail of times and seasons, presented to us in the text. The first part of the day is to be thus occupied. This is to engage our attention through the day, " When thou sittest," &c. This is to be identified with our recreations, " When thou walkest by the way." This is to close all the other duties of the day, " When thou liest down." Now there are spiritual subjects, suited to each of these times and occasions ; to be wise and apt in their use is very desirable. The text enjoins,

4. *Simplicity in the mode of instruction* I think this is included in the phrase, " Thou shalt talk." Nothing is more foolish, and of course useless, than to attempt to convey instruction to children, by orations or set speeches and addresses. If we are to instruct, to impress, to interest, we must talk. Bring down both words, ideas, and style to their capacities ; this is a most desirable attainment, and essential to extended success ; and in this how beautifully Christ the great teacher stands forth as our perfect model. Our efficiency may be easily tested, if we will catechize our children on the points in which they have been taught, and see if they have clearly and distinctly understood them. We add,

5. *Patience and perseverance.* All children are not equally quick, and apt to learn ; the mind, in some cases, is slow of development. Now such instances must not be despised ; they especially need our aid, and compassion for them should induce patient perseverance. To impart knowledge to the juvenile mind has been fitly compared to the pouring of a fluid into a long, narrow-necked bottle, where care, patience, and attention, and perseverance, are all requisite. But we observe,

6. *All instructions must be followed by fervent prayer.* Prayer should precede, accompany, and follow our efforts.

APPLICATION

Our subject I fear is,

1. *The condemnation of many parents present.* Do not trifle with God's commands. You must meet your children at the last day. Our subject,

2. *Shows us the importance of sabbath schools.* These are the true seminaries of the church of Christ. These are the hope of the world.

3. *Efforts for instructing the young should meet with the generous and cheerful support of the pious.*

62

KNOWLEDGE, OBEDIENCE, AND FELICITY

" If ye know these things, happy are ye if ye do them."—JOHN xiii. 17.

WHAT is true religion ? Is not the question important ; is it not necessary ? None will dispute its importance or necessity. One replies, true religion is being of the true church ; and he limits this true church to his own denomination.   Another replies, true religion is having sound opinions and views ; and those are religious who of course agree with the sentiments he professes.   A third replies, true religion is the regular observance of Divine worship, and a general regard to Christian morals.   We reply to each and all of these, and say a person may be invested with each of these, and yet not be religious at all ; he may belong to the purest Christian communion ; he may hold the most orthodox sentiments, and he may lead the most exemplary life, and yet be a stranger to spiritual, practical godliness.   True religion is beautifully delineated in the text ; it is triune in its nature—knowledge—practice—felicity.   If ye know, and do, then happy are ye.   We notice, then,

I. In order to true religion there must be knowledge. "If ye know," &c.   Ignorance is one of the foul antagonists of religion.   It is pernicious and ruinous to the soul ; it is a foul libel on man, and a still fouler libel on religion, when utterance is given to this maxim, that "ignorance is the mother of devotion."   No! ignorance is the mother of crime, and wretchedness, and wo, and it may be of superstition, but knowledge is one of the essential principles of religion.

1. *There must be a knowledge of the true God.*   His nature, character, will.

2. *A knowledge of the scriptures.*   A persuasion of their inspiration and truth ; a knowledge of their contents, especially those parts which relate to our salvation.

3. *A knowledge of ourselves.*   As fallen, sinful, polluted, helpless.   To know the plague of our own hearts, &c.

4. *A knowledge of Jesus Christ.*   As the sent of God—the true Son of the Most High —Mediator, &c.   Of his gospel.   What it reveals, and offers, and requires ; now it reveals God's mercy ; it offers salvation ; and requires repentance, faith, and holiness.   Surely a knowledge of these things is essential to true religion.

II. In order to true religion there must be obedience. "Not every one that saith, Lord, Lord," &c.   Neither knowledge nor talents will do without obedience. "Ye are my friends," &c.   Now in doing these things,

1. *We must have respect to the will of God, as the rule of our obedience.*   Not fancies, or feelings, or impulses, or the conduct of others, but the direct revelation of God.   Have respect to all his commandments.

2. *We must do these things with humility of mind.*   Not in the way of merit and self-righteousness ; but with all lowliness, &c.

3. *We must do these things with cheerfulness and affection.*   From a sense of grateful love to Jesus Christ.   Not from fear or constraint.

4. *We can only do these things in the strength of divine grace.*   God must work both to will and to do.   Not us, but the grace of God within us.

5. *Our obedience in doing these things must be constant and persevering.*   Endure to the end, &c.   We must be so found doing when Christ shall call us.   Labor to the end of the day of life.   Faithful unto death, &c.

III. That religion identified with knowledge and obedience, will certainly be productive of felicity. "Happy are ye."   We do not say it will secure riches, or honor, or wealth, or worldly friends, but it will tend to create happiness.

1. *There will be the happiness of a rightly regulated mind.*   Chaos, and confusion, and night, exchanged for light, order, and day.   A new creation in the soul.   Old things have passed away, &c.   God the soul's centre and rest.

2. *There will be the happiness of internal peace.*   Peace with God—peace with conscience—peace with all men.   The peace of God will keep and rule.

3. *There will be the happiness of conscious safety.*   To have guilt cancelled—fetters burst ; wrath removed.   No longer under the curse, &c., but have the testimony of the Spirit, that we are children of God— now accepted.

4. *There will be the happiness of cheering hope.*   Hope is the telescope of the soul— our anchor in storms—our staff in our pilgrimage.   Hope of victory, full salvation, and eternal life.   Hope of heaven.   Good, bright, solid hope.   Begotten again to a lively hope, &c.

5. *The happiness of divine communications.*   Grace in every time of need.   Heavenly visitation, especially in secret duties, public ordinances.   Oh yes! happy are ye.   Truly so ; increasingly so and shall be eternally so.

APPLICATION

1. *To the religious.* Is your religion of this threefold kind ? Light in the mind—practice in the life—joy in the spirit. Are you not greatly deficient in each of these ?

2. *Invite all to know, obey, and enjoy.* The means of knowledge you have, grace to obey is promised, and happiness must ensue.

63

ON OUR OWN MIND

" Should it be according to thy mind ?"—Job xxxiv. 33.

FEW, if any, of the human family ever endured such severe trials as Job ; and his unyielding confidence in God, his patience, and his humility, are left on record for the instruction of the afflicted of God's people unto the end of the world. We do not marvel that in some things he betrayed the infirmities of a man. The suspicions of his friends as to his integrity were calculated to hurry him into some expressions of haste, and to the adoption of some expressions in self-justification, which otherwise he would not have employed. Our text is the appeal of Elihu, and follows a very fine exhibition of that spirit which should attend us in our sorrows and trials, verses 31, 32. He then asks, " Should it be according to thy mind ?" I observe,

I. WE ARE NATURALLY ANXIOUS THAT THINGS SHOULD BE ACCORDING TO OUR MIND. This is a general, if not universal feeling. Sin entered our world on this principle, and by it, is extensively perpetuated. You see it in all ages ; even children wish to have their own minds ; see the headstrong youth ; the young man ; the person of mature years ; the aged ; all evidence this ; all strive and contend for this ; you see it in all stations, the rich and noble and affluent ; those having rule and authority. But the same feelings extend to the poor, and the indigent. The learned and the illiterate are both living examples of this. This is the broad palpable mark of the profane ; and it is the spot and infirmity of the religious and true servants of God.

II. WE ARE TOTALLY UNFIT FOR DECIDING IN THE THINGS WHICH CONCERN US. We are so because we are more influenced by passion than reason ; because we are so darkened in our understandings and judgments ; because we are at best so shortsighted ; because we are so influenced by sense, and present things. If things were left to our minds, we should never choose trials, disappointments, crosses, afflictions, bereavements. We should not be able to determine on our removal out of time. We should not court temptation, and chastisement, &c. Now all these are indispensable to our well-being, fruitfulness, and future safety. How well then is it for us, that we are not left to determine for ourselves ! Besides our minds are so unsettled ; we are so fickle, and vacillating. The mind we had for things years ago, is now altered. Our present mind will be modified, altered, or probably entirely changed by circumstances. Then how futile to desire that things should be according to our minds !

III. IT IS IMPOSSIBLE THAT THINGS CAN BE ACCORDING TO THE MINDS OF ALL PERSONS. Each one desires his own mind ; but almost every one comes in collision with his neighbor. Now amongst ten thousand various minds, which is to have the ascendency ? It is evident, that not more than one or two can be gratified out of the whole. So that all having their own minds is an impossibility. Why, men are not agreed on any one subject. Every man seeks his own things ; confusion and clashing interests distract and divide our world. A scene of discord vastly worse than that of Babel, would rack and torture our world, if every man had liberty to obtain his own mind.

IV. HOW MANY HAVE BEEN RUINED BY HAVING THEIR OWN MIND ! Our first parents. The inhabitants of the old world resolved, in spite of the warnings of Noah, to eat and drink, &c., and were so found when the flood came. Lot had his own mind, when he selected the well-watered plain of Sodom for his abode ; Pharaoh would have his own mind, and the sequel of his history is found in the overthrow of himself and hosts in the Red Sea ; the children of Israel would have their own minds in the wilderness, and their apostasy and ruin was the consequence. Now, I appeal to you : Should children have their own minds ? should culprits and malefactors ? should violent, wrathful persons ? If so, what misery and horror would fill our world ! Is it not a fearful truth, that men choose the way of death and hell, and thus perish forever, in naving their own minds?

V. IT IS INFINITELY BETTER THAT ONE PERFECT MIND SHOULD CONTROL THE UNIVERSE. Such a mind has God. It is clear, all-seeing, pure, wise, good, and just. He comprehends all, knows all, and can direct all things to a glorious consummation; he is ever of one mind, and never changes nor varies; his power is boundless, his resources infinite, his plans infallible. How delightful, then, that God reigns—reigns in heaven, on earth, and through the universe! His kingdom is an everlasting kingdom, and he ruleth over all.

VI. IT IS OUR HAPPINESS AND REAL WELL-BEING TO BE SUBJECT TO GOD'S MIND. Religion says, "Thy will be done." In heaven all are agreed on this subject; not a discordant sentiment or feeling; and all do it. True religion leads to this. In conversion the sinner bows to God; as piety increases, the will of God is more clearly understood, and more cheerfully obeyed; the language of healthy and sincere Christians is just that of the Redeemer, "Not my will, but thine be done."

VII. CERTAIN THINGS MAY ASSIST US IN COMING TO THIS STATE OF MIND. A persuasion of our own incompetency, "It is not in man that walks to direct," &c.; a retrospect of God's goodness in reference to our past concerns, "Goodness and mercy have followed us," &c.; the daily presentation of our desires to God, "In all thy ways acknowledge," &c. "Commit thy way to the Lord," &c.; a conviction of the transitory character of earthly things, fashion of this world passing away—a looking to the things that are eternal.

64

THE WORSHIP OF THE HEAVENLY HOST

"And the host of heaven worshippeth thee."—
NEHEMIAH ix. 6.

OUR text is connected with the solemn address of the Levites on a day of fasting and especial worship. It contains some of the most sublime thoughts that can possibly occupy the human mind. "Then the Levites," it is recorded, "said, Stand up and bless the Lord your God forever and ever; and blessed be thy glorious name, which is exalted above all blessing and praise. Thou, even thou, art Lord alone, thou hast made heaven, the heaven of heavens, with all their host, the earth, and all things that are therein, and thou preservest them all; *and the host of heaven worshippeth thee.*" The contemplation of superior greatness and goodness has a tendency to elevate and improve the mind, and to inspire the soul with feelings of the loftiest and holiest emulation. Hence we are repeatedly called upon in scripture to consider the lives of those who have been distinguished for godliness, and to make them ensamples for our imitation. The apostle Paul calls upon us to consider the Old Testament worthies, that we may be followers of them who through faith and patience now inherit the promises; and the blessed Redeemer, in that inimitable prayer which he taught his disciples, also directed their thoughts to the holiness of angels—for that is clearly implied in that part of the Lord's prayer, where we are to pray that God's will may be done on earth, even as it is done in heaven; in other words, that man may be as holy, as spiritual, as obedient as angels; and, while Jesus Christ came expressly to shed his blood for human transgression, and turn aside the justly incurred wrath of the Most High, he also came to be our ensample, and "he hath left us," says the apostle, "an example that we should tread in his steps." Our subject leads us to contemplate the angels of God, for it is quite clear that our text refers to angelic beings. Sometimes the term "host" is used in scripture to represent the stars; the starry host; the planets, those numerous magnificent worlds, which God has created in the immensity of space around us; but it is evident our text refers to intelligent beings—to those happy and blessed creatures, who were formed previous to our world's existence, and who have retained all their beauty, and dignity, and purity, and who are incessantly worshipping the God of heaven. Therefore, in our thoughts and meditations let us leave this earth, and travel upward to a higher state, even to the holiest place of all. Let us venture in the exercise of imagination, and by the power of faith, to ascend to that world where God has his immediate throne, and his resplendent dwelling-place; and there, by the assistance of our text, let us contemplate all the host of heaven worshipping God. Let us dwell for a little,

I. ON THE HOST ITSELF.

II. ON THEIR EMPLOYMENT. And,

III. THE PRACTICAL USES WE SHOULD MAKE OF IT.

I. THE HOST ITSELF. The existence of a class of beings, usually denominated angels, is obviously established in scripture. Reference is often made to them both in the Old and New Testament scriptures.

(1.) As to the *nature* of these beings. They are spirits—pure spirits; not clothed with material forms as man. " Who maketh his angels spirits," &c.

(2.) As to their *character*. They are described as perfectly wise, " Angels of light." As good and holy. They are said ever to be hearkening to the voice of God's word; to do his will. Holy angels; without spot; no imperfection.

(3.) Their *number*. Thousands of thousands; analogy from other parts of the creation.

(4.) As to their *orders*. They are called by very expressive titles—thrones, dominions, principalities, powers. We read also of archangels, seraphim, and cherubim. Some of the ancients thought there were nine orders, others eight, others four, and that the angels were under the dominion of archangels. We read, too, of Michael and his angels. We proceed to notice,

II. THEIR EMPLOYMENTS. They serve God; do the bidding of Jehovah. All eye to see—all ear to listen—all heart to love—all wing to fly; but, doubtless, one chief employment is to worship God. In scripture, we have some splendid exhibitions of this, Isaiah vi. 1, 2, Rev. iv. 6, 11. Now, their worship is lofty and dignified, holy and fervent, earnest and sincere, cheerful and incessant. We add, that with the angelic host there are united the spirits of the redeemed, who are made perfect; the souls of holy patriarchs and prophets, apostles, and confessors, and martyrs; and all who have died in the faith and hope of the gospel. Many of our friends and kindred; many of all ages and generations, countries, &c.; elevated to the society, and worship, and joys of the angels. One celestial corporation; one glorious assembly; one vast and happy family. The worship of the heavenly host differs from ours in many respects,

1. *As to the place.* The heaven of heavens; the holiest of all; throne of God in the midst; Deity immediately with them.

2. *As to its character.* More pure and spiritual; nothing gross appertaining to them; nothing indolent and lethargic; spiritual in the highest degree; burning with fervor; brilliant with intelligence; transparent with sincerity.

3. *It is peculiarly humble and lowly.* They stand before the throne as cheerful and ready attendants; they bow down before God, &c.; say nothing of themselves; cast their crowns before him, &c.

4. *Their worship is chiefly praise and adoration.* They extol God, bless him, praise him, adore, &c. All unite in one sublime chorus, " Blessing and power," &c. All their wants are supplied; no prayer; no confession; no supplication; no deprecation.

5. *Their worship is uninterrupted and eternal.* Day and night, &c. Filled with God; absorbed with God; rest in God; nothing above or beyond. Theirs is the fruition—the perfection of bliss.

6. *They seem to identify their worship with the works of God in connection with our world.* That is, they rejoice and adore God in the various displays of his glory with which they are favored. At the creation they sang together; they were the messengers to the patriarchs and prophets; attended at the giving of the law; announced the birth of the Redeemer; sang o'er the plains of Bethlehem; ministered to him in his temptation and agony; hailed his resurrection; were his convoy, &c.; rejoice in the conversion of sinners, &c.; will unite in the lofty acclamations of the glorified in heaven forever.

III. THE PRACTICAL USES TO WHICH OUR SUBJECT MAY BE APPLIED.

1. *It should inspire us with holy emulation.* To resemble them in their character, disposition, and employment.

2. *To think of them in our worship.* Could we then be cold and formal? How dignified, how precious, how sweet is divine worship!

3. *To rejoice in their friendship.* Bless God for their ministering to us. So to live,

4. *That we may be their companions forever.* Let us remember the gracious declaration of the Saviour—that his saints shall be equal to the angels. If so, how poor is this world! how inferior to our great destiny! how unworthy of our attach-

ment! and how necessary is Christian diligence! how indispensable holiness of heart and life! how precious, the fountain opened, &c. There is another world, where there are hosts of angels, fallen, miserable, despairing, &c. ; where they hate, blaspheme, and gnash their teeth, &c. " Choose ye, which shall be your companions forever."

65

NEW YEAR'S COUNSELS TO THE GODLY

" Fret not thyself because of evil doers, neither be thou envious against the workers of iniquity. For they shall soon be cut down like the grass, and wither as the green herb. Trust in the Lord, and do good ; so shalt thou dwell in the land, and verily thou shalt be fed. Delight thyself also in the Lord ; and he shall give thee the desires of thine heart. Commit thy way unto the Lord ; trust also in him, and he shall bring it to pass."— PSALM xxxvii. 1–6.

OUR subject this morning may be properly denominated New Year's counsels. In the merciful providence of God, we have entered upon another year. These divisions of time are calculated to make impressions upon our minds ;—and it will be well for us if these impressions are of a useful character, and if their influence is effective and permanent. I cannot conceive of a series of counsels more adapted really to do us good, than those which we have read, and which form the introductory part of this rich and beautiful psalm. Let us consider these counsels as they are presented to us in the text.

I. NOT TO BE PERTURBED OR ANGRY WITH THE WICKED. I have used the words perturbation and anger, as expressing the meaning of the word " fret." The Psalmist means, do not get your own souls into disorder and confusion, and lose temper and murmur, because of wicked men. Let us however not mistake this counsel. He does not mean that we are to be indifferent to the wicked and their course. The good man is to abhor sin, and hate every evil way ; he is to pray, " Oh let the wickedness of the wicked," &c. " May thy will be done on earth," &c. But how often do men transfer their hatred of sin to the sinner ; and how often do we allow our minds to be confused and irritated, and thus we add our sin to the sin of the wicked! We are in danger of showing a Pharisaical

spirit, and acting as judges of others. We are in danger of assuming a prerogative which belongs to God alone. Look at the apostles James and John, who prayed for fire to consume those who did not receive their message. Forget not Christ's rebuke. " Ye know not what spirit ye are of." We are in danger of envying the wicked. " Neither be thou envious." Perhaps the blasphemer is in purple, and the man of prayer in poverty ; the ungodly in the mansion, and the pious at his gates ; Agrippa on the tribunal, and Paul in chains at the bar. Well, so it is, and it may often perplex us ; but real Christianity precludes envy. To envy, is to sin ; it is a fruit of the flesh ; it is to destroy our own peace ; it will corrode and eat out all enjoyment. " Then fret not, neither be envious," &c.

(1.) Because every man is accountable to God. Leave it with Jehovah.

(2.) We are sincerely to pity and commiserate their state ; but if we are perturbed, and angry, and fretful, we cannot do so, &c.

(3.) Think how transient is their present state, verse 2. " For they shall soon be cut down," &c. What would you think of a person, who should visit a prison, where men under sentence of death were crowded together ; and suppose the prisoners seemed merry, were clothed gorgeously, and gave each other high-sounding names. Would you fret or be envious ? Impossible ! would you not weep, would not your hearts ache, &c. ? verses 9, 10.

II. WE ARE TO CONFIDE IN GOD, AND IMITATE HIS BENEVOLENCE. " Trust in the Lord," &c. ; that is, depend on God—lean on the Lord—look to him for every blessing, &c.

(1.) Trust not in *yourselves*.

(2.) Trust not in *men*. Rich men or princes. " Cursed is the man that trusteth in man."

(3.) Trust not in *riches*, or any of the adventitious circumstances of life. The world is a sea in ceaseless motion. Trust only in the Lord, and trust him wholly, and fully, and always, and for every thing, and forever. Trust the riches of his grace— and the kindness and sufficiency of his providence ; and God shall protect thy life, and satisfy thee with food ; all things needful will be supplied ; God will be thy friend and refuge. " And do good." To the bodies and souls of those around you.

Console the afflicted, relieve the widow, remember the poor, and offer Christ to all.

III. WE ARE TO MAKE GOD THE GREAT OBJECT OF OUR SUPREME JOY AND LOVE. "Delight thyself," &c. Give God our first and chief regards. Look to him as the great source of all blessedness; as the fountain of blessings; meditate on his blessed character and perfection; live near to him by daily prayer and communion; seek his glory in all things; labor to exalt and please God. Do as Noah did, as Enoch did, as Abraham did, as Daniel did, as Jesus did, who ever pleased him. "And he shall give thee," &c. He shall make thee happy, &c. Every heart desires this; every soul thirsts and pants for it. Well, you shall have it; you shall feel his own peace keeping you, &c. His joy elevating, &c. His love shed abroad, &c.

IV. GIVE EVERY THING UP TO BE MANAGED BY THE LORD. "Commit thy way," &c. The course of a person's life is his way. Two things are included.

1. *Our providential course.* The affairs of life. These we cannot manage ourselves. Boast not thyself of to-morrow. Look at that child in a vessel at sea; what would it do? Look at that stranger in a distant land with his guide. Look at that person with a case of legal difficulty. Now as a child commits itself to the captain of a vessel—as the stranger to his guide—the man with his suit to the advocate or counsellor—so we are to commit our way to the Lord, &c. Give up all for him to manage, &c.

2. *Our gracious and spiritual course.* The care of our souls. Our best interests, &c. He will manage it rightly, &c. Keep all secure, and bring us to eternal glory. All shall end well, everlastingly well. Let us regard these counsels. Meditate on them, and practise them, &c.

APPLICATION

1. Admonish the thoughtless.
2. Warn the unbelieving.
3. Direct the inquirer.

66

CHRISTIAN ESTABLISHMENT

"Now he which stablisheth us with you in Christ, and hath anointed us, is God."—2 CORINTHIANS i. 21.

DIVINE grace exerts a uniform influence on the human heart. The manner in which grace operates is very diversified, the instruments also various; but there is a similarity in the effects on the hearts of all who believe. The apostles, although inspired and distinguished by wonderful endowments and miraculous gifts, were still on the same level with other saints, as to the necessity and influence of grace on their souls. This is seen in the text. Now, "he who stablisheth us," &c. Let us look,

I. AT THE BLESSINGS EXPERIENCED.

(1.) Established. There is of course a necessity for this. The tree planted must have time, &c., to take root and be established. The foundation laid, must have time to rest and settle, and be established. The seed sown must have space for sinking into the earth, taking root downward, and being established in order to fruitfulness, &c. The mind must have time to embrace truth and reflect upon it, &c., before man can be established. So with divine grace; time, means, and influence are necessary before Christians can be established.

(2.) Christian establishment is very necessary. It is necessary to our spiritual prosperity. To be moved and unsettled is to be incapable of religious improvement. "Unstable as water," &c.

(3.) It is necessary to our comfort. Vacillation is as wretched as unprofitable. Real peace, and fickleness, are incompatible.

(4.) It is essential to our safety. To be moved from the hope, &c., is to decline and apostatize. Ye did run well," &c. How essential—how important to be established; and this should include establishment in *knowledge*—divine knowledge—knowledge of Christ, and the way of salvation—knowledge of the great doctrines of the gospel, &c. To be men in knowledge. In *faith.* For faith to be strong, invulnerable, &c., that it may not fail. In *love*—love to God—love to his holy law—and in compassionate love to all men. In *obedience*; cheerfully and with heartfelt delight to obey God. To delight to do his will. In our *profession.* A city elevated, impregnable, set on a hill.

II. THIS ESTABLISHMENT OF THE CHRISTIAN IS IN CHRIST. "In Christ." All our privileges and blessings, &c., arise from our being in Christ. Our first parents had no stability in a state of innocency, much less can we in our own imperfect frail nature ; but in Christ our security is firm and sufficient. In his meritorious sacrifice we nave the established favor of God to us. In his intercession the establishing influences of his Spirit. In his example, the established model for our perseverance. In his fulness, establishing grace in every time of need. The tree must have good soil. The Christian tree is planted into Christ. The stone of the structure must have a good foundation—Christ is the foundation stone—built on him—rests on him, &c.

III. THE AUTHOR OF THIS ESTABLISHMENT IS GOD. Now he, &c., " is God." Not ourselves, yet we must use the means. Not ministers, yet we must take heed to the word preached. Not angels, yet we may rejoice in their ministrations ; but God is the source. " Every good gift," &c. Then three things are necessary.

1. *Dependence.* Trusting God. Believing God. He who does so shall never, &c. He will keep him in perfect peace.

2. *Prayer.* Seeking God's blessing. Waiting upon him. Imploring his daily help.

3. *Praise.* Grateful acknowledgment of the past, &c. Giving thanks continually to his name.

APPLICATION

1. The most mature Christian still has need of deeper establishment.

2. Young Christians and new converts should be particularly solicitous for it.

67

THE ANOINTING

" Now he which stablisheth us with you in Christ, and hath anointed us, is God."—2 CORINTHIANS i. 21.

VARIOUS are the figures by which the Holy Spirit is represented in the holy scriptures. He is compared to the air or wind. " The wind bloweth," &c. So when it rested on the apostles, &c. Thus God breathed into man, &c. So Christ to his disciples, after his resurrection, said, " Peace," and breathed on them, &c., John xx. 22. To fire ; thus it rested on them as cloven tongues of fire. " But ye shall be baptized," &c. " Quench not the Spirit," &c. As water. " If any man thirst," &c. He spake of the Holy Spirit, &c.

So also to oil. He shall be anointed with the oil of gladness, &c. ; this is the idea the text contains. Believers are anointed of God, viz. : anointed with the Holy Ghost. See the uses to which oil was applied, and you will at once observe the propriety and beauty of the text.

I. THE SICK WERE ANOINTED IN ORDER TO HEALING. In the beautiful parable of the good Samaritan, oil and wine were poured into his wounds. See also James v. 14. Now in these is set forth the healing influences of the Holy Spirit. It is the work of God's Spirit to heal the broken hearted, Isaiah lxi. 3.

II. THE WEARY WERE REFRESHED BY THE APPLICATION OF OIL. In hot climates this was often indispensable to real comfort. It tended to cool and refresh the debilitated system. Thus David exclaimed, " Thou hast anointed my head with oil," &c. Thus Christ commended the penitent woman who poured on him the precious oil, and said to Simon the Pharisee, " My head with oil thou didst not anoint." Now the Holy Spirit refreshes the soul, revives it, inspirits it, and gives real vigor and comfort.

III. OIL WAS USED TO BEAUTIFY THE COUNTENANCE. One of the blessings acknowledged in the 104th Psalm is, " oil which maketh the face to shine." Now the Holy Spirit beautifies the soul. " He will beautify the meek," &c. David's prayer is to the point. " Let the beauty of the Lord our God," &c. Grace is the true beauty of the soul, it confers beauty which is pleasing to God, and abiding, and heavenly.

IV. OIL WAS USED IN ANOINTING FOR SACRED OFFICES.

1. Kings were anointed with oil. Believers are made kings unto God, they are destined to reign with Christ forever, to wear eternal crowns, to have an everlasting inheritance.

2. Priests were anointed with oil. Believers are a royal priesthood. Spiritual priests offering up spiritual sacrifices to the Lord. This qualifies them, and sanctifies their services, both of praise and prayer.

3. Prophets were anointed. " The Spirit of the Lord is upon me." Every Christian is to teach Jesus Christ. To witness for Christ, and by their conversation, and spirit, and life, to glorify Christ. The Holy Spirit must enable them to do this. Thus believers are anointed of God.

1. Examine yourselves.
2. Seek this.
3. Honor the anointing.

68

BEING SEALED

" Who hath also sealed us."—2 Corinthians i. 22.

In our last discourse, we noticed the anointing of the Holy Spirit, and referred you to the Spirit's operations as likened to oil, on account of their healing, refreshing, beautifying, and consecrating influences. The apostle presents us, in the text, with another figure on the same subject. The Spirit is compared to a seal, and believers are represented as receiving the impression of it in their hearts. A few remarks on the use of seals will elucidate the subject to our minds.

I. Seals were made use of to ratify and render authentic important documents. We have a reference to this in a civil contract, Jer. xxxii. 9, &c. ; in reference to a national covenant, Nehemiah ix. 38. Now the gifts of divine grace, especially the blessings of the new covenant, are by the Spirit sealed over to believers ; for the laws of this covenant are represented as being written on the hearts of believers, and to these the seal of the Spirit is attached.

II. Seals were used to discriminate and mark property. Hence slaves had a mark of their own ; valuable things had the impress of their owners' seals ; see Ezek. ix. 4 ; Rev. vii. 2, &c. Now, it is by the spirit we possess, that our real character is truly known. If we are sons, or children of God, then God hath sent the Spirit of his Son, &c. " The Spirit itself beareth witness," &c.

III. Seals were designed for the preservation of jewels, and other objects of value. Thus, cabinets of jewels are closed, and have the seal of the proprietor upon them ; thus, the stone rolled to the mouth of the sepulchre was sealed, &c. ; thus, confidential communications are sealed. Now, thus does the Spirit seal believers. " They are his jewels," &c. ; his epistles. He only knoweth their value ; the world knoweth them not. He knows and preserves. " None of them have I lost," &c. Our preservation and security are entirely of God. By the power of the

Spirit are we kept, through faith, unto eternal salvation.

IV. By the seal some image or device is impressed. There is one prayer in the Canticles, " Set me as a seal upon thine heart, and upon thine arm," &c. Now, the seal is the Spirit of God, and bears the full likeness of Deity ; a spirit of light, truth, holiness, love, &c. In this image man was created. By the Holy Spirit this is renewed in the heart of the believer. He bears the impression of light, of truth, of holiness, of love. As the impression on the wax corresponds with the image on the seal, so the heart of the believer bears the impression of God's Spirit, and is thus sealed by it.

1. *Men exhibit the likeness of the spirit by which they are impressed.* Wicked men that of Satan. There is the impression of ignorance, delusion, iniquity, malevolence, &c. See this described, Gal. v. 19, &c.

2. *How we should cherish and honor the Holy Spirit.* By prayer, holy meditation, watchfulness, humility, and love. " Grieve not," &c.

3. *The subject affords much comfort.* Sealed to the day of redemption. How consolatory ; how adapted to inspire hope, joy, &c.

69

THE EARNEST

" And given the earnest of the Spirit in our hearts."—2 Corinthians i. 22.

We have previously considered the Holy Spirit under the figures of oil and a seal ; we now have a third metaphorical representation, under the idea of an earnest. The word has reference to the hiring of servants, who at the period of their engagement receive a small sum of money, by which the agreement is ratified, and as the pledge of the reward, or wages, that shall be hereafter given. Now, the Holy Spirit is given to those who become the servants of God, on their reception into the divine family ; and this gift is the earnest of what God will hereafter bestow upon them. This is more fully seen in Eph. i. 13, 14. We observe,

I. The earnest is the same in nature with the final reward. This is essential to an earnest. Now, the Holy Spirit is thus, in the blessings he imparts, an earnest of eternal life ; for this is the final gift—eternal life. Observe, then, some of the features of resemblance. The gift is,

1. *Everlasting spiritual existence, in opposition to the death of the sinner.* Now the earnest is the living spirit in the soul ; spiritual life begun. "It is the Spirit that quickeneth." This is the living water—the life of God within the soul.

2. *A reward of light.* Eternal noon-day splendor. Heaven needs not the light of the sun or moon, &c. God is the light of it ; no night there. The Spirit dwells in the mind as a spirit of light ; by it we are light in the Lord. "God, who commanded the light," &c. No longer darkness, &c.

3. *The reward is one of perfect purity.* No sin in heaven, the holy place ; holiest of all—perfectly so. The Spirit dwells in the people of God, as the spirit of sanctification, transforming, purifying, cleansing, and making meet for the purity of heaven.

4. *The reward is one of celestial victory, and eternal triumph.* The upright have dominions, crowns, &c. "Unto him that overcometh," &c. Now, the Spirit dwells as an earnest in the heart of them ; he imparts courage to the mind—power. By the Spirit, as with a sword, we slay all our adversaries. Our present conquests are those of the Holy Spirit within us.

5. *The reward is one of perfect love.* The infinite love of God to us, and the perfect love of God within us. Now, the Spirit dwells in the heart as an earnest of this. "The love of God is now shed abroad," &c. The Spirit enkindles, sustains, and perfects this love.

6. *The reward is one of unceasing joy and bliss.* There we shall obtain joy and gladness, &c. "Fulness of joy," &c. The Spirit dwells in the heart as an earnest of this. The fruit of the Spirit is joy. As the indwelling Comforter he produces this. It is sometimes unspeakable and full of glory. Thus we see as an earnest, it is of the same nature as the reward. Yet,

II. IT IS INFERIOR IN DEGREE. But a small portion of that reward. Now we know only in part ; now very partially sanctified. It is but as the first sheaf to the great harvest—the drop to the shower —the dawn to the day.

III. IT IS THE GUARANTEE OF THE WHOLE. The rest must follow the earnest, unless the promiser dies, loses his ability, or acts unjustly. These are contingencies which cannot apply to Deity ; therefore the earnest he gives of the Spirit, pledges most inevitably the whole reward.

APPLICATION

1. *Have we the earnest of the Spirit ? &c.* Do we possess a new spirit, different to what we formerly had ? a spirit delighting in God, his word, ordinances, prayer ?

2. *Let us rejoice in it.* How precious in itself, and also in reference to the eternity before us.

3. *By faith in the gospel, the Holy Ghost is imparted as an earnest.*

70

SCRIPTURAL ASSURANCE

"I know whom I have believed, and am persuaded that he is able to keep that which I have committed unto him against that day."—2 TIMOTHY i. 12.

TRUE religion is of heavenly origin, and is at utter variance with the spirit and principles of this world ; true religion generally exposes its possessors to persecution and trouble for Christ and conscience' sake ; but true religion has within itself the elements of comfortable experience, sufficient to sustain the mind in the deepest sorrows and severest afflictions. Let us see these verities exemplified in Paul. His religion was of God—the light and truth of heaven, and it was essentially different to every form of religion then in the world. As a Christian, Paul suffered the loss of all things for his Lord and Master. How long and afflictive the catalogue of his sorrows! but the internal principles of divine grace caused him to rejoice in all his tribulation, and at last to lay down his neck for the testimony of Jesus. This brings us at once to the text. Now a prisoner—ready to die. "For the which cause," &c. Our text is expressive of the essentials of evangelical experimental religion, and in that light we shall consider it.

I. A KNOWLEDGE OF CHRIST IS THE FIRST GRAND ESSENTIAL IN EXPERIMENTAL RELIGION. "I know whom," &c. The knowledge of Christ is the essence of knowledge ; it is knowledge of the highest and most precious kind. Knowledge of letters—of science—of nature—of languages, all are valuable, but none to compare to the knowledge of Jesus. What say the scriptures? " This is life eternal." " Yea, doubtless," &c. But this knowledge of Christ must,

1. *Be scriptural.* Know him as he is revealed in the holy, living word ; the scriptures testify of Christ. We know nothing rightly, perfectly, unless we appeal to the sacred testimony. His nature, person, offices, work, and glory, are all exhibited. The Bible is the word of Christ ; the field of the precious pearl ; the mirror where Christ is visibly beheld. But this knowledge,

2. *Must be personal.* " I know." Not my minister, or my teacher, or my friends ; but my understanding, my judgment, my mind, and spirit are acquainted with Christ.

3. *It must be saving.* Know him as my Redeemer, by the freedom into which he brings my spirit, " If the Son make you free," &c. ; by the forgiveness of my sin, " He came to give the knowledge of salvation by the remission of sin ;" by his purifying grace, " If I wash thee not," &c. Thus, the blind beggar might know much by hearing of Christ, but much more when Christ had said, " Receive thy sight." Thus, the Samaritans knew something from the woman who had talked with Christ, put much more when they came to him. Such know Christ, who can say, " We have found him of whom," &c. " My beloved is mine." " My Lord and my God."

II. Faith in Christ is ever connected with the right knowledge of Jesus. " I know *whom* I have believed." Believed what ?

1. *What Christ has said.* Said of my sinfulness—my misery—my ruin. My help is in himself; what he has said ; his love, and grace, and readiness to save. Believed what ? Why,

2. *What he has done.* Became a man, and poor ; suffered, died, rose again, and ever lives, &c. Believed what ?

3. *What he has promised.* Present mercy ; sufficient grace ; eternal glory.

III. Faith in Christ surrenders the Christian's all into Christ's hands. The salvation of the soul may be justly considered as comprising the Christian's all, for this is really and truly every thing ; but the entire person of the Christian is committed—soul and body. The believer gives himself; his whole undivided self.

(1.) To be preserved and kept by the power of God.

(2.) To be fully laid out for Christ's glory.

(3.) To be sanctified and fitted for future bliss.

IV. The Christian is firmly persuaded of the security of that which is committed to Jesus. Whence arises this persuasion ?

1. *From the ability and love of Christ.* His heart is set upon the eternal salvation of his people, and he has all power to do it. He can work, and none can hinder ; this will be Christ's eternal joy and reward.

2. *From the past experience of Christ's goodness.* What has he not done ? Look at guilt cancelled—debts forgiven—iniquities cleansed—blessings pure and divine imparted—mercies continued. Past safety ; past help.

3. *From the unvarying testimony of the saints in all ages.* Was Enoch disappointed ? or Jacob ? or David ? or Simeon ? or Stephen ? or the martyred saints now in heaven ?

V. The Christian has especial respect to the last day. " Till that day." He refers to the same, verse 18, in reference to Onesiphorus ; a day in which Christ will vindicate, confess, and publicly reward his disciples ; the day of the saint's coronation, reward, and glory. Then Jesus will surrender all that has been committed to him, and say, These I have pardoned, sanctified, and kept, and not one is lost save the son of perdition.

APPLICATION

1. *Have you this knowledge and firm persuasion ?* Are you looking to that day ?

2. *Let each one commit his all to Christ.*

71

HOW TO TREAT OFFENCES

" Moreover, if thy brother shall trespass against thee, go and tell him his fault between thee and him alone," &c.—Matthew xviii. 15–18.

The best of men are but partially sanctified, and therefore are surrounded by infirmities. Such being the case, intercourse cannot be kept up without offences ; such will occur, even among the great, and the wise, and good ; but New Testament direction is fully, explicitly, and clearly given, how we should act under these circumstances. The directions are the very opposite of the feelings of the human mind, contrary to our carnal hearts, and contrary to the course very often taken. Persons often, when offended, become morose and reserved, avoiding the person; or they become vindictive, and try to injure them; or they become angry, and express in passion their displeasure. All this is wrong, evil, to all concerned. Observe the method Christ has laid down.

I. The trespass supposed, whether accidental or designed. Whether it regards reputation, or property, or feelings, &c. Then, the direction given:

II. Seek a private interview. That he may explain, if possible. Better adapted for him to confess. More faithfully and affectionately admonished. State to him plainly, candidly, yet kindly. The motive; you may gain, convince, convert him to a friend, deliver from sin.

III. If this fail, take one or two more. Let them be unobjectionable persons—peaceable persons—prudent persons. These are to witness, and aid by their counsel and influence. If this fail,

IV. Bring it to the church. Let the brethren decide. Do so for these reasons.

1. For the offender's sake. He may hear the church.

2. For Christianity's sake.

3. For the world's sake, that they may see we are neither indifferent nor malevolent. If he refuse to hear the church, then he must,

V. Be removed from Christian communion. This is the last act, and if this is rightly done, it is ratified in heaven, verse 18. Do not let us neglect this order. You object. He is not worthy of all this, &c. This is troublesome, &c.; but it is your duty; Christ demands it!

72

ADMONITION

" Admonish him as a brother."—2 Thessalonians iii. 15.

To admonish, signifies to warn, to reprove gently, &c. The context supposes that some might disobey the epistle, and he then states the course that should be pursued, verse 14. Observe,

I. In the church of Christ there will be cases requiring admonition. Always has been so. So with the apostles, and with the purest church in the world. Ignorance, imperfect graces, temptations, &c., all tend to this. Men drawn aside, &c.

II. On whom does the duty of admonition devolve.

1. *It devolves on some persons officially.* On ministers and elders of the church; on parents and teachers.

2. On the experienced venerable Christian. In some instances, on all believers.

III. The way in which admonition should be given.

1. *The admonitor should be free from the evils on which he admonishes, or his admonition will be powerless, &c.*

2. *He must select an appropriate place and opportunity.*

3. *He must do it in the spirit of Christ, and not in his own spirit.*

4. *He must do it confidentially, and not make it the subject of conversation.* Where admonition fails, there must be rebuke, and if that fails, it must be told to the church.

IV. Motives by which this duty may be enforced.

1. *The relation of the person admonished.* He is our brother; so we ought to feel and care, &c. If sick, or in danger, &c. How much more when the soul, &c.

2. *For the sake of the church of Christ.* We would not that men should apostatize, &c. Satan triumphs; world rejoices, &c.

3. *For our own sake.* We should be condemned, if we saw a man on the verge of peril, and did not cry out, &c. We shall be guilty, &c. Objections to this duty,

1. *It more properly belongs to the minister.* He cannot know every instance, &c.

2. *It will give offence.* Much depends on the spirit, &c. I know persons who constantly do it, and do not offend.

3. *We feel it painful, &c.* But it is not the less necessary, &c. Let all Christians do so to those who are without. Let us warn, entreat, &c.

73

THE WEAK, OTHERS COMFORTED

" A bruised reed shall he not break, and smoking flax shall he not quench."—Matthew xii. 20

Our text must be particularly familiar to every one who reads with attention the holy scriptures. We first meet with it in the forty-second chapter of Isaiah's prophecy; and here in the gospel by Matthew, we see its direct and appropriate application to the Messiah, the friend of sinners, who came expressly to seek and to save, &c. Let us inquire,

I. What the metaphors in the text signify. And,

II. What the declaration in the text includes.

I. What the metaphors in the text signify. The metaphors are two, but alike in spirit and signification.

1. *The bruised reed.* May refer to the musical reed, extensively used by the eastern shepherds while tending their flocks; or it may refer to the common reed, which is easily blown down and crushed. In the one case, the musical reed ceases to yield melodious sounds if crushed, or the common one to be of any use when bruised.

2. *The smoking flax.* Refers to the wick of the lamp, which is just expiring for want of oil, when light is scarcely emitted, and when the odor is offensive. Both metaphors refer to the same spirit, character, and state.

1. *They may be appropriately used to denote the broken-hearted penitent.* The soul crushed with a sense of sin, and an awful apprehension of the divine wrath; the heart which has yielded before the hammer of divine truth; the pierced contrite heart; the lowly abased spirit, where all self-exaltation is dethroned; the whole soul bowed down before God. When the tongue confesses, and the soul loathes its sinful state.

2. *They may perhaps indicate, more directly, a weak and imperfect state of grace.* A low state of spiritual attainment. Where there is little knowledge—little vigor—flickering hope—much weakness and instability, confidence and peace only very imperfectly enjoyed. Or,

3. *A condition of extreme trouble and distress.* Afflictions sometimes bring us low; troubles and trials, especially if they come wave after wave. When the clouds appear after the rain—keen tempest, &c. Let us notice, then,

II. What the declaration of the text includes. Observe, it is negative. He will not break—not quench. The shepherd finds his reed crushed, and as he can easily supply its place, he breaks it and throws it aside; or the husbandman sees he reed beneath his foot, and disregards it.

The flickering light, or merely smoking flax, is extinguished. Not so Christ. He will not break, &c.

1. *He never has done so.* The history of the church contains not one instance; the history of his life, not one case. See how he acted to his disciples—to the afflicted poor. All was pity, kindness, compassion, mercy, gentleness. So you all have felt it, to you.

2. *He never will do so.* For it would be contrary to his nature—to his office—to his delights and enjoyments.

3. *He will do the very opposite of this.* He will bind up and restore—he will heal and strengthen—he will encourage and revive—he will raise up and enliven. Then our subject,

1. *Encourages the timid and fearful.* Christ is as compassionate as he is great—as tender as he is glorious. Go to him by prayer. Cast your souls upon him.

2. *None shall be destroyed but the impenitent.* And because they despise the Saviour.

74

CHRISTIAN HOPE ACCOUNTED FOR

" And be ready always to give an answer to every man that asketh you a reason of the hope that is in you, with meekness and fear."—1 Peter iii. 15.

True religion must not only be enjoyed, but professed; Christ is to be put on; we are to confess him before men; our light is to shine for the good of others; we are to be Christ's witnesses, and confessors to the people. In doing this, the water of life within us springs up, and sends its stream abroad for the good of all around. But more is required of us than even profession; we are to stand forth to vindicate the religion we profess; we are, if necessary, to be disputants in the cause of Christianity; we are to " be ready," &c. Four propositions will bring the subject of the text before us.

I. Christians have a hope within them. Hope is the expectation of future good; it differs, however, from wishing, or desiring. It is an expectation grounded on what is possible and probable, yea, the certainty of what is satisfactorily established. Christians are the children of hope; unbelievers the slaves of fear. The apostle thus speaks,

" Blessed be God," &c., 1 Peter i. 3. The Christian's hope has respect to four things :

1. *An interest in the arrangements of a benignant providence.* The God of providence is the God of grace. Those who are the subjects of his grace are especially interested in a kind and beneficent providence. Of such Christ speaks, when he says, " The very hairs of your head," &c. " The ways of such are ordered by the Lord." " The Lord keepeth them in the hollow of his hand." " If they commit their way to him," &c. " No weapon formed against them," &c.

2. *A full supply of all spiritual blessings.* This supply includes all that they can possibly need, in every condition of their pilgrimage to a better world. Their hope embraces that gracious declaration, " My God shall supply," &c. " The Lord God is a sun," &c.

3. *A safe and blessed dissolution.* Christians have not always an easy transition ; not always a triumphant one ; but always a safe one ; one of peace and hope. " The righteous hath hope in his death."

4. *A certain glorious resurrection, and eternal life.* The hope of eternal life is the grand consummation—the glorious issue— the full redemption of body and soul forever.

II. CHRISTIANS HAVE REASONS FOR THE HOPE THAT IS WITHIN THEM. These reasons are many ; but we refer to the three chief :—

1. *A persuasion of the truth of God's word.* They hope for these things, because they are revealed in the scriptures—published and offered there. There the foundation, the medium, and the certainty of salvation, both present and eternal, are made known. Now, the Christian believes most firmly the truth of this volume ; he considers it as God's own word, and he rests on it as an immoveable rock. " The grass withereth, the flower fadeth, but the word of the Lord endureth forever." Another reason is,

2. *The experience of true religion in the soul.* There is the harmony of their experience with the word of God. They have tested the gospel. It is represented as a word of light—and they are enlightened ; a word of power—and their rocky hearts have been broken ; a word of mercy—and their guilt they feel to be cancelled ; a word of purity—and their evil hearts are cleansed ; a word of comfort and joy—and they have peace ; the word of Christ—and Christ is now within their hearts, the hope of glory. Another reason is,

3. *The concurring testimony of all believers.* The experience of one Christian is in the main the testimony of all ; the general external and internal effects are the same. Persons of all grades, &c., profess to know, to feel, and to enjoy the same. Hence, in the mouths of many witnesses is the reality of religion established.

III. CHRISTIANS MAY BE CALLED UPON TO GIVE A REASON OF THEIR HOPES TO OTHERS.

1. *Fellow-Christians may ask this for their own edification.* " They that feared the Lord," &c.

2. *Penitent inquirers may ask, for their direction and encouragement.* " They shall come seeking, &c., inquiring their way to Zion," &c.

3. *Infidels may ask, to scoff and rail at religion.* To mock ; to gainsay. Now observe,

IV. TO THESE INQUIRERS WE ARE TO GIVE AN ANSWER.

1. *We must be able to do it.* Not ignorant of the great grounds and principles of our faith and hope. Religion not a blind thing, &c.—not mere feeling.

2. *We must be ready to do it.* Have the mind to do it. Not be afraid, nor ashamed, nor reluctant, &c.

3. *We must do it in a right manner.* " With meekness." A calm, quiet spirit ; a modest manner. Not ostentatiously ; not self-complacently ; but with meekness. " With fear ;" that is, solemnly—seriously ; with reverence for God and the truth. Not flippantly ; not with levity, &c.

APPLICATION

1. *Let the Christian rejoice in his hope.* How rich, blessed, and certain ! It ought to lift him up ; make him always rejoice, Rom. xv. 13.

2. *This hope is within the reach of all.* Christ is the hope ; he is offered to you, &c.

3. *Do not reject Christianity until you have a substitute.*

75

PENITENCE AND EXPECTED MERCY

" Who can tell if God will turn and repent, and turn away from his fierce anger, that we perish not ?"—JONAH iii. 9.

Our text relates to Nineveh. Nineveh was a dark, benighted, pagan city, densely populated, and aggravatingly wicked. To this city, Jonah, the prophet, was sent to preach repentance, ere their sins brought upon them the destroying wrath of the Most High. On the preaching of Jonah, the people were convinced of their sins, and fasting, repentance, and prayer were presented to God, that his wrath might be stayed. This humiliation was general, from the king on the throne to the poorest of the city. The king also set the people an example of pious penitence, verse 5. Observe the connection between the text, and the sermon of Jonah, verses 3 and 4. How wise and admirable was the course the Ninevites adopted! What an example for Christian nations and cities! Let us see how it will bear on the condition of every sinner now before God. Three propositions will open the subject to our minds and hearts.

I. As fallen beings, we have all greatly sinned against the Lord.

II. That wrath is threatened against every transgressor. But,

III. There is every reason to believe that sincere repentance may avert the doom threatened.

I. As fallen beings, we have all greatly sinned against the Lord. This is the unvarying doctrine of the scriptures. It applies to all mankind, of every age and nation; of course, it applies to every person in this congregation. When the mind has been enlightened, it is seen and felt. Ignorance of this truth argues that great darkness overspreads the mind. How important that every one should know the plague of his own heart: general statements not enough. To know, to feel, and confess I have sinned, and done wickedly.

1. *We have sinned.* Against both tables of the law—by commission and omission; against the divine government; against redeeming love; against the economy of grace; against the glorious gospel; against the Holy Spirit; against the light and convictions of our consciences! Who can plead exemption? Not one.

2. *We have all greatly sinned.* Both in number, magnitude, and aggravation. Against great light, and great mercies; against a great God; against repeated resolutions. Our sins are like a great mountain—a great cloud—a universal disease. Our sins have been of ingratitude, rebellion, and treason, for all sin includes these. Then many have sinned for years, many years; through youth, through maturer years, even to old age. Well would the lamentation of Isaiah suit us, "Wo is us' wo is us!"

II. That wrath is threatened against every transgressor. God necessarily disapproves, hates, and abhors all sin. As a just and righteous sovereign and lawgiver, he is bound to punish it. His word contains his denunciation against every persevering, impenitent sinner. This wrath involves three things:—

1. *God's righteous disapprobation in this life.* His face is set against the wicked; he is angry with them. Say unto the wicked, it shall be ill with him. "He that believeth not," &c. Every day and moment God is displeased, justly displeased with the sinner.

2. *His curse in the hour of dissolution.* "The wicked are driven away," &c. "The candle of the wicked is put out," &c. His death brings him into the presence of his Judge. How fearful is this! How intolerable the idea!

"What scenes of horror and of dread
Await the sinner's dying bed;
Death's terrors all appear in sight
Presages of eternal night!

"Tormenting pangs distract his breast,
Where'er he turns he finds no rest,
Death strikes the blow, he groans and cries,
And in despair and horror dies."

3. *His fearful wrath through all eternity.* Let a few passages suffice here. "The wicked shall be turned into hell," &c. "Upon the wicked God shall rain fire and brimstone, and a horrible tempest." "Whosoever was not found written in the book of life, was cast into the lake of fire." "These on the left hand of the Judge shall go into everlasting punishment," &c. There shall be weeping, and wailing, and gnashing of teeth, and there the worm dieth not, nor is the fire quenched. Oh, think of eternal horror, eternal pain, eternal agonies, eternal despair! But I hasten with joy,

III. To observe that we have every reason to believe that sincere penitence may avert the destruction threatened. Literally, God is not a man that he should repent, &c. He is of one mind, the same yesterday, &c. " I am the Lord, and change not." But this is a settled principle in his moral government under the gospel, that sincere penitence shall avert the deserved wrath. Observe, this is,

1. *Peculiar to the gospel.* The law does not recognise this ; it says, Obey and live ; disobey and die ! It will not be satisfied with sorrow or amendment ; indeed, it cannot. But the gospel reveals a Mediator between God and man ; one who has propitiated by his death ; one who has borne the desert of sin. A surety, and through his merit, God can be just, &c. " Through this man is preached," &c. The penitence which is effectual,

2. *Must be the effect of the truth upon the conscience.* We have a beautiful instance in the case of the three thousand on the day of Pentecost. They heard, understood, felt, cried out, and became the recipients of the divine mercy. Thus the word acts as a hammer, &c. Christ crucified is to be preached in connection with this. " They shall look on him," &c.

3. *This penitence must be deep and sincere.* Not a mere emotion ; not a transitory sensation ; not a slight impulse, but a sincere feeling in the whole soul. The ardent action of the whole mind. See it in the penitent woman, her shame, her tears, her contrition.

4. *It must be influential.* Work repentance, or change of mind and life. Bring forth fruits meet, &c. The case of the Ninevites. Humiliation, fasting, confession, prayer, &c. Now such penitence shall avail.

(1.) God has said it. " To that man will I look, who is of a contrite spirit." " The sacrifice of God is a broken spirit," &c. " Blessed are they that mourn."

(2.) Sacred history, and the experience of the whole church of Christ, establish it. When did it not prevail ? When was the penitent spurned, rejected, cast out, denied ? Who ever perished, however vile, worthless ? &c.

APPLICATION

1. There is no alternative between penitence and death.

2. Now consider, reflect, and live to God.

3. To all is the offer of mercy sent.

76

PARDONING MERCY CELEBRATED

" And in that day thou shalt say, O Lord, I will praise thee ; though thou wast angry with me, thine anger is turned away, and thou comfortest me."—ISAIAH xii. 1.

IT is evident that the preceding chapter relates to the reign and kingdom of Messiah. The latter end of the chapter clearly relates to the ingathering of the Jews— a time yet to come—a period which will be the spiritual jubilee to the tribes of Israel, and the beginning of the millennium to the world itself. The text refers to the happy and delightful expressions of grateful confidence, which shall be ascribed to the Lord God of Israel. " And in that day," &c. Now while this is clearly the meaning of the passage, yet it is capable without any torturing of a personal application. The text may be assumed by every believer— by every spiritual child of Abraham ; as such we shall treat it on the present occasion. We have,

I. A PREVIOUS STATE REFERRED TO. " Thou wast angry with me." When we speak of anger in Deity, it is not to be supposed that he is influenced by passion as we are. The term indicates his disapprobation and determination to punish. This disapprobation, &c., is never excited towards any beings, but in accordance with his settled equity and holiness of character. God is righteous in all his ways, and just in all his dispensations. We notice,

1. *That man's character and conduct, while in his natural state, are such as justly to expose him to the divine anger.* What does God survey in the sinner ? Ignorance, unbelief, enmity, malevolence, impurity. Not a redeeming trait, &c. Not a lovely feature. His conduct is exceedingly displeasing to God ; he returns not for the mercies received ; he acknowledges no divine benefits, he reverences not God, he yields no obedience ; he does not what God justly and reasonably expects from his rational creatures. Then he breaks his laws, violates his statutes, and does those things which God has sacredly forbidden to be done. In addition to this, he abuses his long-suffering, and despises his mercy. He rejects the gracious message of the gospel, and puts to death again the Son of God. We ask,

2. *How may rational intelligent beings be*

sensible that they are the objects of the divine anger ? " Thou wast angry with me." Now this is clearly revealed in God's holy word. " God is angry," &c. He has expressed it in the most striking and varied language. " His face is set against them that do evil." Then this is ratified by the workings of conscience. Let any one do good secretly, and contrast his state of mind with the feelings arising after the commission of secret evil. In both cases, the cognizance of man shall not be included. What a difference ! day and night—bliss and anguish—heaven and hell, do not form greater contrasts.

3. *The divine anger is of all things most to be deprecated.* Only observe what has been the effect of the divine anger to impenitent sinners. Think of the old world ; of Pharaoh and the Egyptians ; of Sodom, &c. View it written in indelible and awful characters in the history of the Israelites. See the scriptural definitions and figurative representations. It is a desolating flood—a horrible tempest—a devouring fire ; nothing can resist it—nothing alleviate it—nothing extricate the victims of it ; and to the finally incorrigible it will rage with desolating and eternal fury. But notice,

II. THE DELIGHTFUL CHANGE EXPERIENCED. " Thine anger is turned away," &c. This change is experienced in a two-fold form.

1. *The divine displeasure is removed.* " Anger turned away." The cloud blotted out ; no longer under condemnation, &c. This necessarily supposes a change in the creature. His enmity and opposition to God have ceased ; he has seen the evil of sin ; confessed and forsaken it ; and believed in the Lord Jesus Christ. A state of unbelief involves us beneath the divine wrath ; a state of faith brings us from this dire condition. God abhors the high and proud spirit ; but he looks in pity upon the lowly and contrite.

2. *The divine favor is enjoyed.* " Thou comfortest me." We cannot stand in a neutral state with respect to Deity. The instant his anger is removed his favor is enjoyed. This comfort is the light of the divine countenance—it is the possession of the Holy Ghost ; the dove of peace and comfort hovers over the soul. Now guilt, remorse, and the burden of sin are gone, and there is in their stead the smile—the

blessing of God. This comfort is real, not visionary ; suitable, abiding, and inexpressibly precious ; and it is associated with all good, both in this life and in that which is to come. It is the precursor of everlasting felicity. Observe,

III. THE GRATEFUL RETURN PRESENTED. " I will praise thee." Acceptable praise includes,

1. *The offering of a thankful heart.* It must arise from within ; it must have to do with the affections of the soul. Heart gratitude is alone real, and that which God will receive.

2. *It must be free and spontaneous.* " I will." Not I ought, or should, but " I will." I feel borne away with the principle of grateful love to God. This feeling fills the soul ; absorbs all its faculties.

3. *It must be constant.* Never out of time, or unreasonable. " In every thing give thanks." In secret ; in the domestic circle ; in the social means of grace ; in the public ordinances, &c. " I will praise thee every day," &c. Praise God always , in health and sickness, death and eternally.

4. *It must be practical.*

5. *It will be eternal.* " Unto him who hath loved us," &c.

APPLICATION

Let the text be,

1. *The test of our state.* Can we use it ? Is it so with us ? Is God our reconciled friend ?

2. *The test of our spirit and conduct.* Do we love and bless God ? Is it our delight to do so ?

3. *Let it be attractive to the convicted, mourning sinner.* There is a way to divine peace, and to real and heavenly comfort. Christ is that way. Come now to God through him.

77

PREACHING CHRIST

" Whom we preach."—COLOSSIANS i. 28

IN the erection of a building, one of the chief and most important matters is the foundation ; for if the foundation fail, how can the building stand ? In the construction of an arch, the key-stone is that which holds the whole in security. Most systems have their main principles, their cardinal truths. In the human body, some parts are vitally important; in our existence, bread is the staff of life; but you ask, what mean these disconnected observations? I reply, in preaching, Christ is all this to the excellency and value of the sermon. Our discourses are evangelically deficient if Christ is not the foundation—the key-stone —the grand principle and essential truth of the Christian system—the true, living bread of the world. In preaching or suffering, Christ was all to the apostle—" We preach not ourselves," &c. He avowed his desire not only to win Christ, but to have fellowship with him in his sufferings. All his epistles are full of Jesus Christ. This is pre-eminently the case with this epistle. He dwells on his sacrifice, dignity, &c., and then adds in the 27th verse, " To whom God would make known," &c. We preach,

I. ALL CHRIST.
II. CHRIST TO ALL.
III. CHRIST ALWAYS. We preach,

I. ALL CHRIST. In other words, a " whole Christ." We claim for him,

1. *The highest dignity and glory.* He was the angel of Jehovah's presence to the Jews, and he is to us Christians, God over all, blessed, &c. He holds no inferiority to the eternal Father, but claims perfect, essential, unbounded, and everlasting equality. " He thought it not robbery," &c. He is " Immanuel, God with us." His throne is the highest, at the Father's right hand,—the throne of the universe. His authority is illimitable. He created all things—upholds all things—preserves all things—and by him all things consist. On his head are many crowns; the ascriptions of the redeemed, and of seraphim and cherubim, are incessantly given to him " whom we preach." Notice,

2. *We preach him in his perfect humanity and abasement.* A true man; made like unto his brethren, &c.; bone of our bone, &c.; really the second Adam; and in his abasement, we refer to Bethlehem— the stable—the manger—poverty—slander —persecution—at last death. " He humbled himself to death, even the death of the cross." He died as a thief, or a murderer; on a cross between heaven and earth —between two malefactors, &c. " Whom we preach,"

3. *In the glory of his offices.*

(1.) Divine offices as ruler, &c.; but especially his mediatorial offices, as the prophet and apostle of the world.

(2.) As a priest, presenting one sacrifice for man's transgression.

(3.) As the King of Zion, establishing an empire of truth and righteousness, of peace and love on the earth. These offices meet a world's wants.

i. Dark; he illuminates it by his truth.
ii. Lost; he saves it by his death.
iii. In rebellion, he subdues and governs it by his grace. " Whom we preach,"

4. *In his sacrificial obedience and merit.* In his divine and human natures he possesses infinite dignity; in his obedience and righteousness, God's eyes rest on immaculate holiness. His blood has expiatory virtue, and his life once offered removes the curse, and rolls it from our world. The whole is expressed by Isaiah, " All we like sheep," &c., and sung by the redeemed, " Unto him who loved us," &c. " Whom we preach,"

5. *In his illustrious triumphs.* He triumphed over error by his doctrines; over temptations by his endurance; over malice by his meekness; over diseases, death, and devils, by his miracles; over sin by his death; over the grave by his resurrection; and over souls by his gospel and love. Who does not unite with the poet,

" Oh! Jesus, ride on, till all are subdued," &c

But,

II. WE PREACH CHRIST TO ALL.

1. *All stand in need of Christ.* None righteous, &c.; none sufficient to save themselves; no other Saviour for any. Wisdom, righteousness, sanctification, redemption, and eternal life, are nowhere but in Christ. " Whom we preach to all,"

2. *For he is the Saviour of all.* Brother of all; lived for all; died for all. He has the nature of all in the holy place. " Whom we preach to all,"

3. *For he has sent his gospel to all.* The world is the extent of his commission :—

" Wide as the world is his command,
	Vast as eternity his love."

" Whom we preach to all,"

4. *Of every class and rank.*

(1.) Civil—monarch, beggar, rich, poor
(2.) Mental—philosopher, illiterate, civilized, savage.
(3.) Moral—the orderly and the rude,

the correct and the profligate, the best and the worst; also to all ages. We invite children to sing their hosannas to Christ: we entreat the aged to take Jesus in their arms by faith, &c.

III. WE PREACH CHRIST ALWAYS. We desire Christ to find a place in every discourse, and to be its life and glory. "We preach Christ,"

1. *As the essence of all doctrines.* Justification; regeneration; sanctification.

2. *As the substance of all blessings.* Pardon; peace; hope; joy.

3. *As the beginning and end of all duties.* Obedience begins with believing in him, and ends in living to him.

4. *As the model of all virtues.* His life and conversation quite perfect. Practical essons of humility, self-government, lowliness, courtesy, gentleness, fortitude, goodness.

5. *As the sum of all enjoyment.* Ask the forgiven penitent, "I will praise," &c. Ask the tranquil believer, "The peace of God," &c. Ask the dying Christian, "To die is gain." Ask the beatified spirit, "With the Lord to enjoy him; to see him as he is."

APPLICATION

1. *Is Christ yours?* Have you received him? Does he dwell in you?

2. *Are you Christ's?* Your hearts, lives, possessions—all.

3. *Who will become Christ's to-day?* For to you is the word of this salvation sent.

78

THE HELP OF GOD FOR HIS OWN CAUSE, PLEADED

"Arise, O God! plead thine own cause."—PSALM lxxiv. 22.

TRUE religion identifies a man with the things of God. No man who loves God can live to himself, &c. A good man is concerned for the divine glory. His feelings are depressed or exalted, as God is honored or despised. True piety throws its powers of vision through the universe, and rejoices in all that reflects the mind of God, and weeps over the misery, and sin, and ruin which darken so many portions of our world. In the midst of the evil that exists, he perceives the hand of God working, resisting the violence of Satan, circumscribing the limits of human wrath, and giving exercise to the powerful ele-

ments of truth and holiness. Beholding this, the good man's energies are aroused, his spirit encouraged, his ardor excited, and he gives utterance to the prayer of the text, "Arise, O God!" &c. We remark,

I. GOD HAS A CAUSE IN OUR WORLD. The affairs of the universe are in his hands. Our world is a part of that universe. He made it; he upholds it; he governs it. It is under his cognizance; regulated by his agencies, &c. But morally, our world is in a state of revolution. Satan introduced into it the elements of moral evil. By it, it became the region of crime, darkness, misery, and death. To counteract this revolt, and remove its effects, God mercifully set up a cause in our world—a remedial system—a system of restoration to truth, holiness, and salvation. Now, this cause is based on the redeeming love of God; on the mission of Christ into our world; on the setting up of Christ's kingdom, so as to overthrow the kingdom of the evil one. The cause of God and his church are the same. The church is to be the instrument for carrying out Jehovah's designs. God, by his Holy Spirit, dwells in the church, and thus perpetuates and gives efficacy to its influence and exertions.

II. THE CAUSE OF GOD IN OUR WORLD IS DISTINGUISHED BY CERTAIN STRIKING CHARACTERISTICS.

1. *It is distinguished for its knowledge.* Cause of light, and therefore it is bearing down the darkness of the world. Ignorance is the citadel of Satan's kingdom. God is light; diffuses light; makes his church the instrument of light. The seven churches of Asia were likened to seven golden candlesticks. "Ye are the light of the world." "Cities," &c. The church is to arise and shine, &c. Now the word of the divine truth is the light of the church.

2. *It is distinguished for its holiness.* The church is separated from the mass, and is holy to the Lord. Called to holiness; invested with holiness; to exhibit holiness. Thus it is to condemn the sin and defilement of the world, and like salt to save it from corruption and ruin.

3. *It is distinguished for its benevolence.* It embodies the sentiments of the song of the angels at the birth of the Redeemer, "Glory to God," &c. Its aspect towards heaven is purity—towards earth, goodness. Now sin produced misery to man; to his body and spirit; to man personally, rela-

tively, &c. Religion breathes love, peace, goodness ; it exercises candor, mercy, compassion, pity, and tenderness ; it sacrifices self, and lives and works for others. Now, the influence of this benevolence is to diffuse happiness through our world. As sin has rendered man a curse to his fellow-creatures, religion makes him a blessing.

III. THE CAUSE OF GOD, THOUGH COMPRISING MANY ELEMENTS, IS YET ONE. Tyranny and despotism have cursed our world, crushed many thousands beneath their cruel yoke. Liberty, therefore, is the cause of God ; freedom of limb and conscience are the unalienable prerogatives of man. War has made our earth drunk with the crimson fluid of life, and is opposed to God's glory and man's well-being ; peace, therefore, is God's cause. Ecclesiastical systems of error have been the bane of the church, and, riveted by state authority, have been one of the heaviest drags on the chariot wheels of the gospel ; church purity, therefore, is the cause of God. Now, in the gospel of the Saviour are two principles, which, if imbibed and carried out, would overthrow every evil, and bring about the consummation of every good—the love of God, and the love of man ; one as a burning flame ascending to Deity, and the other as a benignant sunbeam shining upon the world. All real good in the world is identified with God's cause.

IV. THE CAUSE OF GOD IS GREATLY IMPEDED AND OPPOSED. Opposed by all the moral evil in the world ; by all the power of Satan. Impeded by the apathy of its professed friends ; impeded by human systems, creeds, and earthly influences ; by the want of devotedness, prayer, and faith of Christians.

V. PRAYER TO GOD ON BEHALF OF HIS CAUSE IS THE CHURCH'S DUTY. What examples we have in the history of the church, where the ardent piety of its people was thus displayed ! How Moses interceded ; how David supplicated, &c. ; how Jeremiah prayed and wept ; how Paul agonized ; how devotionally fervent were the early Christians, the Reformers, the Puritans ; Knox, and others ; and how eminently godly persons do so now ! Thus to pray is pleasing to God—really profitable to ourselves. Such prayer has many promises on which to rest ; such earnest prayerfulness has generally preceded and accompanied the reviva of religion.

VI. GOD CAN MOST EFFECTUALLY ANSWER THE PRAYERS OF HIS PEOPLE. Now, he can do this by the signal acts of his providence, or by the especial influences of his grace, or by both harmonizing with each other. Hence observe how he rescued his people from Egypt ; how he delivered the Jews from the wicked plots of Haman ; how he turned back their captivity by Cyrus ; how he has overthrown empires, raised up instruments, and restricted human wrath and passion ; how he has made the wrath of man to praise him, &c. ; and how he has opened doors of usefulness ; given men the powers to adopt varied kinds of instrumentality ; how he has raised up remarkable agents—Luther, Wickliffe, Knox, Wesley, Whitfield, &c. But we anticipate the full triumphs of his cause by the universal diffusion of his truth ; by the erection of the cross, " And I, if I be lifted up," &c. Providence subserving the means of grace ; and this shall be " until the kingdoms of this world," &c. " Till the knowledge of the Lord," &c. " Till all flesh shall see his salvation."

APPLICATION

1. *Who are with Christ in this cause?* How are you feeling and acting ? What doing for its extension ? &c. Oh ! labor and pray.

2. *Who are indifferent?* More concerned about their own temporal affairs.

3. *Who are opposed to it ?* That is a fearful position. We urge you to abandon it. Seek the mercy of the Lord, that you perish not, &c. And now shall not this be our prayer, " Arise, O Lord !" &c.

79

ON A REVIVAL OF RELIGION
" Wilt thou not revive us ?"—PSALM lxxxv. 6.

To revive signifies to restore ; to increase ; and a revival of religion supposes its previous existence. The necessity and importance of religion we do not stay to establish. It is presumed that this is felt to be of the very highest moment ; of both individual and general interest ; essential to man's best interests both in time and eternity. Observe what our text supposes.

I. THE COMPARATIVE LOW STATE OF RELIGION. We use the term comparative, because that which is only a low state of religion with one, may be ardor contrasted with that of another. Look at this subject in relation to,

1. *Individuals.* What a limited state of knowledge, faith, peace, hope, joy, &c.; what little devotedness; what formality, earthliness; what selfish manifestations; what feebleness of action for Christ and his cause; how little of the mind of Christ, and the power of high-toned piety.

2. *As to churches.* Here, also, great diversity of state; but take the more prosperous. How few really enlisted in active support of the great movements of the age. How few of the most flourishing churches inspired by glowing zeal; living in all things to God, for souls and eternity.

3. *As to the universal church of Christ.* In its catholic aspect. How feeble its instrumentality—how limited its resources—how contracted its sphere — how few its leading master minds and its members, as contrasted with the subjects of the kingdom of Satan—how little effected—how very much to be done. What solicitude, therefore, should it excite among Christians of all sections of the church.

II. The importance of a revival of religion.

1. *To each individual Christian.* It will be their dignity, elevation, riches, and true felicity. This is their fertility and meetness for eternal glory.

2. *To the great cause of the Redeemer.* Its beauty, vigor, grandeur, extension, and consummation, all depend on the revival of religion.

3. *To the world at large.* How are its darkness, guilt, misery, and wo to be removed without a revival of religion? The spiritual salvation of the world hangs upon it.

III. The means to be adopted for securing a revival of religion.

1. *An increase of personal piety among the disciples of Christ.* This applies to every Christian, especially in humility, faith, and benevolence.

2. *A better organization of the friends of the Redeemer.* The army is large, but the real active force exceedingly few. In churches comprising hundreds, perhaps not more than one in ten is really engaged in active effort for the extension of the Redeemer's kingdom. Some system of division of labor, &c., must be adopted to remedy this great evil.

3. *The removal of certain great impedi-*ments. The disunion of real Christians; the overthrow of sectarianism, &c.; temporal poverty, and excessive physical toil. We must expect and labor for this. Civil freedom and happiness are favorable to true piety, and its revival throughout the world. It is to be regretted that persons in our own country have so little time to spare for mental and moral improvement. Tyranny and oppression will all be swept away as the truth of the gospel wins its widening course. Ecclesiastical secularities are also great impediments.

4. *The united prayer and self-denial of the church.* Prayers more direct and fervent—more pleading—more agonizing.— Prayer meetings for this end more common, and better frequented. Christians more self-denying. A willingness to give up our own feelings, &c., for the honor of Christ, and the extension of his kingdom.

IV. The probable success of these means. "Wilt thou not?" &c. That God is willing to answer this appeal is evident; for,

1. *He desires it.* It is asking for what is agreeable to him. His bowels yearn over this miserable world; his affections are upon it; he wills the salvation of each and of all.

2. *God has engaged for its accomplishment.* How many the predictions; how great, and radiant, and glowing the promises! and not one shall fail. The celestial heavens are bestudded with them. A galaxy; a milky way.

3. *God has revived his cause in answer to prayer.* His word records instances of such a kind. Two instances must suffice: Neh. viii. 16; Acts iv. 31. In Scotland, in the sixteenth and seventeenth centuries; in England, Ireland, and Wales, in the eighteenth century. Then what ground of hope there is; what reason to unite and plead, "Wilt thou not?" &c.

APPLICATION

1. *Who feels the propriety and force of the text?*

2. *Will you pray, and labor, and toil?* Assist to remove the impediments, and to keep the machinery in motion.

3. *It will be effected by us, or without us.*

4. *See what persons do for sin and false religions.* Pleasure-takers; infidels; pagans.

80

JEHOVAH'S GRACIOUS DECLARATION ABOUT THE WICKED

" As I live, saith the Lord God, I have no pleasure in the death of the wicked."—EZEKIEL xxxiii. 11.

I KNOW not of a more solemn yet interesting passage in the holy scriptures, than the text we have just read in your hearing. Whether we consider the speaker, or the solemn declaration given, it demands our most serious and prayerful consideration. The speaker is Jehovah, the eternal and ever-blessed God, the fountain of purity, and goodness, and truth. The declaration relates to the death of the sinner. Not the death of the body, but of the soul, that which includes the righteous infliction of wrath in the world to come. The death of deaths; the death that never dies. The declaration affirms that this is not the pleasure of God. He has not appointed, or decreed, or necessitated it. He does not desire it. He confirms this by a solemn asseveration or oath, " As I live." Notice,

I. TO WHOM THE TEXT REFERS.

II. THE EVIDENCES BY WHICH IT IS CONFIRMED.

III. THE IMPRESSIONS IT SHOULD PRODUCE UPON OUR MINDS.

I. TO WHOM DOES THE TEXT REFER? " The wicked." The transgressor. We readily believe that God wills not the death of the righteous. He cannot do this. But the text refers to the very opposite of these. Those who are far from God. Haters of God. Disobedient, &c. Now the term includes all who are unrenewed in their hearts. Hence, in the sight of God, all who are in their natural state are such. But the text will apply,

1. *To the flagrantly wicked.* Notorious sinners. Men who have exceeded those around them in crime. Daring, desperate, prominently vile. Bearing the mark of the beast in their foreheads. Who glory in their shame. Yes, our text applies to the very vilest of these.

2. *To the aged wicked.* God does not will the death of the hoary-headed rebel. He whose childhood was folly — whose youth was riotous—whose maturer years were criminal, and whose old age is evil and perverse, yet in the eternal death of him, God does not delight.

3. *The influentially wicked.* He does not delight in the death even of the ringleaders of evil ; yet this is a fearful state to be in. Alluring others to dreary regions of wo. To be champions for vice ; to spread the deadliest poison around ; to mature others for endless torments ; yet these are included in the gracious declaration in the text. Of these, then, none are excluded, no, not one of the countless myriads of the human race.

II. THE EVIDENCES BY WHICH IT IS CONFIRMED. How does it appear that God has no pleasure in the death of the wicked ?

1. *In not leaving the sinner to the results of his crimes.* God had only to be passive and leave the sinner to his own ways. Guilt made man anxious, wretched, and miserable. Like poison, it would have worked death—as fire, it would have consumed the spirit. Had God left man the prey of his own freely chosen evil, he must have been eternally lost. God's interference was for the sinner's recovery, it was essential to his rescue, and consequently establishes the truth of the text, that God has " no pleasure in the death," &c.

2. *The marvellous provision for man's restoration is another evidence.* God made provision for the salvation of man, that provision was the sacrifice of his own Son. He laid our iniquity upon him. He transferred the sufferings of the guilty to the holy and just One, who suffered for us, that he might bring us to God. This provision is truly marvellous, it surpasses understanding. It is too high, too vast, too sublime, too profound, for human comprehension. The whole economy of redemption exhibited in every unfolding of it the great truth of the text. Wherefore the abasing advent of the Son of God ? Wherefore the sorrowful and afflictive life, the cruel and shameful sufferings, the intense agonies, the inexplicable passion, the bloody and ignominious death of the holiest person in the universe, if God delighted in the death of the sinner ? The song of Bethlehem— the doctrines of Jesus—the sufferings of our substitute—all, all testify that God " has no pleasure," &c.

3. *The gracious principles on which salvation is tendered is a further evidence of the truth of the text.* To show the divine solicitude for man's welfare, the blessings of salvation are brought down to his moral exigency and condition. Every impediment is removed. Every blessing prepar-

ed, and God only requires the acceptance of his mercy, on his own gracious terms of appointment. No oppressive toil—no hard exertions—no painful penances—no preparatory self-preparation. The object of his hope is lifted up, and he has just to look, and as Moses, &c. The bread of life is presented, and he has but to receive it. The fountain of healing is opened at his feet, and he has but to step in. The proclamation of liberty is made, and the door of emancipation is opened, and he has but to go forth and enjoy the liberty and happiness of the children of God. Here then we see in the adaptedness of the gospel provision, that "God has no pleasure," &c.

4. *The long-suffering of God, and his forbearance to the impenitent, further ratify the truth of the text.* Every sinner deserves to die. God could justly punish with death on the first rejection of his gospel. God has power to do it. The sinner is always in his power. But how does the Lord act towards the wicked? He restrains his wrath—he bounds his vengeance—he extends the reprieve, he does vastly more than this, he keeps in activity a variety of means for his rescue and salvation. He sends days and years of these—he sends sabbaths and ordinances—he sends ministers and friends—he sends promises and threatenings —he sends comforts and afflictions, and all for what? That the wicked may not die, to exhibit his unbounded mercy, and to prove that he has no pleasure in the death of the wicked. We shall only add,

Finally, the solemn asseveration or oath in the text. An oath is a solemn, deliberate affirmation, made as before God, and calling his cognizance to what is attested. Jehovah cannot testify before a greater, for he is the only God, and beside him there is none else ; but to vindicate his tender mercy and compassion for the welfare of the wicked, he stands forth, and before angels, men, and devils, he proclaims by his own eternal immutability, "As I live," (not only in myself, by my eternal self-existence, but as the fountain of life and being to the universe itself,) "I have no pleasure in the death of the wicked." Let us briefly notice, then,

III. The impressions it should produce upon our minds.

1. *We should be impressed with our own personal responsibility.* Many would cavil with circumstances, and reason about ne-

cessity, and thus remove the blame from themselves, and affirm his desire for our destruction. Every man must give an account, and God will reward every man, &c.

2. *We should be affected by God's gracious conduct towards us.* What love and mercy is here exhibited ! It ought to melt the hardest heart. It ought to constrain the most desperate rebel, &c.

3. *We should co-operate with God so as to secure the great salvation.* Nothing is requisite but to act with God. To will as God wills; agreement here will secure present reconciliation and eternal happiness.

4. *We should do all in our power to prevent the wicked from dying.* Every minister. Every Christian, feel, pray, labor, &c., or we are not like God.

81

ADAM AND EVE

"So God created man in his own image : in the image of God created he him ; male and female created he them."—Genesis i. 27.

The history of our first parents cannot but be interesting in whatever light it is considered. Of their nature we are partakers. In the results of their conduct we are involved, and therefore from their example and history, valuable instruction must be derived. With the leading events in their lives scripture is replete, and therefore to its divine and authentic records let us appeal. We may contemplate them,

I. In their primeval purity and blessedness. The offspring of God ; made by him, and for him ; but especially formed under peculiarly interesting circumstances. The last and fairest of the divine works—the result of the divine council— and formed in the divine likeness — created with a spiritual nature, immediately proceeding from God, chapter ii. 7. Intellectual, holy, happy—in their understanding, reflecting the divine knowledge —in their judgment, the divine truth— in their affections, the divine goodness— in their conscience, the divine purity—in their will, the divine dominion. All the faculties and passions nicely balanced. All their powers in a state of transparent beauty and harmony. God enthroned in their affections, adored in their spirits, and obeyed in their lives. In their earthly condition, having the supremacy over all terrestrial creatures; invested with entire, indisputable dominion; the earth their domain; Eden their royal abode; angels their friends and companions, and all creatures their willing and obedient servants; above all, God their joy and supreme good. In this state they had ability to abide. Subject to Deity by a law the most easy, beneficent, and practicable; but alas! how soon is this picture of moral beauty and felicity reversed. Behold them,

II. IN A STATE OF TEMPTATION AND PERIL. Tempted by the devil. Tempted to disbelieve God in reference to the forbidden fruit—tempted to disobey his explicit commands—tempted to exalt themselves to an equality with God. These temptations were addressed to the weaker vessel, when alone, and alas! they were successful and prevailed. She beheld, and hearkened, and desired, and ate. Adam also from her received the fruit of sin, and fell into the same condemnation. With this act fled innocence, peace, and purity. Shame was the immediate result, and fear and dread followed in its train; thus sin and wo were introduced into our world. Observe them,

III. UNDER ARREST AND EXAMINATION. By the darkness of their minds, they had supposed it possible to flee from God. How foolish, how futile! His voice arrested them. Their fear and shame are confessed, chapter iii. 10. The heart-searching interrogation is presented. "Hast thou eaten," &c. Self-justification — man throws the blame on the woman, and the Being who had given her to him. "The woman whom thou gavest me," &c. And then reluctantly the admission, "I did eat." The woman throws the blame on the serpent. Ah, sin was found so degrading and miserable, that its perpetrators were most anxious to disown it. And now notice them,

IV. RECEIVING THE RIGHTEOUS SENTENCE OF GOD. On the woman was pronounced sorrow in conception and child-bearing, and subjection to her husband, verse 16. To the man toil, perpetuated through the course of his existence. "In the sweat," &c., ver. 19. And on both, the dissolution of the body. "Dust thou art," &c. And now the seeds of death began their operation, influence, &c. Every step was one towards the house appointed for all living; but in addition to this sentence, sin had effaced the moral beauty and excellency of their spiritual nature. The

gold, alas, how dim! the fine gold how changed! The crown of dignity had now fallen from their head, and the sceptre of royalty from their grasp. The spirit was bereft of its virgin purity, and the moral glory had departed; instead of peace was anxiety; instead of joy, remorse; instead of tranquillity, distraction; instead of health, disease; instead of the divine smile and approbation, the holy displeasure of God. Notice,

V. THEIR EXPULSION FROM THE ABODE OF HOLINESS AND BLISS. As traitors their inheritance was forfeited, as rebels they were excluded those peaceful scenes of purity and joy. God himself exercised the sentence. "So he drove out the man," &c., and a flaming sword prevented their access to the tree of life. Now, alas! sinners, polluted and wretched, and expelled the paradise which had been prepared as a residence of dignity and enjoyment. But observe them,

VI. AS THE SUBJECTS OF GOD'S MERCIFUL INTERPOSITION. In the midst of wrath, mercy was remembered. Compassion triumphed over judgment; and when the cloud of punishment seemed so black and terrible as to exclude all hope, a ray of celestial light streaked the agitated horizon, and a promise of redemption and deliverance given in those joyous words, that the woman's seed should bruise the serpent's head. Doubtless religious instruction and direction were given. The mode of access to God revealed; the way of their gracious acceptance clearly made known; and the terms of their final salvation fully detailed. Let us,

1. Mourn over the evil of sin.
2. Rejoice in the remedy provided. And,
3. Personally seek the salvation the gospel proclaims.

82

FAITH AND SACRIFICE OF ABEL

" By faith Abel offered unto God a more excellent sacrifice than Cain, by which he obtained witness that he was righteous, God testifying of his gifts: and by it he being dead yet speaketh "—HEBREWS xi. 4.

How awfully prolific and rapid in its dire progress is sin! The first man born into our world was a murderer; not only a murderer, but a fratricide—the murderer of his brother. How greatly mistaken was the mother of all living when, at the birth of Cain, she exclaimed, "I have gotten a man from the Lord," imagining that he was the promised seed who should bruise the serpent's head. Her second son was a martyr, and one destined to lead the van among those who suffered death for the testimony of Jesus. Our subject however this morning refers to his faith, and the sacrifice he presented to God. To this then we would call your serious and prayerful attention.

I. ABEL OFFERED SACRIFICE UNTO GOD. The immediate and precise origin of sacrifices is not revealed. It is exceedingly probable that when God revealed the promise of a Saviour to our first parents, he gave them direct instructions on the subject of sacrifices, and we have no doubt the skins with which he clothed them were the skins of animals which had been thus presented. Animal food was not then allowed. To slay animals expressly for their skins is improbable, but to suppose the beasts slain for sacrifice, and the skins thus appropriated, seems reasonable, and leads us at once to the very probable institution of sacrifices. Doubtless God revealed the nature of the sacrifices, and the symbolical end they were to answer. Abel's sacrifice was the firstling of his flock. A lamb, the best and most choice his flock could yield. This was afterwards incorporated in the Jewish ritual as the great annual offering. The victim which Abel presented was slain. Doubtless a rude altar of stones was erected, and on this the lamb was presented to God.

II. ABEL'S SACRIFICE WAS MORE EXCELLENT THAN CAIN'S.

(1.) Now we presume it was the offering prescribed by God. God will not own or bless will-worship. In religion God leaves no room for fancy or human invention.

(2.) Abel's offering was better, as being more suited to a sinner. Homage, reverence, gratitude, &c., become holy beings, something more is necessary from the guilty. A sinner requires a mediator, a way of access to God. Cain's sacrifice only savored of natural religion. God's claims as a Creator and Benefactor must not be forgotten ; but we must never forget, as guilty beings, that we need pardon, and as polluted, a laver of purification. Praise and veneration will not do instead of repentance, confession, and faith.

III. ABEL OFFERED HIS SACRIFICE IN FAITH. And his faith,

1. *Would regard his own unworthiness and guilt.* "The whole have no need of a physician," &c. The act of killing the lamb, would lead him to reflect on the just desert of sin. By sin came death. "Here I see the claims of God's offended justice and broken law, thus my life might have been poured out."

2. *His faith regarded the great sacrifice of which his lamb was but an emblem and a type.* The ancient sacrifices were designed to keep up and prefigure the great propitiation for sin. The ancient saints rested not on the victims slain, but on the Lamb of God, who should be offered in the latter days for the sin of the world.

3. *His faith would regard his own interest and dependence on that sacrifice.* He offered the sacrifice for himself, he felt personally concerned. Here he rested his hope, and believed God would accept him through the promised Messiah. He believed what God had testified, and on that great Victim he rested all his expectation of God's favor, and eternal life.

IV. GOD TESTIFIED HIS APPROBATION OF ABEL'S SACRIFICE. "He obtained witness," &c., "God testifying," &c., see Gen. iv. 4.

1. *How did God witness?* He could have done so by an audible voice, but doubtless by fire consuming the victim. Some commentators render "he had respect,"—"kindled with fire." This was the way in which God accepted the sacrifices under the law, see Lev. ix. 24.

2. *What did God witness?* "That he was righteous." Offered what pleased God ; obeyed God's sacrificial law ; but it doubtless means that he was justified, forgiven ; that God expressed his favor, and accepted him through the great sacrifice ; that his heart was penitent, humbled, believing.

V. ABEL BY HIS FAITH AND SACRIFICE STILL GIVES INSTRUCTION TO MANKIND. "By it he being dead," &c. Now in what does Abel instruct us ? He saith,

1. *That sinful man may have access to God.* Can man approach a holy Being ? Will he not perish ? No, God is accessible even to the guilty, the sinner may bow down and not perish, "for his mercy endureth forever." He saith,

2. *That the way of sacrifice is the only way which God approves.* "Without shedding of blood," &c. All our blessings are

through Christ's death. No pardon or holiness without it. He saith,

3. *That faith is essential to acceptance.* Unbelief insults God—rejects his mercy. Throws discredit on his word. Faith trusts all and every thing, where God has laid the only foundation. As the poet has sung,

" Believe, and all your sin's forgiven ;
  Believe, and you are heirs of heaven."

4. *That true religion may expose to severe suffering.* It may cost us our wealth, liberty, reputation, yea, life itself. "If a man will lose his life," &c. It cost Abel his. He was slain by his brother.

Finally, it teaches us, that God's favor will amply repay for all it may cost. Abel paid a great price, but was. it not worth it? You do not doubt it. Myriads have paid the same, and not one has ever regretted it. Not one that would not cheerfully pay the same cost again. Go through the whole army of martyrs, behold them in their white robes, see their glittering crowns, their waving palms. Ask you, who are they ? These are they " who came out of great tribulation," &c. If they had a thousand lives, they would sacrifice them all for Christ— all for salvation—all for eternal life. Believers, cleave to Christ. Sinners, come to him and live.

83

CAIN

" And bare Cain, and said, I have gotten a man from the Lord."—GENESIS iv. 1.

SUCH is the brief account of the entrance into our world of the first of woman born. The first promise had inspired our progenitors with the hope that Cain was the woman's seed who should bruise the serpent's head. Little did they think that that child was to be the cruel persecutor and murderer of his brother, and that age upon age must pass away before the appearance of the incarnate Redeemer of the world. Let us just glance at the leading particulars in the life and character of Cain. Observe,

I. HIS PECULIAR CONDITION AS THE FIRST-BORN CHILD. What anxieties he would occasion ; what attention elicit ; what hopes and desires excite ; the first infant, with all the accompanying weakness, &c., of that state. How dignified in his parentage, notwithstanding their fall, &c. ; how copiously towards him would maternal kindness flow ;

how every action would be observed ; how his growth and advancement towards maturity watched, &c. Notice,

II. HIS RURAL OCCUPATION. " A tiller of the ground." Though the eldest of Adam's progeny, yet he was not nursed in the lap of luxury and indolence. Industry is an honor to any man, however exalted. His labor was of a useful kind, adapted to increase his physical health and enjoyment. He had before him the beauties of nature —around him the wonders of creation— and above him the glorious heavens, in the height of which sat enthroned the Maker and Lord of the universe. His occupation was favorable to meditation, to seriousness, and communion with God. It was adapted also to promote gratitude to God, and dependence upon the communications of his rich and essential blessings on the culture of the accursed ground. The earth he tilled proclaimed the injury it had sustained through sin, and also would admonish him as to his final dusty bed. Consider him,

III. AS AN UNACCEPTABLE WORSHIPPER. It seems highly probable that God had revealed to our first parents the nature and character of that service he would require from them ; and, doubtless, the offering of sacrifices was an essential part thereof. Thus the worshipper would be led to perceive the evil and desert of sin, and to look forward to the great sacrifice which should in the end of the ages take away the sin of the world. But Cain's offering " was of the fruit of the ground," in which God was recognised only as the Lord of nature ; a mere acknowledgment of his being and government, such as holy creatures might with propriety have presented. But neither Cain's spirit nor worship had the least reference to his sinfulness, or the necessity of divine mercy. In this it is contrasted with that of Abel, verse 4. As such, it was rejected of the Almighty. Observe him,

IV. AS A VICTIM OF FRATERNAL ENVY AND MALEVOLENCE. He discovered that his offering was rejected, while God honored Abel by a gracious acceptance of the sacrifice he had presented ; and now envy —that foul Satanic passion—took possession of his soul. It is said, " He was very wroth, and his countenance fell." His soul disdained his God, and hated his brother ; he indignantly abhorred him for his excellence, and the worst of all feelings now rankled in his bosom. Alas ! he was now the slave of the destroyer, that wicked one, who was a murderer from the beginning. A great proportion of the crime and misery of our world is to be traced to the sin which had now full possession of the soul of Cain. We are called to view him,

V. As a guilty fratricide. God had expostulated with him on his wrath, and sullenness, and envy; he had cleared himself of partiality, and had assured him that if he did well he should be accepted; he had thrown the responsibility entirely upon him, see verse 7; but it was all in vain; the demon of hate still kept possession, until at length " he rose up and slew his brother." Thus did the influence of Satan and man's depravity prevail; thus did excellency and real piety suffer; and thus did the accursed earth drink in the precious blood of one of the saints of the Most High. Abel had lived in the divine service and favor; was hated and persecuted for his superior and godly spirit; died a martyr; and was the first of the human race to realize the blessedness and glory of the eternal world. Observe,

VI. Cain a guilty culprit in the presence of the supreme Judge. How overwhelming the solemn interrogation of Jehovah, " Where is Abel, thy brother?" the cool and wicked falsehood he uttered, " I know not;" the heartless, evading question, " Am I my brother's keeper?" then the solemn declaration of God, " What hast thou done? the voice of thy brother's blood crieth," &c.; the pronouncing of the curse, " And now art thou cursed from the ground," &c., verses 11, 12. His misery now filled him with horror, and overwhelmed, he exclaimed, " My punishment is greater than I can bear." Divine mercy was richly mingled in God's dealings with him. He was allowed to live; his life was pronounced sacred, verse 15; his punishment was evidently limited to this life; his after-life is not stated; but we fear he remained a child of the wicked one.

REMARKS

1. Unbelief is one of the reigning principles of the carnal heart, and is full of evil fruit.

2. How fearful a sin is envy; how to be guarded against.

3. How essential is the fear of God.

4. How all-important an interest in Christ Jesus.

84
GOD'S TESTIMONY CONCERNING ENOCH

" By faith Enoch was translated, that he should not see death; and was not found, because God had translated him; for before his translation he had this testimony, that he pleased God."—Hebrews xi. 5.

In every age and dispensation, God has had his illustrious servants exhibiting to all around the power of religion, and the beauties of holiness. In the first age of the world, there was the pious Abel, the first of the noble army of martyrs; in the period which intervened between that time and the flood, there was the holy Enoch, of whom our text speaks; at the time of the deluge, there was the righteous Noah. So we see that each period, however dark and wicked, had its pious luminaries, its sacred stars, which lit up the moral hemisphere, and showed men the true pathway to a blissful immortality. We now direct your attention to Enoch. Observe,

I. His personal holiness.
II. His internal assurance.
III. His glorious reward.

I. His personal holiness. This is thus expressed by the Holy Spirit: " And Enoch walked with God." In the Greek translation of the Old Testament scriptures, it is rendered the same as in our text, " He pleased God." Three things have ever been requisite in pleasing God:—

1. Faith. " By faith Enoch," &c. " Without faith it is impossible," &c. Faith is the firm persuasion of the truth of a testimony or record. To reject or disbelieve such a testimony, is to make the person testifying a liar, the greatest possible insult you can offer. This is what unbelief does to God. He that believes not the record God has given, &c., makes God a liar. How horrible the idea! What God testified to Enoch we know not, or how; whether by vision, an audible voice, or by immediate inspiration. Whatever was the method of God's communicating his testimony, Enoch believed God; he believed all the Lord testified; and this was the basis of all his religion, the root of that pious tree which bare such holy fruit, and was finally transplanted to the blissful regions of the heavenly paradise. In pleasing God there must be,

2. Affectionate communion. God must be supremely loved—the object of our

soul's delight; he must have the palace of the heart—the throne of the affections. The soul was originally created for this; capable of it; and this must be the centre around which the mind must revolve, and the end to which all its delights must tend. Thus God will be in the thoughts, in the imaginations, in the mental exercises of the mind. He will be with us, and we shall be with him, in secret, in public, by the wayside, by day, and by night. We shall have continual fellowship and spiritual intercourse with him. In pleasing God there must be,

3. *Constant and progressive obedience.* "Be followers of God as dear children." We are to imitate Deity. Thus Christ, the good shepherd, says, "My sheep hear my voice, and follow me." God's voice must not only be listened to, delighted in, but also obeyed; and there must be constancy in this; it must be the wont and custom, the habit and practice. There must also be advancement; going onward. The child can walk but feebly, or a little at a time; but it gains strength, and then can do so easily and more extensively.

II. His HAPPY ASSURANCE. "He had this testimony," &c. Now, we may be assured of having the approbation of another in several ways. Take the case of a child and its father, or the subject and sovereign.

(1.) Now, if either give certain commands in which they exhibit great interest, and to which they attach great importance, then by obeying those commands, and carrying out those designs, we rationally conclude that we possess their approbation.

(2.) This will be still more forcibly deduced, if we feel that we have the same spirit, enter heartily upon the same pursuits. Thus, supposing the emperor of China is sincere in his denunciations against opium, every Englishman must please him who labors to prevail with our countrymen to abandon that traffic. Now this may be still more effectually ratified,

(3.) By a written, or a verbal attestation. Let a child show the father's letter wherein his approval is attested, or state the sentiments he has uttered; let the subject refer to his king's eulogy, and then the matter is placed beyond all doubt. The Christian has this threefold testimony:—

i. He compares his life by the divine word, and he reads his conformity to that.

He sees some faint resemblance in that infallible mirror.

ii. He searches his own spirit, and he feels that it agrees with the Spirit of God; with God's desires and delights; and in this, that it is the opposite of what it was.

iii. God's Spirit imparts the approving light of his countenance and breathings of peace, just as when Christ visited his disciples, and breathed on them, and said, "Receive ye," &c. The apostle says on this subject, "Because ye are sons," &c. Gal. iv. 6; Rom. viii. 14, 16. "For as many as are led," &c. This testimony is exceedingly valuable,

(1.) As it regards our safety.

(2.) As it regards our comfort; for both of these entirely depend on having this testimony, &c. Observe,

III. His GLORIOUS REWARD. "Was translated," &c. This is sometimes spoken of in reference to character and state. "Translated from the kingdom of darkness," &c.; but here it refers to the removal of Enoch from this world to the heavenly glory. "He was not," &c. He did not remain on earth; he was not found in his usual sphere; it is probable his friends were surprised when they missed him, and knew not whence he was removed. God, however, declared that he had taken him, or in the words of our text, "translated him." He was thus exempted from the stroke of death; he was delivered from the corruption of mortality; he entered not the house appointed for all living; his remains did not see corruption; but it is clear that he underwent some important change to fit him for the joys of immortality. 1 Cor. xv. 50.

APPLICATION

1. *Learn the doctrine of a future state of existence.* And in respect both of body and soul. This is but the dawn of our being—the infancy of our existence; the body shall live again. There are already three glorified bodies in heaven—Enoch's, Elijah's, and that of our blessed Redeemer. These are the first-fruits of a glorious harvest.

2. *The sure path to a blessed immortality.* Walking with God, and thus having the testimony, &c. Believers, cherish this. Sinners, be anxious for this, &c. Let all think how important it will be in the day of death and of judgment.

3. *The great, essential principle of saving religion is faith.*

85

THE FEAR AND FAITH OF NOAH

" By faith, Noah being warned of God of things not seen as yet, moved with fear, prepared an ark to the saving of his house ; by the which he condemned the world, and became heir of the righteousness which is by faith."—HEBREWS xi. 17.

WE now proceed to contemplate the third distinguished worthy presented to our notice in this illustrious chapter of the believing heroes of Old Testament history. The same striking encomium is passed upon his devoted spirit and conduct as on that of Enoch ; see what is said of Noah, in 6th chapter of Genesis, 9th verse, &c. Our text, however, refers to the great leading events in his life ; his deliverance from the flood, which God brought upon the old world. This is very concisely, yet clearly presented to us in the words of the apostle, " By faith, Noah being warned," &c. In reference to Noah, notice,

I. THE WARNING HE RECEIVED. We read the warning, Gen. vi. 13, 14. The cause of this awful threatening was the universal spread of deep-toned iniquity and corruption, Gen. vi. 1–5, 12. The nature of the threatening was the universal destruction of all flesh. This God threatened he would accomplish by a flood of waters, verse 17. This warning related to *unseen things.* There was nothing to indicate this in all the range of nature around him. The sky, and earth, and sea wore their usual aspect. The man of observation might look round, and yet nothing confirmed the intimation ; the man of science might appeal to the laws of nature, &c. The worldlings of that day would not spare one hour to examine the question, nor the men of pleasure have one scene of banqueting less ; the great mass of the people would ridicule and laugh at the folly of the eccentric, fanatical Noah ; yet, despite of all this, the warning was received in the spirit of pious reverence by that godly man. Notice,

II. NOAH'S CONDUCT IN REFERENCE TO THIS WARNING.

1. *He believed God.* He regarded the threatening as coming from the faithful and true Jehovah. Faith in God's testimony was the spring of Noah's conduct. This is the basis on which the structure of his after life was built.

2. *His faith produced fear.* He feared the evil threatened—the wrath denounced. God is greatly to be feared ; his wrath is terrible. This is the characteristic of the Lord's people, that they have his fear before their eyes. " The fear of the Lord is the beginning of wisdom." They are in the fear of the Lord all the day long.

3. *His fear was connected with active obedience.* He obeyed God. God told him how he might escape by the construction of an ark, Gen. vi. 14. Here the duty was formidable, expensive, connected with great toil, and which would expose him to general contempt ; but his faith was operative. " He prepared the ark," &c. ; as prescribed by God ; the identical vessel in all things, as God had ordered. His obedience was *full, minute,* and *explicit,* see verse 22. " Thus did Noah ; according to all that God commanded him, so did he." This is genuine, acceptable, saving religion. Notice,

III. THE REWARD WHICH FOLLOWED THE PIOUS COURSE NOAH ADOPTED. We see the importance of *believing God's word,* and thus fearing his wrath, and gratefully accepting the method of escape he has provided. Two things specified :—

(1.) He condemned the world ; his preaching, and practice, and building the ark, all condemned the world ; left it excuseless ; justified God's dispensation.

(2.) He became heir of righteousness ; that is, he became before God and men a righteous character, and therefore entitled, through the mercy of God, to the reward which had been promised. But the reward itself,

1. *Consisted in his own preservation.* He escaped the vengeance of God ; his life was spared, the greatest earthly blessing he could enjoy ; and this was but a shadow of the great and eternal salvation which as a righteous man he would enjoy forever.

2. *His family were also interested in the deliverance.* God often blesses individuals for the sake of others. There is a real blessing in being piously connected ; but that will not save, if they personally reject the piety of their relatives ; see the case of Lot and his daughters, &c. The advantages and privileges are greater ; but if abused, their condition is the more signally awful. Noah's sons, and their wives, evidently obeyed Noah, regarded his commands, went with him readily into the ark,

&c., and thus were delivered with him. Oh ! how joyous to be saved, and those related to each other, all saved together.

APPLICATION

1. *God has revealed the certainty of a future judgment.* He has recorded the method, and the sublime grandeur of the great day ; he has reiterated this solemn warning ; of this we see no indication. The scoffer asks, Where is the promise ? &c. Men generally neglect and despise it ; but the day will come. The flood was delayed 120 years, yet it came at length ; so will the final day of God.

2. *God demands your belief of this great and solemn warning.* He calls you to fear, &c.

3. *He has revealed a way of safety.* His Son is the ark ; the door of this ark is open ; he urges you to enter ; on this your safety depends ; no other way. Are you believing—fearing—obeying ?

4. *Are you laboring for the security of your children ? &c.* They are all equally welcome with you ; but each must personally enter.

86

ABRAHAM'S BELIEVING PILGRIMAGE

" By faith Abraham, when he was called to go out into a place which he should after receive for an inheritance, obeyed ; and he went out, not knowing whither he went. By faith, he sojourned in the land of promise, as in a strange country, dwelling in tabernacles with Isaac and Jacob, the heirs with him of the same promise. For he looked for a city which hath foundations, whose builder and maker is God."—HEBREWS xi. 8–10.

AFTER God had frustrated the Babel builders, and confused their speech, sacred history refers us to the origin of distinct nations, and the fact of God choosing Abraham to be the father of the Jewish people, and one whom God engaged to bless and make a blessing. To this eventful period the text refers ; see Gen. xii. 1, &c. Thus Abraham acted through the influence of faith. He believed God ; he forsook all for God ; he went where God directed ; he considered himself but as a stranger ; and, finally, he looked for a more fixed and abiding habitation.

I. ABRAHAM BELIEVED GOD. For this he holds a most eminent and exalted station in the sacred pages of truth ; so much so, that he has the honored appellation of " father of the faithful." His confidence in God was so full, and entire, and unshaken, that he was styled the friend of God. Now, as faith is the foundation of every holy work, in proportion as this is strong and vigorous, will every virtue thrive, and flourish, and bear fruit. It is like gold, the most precious of all metals ; but we are enriched according to the abundance we possess of it. Weak faith is valuable ; but it is strong faith gives glory to God. Weak faith will walk safely on a calm lake ; but strong faith will not sink in the tempest or the storm. How desirable it is to believe God ! all God says, and at all times. Faith has an eagle's wing, and an eagle's eye ; it can rise to the greatest possible elevation, and it has a lion's courage amidst confusion and persecution ; even when the sea roars, and the earth shakes, it sits with firm security, and sings " defiance to the gates of hell !"

II. ABRAHAM FORSOOK ALL FOR GOD. His own country ; his father's house. In this,

1. *He gave up what he possessed for that which was promised.* He had an interest in his father's house, and his own country. These were in hand, in possession ; and, doubtless, were far from being despicable. He left, however, his own land, and his father's house, for that which was named in the promise.

2. *He gave up the present for the future.* Present subsistence, and present patrimony, for some good to be hereafter bestowed. Now, in these we see the nature of the demands religion makes. Abandonment of our carnal possessions and pleasures for those which God promises ; to give up the society of the world for the church ; to resign present profits for future advantages ; to lose sight of earth and time for heaven and eternity. Abraham became as it were isolated from the world to be united to God ; a true picture of spiritual religion. We cannot enjoy the world and God ; nor love both ; nor serve both. We may use the world ; but it cannot be pre-eminent, and God be glorified.

III. HE WENT WHERE GOD DIRECTED. True religion has,

1. *An ear to listen to God.* "Speak, Lord, for thy servant heareth." God spake

to Abraham, and he reverently heard the will of God propounded to him.

2. *Feet of cheerful obedience.* Having heard and understood, he "obeyed." Acted as God directed ; walked as he chalked out the way. God said, This is the way, and Abraham walked in it.

3. *Unsuspecting surrender of all into the Lord's hands.* "Not knowing," &c. God knew, and this was his comfort, &c. It is not necessary for a passenger to understand navigation to reach the port, &c., in safety ; or for a child to know the way, when its father holds its hand ; or the patient, anatomy or medicine, when the skilful physician is present.

IV. ABRAHAM CONSIDERED HIMSELF A STRANGER. As such he acted and lived. He conducted himself as a dying man in a dying world ; he knew this was not his rest, or home, or portion ; and this is precisely the spirit we should feel and cherish. A little reflection might convince every one of the propriety of this. This world is merely a land of passage : eight hundred millions are ever crowding its surface ; but they are all moving. "One generation passeth away," &c. Some are just leaving it—others just entering—but all are moving. Hence life, as a river, is ever emptying its countless drops into the ocean of eternity.

V. HE LOOKED FOR A MORE FIXED AND ABIDING HABITATION. Here he recognised his own immortality ; he associated with future existence a union with kindred spirits ; he beheld above not a desert but a city —the city of God—the new Jerusalem— the palace of Jehovah. He saw its foundations were firm ; yea, firmer than a rock, the very being, and purposes, and perfections of God sustaining it. Its grandeur was worthy of its artificer. "Builder and maker is God." He looked for it by faith, and daily hope, and constant prayer ; he reckoned upon it as his own ; he lived in reference to it ; and daily felt himself getting nearer and nearer.

APPLICATION

1. *Have we obeyed God, and given up the sinful pursuits of the present world?*

2. *Are we walking by faith or sight?* Abandoning present temporal gain, for future spiritual and eternal glory.

3. *Urge all to set out.*

4. *Believers to persevere, &c.*

87
JACOB WRESTLING WITH THE ANGEL

"And Jacob was left alone ; and there wrestled a man with him until the break of day. And when he saw that he prevailed not against him, he touched the hollow of his thigh ; and the hollow of Jacob's thigh was out of joint, as he wrestled with him."—GENESIS xxxii. 24, 25, &c.

THE patriarchs and early saints possessed not the valuable direction of a written revelation. In that early age there were none especially inspired either to teach or prophesy to the people. To make up for this, God often revealed himself to his saints, especially by visions and dreams of the night. Oftentimes too did Jehovah appear and discourse with them, assuming sometimes the form of a man, and at other times the appearance of an angel. Jacob was favored with two of these especial manifestations. At Bethel, where he saw the ladder reaching to heaven, and on the occasion to which the text refers. Notice,

I. THE CIRCUMSTANCES IN WHICH JACOB WAS PLACED.

II. HIS MYSTERIOUS CONFLICT.

III. HIS WONDROUS VICTORY.

IV. THE BLESSINGS BY WHICH IT WAS FOLLOWED.

I. THE CIRCUMSTANCES IN WHICH HE WAS PLACED.

1. *He was returning into his own country.* He left it through fear of his incensed brother. More than twenty years had passed over. His return was under God's direction, ver. 9. "In all thy ways acknowledge," &c. "Commit thy way," &c.

2. *His brother was announced as coming in wrath to meet him.* He had wisely and piously sent a message of kindness to Esau, v. 3, &c. ; but his resentment was aroused, and Jacob is informed of his hostility, &c., ver. 6.

3. *He had prudently arranged his temporal concerns.* His peril seemed awfully imminent. What could he do ? (ver. 7.)

4. *He had fervently poured out his soul to God.* He followed up all with earnest prayer. He pleaded God's promises, ver. 9 to 12. Having done this, he sent over the brook his flocks, and also his family.

5. *He was now enjoying devotional solitude.* "Alone," so far as mortal beings were concerned. "Alone," to press his suit with God. "Alone," to confess his

sins, and to open all his heart to the Lord. Notice,

II. HIS MYSTERIOUS CONFLICT. This conflict was mysterious indeed ; we have nothing like it on record. It was not merely mental. His body and soul were engaged ; but who was the glorious being, &c. " A man," says the text ; but in verse 28, he is said to have " power with God." See Hosea xii. 4, 5. None other than Jehovah Jesus. God in the appearance of humanity. God anticipating his incarnation, &c.

(1.) How unequal the conflict !

(2.) How protracted ! lasted for several hours.

(3.) To show the weakness of Jacob, and his own power, he touches him and disjoints the hollow of his thigh ; but still Jacob maintains the struggle.

(4.) He solicits permission to retire. " Let me go, for the day breaketh." How easily he could have done so ! but he honors Jacob's perseverance, and elicits his strongest faith. God will not oppose physical might to moral power. He allows moral influence to prevail.

(5.) Mark, Jacob resolves not to yield without the blessing. " I will not," &c. What pious valor, decision, energy, perseverance ! And now observe,

III. THE WONDROUS VICTORY HE ACHIEVED. God allows omnipotence to yield to the influence of faithful prayer. In token of the victory,

(1.) He obliterates his former name. No more Jacob, i. e. Supplanter, the sins and frailties of the past blotted out, see chapter xxvii. 34, &c.

(2.) A new name is given, " Israel," a name of honor and holy distinction. " One who has power with Jehovah," one who has prevailed with the divine majesty of heaven and earth. The title was one of great honor, and everlasting renown ; a name too which should descend to thousands of thousands, and to generations then unborn. Then notice,

IV. THE BLESSINGS BY WHICH IT WAS FOLLOWED. Verse 23. " And with men," &c. This victory was the assurance that men should not overcome or destroy him, the less victory would certainly follow the greater.

(1.) The mind of Jacob was filled with sublime yet sweet conceptions of God's glory. He called the place, " Peniel," &c.

(2.) He marvelled at his own preservation. " And my life is preserved."

(3.) The wrath of his brother was turned aside. His heart was in the Lord's hand, and he subdued and softened it. " If a man's ways please the Lord," &c.

(4.) He retained, however, the sense of his weakness. " He halted upon his thigh." Lest he should be exalted above measure. To keep him prostrate before the Lord, &c.

APPLICATION

1. *The marvellous potency of prayer.* How wondrous its achievements ! What hath it wrought ?

2. *The secret of its power is fervor.* Persevering fervor. What was emblemized by Jacob's wrestling ? Not fainting ; not ceasing ; but pleading, and pressing our suit. Let us long for, and seek the spirit of prayer, and the grace of supplication.

3. *Let the prayerless now see the value of prayer.*

88

PHARAOH AND JACOB

" And Pharaoh said unto Jacob, How old art thou ?"—GENESIS xlvii. 8, 9.

OUR text introduces us to one of the most striking scenes of Old Testament history. We have before us three distinguished individuals ; the monarch of Egypt ; the prime minister, raised by extraordinary providences from a captive to that exalted station ; and the devout Jacob ; the man who, as a holy prince, had power with men and with God, and who was named Israel because he prevailed. Joseph is introducing his venerable and beloved father to Pharaoh, who with affable condescension and kindness, thus addresses the hoary headed saint, " And Pharaoh said unto Jacob," &c. Let us consider the question, the reply, and the lessons it suggests.

I. THE QUESTION ASKED. " How old art thou ?" We observe this is,

1. *A very common question.* How often it has been asked in our hearing, of us, and from us to others ! We may generally form some idea, but not always correct, some persons look much younger. Read the account of Moses, Deut. xxxiv. 7. Also of Joshua, xiv. 10, &c. ; others look aged early—labor,

sorrow, constitutional weakness, afflictions, &c. Some become old early by emaciating sins, &c. The wicked often do not live out half their time.

2. *This question is interesting.* How marvellous is life! The wonder is that we live, not that we die. How mysteriously is life sustained, what pulsations! what inspirations and respirations of the lungs! how many vessels have to be acting so that the machinery may not stand still! as the poet says,

" Our life contains a thousand springs," &c.

besides, the dangers are so numerous, &c.

" Dangers stand thick through all the ground,
    To push us to the tomb;
And fierce diseases wait around,
    To hurry mortals home."

3. *This question is solemn and momentous.* It is connected with great responsibilities, mercies, privileges, opportunities, gratitude, improvement, and duties demanded; oh! weigh this, and then how momentous life becomes! But, also, because it is connected with eternity; our cradles rock us to the tomb; whatever we do, wherever we be, we are travelling to the grave; yes, and to eternity.

" Lo! on a narrow neck of land,
'Twixt two unbounded seas I stand," &c.

To elderly persons, how affecting this should be to you; the morning and the afternoon, the spring and the summer are gone, and the evening and the autumn are passing away. Observe in reference to this question,

II. THE ANSWER GIVEN.—Mark,

1. *The age specified.* 130 years, a very extended age, yet it was short when contrasted with his predecessors; his father Isaac lived 180, his grandfather 175, his great grandfather 205, and many of the antediluvians approached to 800 and 900 years; yet 130 to us appears very long. In the time of Moses, the great majority did not survive 70, and now a generation is computed at 30 years; these are statistics well worthy of our consideration.

2. *He represents his years as being few.* There is the most marked difference in past time and the future; how short a period is a year in the retrospect! Ask the aged, and they all agree, that a long life is as nothing; one says it is as yesterday, another says it is as a tale, &c., a mere vapor,

man's life is but as a shadow, a flitting cloud, &c.

3. *He describes his years as being evil.* That is, years of sorrow and affliction. Jacob's were so in many cases. His own private anxieties—exiled when a youth, servant for twenty years to his uncle, much domestic trouble. There stands the tomb of Rachel; then Joseph is in his opinion slain; his sons, some of them profligate others cruel, most of them ungodly. In his old age exposed to adversity through famine; he was the man who had seen trouble; fears within and fightings without; and this is a fair sample of human life; most of you know it. A wilderness — a rough sea—a perilous desert.

4. *He describes his whole life as a pilgrimage.* " The days of the years," &c. I like this form of speech. We should not forget that our years are formed of days; we cannot tell what a day may bring forth " So teach us to number our days," &c Altogether it is a pilgrimage. Incessant change—mutability itself—a continuou-progression. Not at home in the body " strangers," &c. Thus the saints have always felt. " They confessed," &c. Now let us notice,

III. THE LESSONS WHICH IT SUGGESTS.

1. *Let us form a true estimate of life.* It is short and sorrowful. Let us settle this in our minds, we shall then treat the world as such, and expect such treatment from it.

2. *Let us ascertain if the great ends of life are accomplished by us.* The ends for which we should live.

(1.) For ourselves. To secure our own salvation and spiritual improvement.

(2.) For the good of others, our families, the church, and the world.

(3.) For God. To glorify Him, to show forth our love and gratitude, &c. He formed us for this, &c.

3. *Let me ask the elderly if they are distinguished for the graces and virtues which should distinguish old age.* Should not such excel in knowledge, experience, patience, self-command, spiritual-mindedness, charity, &c., such should be ensamples and counsellors to the young, &c.

4. *Old age without piety is a fearful state.* Think of the sins of sixty or seventy years, of the abused blessings, and neglected privileges; what a mountain of guilt, &c. Travelling from God and heaven towards

perdition, how awful your influence on others, &c.

5. *The aged sinner may be forgiven.* God's patience yet waits, His mercy still lingers. The door is still open, but do not delay or trifle. Be intent, &c.

6. *May all present set out on the heavenly pilgrimage.*

89

ESAU

"Lest there be any fornicator, or profane person, as Esau, who for one morsel of meat sold his birthright," &c.—HEBREWS xii. 16, 17.

VERY much has been improperly said and inferred respecting Esau. By some he has been represented as the type of the abandoned, and as bearing the broad seal of God's eternal reprobation. Surely such forget, that by representing him as hated of God and predestined to wo, with all feeling minds they must enlist pity for his wretchedness, and sympathy on account of his doom. Thus reasoning, God has been greatly dishonored, and, in opposition to his solemn asseveration, he has been declared a respecter of persons. The literal scriptural account will vindicate Jehovah, and throw all the blame on Esau himself. Hating and loving, in the words of scripture, often signify ardent, and less devoted affection. Jesus says, "Except a man hate father and mother, wife and children," &c. So it is said, "God loved Jacob, and hated Esau." God's disapprobation of Esau was owing to the profanity of his character, and to that the text refers.

I. LET US LOOK AT ESAU'S PROFANE BARTER, AND CONSIDER THOSE WHO IMITATE HIS CONDUCT. Esau, as the first-born of Isaac, possessed many privileges, and was heir to many blessings. These privileges were two-fold.

1. *Temporal.*

(1.) He had pre-eminence of authority and power over the rest of the family.

(2.) He had a double portion of the paternal estate.

2. *Spiritual.*

(1.) From the first-born, before the law, descended the priesthood of the family.

(2.) Of him and his seed was the Messiah to spring.

(3.) He was first to receive the especial blessing of the father, which was uttered in the spirit of prophecy, and was associated with peculiar and precious promises. Now, this birthright he sold. The circumstances are given to us, Gen. xxv. 29, &c. Was not this an extremely foolish barter? To prefer one plain meal to his birthright? How can it be accounted for? It was the result,

1. *Of inconsideration.* He did not ponder and weigh the matter; he acted hastily, &c.

2. *Appetite was another cause.* So powerful that he could not restrain it until food was prepared, &c.

3. *An irreverent depreciation of spiritual things.* He held the birthright in low esteem; he was a worldly and carnal man. A small amount of piety would have given to it a high sense of value. He was deficient alike in personal piety towards God, and filial piety towards his father; the two are often wedded. Such was the profane barter; but many have acted as unwisely, and with equal profanity. Look at Gehazi, the servant of Elisha, who for a number of garments lied to Naaman and his master, and became the subject of a fearful leprosy; look at Judas, who for thirty pieces of silver, &c.; look at Ananias and Sapphira, who to retain a portion of their property, lied to the Holy Ghost; look at Herod, who dared to receive the flattering homage of the crowd, and was eaten up of worms. All these were bad bargains, equally with Esau's. Are there none here who are acting with equal profanity? Those who sell themselves for vanity; seek the applause of their fellow-creatures, &c.; make this their God. Those who sell themselves for money; for this will do any thing; they sacrifice truth, honesty, goodness, &c.; all is devoted to this, &c. Those who sacrifice themselves on the altar of pleasure; lovers of pleasure, &c. Those who exchange their souls for rioting and excess; in most cases these bargains are worse than that of Esau. He did obtain a good— a meal; he had his hunger alleviated; but how often the sinner receives evil, and evil only, for the fearful price he pays. We have more light than Esau had, &c. He regretted; but not so with many around us, &c. This leads us to notice,

II. ESAU'S UNAVAILING REPENTANCE. He evidently altered his mind—saw his folly— labored to undo the deed. He was very urgent, and sorrowful, and intent; but his repentance,

1. *Seems to have been carnal in its motives.* He regrets not his depravity; he acknowledges not his sin; he does not abase himself before God. Doubtless, the worldly part of the blessing was what he chiefly deplored.

2. *His repentance was too late.* The word was pronounced; Isaac could not recall it; the blessing was irrevocably transferred. Esau's repentance, I fear, is but too common in the stead of repentance unto life. We may exclude one sin for another; we may abandon a sin on account of its influence on our health, or reputation, or property; we may give up vices from necessity, not having the power of gratification; we may do so through sheer dread of future consequences, and not from dislike to the sin; we may alter our mind when it is too late; the conscience may become seared and callous; the Spirit may cease to strive; put it off till the door is shut. Many have wept on their death-beds in vain; many in the prison-house of hell, for " there is weeping, and wailing, and gnashing of teeth," &c. Then what is the application of the whole?

1. *Let me glance at your condition.* You have an immortal spirit of amazing powers, &c.; you are responsible to God; you are sinful, exposed to death, but redeemed. Christ has opened a way of life. The gospel reveals it, &c. You can accept, or reject.

2. *Let me glance at your duty and interest.* Now to accept of the blessing of salvation. This year, though nearly finished; this night, though almost ended; by earnest prayer and faith turn to the Lord. Let the soul's salvation be preferred to all things.

3. *Let me exhort you in reference to the sins and dangers of this season.** Now is a time of peculiar danger, frivolity, mirth, carousing, indolence, &c. Oh! be on your guard, especially you young persons. You who have made a Christian profession, let your consistent conduct reprove and silence gainsayers.

90
THE CHOICE OF MOSES

" By faith Moses, when he was come to years, refused to be called the son of Pharaoh's daughter; choosing rather to suffer affliction with the

---
* Preached during Christmas festivities.

people of God, than to enjoy the pleasures of sin for a season. Esteeming the reproach of Christ greater riches than the treasures in Egypt; for he had respect unto the recompense of the reward."—HEBREWS xi. 24-26.

AMONG all the illustrious Old Testament saints, Moses occupies the most dignified and promising place. His whole life was one of signal and illustrious events. The impression that he made at his birth, by his captivating beauty, so that his parents resolved to save him, not fearing the edict and wrath of the king; his amazing preservation, when floating in the fragile ark on the waters of the Nile; his favorable reception into the palace of Pharaoh, under the auspices of the king's daughter; his amazing privilege of obtaining learning and influence in the court of royalty; but now we no longer watch the workings of providence for him, but we see him also operating with that providence, and taking his stand with his afflicted countrymen after the flesh. There were many then living who might sway the sceptre of Egypt, but probably only one in all things fit to be the emancipator and ruler over Israel. To this our direct attention is called, " By faith," &c. You are aware how the Israelites entered Egypt during the time of Joseph; how they multiplied, so as to become an immense people; how they were cruelly entreated and oppressed by their tyrannic taskmasters; how their increase was attempted to be bounded by the destruction of their male children; and now the crisis of deliverance is drawing near. Moses is to be the great agent in God's hand. " And by faith," &c. Observe,

I. THE CHOICE MOSES MADE.
II. THE THINGS MOSES SACRIFICED.
III. THE TIME IN WHICH HE MADE THIS CHOICE AND SACRIFICE. And,
IV. THE GREAT PRINCIPLE BY WHICH HE WAS ACTUATED.

I. THE CHOICE MOSES MADE. He chose,
1. *The condition of his afflicted countrymen.* Men generally aspire to the society and circle of those above them; men generally choose the society of the affluent and influential, or of the intellectual and cultivated. His countrymen were poor, in the lowest walks of life; they were slaves in the direst bondage; they were treated as the refuse of the nation. Not noble after the world's reckoning; not rich; not walk-

ing in the paths of honor, or literature, or science ; but slaves groaning in bondage ; yet he chose them—became one with them ; as he could not at once raise them to earthly dignity, he descended step by step, and became their friend, and companion, and brother. Before you censure Moses, do not forget they were the people of God ; the objects of God's smile, and love, and care ; and were destined to act a more remarkable part in the drama of the world's history than any other nation under heaven.

2. *He chose religious reproach.* "The reproach of Christ." Literally, of the Messiah. The Israelites were the descendants of Abraham, and Isaac, and Jacob. Unto them God had promised to send the Messiah. These prophecies and promises they cherished ; in them they trusted ; for these they hoped. No doubt their services and conversation respected the coming of the Messiah ; and for this belief and worship they were reproached. The Egyptians were idolaters, ignorant of the true God ; therefore the Israelites were despised, and reviled, and scorned, and treated as fools and fanatics. True fervid piety has ever thus been treated. But the reproach of Christ, is it not better than to be reproached by God, or the reproach of conscience ? Now this was the choice of Moses. Observe,

II. THE THINGS MOSES SACRIFICED. Now by these we are to determine the heroism, the patriotism, the piety of the act. He was not shut up to the condition of the Israelites, or to the reproach of Christ ; he had worldly glory, wealth, and pleasure at his command.

1. *He sacrificed the dignity of a prince.* He had been the adopted of royalty ; but he severed the connection, and refused to be called the son of Pharaoh's daughter ; he traced his lineage back to Israel, and to that stock, though now in poverty and oppression, he adhered. Survey the contrast ; a prince-royal—and a slave. Yet he despised the one, with all its authority and glittering show, and preferred the other. A sceptre did not fire his ambitious eye ; a throne did not absorb his thoughts ; a crown did not elicit his desires.

2. *He sacrificed the riches of royalty.* Egypt at that time was one of the oldest and wealthiest monarchies ; her coffers were full of treasures ; as a royal prince, they were within his grasp ; but the golden

dust of the nation, the crowns and diadems of the court, corrupted not his soul, nor fascinated his heart.

3. *He sacrificed the pleasures of a palace.* And what sensual enjoyments were not within his reach ? What could mind devise, or heart desire, or imagination conceive, which were not at his hand ? These pleasures of sin formed the atmosphere of his royal residence ; these flowers of enjoyment grew at his feet ; these retreats of gratification were ever at his command ; but he magnanimously, and in the fear of his God, sacrificed the whole. Observe,

III. THE TIME AT WHICH HE MADE THIS CHOICE AND SACRIFICE. "When he was come to years." He was now forty years of age ; in the very prime and vigor of life. It was not, therefore, a mad eccentricity of youth, much less the cynical declaration of old age, satiated with enjoyment ; but when he could best reason upon the value both of his choice and sacrifice. He had long enjoyed the dignities and the honors of royalty ; he was now nearer to the climax of earthly glory ; he was now possessed of sufficient experience to determine with wisdom, &c. ; his resolution and conduct we have placed before you. Well may we inquire, therefore, as to,

IV. THE GREAT PRINCIPLES BY WHICH HE WAS ACTUATED. These are placed in the text :—

1. *Faith.* "By faith," &c. He believed to be of the seed of Abraham was truer dignity, than to be the son of a pagan princess ; he believed to be one of God's poor people was more exalted, than to be the sovereign of an idolatrous nation ; he believed to be the reproached, as one hoping in the Messiah, was better than to enjoy the smiles and plaudits of the courtiers of a palace ; he had faith in God, as a true God, and in the Messiah he had promised. Another principle,

2. *Was sanctified self-interest.* "He had respect," &c. He knew of the prophecies and promises connected with the faith and service of God. Now, this faith weighed the grandeur of the honors, and riches, and enjoyments of Egypt in the right scale ; and he found it better for him thus to choose, and thus to sacrifice. Egypt's royal honors and treasures were but for a season ; the short span of life ; evanescent ; "For the fashion of this world," &c. He saw, too, that poverty and reproach, &c., were

also very transient ; but he saw the rewards of faithful obedience to Christ as having reference to heaven, and to eternity ; that they were celestial and everlasting ; " He, therefore, had respect," &c.

APPLICATION

1. *I ask, was his choice wise ?* I appeal to the honors he had on earth ; I appeal to the communications of heaven ; to the revelation of the divine glory ; to Pisgah's top ; to the heaven of heavens. Nearly 4000 years have transpired since the decease of Moses ; where are the honors, treasures, and enjoyments of Egypt ? Where the renowned Moses ?

2. *Then imitate his conduct.*

3. *Act upon the same principles.*

4. *And ensure the same high reward.*

91

THE BURNING BUSH, AN EMBLEM OF THE CHURCH

" And the angel of the Lord appeared unto him in a flame of fire, out of the midst of a bush : and he looked, and behold, the bush burned with fire, and the bush was not consumed."—Exodus iii. 2.

Our text relates to a series of wonderful persons and events : Moses, the great Jewish lawgiver, and deliverer of the children of Israel ; an Angel, yet not one of the ordinary intelligences, but obviously the uncreated and ever-blessed Son of God, verse 4 ; an interesting phenomenon — a bush enveloped in flame, and yet unconsumed ; that phenomenon symbolizing the condition and preservation of the seed of Abraham, who were now enduring the sore and grievous oppression of Pharaoh in Egypt, and yet by the providence of God were sustained and preserved. But we have selected the text with a view to its application to the church of God in all ages, and desire to ground upon it the following propositions :—

I. The true church of God is not associated with earthly grandeur and magnificence. What is the emblem in the text ? The lofty oak—the towering cedar ? no ; the bramble bush, of apparently mean and low appearance. Nothing in it to please the eye ; nothing to fascinate the imagination ; nothing to attract the notice of the intellectual and great. But what is God's church ? Why, what it ever has been, and must be—the body of those who believe in God, and obey him. Now wherever these are found, in whatever class of society or nation, they are the true church of God. Of course, there never has been a nation of such ; and therefore never, in the true sense of the term, a national church of God. Now, the truly and sincerely pious have ever formed the minority of any and every sectional denomination, and as such, have always been among the despised and contemned of the human family. Ask the opinion of the world respecting this pure, unsophisticated, spiritual piety, and they laugh at it, deride it ; ask the nominal members of the visible church ; they despise them, and look with contempt upon them as fanatics, puritans, and righteous overmuch. Few of the members of the church of Jesus are found in king's houses ; few in the mansions of the noble ; few among the great and renowned of this world. Even yet the church of God is a little flock, and appearing to the eye of sense as one of the things that are not. The present position of the church is like that of the bush in the desert. Where was this marvellous phenomenon seen ? Not in heaven ; not in Eden ; but in the desert. Behold the sterility and dreariness, and see the moral aspect of the world ; behold the dangers of the desert from beasts of prey, and awful storms, and see the imminent perils which surround the earth in which we live. But allow me to remark, that the church of God is in this world for the world's advantage. The church of Christ is the very conservation of the world. It bears it up ; life-boat ; hospital for its morally diseased ; illumines it with the light of hope, and by its sanctifying influence shall finally make it to bud and blossom as the rose ; see Isaiah xxxv. 1, &c.

II. The condition of the church has ever been that of trial and suffering. It was planted amidst persecution ; and was not one of its earliest members a martyr to the envious feelings of his brother ? Behold it afterwards assailed with the ridicule of the old world ; then riding on the bosom of the waters of the deluge ; then mourning under the despotic decree in Egypt ; afterwards in captivity by the waters of Babylon ; now emerging into notice beneath the wings of the Sun of Righteousness, but immediately hated and persecuted to the death of the Messiah; after the death of Christ, apostles, confessors, and unnumbered hosts of its disciples, moistening the very soil of the world with their blood; passing through ten fiery persecutions, until hell had exhausted its resources of torment, and the world appeared one vast aceldama, or field of human gore. But allow me to refer to one peculiar and fearful instance of suffering to which the church of God has been exposed. No sooner was the Christian religion secularized, than it became the instrument of torture and oppression. Liberty of conscience was assailed; spiritual purity despised; and the best and worthiest of its members galled and injured by those in the earthly ascendency. What myriads have been persecuted to the death by papal Rome! The woman of Babylon is dyed scarlet with the blood of the martyred saints! Every state church has been a persecuting church. How was it that the rivers of Scotland became like the crimsoned Nile of Egypt? By prelacy, which was thrust upon the people at the point of the bayonet, and by the mouth of the cannon. What has been the state of conscientious Nonconformists in England? In 1662, two thousand ministers were ejected on St. Bartholomew's day from the church of England, because they could not assent and consent to every thing in the Book of Common Prayer. An act was passed, that no man should hold an office of civil trust, unless he took the sacrament at the church of England; another act, that no congregation of more than five adults should meet for worship except in the church of England; another, that no minister should live within five miles of a borough or city, and that schools should not be taught except by ministers of the church of England. During the reign of Charles II., eight thousand persons died in prison, and from that period to the restoration, fifty-two thousand more. Pagans have persecuted the church of God; Mahometans have done so; the world has done so; but not all together a hundredth part with the persecution that has been exercised by the dominant party over the sects who could not conform to her principles and forms. How has humanity thus been disgraced—religion rendered odious to the heathen—skepticism confirmed! How have demons rejoiced, and, if possible, angels wept! What a book of martyrs will be opened in the day of doom! What a scroll of lamentation, sorrow, and wo will then be spread before an assembled world!

III. THE CHURCH OF GOD HAS WITHIN IT THE ELEMENT OF PERPETUITY. "Not burnt." Not consumed. Look at this,

1. *As a striking fact.* Is it not so? How wonderfully the church of God flourished in Egypt—has flourished in all ages; the fire has purified, but never consumed. It has survived all opposition; has had earth and hell against it; and yet lives, yet prospers; the gates of hell have not prevailed, &c.

2. *For this there is a sufficient reason.* God was in the bush; he spake out of it. This is the secret of its life and perpetuity. His wisdom has baffled the counsel of the wicked; his arm supported the church; he took away the consuming principle from the fire; made the wrath to praise him, &c., Psalm xlvi. 1, &c. Where are the enemies of the church of God? Where Pharaoh? Balak? Herod? Where the Roman emperors? Where Julian? Where the judges of the Inquisition? Where the officers of the Star Chamber? Where the impious Bonner? the iron-hearted Jeffries? Where are they all? Gone down to the grave with infamy! "So let all thine enemies perish, O God!" &c. But where is the church? Living—prospering—growing; extending its boughs to the South Seas—to Australia—to China; and is destined to become a universal praise throughout all the earth.

APPLICATION

1. *Understand the nature of Christ's church.*

2. *Abhor persecution.* Value and hold sacred all the precious boon of liberty of conscience.

3. *Look to Jehovah for success.* He can help, and he will; he ever has done so.

4. *Sympathize with the persecuted and the tried.* The true church is yet exposed to suffering; as in France, Switzerland, Scotland, &c.

92

THE MYSTERIOUS PILLAR

"And the Lord went before them by day in a pillar of cloud, to lead them the way; and by night in a pillar of fire, to give them light; to go by day and night."—EXODUS xiii. 21.

THE dispensation of Moses was a dispensation of miracles; the manifestation of God to Moses was miraculous, when he revealed himself to him in the burning bush; it was by successive miracles God compelled Pharaoh to let the Israelites depart from Egypt; and the history of Israel, from leaving Egypt to entering Canaan, was but one chain of wonderful events. This morning we select one of these divine manifestations for the subject of our meditation. " And the Lord went before," &c. Let us consider it,

I. LITERALLY AS A DIVINE INTERPOSITION ON BEHALF OF THE ISRAELITES.

1. *The pillar of cloud was miraculous, or supernatural.* It was not a common cloud, but the cloud of the divine presence; that which veiled from them the grandeur and overwhelming glory of God. God has generally thus shrouded himself, when he has held audience with his people. It overspread the mountain; it filled the holiest place in the tabernacle; it covered the mercy-seat; it filled the temple, &c. So it was now the symbol of God's presence with his people.

2. *It was the constant and infallible guide of Israel.* Hence its appearance was altered to suit the alternate seasons of day and night. It never left them; no, not for a moment. By day, it was a *cloud;* by night, as a pillar of *fire.* God is an ever present and ever suitable help to his people. He is with his people at all times, and under all circumstances. Day of prosperity, night of adversity; day of health, and night of affliction; day of life, and night of death.

3. *This pillar was the defence of Israel.* Hence, when in peril from the Egyptian host, instead of being in front of the camp of Israel, it removed and went behind, and intervened between them and their enemies. All our security is of God. We should have no might against our foes, if the arm of the Lord was not on our side. See the sufficiency of the defence; the omnipotent Deity. Before the Egyptians could have injured Israel, they must have overcome Jehovah. Well might the church sing, "The Lord is on our side, therefore we will not fear," &c. "The Lord of hosts is with us," &c.

4. *The pillar of cloud and fire was the joy and confidence of Israel.* How delightful to know that God was for them; to have with them the token and sign of his presence. Nothing can be equal to a sense of the gracious presence of God. If so, I cannot err—I cannot faint—I cannot be destroyed; all must be well. The form of the cloud was calculated to produce this confidence. It was a pillar; not like other clouds. There was the appearance of order and arrangement, of firmness and stability. The providence of God is subservient to the designs of grace, &c.

5. *The pillar of cloud, &c., was the oracle of the Israelites.* From thence came the voice of God to Moses, verses 15–26. See Exodus xxxiii. 9. Now this clearly shows us, that if we are to secure the guidance and protection of God, we must hearken to the voice of the Lord; we must obey the word of the Lord. Now, God no longer speaks to us from the cloud; but the apostle says, " We have a more sure word of prophecy," &c. 2 Peter i. 19. Let us consider the pillar, &c.,

II. AS TYPICAL OF THE LORD JESUS CHRIST.

1. *It typified the constitution of Christ's person.* Symbol of God's presence; in it dwelt the Deity; it was the garment of Jehovah. So God came to us in the person of Jesus. " His name shall be called Immanuel." " God with us." " And the word was made flesh," &c. Now, the cloud was the emblem of Christ's body; hence " God was manifest in the flesh."

2. *It typified Christ's redeeming work.* The pillar of cloud was connected with the deliverance of Israel, and the overthrow of their enemies. " So Jesus came to save his people," &c. One exceedingly appropriate passage, Luke i. 68–72. In doing this, he delivered us from the bondage of iniquity, &c. He also came that " he might destroy the works of the devil." Observe,

3. *It typified Christ as the light and guide of mankind.* Jesus is described as a " light," &c. He said, " I am the light of the world." He came to reveal the way to God—the way to heaven. He marked the path through this world to eternal glory. So fully he did this, that he said, " I am the way," &c.

4. *It typified Christ's glorious presence with his church.* When his church was sent forth in the persons of the apostles and disciples, he said, " Lo! I am with you," &c. And to the church he is all and in

all. He guides—protects—cheers; he is its glory, and its defence; he is the oracle of the church. God says to his people, "Hear ye him." The word and ordinances are the signs of his presence.

APPLICATION

1. *Let the subject greatly encourage the people of God.* Christ is with you. He will never leave; he will conduct to glory. Believe, love, and obey him.

2. *He is the only director to glory and eternal life.*

93

MANOAH AND HIS WIFE

"And Manoah said unto his wife, We shall surely die, because we have seen God," &c.— JUDGES xiii. 22, 23.

BEFORE the time of Moses and the prophets, God often manifested himself to the patriarchs, by appearing in the form of a man, or by visions of the night; afterwards, these supernatural appearances became more rare. A few visits, however, are recorded. Among these is the striking instance to which the text refers; see verse 3, &c. This vision was repeated, verse 8, &c. It is obvious from the name assumed, that this angel of the Lord was the Son of God, his name being "Secret, or Wonderful." We see in this subject an exhibition of weak faith and gloomy fears; and of strong faith and cheering hope.

I. WE SEE THE EXHIBITION OF WEAK FAITH AND GLOOMY FEARS. "We shall surely die," &c. Here Manoah was evidently bound by the fetters of a superstition, which has prevailed in all ages, that supernatural appearances were premonitions of death. We do not marvel that sinful beings should be agitated and alarmed. There was a time when angels conversed with our first sire, and when our parents held joyous communion with God; but sin dissolved the fellowship, and clothed man with the garment of sin, and shame, and fear. Where unbelief reigns, or where faith is feeble, a view of the divine character and glory is calculated to overwhelm the soul if you,

1. *Contemplate the divine holiness, and our own pollution.* God spotless; man depraved. "From the crown of the head," &c. Contemplate,

2. *The divine justice, and man's guilt.*

One swaying a sceptre of righteous, impartial equity; and man laden with guilt, his sins crying for vengeance.

3. *The divine truth, and our excuseless condition.* The edict has been declared, that "The soul that sinneth shall die." Shall God lie, or the sinner be punished?

4. *The divine ability and our helplessness.* God has power to execute all he has said. If he resolve, we cannot escape.

5. *The divine conduct in reference to the guilty, and our equal guiltiness.* He has stepped forth to punish; he has whet his glittering sword; he has poured his vengeance—and why not upon us? Why should we escape? Now, in all these points weak faith reasons, and that plausibly, against itself. "We shall surely die," &c. Let us now turn our attention to the display,

II. OF STRONG FAITH AND CHEERING HOPE. "But his wife said," &c. Now here we see the very opposite reasoning and inferences from the same premises and facts. The reasoning of Manoah's wife refers to three particulars:—

1. *She concludes favorably, from the acceptance of their sacrifice.* "If the Lord," &c. Now, the acceptance of the offering was evidently a token for good. It has been so in all generations; it was so with Abel, &c. Now, the Christian may reason thus, from two important considerations:—

(1.) From God's acceptance of Christ's sacrifice. All previous ones derived their virtue from this. Christ has presented an effectual and all-efficient one. "It speaks better things," &c. This the Christian pleads, and from this derives his hope.

(2.) From God's acceptance of us through this sacrifice. "The sacrifices of God," &c. Now, the Christian has presented this; he has laid himself on the sacred altar; "God has mercifully heard and accepted," &c.; but if he had resolved to destroy, he would have accepted neither.

2. *She concludes favorably, from the revelation he had made.* This to her was a most interesting revelation, and it was evidently one of great favor. Now, thus the Christian also may reason. God has revealed his mind to us, and it is emphatically a revelation of mercy and hope; a revelation of grace and compassion. The scriptures were given that we might have abundant consolation, and good hope.

3. *She reasoned favorably, from the promise which the angel gave ;* verse 5. Now, the revelation which God has given us is also one of great and precious promises; and these promises all meet in Jesus Christ, the great deliverer, and are all yea and amen, &c. Our deliverance from evil, by his power and grace, is the leading promise, and is associated with a series of promises referring both to time and eternity. Now, surely these are striking evidences that God does not mean to destroy us.

APPLICATION

1. *That the germ of religion is confidence towards God.* To believe his love to us; to receive it; to trust in it; venture our souls fully on it. This is the province of faith. How desirable, therefore, that it should be strong and vigorous!

2. *We often see striking displays of Christian confidence and courage, where we least expect to see them.* We should have expected strong faith in Manoah. He should have been the shield to his wife's fears, &c. ; the stronger vessel; but morally he is the weaker, and his wife has to reason away his fears and dread. This is not the only instance. We see the like in the holy women who dared to go with Christ to the cross, &c. Priscilla, in concert with her husband, undertook to teach even the eloquent Apollos the way of the Lord more perfectly.

3. *Have we a lively and cheering hope in the mercy of God, through Christ Jesus ?* Let me urge this upon you. How necessary this is! We preach to you for this. Do you feel this? Have you confidence in God's love ?

94
BOAZ AND RUTH

" And Boaz answered and said unto her, It hath fully been showed me, all that thou hast done unto thy mother-in-law since the death of thine husband ; and how thou hast left thy father and thy mother, and the land of thy nativity, and art come unto a people which thou knewest not heretofore. The Lord recompense thy work, and a full reward be given thee of the Lord God of Israel, under whose wings thou art come to trust."—RUTH ii. 11, 12.

IN the days of the judges of Israel, a man of the name of Elimelech, with his wife Naomi, went to reside in the land of Moab in consequence of the famine which prevailed in Bethlehem Judah. During his residence there, his two sons married with the daughters of Moab ; the name of one of these was Ruth, the person addressed in the text. It came to pass in this mutable and dying state of things, that both Elimelech and his two sons died, and thus Naomi, Ruth, and Orpah were left to exclaim, in the bitterness of the grief of widowhood, " Lover and friend thou hast put far from us, and our acquaintance," &c. Naomi determined to return to her own people, and Ruth, who evinced the deepest affection for her, resolved to accompany her. When Ruth was advised to act as her sister-in-law had done, she exclaimed, " Entreat me not to leave thee," &c. i. 16. Ruth did accompany her, and her kindness had been made known to Boaz, a rich and near kinsman with whom she had now her first interview, and who thus addressed her in the text. " It hath fully," &c. We design to accommodate the subject to those who abandon the world and unite themselves with the church of God. Observe,

I. THE ABANDONMENT. She had forsaken her country and friends. Every believer in the day of his conversion must do the same. We must abandon,

1. *Our original state and condition.* Metaphorically we are said to be far from God. Aliens—outcasts, ready to perish. We are in the region of the shadow of death. On the dark mountains of iniquity. Now, like the prodigal our steps must be retraced. We must not remain in the land of rebellion, in the enemy's country. Like Abraham, we must come out, &c. Like Ruth, we must take our departure.

2. *We must abandon associates and friends.* " And hast left thy father," &c. We cannot be confidential bosom companions of the ungodly, and yet love and serve God. The friend of the world is the enemy of God. Religion is entirely personal. A man must be so for himself; he cannot take his acquaintances with him, and therefore must go without them; he cannot take his family ; mother, wife, &c. Suppose Ruth had tried this ; her efforts would have been vain, they did not see as she did, nor feel as she did. We must not therefore wait for others, but be in earnest for ourselves. When one wanted to go and bid adieu to friends, Christ said, " If any man love," &c. So when one wanted to bury his father, he said, " Let the dead," &c. Now we observe,

(1.) That this abandonment is difficult. It is not congenial to flesh and blood; it is therefore represented as a sacrifice. "Present yourselves," &c. "Strive to enter in," &c. And it is so difficult that we notice,

(2.) It can only be done by faith. Abraham did it by faith; so doubtless did Ruth. Faith recognises the peril of our state, the necessity of repentance, &c. A faith losing sight of present pleasure and riches, for future pleasures, and enduring treasures of righteousness. By faith Moses did thus. Consider minutely his case. Observe,

II. The choice. "And art come unto a place," &c. Now in choosing the people of God for our people we resolve,

1. *To conform to their maxims and habits.* To walk with them; to unite with them in their duties; to adopt their costume; to speak their language, and to be incorporated with them in all their services and engagements. We resolve,

2. *To share their burdens and perils.* This is the end of society, to sympathize and aid each other. "Bear ye one," &c. Thus it is in the body, the hand assists the foot, &c. Thus Ruth had identified herself with Naomi; now this can only be done by cherishing a liberal and benevolent spirit, feeling our kindredness, &c. This choice may properly include,

3. *A desire to participate of their various blessings.* If Ruth resolved to leave all for Naomi, why not enjoy Naomi's advantages? "We will go with you," &c. Yes, and we say to those who are without, "Come with us," &c. There is no monopoly in spiritual blessings, there is bread enough and to spare. We do not envy the new convert the fatted calf, &c. Notice,

III. The prayer. "The Lord recompense thee," &c. We ought to pray for one another; especially for young converts. Now this prayer is,

1. *Very comprehensive.* "Recompense." "A full reward." The blessings of the God of Israel were princely; satisfying; delighting the soul; inconceivably precious. God oftentimes gives a recompense in kind; he did so to Ruth; he did so to Job; at any rate they shall have the principal, and a hundred-fold interest in the world to come. This prayer is,

2. *Certain in its realization.* The Lord can fulfil it; he will fulfil it. His nature disposes him; his promises pledge him. His Son intercedes, &c.

3. *This prayer was connected with a congratulatory declaration of safety.* "Under whose wings," &c. How checkered is the dream of life, and how exposed is man to danger! God is the pavilion, &c. Our rock, and fortress. Under his wings we may indeed trust; here is comfort and security. Who will harm you? &c. "The Lord God is a sun and shield," &c.

APPLICATION

1. *How desirable that providential visitations should be sanctified!* The death of Ruth's husband was the means of her uniting with God's people.

2. *How necessary to cherish and perfect good desires!* She thought, resolved, acted. Have you done so?

3. *Decision in religion will have its reward.* "As long as he sought the Lord," &c.

95

ELIJAH'S SINFUL FLIGHT

" But he himself went a day's journey into the wilderness, and came and sat down under a juniper tree : and he requested for himself that he might die," &c.—1 Kings xix. 4.

Nothing is calculated to edify us more than an acquaintance with the experience of saints who have gone before, and who, having borne the burden and heat of the day, have entered into rest. We are exhorted " to be followers," &c., but how can it be, unless we are intimate with their history, and study their character? Elijah was a very illustrious servant of God. His life is full of the marvellous, and we wonder how persons, who have received a religious education, can prefer the reading of works of mere fiction to the astonishing facts recorded in the prophet's life. Our subject, however, presents him to our notice under unfavorable circumstances. His sun at this time, if not eclipsed, is overcast with dark and intercepting clouds. To profit by the theme the text supplies, let us inquire,

I. What was the state of mind he displayed. We perceive a display,

1. *Of great fear.* The preceding chapter relates his signal triumph on mount Carmel. It details the extraordinary success of prayer—the prayer of Elijah. The heavens, which had been as brass, nad sent down refreshing rain on the previous dry and

parched earth; but now he is unnerved, his courage fails, his heart sinks, his spirit drops. At what? At the oath of the impious Jezebel. Read from the first verse to the text—he who stood before four hundred and fifty idolatrous priests, and had commanded them to be slain, as you will see in the fortieth verse of the previous chapter, now begins to fear, and manifests the utmost dread.

2. *We observe manifest impatience.* He is evidently fretting himself. His spirit is ruffled—the equilibrium is lost—the nicely poised balance of feeling is deranged, and his whole demeanor indicates haste, restlessness, and rashness. Doubtless he was weary and exhausted by his journey, but to give himself up to haste, was decidedly wrong. How necessary is self-government and self-possession! How delightful in patience to possess our souls—to be passive in the hands of Deity! Elijah had previously displayed amazing perseverance, but faith and patience seem now both to fail.

3. *He presented an unhallowed prayer to Deity.* Many have supposed that he had had intimations of his translation, but being now out of humor with his condition, says, "I forego the superior transit, let me die," &c. We do not say that this desire is always unhallowed. Paul said, "he had rather depart," &c. The mariner may wish for the haven, the prisoner for liberty, the traveller for his home; but it is not right to desire, except in deference to God's will; rather with Job, say piously even in great suffering, "I will wait," &c., than seek it by prayers not authorized. We have no such directions. No promise to such a prayer. Elijah had much to experience, much to teach, and much to do, before his labors could terminate. Let us, then,

II. ENDEAVOR TO ACCOUNT FOR IT. We do this on the ground of human infirmity, infirmities which attach to the good, and the holy, and eminently pious. Elijah was a moral sun, and yet there are spots upon the sun. We have no spotless examples but one, who, though he was made sin for us, yet knew no sin. It is amazing, too, that the failings of pious men have ever been in those points of character for which they were most eminent. Look at Abraham, ingenuous, implicitly trusting in God, and yet concealing the truth respecting Sarah to Pharaoh, and who fell into the same sin precisely with Abimelech after-

wards. Look at Lot, whose righteous soul was vexed, &c.; and yet in solitude became the victim of sin, and that sin incest. Look at Moses, the meekest man; see his condemnation of the evil spirit of his countrymen, and yet the sin that excluded him from the land of promise, was rashness and impetuosity. Look at David, the man of inward purity,—after God's own heart, and yet he falls into the polluted snare of sensuality. Look at Peter, the heroic disciple who avows his resolution to live and die with Christ, yet first follows afar off, and then denies, &c. Look at John, the loving disciple, yet he was one who prayed that fire from heaven might consume the Samaritans, because they received them not. Now these were not mere accidents, but a continuous series of proofs that good men may not only fail, but fail in the very things for which they are pre-eminent. This may arise,

(1.) From too much self-confidence. We fear this or that sin, but feel assured that we shall not fall into others. And this,

(2.) Causes unwatchfulness. Our excellencies and virtues require watching. We are vulnerable all over. No part can be left unguarded with safety. Let us consider,

III. HOW WE MAY IMPROVE BY IT.

1. *It should lead us to diligent self-examination and circumspection.* Prove ourselves, &c. Try to ascertain our real state. Be faithful, &c. Be jealous, &c. Take heed to our spirit and temper, &c. Oh, yes! on the temporary defection of Elijah, it is written, "Let him that thinketh he standeth, take heed lest he fall."

2. *It shows the importance of continually depending on the grace of God.* His grace is sufficient. Not our knowledge, or talents, or graces, or experience, &c. He is to us God all-sufficient, &c.

3. *It points out the value of Christian magnanimity.* "Add to your faith, virtue, or courage." "The fear of man bringeth a snare." How necessary are holy resolutions! "Be strong, quit yourselves like men." "Be strong in the Lord," &c. How happy when, like Joshua and Caleb, we can be vigorous and hopeful; or, like the three Hebrew worthies, and Daniel, firm and invincible; or, like those described by the apostle, who accepted not deliverance, that they might obtain a better resurrection.

4. *It may console Christians when bowed down by a sense of their infirmities.* Our adversary suits his wiles to our circumstances and feelings. When confident, he would incite us to presumption—when depressed, he would sink us to despondency. Let feeble saints remember Elijah, and not be swallowed up with sorrow, and especially Elijah's God, who is as pitiful as ever, who knows our infirmities, and remembers that we are but dust.

Finally, *Our subject shows us the worth and propriety of that prayer,* "Hold thou me up, and I shall be safe."

96

ELISHA'S ENEMIES AND GUARD

" And when the servant of the man of God was risen," &c.—2 Kings vi. 15–17.

THE faithful servants of God in all ages have been hated, and often put to death on account of the obnoxious messages they have had to deliver to the enemies of Jehovah. How great must have been the wrath of Pharaoh when Moses delivered to him the demands of God, in reference to his oppressed and suffering people ; but he feared not the wrath of the great king, &c. So you remember how Elijah was called to deliver the most unwelcome truths to Ahab and Jezebel, but in the fear and strength of God he dared to do it. This has been the command of God, that they must declare faithfully his truths, whether men will hear or forbear. Elisha had been fulfilling his prophetical duties faithfully in reference to the king of Syria, and he came therefore with horses and chariots, against the man of God. Elisha's servant, having risen early, beheld the warlike host, and came to his master, saying, "Alas !" &c. And he answered, "Fear not," &c. Let us consider several propositions, by which the text may be rendered instructive and edifying.

I. THE PEOPLE OF GOD ARE SURROUNDED BY A HOST OF ENEMIES. The aspect of those seen in the text was exceedingly terrible. "A host," &c. Their appearance too was warlike and formidable, " horses and chariots." I take no notice on this occasion of the enemies within, the legion of doubts and fears, &c. Nor of our adversaries in the world. " Marvel not that the world hateth you." But there is a host of fallen spirits ; Satan and the powers of darkness. We wrestle not with flesh and blood, but with principalities and powers, and spiritual wickedness in high places. The leader of this host of spiritual foes, is described as our adversary ; the destroyer, the prince of darkness—the devil ; he is likened to a roaring lion, &c. He is in league with all the fallen spirits to do evil, to war against God and to destroy souls. There are several features in this host of malevolent spirits of an awful kind.

1. *Their invisibility.* Not observed by our eyes. May injure us unnoticed ; may direct all their missiles unperceived.

2. *Their power and energy.* Angels excel in strength ; fallen spirits doubtless possess it in an awful degree. In the case of Job, by a great wind they smote the four corners of the house, so that it fell to the ground ; in the case of bodily possessions, how it brought to extreme wretchedness and misery those who were its victims !

3. *Restlessness and activity.* It is probable, that as spirits, they weary not, know nothing of fatigue ; so that they can keep up incessant hostility. Then there is,

4. *Their extreme malevolence and hatred to us.* Inspired with deepest envy ; full of bitter hate and wrath ; longing to destroy and tear to pieces ; desiring to blot out all excellency, and involve in misery, black and hopeless as their own, all the creatures of God.

5. *Their access to the mind is another fearful faculty they possess.* They can act upon the understanding, judgment, imagination, passions, &c. This is clearly expressed when in reference to wrath, &c., we are called not to give place to the devil.

Finally. *There is their number.* It has been conjectured that the countless myriads of the redeemed are destined to occupy their vacated thrones. The poet has said in reference to them,

" They throng the air, they darken heaven,
    And crowd this lower world."

What a fearful enemy ! We remark,

II. THAT A CONTEMPLATION OF THIS ADVERSE HOST IS CALCULATED TO PRODUCE FEAR. And his servant said, " Alas ! my master, how shall we do ?" &c. Our fears may arise,

1. *From a sense of our own weakness.* Our knowledge cannot grapple with their intelligence and craftiness ; our power of resistance with their deadly missiles. The lamb is not more unable to combat the lion, or the dove the vulture, than man these evil foes. How shall we do ?

2. *From a conviction of our tendency to evil.* They worsted our parents in their original purity. How inferior our ability! We have the very seeds of evil within us. Much ignorance, and error, and unbelief, and superstition, and fear, and passion. Their fiery darts ignite these elements of sin. We have traitors within the citadel, who would open the gates and betray us. Hearts of unbelief, &c.

3. *From the recollection of those who have been ruined by this host.* Our world has been made to resemble a valley of dry bones. The number of those slain is thousands of thousands ; many of these we have known ; need we wonder, therefore, that the people of God should exclaim, " Alas ! what shall we do ?" We observe,

III. THAT GOD HAS ABUNDANTLY PROVIDED FOR THE SECURITY OF HIS PEOPLE. " The mountain was full of horses," &c. God is the great defence and protection of his people ; the munition of rocks. He is as a wall of fire, &c. Then, in addition to this, he has appointed a perfect panoply of spiritual armor for our defence ; this is described by the apostle Paul, " Put on the whole armor of God." But our text introduces another kind of defence ; it is that of angels ; the spirits of light and glory ; the hosts of heaven, &c. You know it is written, " The angel of the Lord," &c. " He will give his angels charge," &c. " Are they not all ministering spirits," &c. It is also written, " Who maketh his angels spirits, and his ministers a flame of fire." These were often employed to serve the patriarchs—to instruct, counsel, and deliver the prophets ; they were now the body-guard of Elisha ; they are often the watchers, keepers, and deliverers of the saints. This is a cheering consideration, when we reflect on the presence of the evil malignant spirits, that however terrible, yet around our path " there are horses of fire, and chariots of fire." But we observe,

IV. GRACIOUS ASSISTANCE IS ESSENTIAL TO OUR RECEIVING COMFORT AND ENCOURAGEMENT FROM THE DEFENCE GOD HAS APPOINTED. The servant saw the foe, but not the guardian host. A striking exhibition of the influence of fear and unbelief. We fear and tremble when the eye of faith is closed ; but we exclaim by faith as Elisha did, " Fear not ; for they that be with us," &c. Now to realize this, and have confidence from it,

1. *God has given us his word.* He has filled it with declarations of love and mercy ; full of promises, &c. ; and we must open our eyes and believe these, if we would have spiritual consolation. A believing view of the scriptures will enable us to exclaim, " They that be with us," &c. He has,

2. *Promised us his Holy Spirit.* By the Spirit we shall be instructed in the warfare, &c. Equipped for the conflict. It is thus written, " When the enemy shall come," &c. Now this must be believed and personally realized, and then we shall exclaim, " They that be with us," &c. He has,

3. *Given us striking examples of delivering goodness.* Look at Jacob fearing the wrath of Esau—look at the Israelites in the wilderness—look at David exposed to the envy of Saul—look at Daniel, &c.—look at Peter in prison, &c. What do these things teach, but the same truth, " They that be with us," &c.

APPLICATION

1. *The Christian life is a warfare.*

2. *God is the strong tower and refuge of his saints.*

3. *Faith in him will render us invincible.*

97

DAVID'S DISTRESS AND CONSOLATION

" And David was greatly distressed ; for the people spake of stoning him, because the soul of all the people was grieved, every man for his sons and for his daughters : but David encouraged himself in the Lord his God."—1 SAMUEL xxx. 6.

IN reading the text, a variety of scripture passages are forced upon our remembrance : " Man that is born of a woman," &c. " Many are the afflictions of the righteous," &c. " It is through much tribulation," &c. Many of David's psalms come to us bedewed with the tears which were shed when they were composed. The history of our text shall be the introduction. At a time of difficulty, David fled into the land of the Philistines, and dwelt with Achish, king of Gath ; the king gave David Ziklag for his abode ; a war broke out between the Israelites and the Philistines, and Achish sought David to aid him in the warfare. Here were two extreme difficulties : he must fight for his benefactor, and against his country—or for his country, and against his benefactor. In either case, gratitude or piety would have been sacrificed. The lords of the Philistines, however, jealous of him, refused him as their ally ; therefore, he returned back. But mark the scene he beheld, when he reached his residence, verse 1, &c. Let us consider,

I. DAVID'S GREAT DISTRESS.

II. THE NATURE AND SOURCE OF HIS ENCOURAGEMENT.

I. DAVID'S GREAT DISTRESS. Look at several particulars :—

1. *It was a severe domestic calamity.* Their city burnt—property perishing—but chiefly the captivity of their wives and children, taken by a rude, violent, lawless soldiery ; exposed to suffering, violation— probably death. The absence of our friends is often a sore trial ; their afflictions exceedingly painful ; their death one of the severest strokes of providence ; but, I ask, would not death be preferred to such a captivity as we have described ? How exposed we are to relative afflictions ! In proportion to the extent of that relationship, they are so many channels of grief ; in proportion to our tenderest regards there is the possibility of the greater anguish and deeper sorrow. The loss of a Joseph—of a Rachel—of a friend like Jonathan—of an only son, &c.—of a beloved brother ; but here, by one fell swoop of adversity, their wives, and their sons, and their daughters, were seized by an ungodly and excited army.

2. *It was a sudden and an unexpected calamity.* Sometimes we have premonitions and signs of coming sorrow ; then there is time to prepare, to anticipate, and to fortify the mind by serious and pious contemplation ; but this was sudden and unexpected. He was returning to his home, and expecting to find his habitation in peace ; expecting a hearty welcome, a kind reception ; especially to enjoy the sweet and tender reciprocation of domestic affection. But, alas! how blighted were his hopes—how sorrowful his countenance— how overwhelmed his spirit. A city in ashes—dwellings in ruin—beloved friends borne into captivity. What could exceed the shock ? what embitter such a cup ?

what deepen such a trial ? You do not wonder at David's distress. View him as a man—as a husband—as a father—as a child of God. His distress was natural, in accordance with true piety, and with the most generous feelings of kindness and benevolence. Hence observe,

3. *The immediate effect of this calamity ;* verse 4. Their grief was loud ; it vented itself in wailings, &c. ; it flowed in tears ; it exhausted the physical strength ; they could weep no more. Ah! cries and tears are the resource of nature, which, if blocked up, would often produce the sullenness of deep melancholy, the ravings of phrensy, or the instant disembodiment of the spirit. Tears, and cries, and groans, are the natural results of sorrow, affliction, and distress. Happy when it does not become the sorrow that worketh death. We turn from the distress,

II. TO THE NATURE AND SOURCE OF HIS ENCOURAGEMENT. Observe,

1. *The great object of his encouragement and comfort.* God ; the Lord God ; the ruling Jehovah of the universe. He went at once to the Great Supreme. A link in the chain of providence seemed to burn with calamity. He went upward to the Being in whose hand was the whole chain. To whom could he so well refer as to the God whose presence is everywhere — whose eyes observe all—whose power is above all —whose righteousness regulates all—and whose resources include all things in the immaterial or material parts of the universe ? But observe,

2. *The interest he personally had in that great object.* One word here of infinite value. "His God." See you not the difference between the God, or their God, and my God. Look at the beautiful address, Psalm lxiii. 1 :—

> "The God that rules on high,
> 　And thunders when he please ;
> That rides upon the stormy sky,
> 　And manages the seas :
> 　This awful God is ours,
> 　Our Father, and our Love," &c.

3. *The grounds of his encouragement and confidence in God.* I need not say more of the perfections of God, or his relationship, &c. ; but we may add to these,

(1.) *His government.* He knew that all things and events were under God's control, and that he was a wise, just, and good God. "Though clouds," &c. ; though obscure, or dark, &c., yet always right. He knew that none could seize the reins, or prevent the rule of Jehovah, or defeat his designs.

(2.) *His especial and particular providence.* That this government especially had respect to the righteous. If he cared for the grass, &c.—for the lions—for the ravens—and for sparrows, then still more so for his people—" The very hairs of their head," &c. " The Father knoweth that ye have need," &c. Objects of especial love, and divine delight.

(3.) *In his gracious declarations.* Look at the figures he has chosen. Walls of Jerusalem ; shield ; tower ; refuge ; pavilion, &c. Father's paternal care ; mother's tender love ; an unchanging friend, &c.

(4.) *In his great and precious promises.* None of these speak of 'exemption from trouble, but support in it—deliverance from it—sanctification of it—happy influence, and glorious issue out of it.

(5.) *In his past experience of God's love.* God had done great things for him. Read the preceding portions of his history ; the events of his life. He is now called to review this, and then he encouraged himself in the Lord, &c.

APPLICATION

1. *We may have distresses similar to David's.* Why and wherefore, if it be the will of God, should we be exempt ?

2. *We may have David's consolations.* David's hopes were not blighted. He sought to know the will of God ; he adopted means, and regained his family and his friends. Therefore,

3. *There is never any need for despair.*

4. *How wretched they who have deep trials, and no religion !*

98

DAVID AND HIS HOST IN THE CAVE OF ADULLAM

" And every one that was in distress, and every one that was in debt, and every one that was discontented, gathered themselves unto him ; and he became a captain over them."—1 SAMUEL xxii. 2.

OUR text relates to a literal incident in the life of David. From fear of Saul, he had taken refuge in the cave of Adullam, and here he was joined by those of his own family, and his father's house. Here, too, he collected together a small army, and our text describes the character of those who fled to his standard, " And every one that was in distress," &c. We design to apply the subject, by way of accommodation, to one greater than David, even to David's Lord, and to those who became soldiers under the Captain of Salvation. Notice,

I. THE DESCRIPTION OF THOSE WHO GATHERED THEMSELVES UNTO DAVID. And,

II. WHAT HE BECAME UNTO THEM.

I. THE DESCRIPTION OF THOSE WHO GATHERED THEMSELVES UNTO DAVID. " And every one," &c. Now, this description will particularly apply to those who, sensible of their misery, come to Jesus Christ for life and salvation. We apply the passage to the awakened conscious sinner, who is bowed down by penitency at the foot of the cross. Observe, they were such,

1. *As were in distress.* There is such a thing as worldly distress, and worldly sorrow ; these often work death—drive to distraction—involve in ruin. There is distress arising from bereavements, &c.— Thus David, " I am distressed for thee, my brother Jonathan," &c. ; Rachel weeping, &c. Distress arising from bodily affliction : wearisome days, sleepless nights, &c., severe pain, &c. ; but the distress of the penitent arises from none of these sources. It is distress of soul for sin ; distress, like the psalmist's, when he discovered himself in the horrible pit, &c. ; like the publican's ; like the prodigal's, " I have sinned against heaven," &c. ; godly sorrow for sin, &c. Observe,

2. *They were such as were in debt.* Or, as it may read, every one that had a creditor. Now, every sinner is a debtor to the justice of God. We were bound to serve and obey, and we have all trespassed. From the goodness of God, we have received unnumbered blessings, and have not returned, &c. ; the mercy and forbearance of God, we have not improved, &c. Our debt is great, immense, overwhelming, what we can never pay. Observe,

3. *They were discontented.* In the margin we have a better rendering, " Bitter of soul." This would arise from their reflecting on their debt and distress. Were destitute of enjoyment ; almost overwhelmed ; anxious for deliverance ; in a state of desperation. Now, the awakened sinner

feels thus. He is bitter of spirit ; his heart is sad ; his condition deplorable ; darkness surrounds him ; he is filled with anxiety, " What shall I do to be saved?" &c., weary and heavy laden, he intensely longs for rest; he groans for freedom, &c. Now, it is said that they gathered themselves to David.

(1.) They had evidently heard of him, and where he was ; so have those who are awakened, &c. You have read of Christ, and heard of Christ, and the tidings have been such as to interest you.

(2.) They know their condition could not be worse. Now this is generally felt by those who seek the Lord ; they are perishing of hunger ; a change must be rather favorable than otherwise.

(3.) They therefore hoped, and gathered themselves unto him ; they ventured, and came to him ; they had thought, reflected, considered, resolved, and now they act. So it is with the anxious soul ; prayer is poured out, hope is cherished, faith exercised ; the hand is stretched out, and laid on the head of the sacrifice :—

" 'Tis just the sentence should take place ;
'Tis just ; but, oh ! thy Son hath died."

(4.) Observe the subjection which is expressed, " They gathered themselves unto him," that he might be " over them." Were subject to him. It is thus only we can come acceptably to Jesus ; it is thus only Christ will receive us. We must be under his authority and laws. As the disciple is under his teacher ; as the subject is under the sovereign ; as the patient is under the physician ; as the child is under the parent, we must yield ourselves to the Lord, &c. Notice,

II. WHAT HE BECAME UNTO THEM. " He became a captain over them." That is, their head, leader, and commander ; he undertook their cause. All the ideas included in the similitude of captain, are amply sufficient for a discourse ; we shall, therefore, notice the happy results arising from gathering ourselves under Christ, and Christ becoming a Captain over us.

1. *He delivers from distress.* The weary and heavy-laden find rest ; the prodigal finds a home ; the traveller, a refuge ; the friendless, a friend ; the poor, the bread of life.

2. *He discharges our debt.* Insolvent ; nothing to pay ; owing more than ten thousand talents ; yet when we come to him trembling for the consequences, he says, " Be of good cheer, thy sins are forgiven thee." He frankly forgives all ; he is exalted a Prince and a Saviour, &c.

3. *He gives true content, peace of soul.* He takes away the cup of bitterness ; he takes away the gall and the wormwood ; he takes the restlessness and anxiety away, and says, " Peace I give unto thee, my peace I leave with thee," &c. He implants that kingdom in the heart, which is not meat and drink, but righteousness, joy, &c. Let us inquire, Have you gathered yourselves to Christ ?

1. *Some of you have.* Then our subject is one of happy experience. Cleave to Christ ; honor and extol him.

2. *Some of you are doing so.* Be determined ; be prompt ; venture on him, &c.

3. *Some have not decided.* Unto whom will you go ? or how will you bear the distress, the debt, the bitter spirit ? Oh ! think, consider, repent, &c., and do it now.

99

MEPHIBOSHETH

" And the king said, Is there not yet any of the house of Saul, that I may show the kindness of God unto him ? And Ziba said unto the king, Jonathan hath yet a son, which is lame on his feet."—2 SAMUEL ix. 3.

NOTHING is more calculated to give us just views of the things of time, than seriously contemplating the movements of the providence of God. Just views of divine providence would make us sober, serious, prayerful, and contented. We often live for years without at all thinking of the way in which the Lord our God hath led us. This is both unwise and unprofitable. The word of God contains many striking exhibitions of the wonders of providence, both in the history of nations and individuals. The history of the people of Israel is one vast chain of connected wonders. Their formation, their rise, their glory, their decline, their dispersion, and yet their preservation, furnish ample materials for meditation and astonishment. How interesting in this respect is the history of David ! What a life of joy and sorrow, honor and humiliation, good and evil ! In his life there are some of the finest displays of real goodness and tender feeling the word of God contains. An instance of this sort is contained in the narrative connected with the text. Let us glance at the more prominent things which it contains.

I. OBSERVE THE MUTABILITY OF WORLDLY GREATNESS. About thirty-four years before this, you will witness the appointment of Saul as the first king of Israel. Many things of the most flattering kind connected with him. His majestic appearance; his sacred anointing; his possession of another spirit from God. He had a rich kingdom, a powerful army, and a numerous family; but what changes have transpired! He apostatizes from God; he becomes a curse to the people; his life is laden with trouble, his heart tortured with envy, until he becomes the victim of despondency, and finally, he expires by his own hand; his numerous family are scattered; and in a few years only one individual of the royal race of Saul is to be found. Let it teach us the evanescence of earthly things; how uncertain is worldly glory and grandeur!

II. OBSERVE THE EFFICIENCY OF THE FAVOR AND BLESSING OF GOD. And here we must contrast David with Saul; and if you look back to his history, you find him dwelling with his father in rural life—a shepherd; but God brings him out of obscurity —gives him a noble spirit—introduces him to the court as he who had slain the impious Goliath. The same care follows his steps, delivers his life often from jeopardy, and finally places him on the throne of Israel. Who does not see the providence of God in all this? It could not have been, had not God been with him. "God's blessing maketh rich," &c.; his favor is better than life. Observe,

III. THE EXHIBITION OF A TRULY MAGNANIMOUS SPIRIT IN DAVID TOWARDS THE HOUSE OF HIS BITTEREST ENEMY. "Is there any yet?" &c. For what purpose? That I may erase them from the eartl? that I may sit secure on my throne? that I may revenge the unrelenting malignity of Saul, their father? Oh, no; but that I may show him kindness. This is true magnanimity, real greatness. It has been said, to do good to those who love us is natural; to do evil to those who do us good is devilish; but to do good to those who do us evil is godlike. It is imitating Him who "causeth his sun to shine," &c.; it is imitating the blessed Redeemer, who died for his enemies, and who employed his dying breath in praying for his murderers, "Father, forgive them," &c. Oh! how hard a lesson, but how necessary! "Love your enemies," &c. "Bless them that curse," &c. "For, if ye forgive not," &c.

IV. WE SEE A STRIKING INSTANCE OF GENUINE AND DISINTERESTED FRIENDSHIP. Friendship is the affection of kindred hearts and minds. It never existed in greater purity and ardor than between David and Jonathan. Who can read the ode composed by David on Jonathan's death, and not be affected: "How are the mighty fallen in the midst of the battle! Oh, Jonathan! thou wast slain in thine high places. I am distressed for thee, my brother Jonathan; very pleasant hast thou been unto me: thy love to me was wonderful, passing the love of women," 2 Sam. i. 25, 27. Now, this friendship did not die with Jonathan; see verse 1. And here the son of Jonathan is brought under the monarch's notice, &c. This reminds us of the dealings of God with sinners. God is graciously disposed to us through the merit of Jesus. It is the language of divine benevolence, &c.; it reminds us of what Christ expects from us. We profess to be his friends. If so, what would we not do for Christ? How we would honor him, clothe him, entertain him, &c. This we cannot do; but we have his friends all around us—his children; and he says, "Whosoever giveth a cup of cold water," &c. "As much as ye do it," &c.

V. WE SEE A REMARKABLE INTERPOSITION OF PROVIDENCE ON BEHALF OF THE FATHERLESS AND AFFLICTED. In the first instance, God had provided this afflicted child with a friend in Machir, verse 4; and now he is received into the palace of David.

APPLICATION

Observe,

1. *The reward of pious benevolence to the seed of the godly.* Jonathan had been David's friend in the day of adversity, and God blesses and befriends Jonathan's son through the medium of the same David. God will not forget pious benevolence and liberality.

2. *The advantage of pious ancestors.* There was nothing in Mephibosheth to call for all this; but there was in his father Jonathan. Who can tell what blessings we inherit through the influence of our godly predecessors? see Psalm ciii. 17; Prov. xiii. 22.

3. *We are reminded of the rich provision of the gospel for the humble, penitent sinner ;* verse 7, to the end. A sense of unworthiness, and a believing reception of the message of grace, will ensure to us all the blessings of life and salvation.

100

DAVID AND HIS FAMILY

"And David returned to bless his household."— 2 SAMUEL vi. 20.

OUR subject is to heads of families a subject of great importance on very many accounts. The family is composed of distinct individuals, each having their own responsibility—parents, children, servants, masters, &c. The family (I mean the Christian family) is connected with the church of Jesus Christ—indeed ought to be a church in miniature. The family is also connected with the world ; and the influence of every family is for the good or evil of mankind in general. True religion qualifies man for every sphere. It makes him first a good man ; then a good relative character ; a good citizen ; and a blessing to the world. The example in the text is one of very great interest in reference to our subject. David had been very piously and actively engaged during the day ; he had brought the ark of the Lord into the city of David ; he had been filled with the spirit of holy joy and exultation ; and then he concludes the whole by returning to bless his household. We inquire, then,

I. IN WHAT WE MAY BLESS OUR HOUSEHOLD. We cannot bless the members of our families with saving grace ; we cannot convince, convert, or sanctify them ; but we can use those means which under God are most likely to be efficient in obtaining these all-important results.

1. *We must establish family order and discipline.* And nothing can be really well done without these. The merchant adopts a system of order ; the student the same. The gardener does not throw his seeds at random, or leave his ground open and exposed, without fence, &c. Every family should be regulated by the laws of order, and be under wise arrangement ; each should know their place, and keep it. In some families, children rule ; in others, servants ; and in many, there is no rule at all. To extract comfort from such dwellings would be a miracle indeed ; besides, it is the greatest mischief to the individuals themselves. They become spoiled and ruined, unfit for society, and often pests to the world. Not much good can be done without order, and to this, discipline must be added. Tempers, dispositions, and actions must be brought under restraint, and, if needs be, punished. How many are ruined through indulgence ! I do not plead for the instant use of physical correction, but for the due use of authority, and parental restraint. Eli's sin was, " his sons made themselves vile, and he restrained them not."

2. *We must set up domestic worship, and regularly maintain it.* God has declared that his curse rests on the families who call not on his name. Joshua said, " As for me," &c. So " David returned," &c. Family worship should include reading the scriptures, prayer, and praise ; it should be regular ; should include the whole family ; be simple, and short. Singing will generally make it attractive to the younger branches.

3. *We must exhibit before our families the spirit and practice of the gospel.* Nothing will give a more utter distaste to religion, than direct contradiction between our profession and lives. Proud followers of an humble Saviour ! passionate, covetous, unjust, want of truth and fidelity. Our example must lead the way ; we must take them with us, &c.

4. *We must present for our families earnest and affectionate prayer.* Seek God's blessing to succeed our labors. Surely we shall feel it both a duty and delight to pray fervently for our households. If we are called to pray for all men, how much more for our own families !

5. *We must provide for our own families the means of religious instruction and public worship.* We must lead them to the house of God ; instil into them habits of reverence for divine things ; ascertain that they know the essentials ; converse with them ; place religious books within their reach, &c. Let us notice,

II. SOME THINGS ESSENTIAL TO THE DISCHARGE OF THESE DUTIES.

1. *There must be unanimity in the heads of families.* Not two heads ; not one correcting, and the other indulging. Father and mother must act in unison, both having

the same object. Children must not be trained to fear one and love the other. How many have been ruined thus!

2. *We must possess much wisdom and self-control.* Time, place, and circumstances, all to be considered. Provoke not your children. Masters must not be overbearing, &c. If we are violent and unreasonable, our families will dread and dislike us.

3. *We must seek the assistance of God's grace.* Our work is difficult and arduous, and we are short-sighted, feeble, &c. God alone, the head of all families, can well direct and qualify. Observe,

III. SEVERAL MOTIVES BY WHICH THIS COURSE MAY BE ENFORCED.

1. *We appeal to human affection.* Surely this should include the mind and soul; the intellectual and deathless spirit; their moral and their eternal condition.

2. *We appeal to our responsibility.* This is our duty. Who shall do it, if we do not? What will be our reply at the last day?

3. *We appeal to our own mercies.* God, our heavenly Father, how he instructs, counsels, and blesses us. So many of us owe much to our earthly parents.

4. *We argue from the advantages which may result.* To see our children wise, respectable, and pious; ornaments to the world; members of the church, &c. If it fails, our conscience will not upbraid us; we may boldly face them at the last day.

APPLICATION

1. *What say you, Christian parents?* What plea do you present? Do you object for,

(1.) Want of time.

(2.) Want of ability.

(3.) Want of hope. We reply,

2. *Can time be better spent?* God will give you ability. Duty is yours.

3. *We shall meet our families at the last day.*

101

DAVID'S ADDRESS TO SOLOMON

" And thou, Solomon, my son, know thou the God of thy fathers," &c.—1 CHRONICLES xxviii. 9.

THIS was David's advice to Solomon. A monarch's advice to his successor; a parent's advice to his son; and a godly man's advice to his posterity. Who can read it, and not admire the sentiments it contains? who can meditate on it, and not feel its supreme importance? It inculcates religion, that one thing needful; it urges it on the attention of youth, when it is so eminently beautiful and useful; it enforces the advice by a promise the most interesting, that God will be found of those who seek him; and it concludes the lesson by an admonition the most solemn, if we forsake God he will cast us off forever. Consider, my young friends,

I. THE ADVICE AND COUNSEL THE TEXT IMPARTS. This advice refers to two things:—

1. *To the knowledge of God.* " Know thou." Now, in a knowledge of God,

(1.) *There must be the admission of his being.* " He that cometh," &c. The existence of the supreme Creator and Ruler of the universe is a sentiment almost universally entertained by civilized men; only a very few who say " There is no God," and they rather speak the sentiments of their hearts, than the conclusions of their minds. If you have doubts here, just think of the great difficulties which these doubts create. A universe originally from nothing; a world without a maker; order, beauty, arrangement, all the offspring of chance. I will not dwell on this, satisfied that you heartily and fully admit the existence of one great and blessed Deity. In the knowledge of God,

(2.) *There must be a right apprehension of his character.* What is he? A Spirit— an eternal, unchangeable Spirit; a Spirit filling all things, knowing all things, governing all things; a Being glorious, almighty, infinitely wise, unboundedly good, yet righteous and pure; in reference to our world, a God of mercy; full of compassion, &c.

(3.) *There must be a clear conception of his will.* What does he hate? Sin. What does he love? Holiness. Go through the list of sins, and it extends to all sin; go over the whole of the graces and virtues, and his love extends to each and all. But that we may not err, we have his mind revealed. He has written his statutes, and hear what a giant spirit says of it: " All scripture," &c. 2 Tim. iii. 16. An attentive regard to this book is indispensable to a true knowledge of God. In this sublime mirror we behold him in all his glory. The true knowledge of God includes,

(4.) An experimental consciousness of his favor. To know how we stand in reference to God, and God in reference to us; to seek the assurance of his love to us. If we have not repented and sought mercy, nor believed in Christ Jesus, then our state is that of enemies—carnal—under his displeasure—exposed to his wrath; his face is set against such, &c. "He is angry with the wicked every day." But to know that we have seen and felt the evil of sin; loathed, forsaken, and repented of it; prayed for, and found pardon; to have a good conscience, one made so by the blood of sprinkling; to enjoy the Holy Spirit, &c. Observe, this knowledge of God is connected in the text,

2. *With obedience to him.* "And serve him." Take his yoke upon us; engage ourselves to him, by the consecration of all we are and have; give ourselves to God; to obey him, and hearken to his voice in all things. This service,

(1.) *Must be sincere.* "With a perfect heart." That is, with a whole heart; not divided, not feignedly, nor formally, but in uprightness, and truth, and in reality. Neither must our obedience be circumscribed by our opinions, or feelings, but have respect to all his commandments and statutes. This service,

(2.) *Must be free and voluntary.* "With a willing mind." Cheerfully; with readiness and delight. The renewed man can say, "I delight to do thy will, O God!" The good man delighteth in the law of the Lord. That which is not done willingly has no real virtue in it; nor will God accept the service of terror or superstition. I add, that this knowledge or service of God must be followed by,

3. *A constant seeking of God.* "If thou seek him," &c. A good man has often occasion to seek God.

(1.) He seeks his grace in the exercise of believing devotion.

(2.) He seeks his guidance through all the perplexities of life.

(3.) He seeks his preserving protection from his numerous adversaries.

(4.) He seeks his counsel in all his engagements; acknowledges him in all his ways, &c. And,

(5.) He seeks fellowship with God. Enoch, it is said, "walked with God," &c. David said, "I will walk before the Lord," &c. Observe,

II. THE MOTIVES BY WHICH THIS COURSE IS ENFORCED. The

1st. *Is addressed to our hope.* "He will be found of us." Now, this is a great scriptural truth. God will be found of all who seek him as he has directed; he will reject none; but to the young there is an especial promise, "They that seek me early shall find me." Youthful piety is peculiarly acceptable; and in finding God, we find all the soul's chief good and portion, light, joy, and salvation; peace, rest, and consolation; providential direction and safety; the blessings of time, and glories of eternity. In God is dignity, enjoyment, riches, blessedness. "All other things shall be added," &c. "Godliness is profitable," &c. The other motive,

2. *Is addressed to our fears.* "But if thou forsake him," &c. Live without him; neglect his words and ordinances, &c.; he will cast us off.

(1.) He casts men off from his gracious restraints; and how fearful they become! given up to all sin; run headlong into vice, &c.; given up to a rebellious mind.

(2.) He casts men off from his providential solicitudes; withdraws his paternal regards; allows them to reap as they have sown; then want, rage, shame, reproach, disease, and often premature death, is the result.

(3.) He casts the incorrigible into hell. "The wicked shall be turned into hell," &c. "The wicked are driven away," &c. Now, such are the motives. In applying this subject,

1. *Let me suggest a few things to those young persons who have obeyed the voice of the text.*

(1.) Entertain lowly views of yourselves.

(2.) Cherish the fear of God daily.

(3.) Remember that personal, practical godliness must be always sought. Cherish a spirit of intense devotion.

(4.) Cleave to your Bible, "Whereby shall a young man cleanse," &c.

(5.) Be watchful in an eminent degree.

2. *To those who are resolving to act upon the spirit of the text.*

(1.) Then carry out your resolutions this very night. Go to your chambers, and prostrate yourselves before God.

(2.) Avoid your evil companions, though they may not be profligates, &c., yet if they are neglecters of religion.

(3.) Seek the society of the pious, &c.

" He that walks with wise men," &c. " I will be the companion of them that fear God," &c.

3. *To those who care for none of these things.* You have been instructed, admonished, warned, invited. Now, the responsibility is your own ; to God you must give an account.

102

JEHOVAH'S DWELLING ON EARTH

" But will God indeed dwell on the earth ?"— 1 KINGS viii. 27.

THE text is connected with the dedication of Solomon's temple. The whole description is solemn, impressive, and magnificent. A moveable tabernacle was now superseded by one of the most splendid erections on which the sun of heaven ever shone. In the vastness of its dimensions, in the costliness of its materials, and in the resplendent appearance of the whole, it so far exceeded all previous erections, as to be worthy of its great design—a temple for the living and eternal God. Three circumstances worthy of notice were connected with its history : God himself was its artificer ; it was erected according to the plan which Infinite Wisdom directed ; it was the result of the voluntary free-will offerings of the Jewish nation, from Solomon on the throne to the peasantry of the people ; it was dedicated to God by the fervent prayers and thanksgivings of the people, through Solomon, their king. How truly grand and affecting was that dedication ! The king takes the lead in the services. Then Solomon assembled the elders of the people—the priests and Levites in their sacerdotal vestments, in connection with the chief of the men of Israel, form the august and memorable convocation. Solomon then, standing before the altar, stretches forth his hands, and lifting his eyes towards heaven, thus addresses the infinite Majesty of heaven and earth, verse 23. The text is a kind of parenthetical exclamation ; a solemn pause in the midst of his supplications, " But will God ?" &c.

I. LET US EXAMINE THE VARIOUS TERMS WHICH THE TEXT CONTAINS.

II. GIVE A SCRIPTURAL SOLUTION OF THE QUESTION PROPOSED.

I. LET US EXAMINE THE VARIOUS TERMS OF WHICH THE TEXT IS COMPOSED. The text refers to the divine Being dwelling on the earth.

1. *Let the earth be the first subject of our consideration.* The earth is represented as the footstool of Deity. It was originally given to the children of men ; it forms a beautiful part of the divine dominions, and is full of the goodness of the Lord ; it bears evident marks of the footsteps of Deity ; worthy of its great Artificer ; the scene of the divine wonders and glory. But through the entrance of sin, it has been spoiled and cursed. Eden has been converted into a desert ; paradise into a howling wilderness ; now the seat of Satan ; the usurper has seized upon it, as though it was his rightful dominion. It is the Egypt of the hellish despot—the place of his cruel oppression— the scene of crime, and darkness, and wo ; so that the earth is like one vast aceldama, or scene of horror and blood. It is the site of avowed enmity and rebellion against the Most High, and is in treasonable league with the powers of darkness. Well may we ask in reference to it, " Will God indeed dwell on the earth ?" in a world so guilty, so polluted, so vile ? Let us now consider,

2. *The glorious and blessed Being referred to in the text.* " Will God ?" Think of his magnificent celestial dwelling ; his imperial exalted palace ; his sublime throne, exalted infinitely above seraphim and cherubim. It is well also to think of the extent of his dominions. Has he not worlds upon worlds, beyond number or calculation ? Lift up your eyes on high. Behold the vastness and grandeur even of the solar system, compared with which our world is a mere speck, an atom ! But reflect upon the starry worlds beyond the influence and attraction of our sun, which are most probably the suns and centres of other systems, scattered in the immensity of space, unexplored, and inexplicable to the inhabitants of our world. Well may we ask, " Will God ?" &c.

3. *Now consider the word " dwell."* Will he " dwell ?" We know he will observe ; his omniscience beholds the whole of it at one glance, &c. Heaven, and earth, and hell are all open before him, &c. He will govern the earth, for he ruleth over all ; his dominion is a universal dominion ; he doeth according to his will, &c.; his presence will, and must pervade all space. " Whither shall we flee," &c. " But will he

be well?" &c. Make it his residence, his abode. Now lay the emphasis of the text,

4. *On the word "indeed."* Really, manifestly; in some certain, peculiar, especial sense. Shall its inhabitants know and discern his dwelling in their midst? Such are the terms of which the text is composed. Well may we pause, and linger, and adore. Well ought we to pray that the Eternal Spirit would guide our minds in pursuing the solemn and momentous investigation! Where shall our appeal be made? To the ancient oracles of paganism? They ask, "What God?" &c. In the range of paganism there are innumerable deities, greater and minor: gods of the winds and of the waters; of the tempest and the calm; of the mountains and the valleys; but of the great, living, and eternal God, they are utterly ignorant. We appeal to the massive tomes of ancient philosophy, and there are profound research, subtle disquisitions, &c., innumerable conjectures; but we close these huge collections, satisfied that the world by wisdom knew not God. We ask the Deist—the votary of modern rationalism—and, instead of meeting the question with due seriousness, he treats the subject as visionary, and in place of a reply worthy of an intellectual being, you have the curled lip of scorn, the sneering look, and the vapid declaration that the great God is too much absorbed with his own perfections to care at all for this earth, or its puerile inhabitants. Let us, then,

II. Give a scriptural solution of the question proposed. Our subject convinces us of the necessity of a divine revelation; and to that revelation, then, our appeal must be made.

1. *God did dwell in the midst of his ancient Israel.* Not only had they occasional august manifestations of the divine glory, but he appeared for them in their redemption from the Egyptian yoke; guided and guarded, &c.; "In the pillar," &c.; but especially see this, Exod. xxix. 43, xl. 4. So also, when the temple was dedicated, 1 Kings viii. 10, 11; so also the Lord said, "Now have I chosen and sanctified this house, that my name may be there forever, and mine eyes and my heart shall be there continually."

2. *God dwelt on the earth, in the glorious incarnation of his beloved Son.* It was to this the apostle referred, "We beheld his glory, the glory," &c. Jesus thus taught his disciples, "Whoso hath seen," &c. To this the apostle refers, "In Christ dwelt all the fulness," &c. This is the great mystery of godliness, "God manifest in the flesh," &c. This was evidenced in his teaching, miracles, death, and resurrection. "He spake with the power and majesty of God." Diseases — sorrows — winds — the dead, obeyed. The devils, too, confessed and fled before him. No wonder, when the elements of nature obeyed him, that the people exclaimed, "What manner of man," &c.

3. *God dwells in his church, by the presence of his Spirit.* Deity, enrobed in flesh, hath ascended on high, even to the right hand, &c. But according to his promise, he sent down the Divine Spirit to dwell with his people, to the end of the world, John xiv. 16. Thus he dwelt miraculously on the apostles and first disciples, and thus he now dwells in his own spiritual church as the guide, the sanctifier, and the comforter of the saints. He it is who constitutes the vitality of the kingdom of Christ; he perfectly builds it up; he succeeds the efforts of his servants, giving testimony to the word of his grace, and enabling the devoutly pious to worship God in spirit and in truth.

4. *God graciously dwells in the heart of every believer.* How overwhelming that stupendous passage in Isaiah lxvi. 1, 2. How delightful the saying of Christ, "If a man love me, he will keep my words, and my Father will love him, and we will come unto him, and make our abode with him," &c. "Hereby," says John, "we know that we dwell in him, and he in us, because he hath given us his Spirit." "Know ye not that ye are the temple of God, if so be God dwell in you?"

5. *God will dwell on the earth, in the universal dominion which he has engaged to set up.* The earth is redeemed, and God has sworn that truth and righteousness shall again adorn it, so that it shall be one garden to the Lord. "That his knowledge shall cover the earth," &c. That his tabernacle shall be among men, and that he will dwell among them; that one song of triumph shall be heard from the rising to the setting of the sun, "Hallelujah! the Lord God omnipotent reigneth! Hallelujah! for the kingdoms of this world," &c. Well may we exclaim, "Blessed be the Lord God, the God of Israel, who only doeth wondrous things," &c.

APPLICATION

1. *What an exhibition of the condescension and grace of God!* That he should hate, punish, destroy, &c., would be no marvel ; but he loves, pities, descends ; makes the earth the scene of mercy, long-suffering, and grace.

2. *How desirable that the presence of God should be secured and enjoyed in this church and congregation.* This will be its beauty, its exaltation, its establishment, its prosperity, and security. To secure this, the cross of Christ must be exalted. If Christ be honored, God will honor you. Let Christ be preached, and God will bless and succeed. To secure this, the Spirit must be constantly and fervently sought. House of prayer. He will give the plenitude of spiritual influence ; like the copious rain or the early dews. He will cause showers of blessings to descend on his chosen hill. But to secure this, a peaceful atmosphere must be maintained. He is not the God of confusion, but of peace. This is his own element. Here the Dove will hover round you, and over you, &c.

3. *I ask another question.* Will men dwell with God in heaven ? The place—heaven ; God's palace, &c. Men, worthless, &c. Oh ! yes ; they shall come from the east, and the west, &c. Who ? The believer ; the faithful servants of Christ. Then forget not, but seek this better country.

103

A RECOGNITION OF PIOUS VOWS

" Thy vows are upon me, O God ! I will render praises unto thee ; for thou hast delivered my soul from death ; wilt not thou deliver my feet from falling, that I may walk before God in the light of the living ?"—PSALM lvi. 12, 13.

MUCH is said in the scriptures of the Old Testament on the subject of vows. The earliest vow recorded, is that of Jacob in connection with the vision of Jehovah at Bethel. " If God be with me, and will keep me," &c., Gen. xxviii. 20. Hannah also vowed unto the Lord in reference to Samuel, resolving to dedicate the child to the Lord forever, 1 Samuel i. 21, 22. All of you remember the rash vow of Jephthah, and its sequel of unhappy results in reference to his daughter. It is said that the sailors of the vessel in which Jonah was endeavoring to escape, after they had thrown him into the sea, " offered a sacrifice, and made vows," Jonah i. 16. In several portions of the Psalms, the inspired and holy man of God refers to vows ; thus he openeth one of his beautiful and sacred odes, " Praise waiteth for thee, oh God, in Zion, and unto thee shall the vow be performed," Psalm lxv. 1. Again he says, " So will I sing praise unto thy name forever, that I may daily perform my vows," Psalm lxi. 8 ; but I confine the subject at the present to those who have vowed allegiance to the Lord, and are this evening intending to ratify that vow by commemorating the love of Jesus at his sacramental table ; to you then who are now uniting yourselves to the people of God, our subject will be especially directed. We ask,

I. WHAT THE VOWS OF THE BELIEVING PENITENT SHOULD COMPRISE. Their vows should include,

1. *A resolution to forsake the service of Satan and sin.* To abandon and utterly forsake the way of transgression and death. To this we are often invited, exhorted, &c. Great promises made to such. The apostle refers to the believing Romans as having done so, Romans vi. 16, 17.

2. *A resolution to yield body, soul, and spirit to God.* The apostle says, " Yield yourselves to God"—" I beseech you, brethren," &c., Romans xii. 1. This is a reasonable service—a dignified service—a happy service ; one which appeals to us from the cross. " Ye are not your own," &c. Christ must have heart, tongue, and life.

3. *To present constant homage, reverence, and supreme love to God.* God demands this, and it is our highest interest and felicity to yield it to him. The loftiest angels do this—his greatness, and glory, and power, claim our homage and reverence—his goodness and love, our supreme affection. God must have the heart—occupy the throne—sway the sceptre.

4. *To identify Christ's cause with our dearest interests.* Christ's cause must be sacred to those who love him. Apostles and confessors valued it more than worldly honor, riches, ease, liberty, or life. They toiled, and suffered, and died for it ; now it ought to be as precious to us ; and the resolve of the Christian convert should be, " If I forget thee, Jerusalem," &c. This must be continuous, daily, &c.

5. *Unfeigned attachment to God's church and people.* " Peace be within thy walls," &c. " For my brethren and companions' sake, I will now say," &c. Consecration to God must be followed by close and constant union to the followers of Christ. " They that believed were together," &c. Now, these feelings of attachment must be visible, distinct, and manifest ; we are to do good unto all men, but " especially to the household of faith." Now, these vows are to be taken, and sustained and honored by the exemplification of the principles they involve. Notice,

II. THE SPIRIT IN WHICH THESE VOWS SHOULD BE MADE. In the joyful spirit of praise. " I will render praise unto thee," &c. Now here he affirms,

1. *What God had done for him.* " Delivered my soul from death." The soul in its unrenewed state is dead, " dead in trespasses and sins"—dead to God—dead to holiness, &c.—dead also judicially under the righteous sentence of eternal death ; exposed to the wrath to come. Now from this death the soul is delivered—delivered meritoriously by the sacrifice of Jesus Christ—he came to deliver from the wrath to come—delivered really by the gracious and merciful influences of the Spirit of God. When the sense of guilt and condemnation is taken away—when the Spirit testifies with our spirits that we are the children of God, &c. What a great and blessed deliverance this is. Now for this deliverance, .

2. *He will cherish a thankful spirit.* " I will render praises," &c. Thus the prophet breaks forth, " O Lord, I will praise thee," &c. Now these praises are to include thanksgivings at all times, places, and occasions. " Praises" in the plural, so that the vows of God are to be honored by a spirit of holy, delightful praise—a spirit of cheerfulness and joy. We cannot be too ardent, intent, and frequent in the praises we render to the Lord ; so to praise God, as never to allow the least feeling of self-righteous complacency to attach to ourselves. Notice,

III. THE PIOUS APPEAL HE MAKES TO GOD IN REFERENCE TO THE FUTURE. " Wilt not thou deliver my feet," &c. He recognises,

1. *Perils in his way.* Satan lays his snares in the pathway of the Christian. There are many worldly allurements, &c. Now we must remember this—not be for-getful, or careless, or presumptuous ; not lean on our own strength; many have fallen—Noah, Lot, David, Solomon, Peter, &c.

2. *He trusts to God for security.* " Wilt not thou deliver," &c. Now in perplexity, seek counsel of your Christian friends, especially of your minister. Go to your Bible, and frequently to the closet of secret devotion ; but after all trust only in God's delivering arm. " Hold thou me up," &c. Cherish a constant sense of this.

3. *He exhibits the prevailing desire of his soul.* " To walk before God," &c. Always to recognise God, to set the Lord before us—to act in all things, to please and glorify his name ; and in this holy course to " walk," to make constant advances, to go " from strength to strength," &c. " One thing I do, forgetting the things that are behind," &c.

APPLICATION

1. *Perhaps most persons here have been vow-makers.* At one time or another you have resolved to give yourselves to God ; perhaps in affliction—in severe trouble—in peril—in bereavements ; but in general, how evanescent they have been ! " Oh, Judah ! what shall I do unto thee ?" " Oh, Ephraim !" &c. " Unstable as water," &c.

2. *There are some here who have vowed, and kept their vows.* What a mercy ! Let God be exalted. Render praises, &c. Especially you who are for the first time to be recognised as the followers of Christ. Oh, study the text, pray over it, &c.

3. *Who will now avow his resolve to give himself entirely to God ?* Let this be the great crisis—the eventful turning point—the time when it shall be said, " Behold, he prayeth," &c.

104

HISTORY OF HEZEKIAH

PART 1—HIS MORAL CHARACTER

" For he clave to the Lord, and departed not from following him, but kept his commandments, which the Lord commanded Moses. And the Lord was with him ; and he prospered whithersoever he went forth."—2 KINGS xviii. 6, 7.

HEZEKIAH was one of the most pious kings of Judah. He lived in the fear of the Lord, and was jealous for Jehovah's glory. Previous to his reign the people had greatly departed from the true God, and sunk into gross and wicked idolatries. See former chapter, v. ix. 11. Now, Hezekiah immediately set on foot an entire reformation. It is said of him, that " he did that which was right in the sight of the Lord," viii. 38; and then follows our text, " For he clave unto the Lord," &c.

I. THE PIOUS COURSE HEZEKIAH PURSUED. Now, this is expressed in the following particulars:

1. *His adherence to God.* " He clave unto the Lord." This implies union with the Lord. Oneness with him ; attachment, preference, and decision. When Barnabas visited the disciples at Antioch, " he exhorted them to cleave unto the Lord," &c. It includes,

(1.) The judgment cleaving to the truth of God.

(2.) The will cleaving to the ways of God.

(3.) The affections fervently going out after God ; loving and delighting in him.

(4.) The soul's trust and confidence implicitly resting upon him. Many things are opposed to this cleaving to the Lord. Satan tries to beguile us ; world to fascinate our hearts ; unbelief would be constantly turning aside from him ; cleaving to the Lord requires the resolute determination of the soul to adhere to God under all these circumstances.

2. *He kept his commandments.* No acceptable religion without this. Knowledge, profession, attendance upon ordinances, all worthless without this. This is the evidence of our sincerity. Love to God will make his commandments pleasant and delightful. " This is the love of God," &c.

3. *He persevered in the way of holy obedience.* " And departed not," &c. Some ran well but were hindered. Impulse and excitement often prompt to a certain line of action, and then, when the novelty is over, they turn aside. Many are drawn aside by the pomps and vanities of the world ; many by sordid love of gain ; many by fear of man, or of suffering ; Hezekiah held on his way and departed not, &c. This preservation is necessary—essential. The end must crown the whole. " He that endureth to the end," &c.

II. THE DISTINGUISHED BLESSINGS WHICH HE ENJOYED. He was favored,

1. *With the divine presence.* " And the Lord was with him." This is a very comprehensive form of expression ; it includes every desirable good ; it is what God promised to Jacob, Gen. xxviii. 15. What Moses so earnestly prayed for. " If thy presence go not with us," &c. It is that which formed the great desire of David for his son Solomon, 1 Chron. xxviii. 9. The presence of the Lord is the good man's safety. " In the Lord Jehovah is everlasting strength." " A very present help," &c. The presence of the Lord is the good man's guide. He led Israel, and also all who trust in him by a right way, &c. It is his comfort. His presence makes our paradise, &c. He was favored,

2. *With continued prosperity.* " And he prospered," &c. It is said of another, " So long as he sought the Lord," &c. Now that is prosperity, when all things are tending to one great and glorious consummation ; not because a man is getting rich, or elevated in the world ; what are these, if they are in the way of sin and death ? When the mind and heart are in a state of cultivation and improvement for another world, yet " godliness is profitable unto all things," &c. A pious man enjoys what he has, much or little. " Godliness with contentment is great gain," still greater with a brightening hope of immortality and unending life. Real prosperity is of God. His favor and smile are essential to it.

APPLICATION

1. *How many are imitating the good Hezekiah ?* cleaving, following, obeying God.

2. *What encouragement for all to do so !*

3. *Will not some commence to-day ?*

105

HISTORY OF HEZEKIAH
PART 2—HIS SICKNESS

" In those days was Hezekiah sick unto death. And the prophet Isaiah, the son of Amoz, came unto him, and said unto him, Thus saith the Lord, Set thine house in order, for thou shalt die, and not live. Then he turned his face to the wall, and prayed unto the Lord, saying," &c. &c.—2 KINGS xx. 1–6.

WE previously referred you to the piety and persevering decision of Hezekiah. He effected a great national reformation ; and he personally clave unto the Lord, and departed not from following the Lord, &c. It is said of him, that God prospered him whithersoever he went forth. This world, however, is a state of mutability ; here we ought not to calculate upon our temporal blessings as abiding. Like the agitated ocean is the sea of human life : there is nothing changeless, fixed, and certain. One of the sources of trouble to man, is the affliction of body to which he is liable. Sin has sown the seeds of disease and death in our mortal system, and pain and sickness are the necessary consequences. Our subject relates to the affliction of Hezekiah, and his gracious recovery from it. Observe,

I. THE SICKNESS WHICH HE ENDURED.

1. *The sickness itself.* The nature of Hezekiah's affliction is not stated, (supposed to be the plague,) it was evidently, however, severe and dangerous, ver. 1. He was confined to his bed. Now, in his visitation, observe,

(1.) Hezekiah was not exempted, although in the prime of life, in the very midst of his days, (he was now between thirty and forty years of age.) We do not wonder at helpless children and the infirm aged ; but every period of life is alike vulnerable, &c.

(2..) His worldly elevation did not exempt him ; he was a monarch, had his crown, sceptre, throne of state, retinue, &c. ; all these are worthless as to the prevention or the removal of pain.

(3.) His eminent godliness did not exempt him. Afflictions come alike to all ; piety enables us to bear them with patience—it sanctifies them, and obtains good out of them ; but does not exempt, &c.

(4.) His extensive usefulness did not exempt him ; he filled a most important station, and that well ; he was a blessing of real worth and importance to the kingdom ; yet he was sick even unto death. Observe,

2. *The intimation he had of its fatal termination.* The prophet Isaiah, &c., ver. 1. The message evidently meant this, Thy sickness is of a mortal kind, it must naturally prove fatal ; such was its character and tendency. Notice,

3. *The direction given him.* " Set thine house in order," &c. This direction was a favorable sign as to Hezekiah's piety. He was a godly man, as such his state was secure ; he had lived to the Lord, so was ready to die, &c. ; but it was desirable that his household affairs should be arranged

and fixed. This is of importance to all persons, especially to a king, and still more so to a king who had been extensively engaged in the service of God. Let me pause in the narrative to make a few observations.

(1.) Some persons neglect a proper settlement of their temporal concerns ; and often family broils, litigation, and strife, &c., are the result.

(2.) Others do this, but neglect personal preparation for dying. They are exact, and prompt, and minute about property, &c., but they neglect their souls, are careless about religion and eternal things ; or, perhaps, professedly leave it to the last. What folly and infatuation ! surely the soul is the chief ; eternity most momentous ; heaven the most precious.

(3.) Others neglect both. They neither set themselves nor their houses in order. They will not entertain the subject. By turning their backs upon it, they persuade themselves the evil day is postponed.

(4.) The godly man does both. First he seeks the kingdom of God, &c. First regards the soul, and seeks for it a title and meetness for a better world ; lays up a good foundation for the future ; then he considers how he can render his riches and influence more useful to mankind after his decease, that being dead, his spirit and holy efforts may live after him ; he will be anxious that his family, the church, and the institutions of mercy, may all flourish after his decease. As we cannot enter now on the other parts of the subject, we take four views of sickness of body to which all men are liable.

1. *The origin of all sickness is sin.* But for this our bodies would have been painless and invulnerable, the seat of abiding pleasure ; such they were when they came from the hands of the great Artificer. Sin has undermined it, weakened it, and diffused through every fibre and pore the seeds of frailty and death.

2. *Most persons are called to bear it.* Few live to any great age without experiencing it. Most now present, many this day, &c. We ought rather to calculate upon it. No marvel that we are so, but the reverse.

" Our life contains a thousand springs,
    And dies if one be gone ;
Strange that a harp of thousand strings
    Should keep in tune so long."

3. *In sickness we should recognise the hand of God.* Does not spring out of the dust. To the righteous, fatherly chastisement; to the wicked, often warning; admonitory to all; yet much sickness is from the manifest disregard which persons pay to the laws of nature. Health is a gift to be preserved, &c., valued, &c. How many are sick through transgression; many too through neglect; but all may derive good therefrom, by reflection and prayer.

4. *There will be no sickness in heaven.* World of health. No sickness or death, &c. "Sighing and sorrow shall forever flee away," &c.

APPLICATION

1. *Let health and life be improved, &c.*
2. *In all states, seek the favor of God.* "Glorify him with your bodies and souls," &c.

106

HISTORY OF HEZEKIAH

PART 3—HIS RECOVERY

" In those days was Hezekiah sick unto death. And the prophet Isaiah the son of Amoz came to him, and said unto him, Thus saith the Lord," &c. —2 KINGS xx. 1–6.

WE formerly adverted to the sickness of Hezekiah and the message of Isaiah, concerning its fatal termination, "Set thine house in order," &c. We have now to observe the effects which this message produced; it was a very momentous one. Truly the most solemn which can be addressed to an immortal being. It was particularly so to Hezekiah in the meridian of life; in the midst of the great work in which both the glory of God and the well-being of the nation were concerned. The effects of this message were, "Hezekiah wept sore." He was in great trouble and distress of mind. It does not appear that this arose from immoderate love of life, or distressing fear of death, or from awful forebodings of the future. But,

(1.) There was doubtless the instinctive love of being. This is of God's own planting, worthy even of the pious. To be cherished, &c.

(2.) Love to the kingdom of Israel; no successor; national confusion.

(3.) Love to God's cause. The reformation scarcely finished; the blasphemers,

the enemies of God, were now conspiring to overthrow. Such it appears were the reasons of Hezekiah's distress, worthy of him as a man and as a servant of God. Notice then as the leading division of the subject,

I. THE COURSE WHICH HEZEKIAH ADOPTED. He had recourse to prayer. Prayer is the remedy of the afflicted spirit. "If any man is afflicted, let him pray."

1. *His prayer was divine in its object.* He prayed to the Lord. How vain is every other refuge!

2. *It was direct and intimate.* "He turned his face to the wall." He shut out the world; withdrew from earth; sought immediate audience with Jehovah. What a sight! An afflicted mortal ascending to the throne of grace, with a petition for mercy; what a privilege to be allowed to do so. To be made welcome.

3. *It was fervent and earnest.* "I beseech thee," &c. His heart was poured out; his soul's earnest longings were presented. With tears he supplicated, &c.

4. *It was connected with reference to his own integrity.* Now this was not self-righteous. Not boasting. He did not plead it as a merit; he referred to his sincerity as a truth, &c. Not divided in his attachments, &c. He had enjoyed tokens of God's approbation; now this was all true—he could appeal to God, &c. We find Job referred to his previous life. Paul also, who felt himself less than the least of all saints, had to refer to his sufferings and labors in the cause of God; this is the privilege of the righteous, that they have constantly the rejoicing of a good conscience, &c.

5. *Yet it was evidently submissive to God's will.* His prayer is remarkable in this respect. He does not mention his life or recovery; he thought it best to pray in general terms, and left particulars with the Lord; no doubt his petition included restoration, yet it is clear he left it to the Lord. How wise and safe is this! Not our will, &c. Observe,

II. THE RECOVERY WHICH HE EXPERIENCED. The decree of mortality was reversed; his life was prolonged. In saving his life God referred,

1. *To the success of Hezekiah's prayer.* "I have heard thy prayer, I have seen thy tears," &c. God is the hearer and answerer of prayer. How potent, how almost almighty is prayer, &c. When prayer

has been fervently presented, it has stayed divine wrath. God exclaimed to Moses, " Let me alone," &c. It is right and desirable at all times. No case too extreme. Even when God said, " Thou shalt die," Hezekiah's prayer was successful. " Is any afflicted, let him pray." Hezekiah's recovery was connected,

2. *With the use of means,* verse 7. We cannot doubt the perilousness of the case without God's interposition. The disease was a fatal one, only God could stay it; but God is the author of means. In the use of wise and proper means we may expect God's blessing. Many of Christ's miracles were connected with means. Clay and spittle, &c.

3. *It was attested by a miraculous event.* Hezekiah seemed exceedingly anxious; death probably appeared at hand; hope had expired, and he sought of God a sign. Many cases of a similar kind, Gideon and the fleece, &c. This is always the sign of weak faith; nothing can be stronger than God's word. Deity might be justly offended; but he remembers our frame, &c. He does not break the bruised reed, &c. The sign is specified, verses 9, 10.

4. *His recovery was connected with other blessings.* God gave more than was asked, verse 6. Probably Hezekiah desired to live chiefly for these things. God anticipates and gives liberally, &c.

5. *His lengthened life was definitely stated.* " Fifteen years." To a man on the borders of death, fifteen years is a considerable period; but what in itself? look back upon the last fifteen you have spent. To know the precise time of death is not desirable; it is not best generally, but it was with Hezekiah. God's ways are not our ways, &c.

APPLICATION

1. *Let the subject teach us the mutability of earthly affairs.* We know not what a day, &c. Do not expect to live without sorrow and crosses; this is indeed a valley of tears.

2. *Let it teach how important an interest in God's favor is.* God is all-sufficient.

3. *How important to redeem our time.* " So teach us to number our days," &c. " Be ye therefore ready," &c.

107
HISTORY OF HEZEKIAH
PART 4—HIS UNGRATEFULNESS

" But Hezekiah rendered not again according to the benefit done unto him."—2 Chronicles xxxii 25.

WE should not have been surprised if the text had been recorded of Cain, who with haughty self-complacency offered his sacrifice to God, but whose offering evidently had no respect to his own sinfulness or the provision of a Saviour; or if the text had been spoken of the murmuring Israelites, who were filled with discontent and murmuring despite of all the miracles which God wrought for them in the desert; but the text is spoken of Hezekiah, the good king Hezekiah, whose prayer obtained a long respite when the sentence of death had gone forth.

I. CONSIDER THE TEXT IN REFERENCE TO HEZEKIAH. Two inquiries will elucidate the first part of our subject.

1. *The benefits he had received.* We speak not now of the regular bounties of the divine providence and goodness; nor yet of the especial favors of God's grace. Two events had recently transpired; he had been sick, nigh unto death; the solemn mandate had been addressed to him, " Set thine house," &c. But God had heard his prayer, and, moved with compassion, had healed him, and added fifteen years to his life. What an interposition of mercy, &c. The powerful Assyrian monarch, with an army so numerous and powerful as to fill the Israelites with the utmost dismay, was at his gates. God sent his angel, and in one night 145,000 of the Assyrian army were slain. Without battle, without the aid of Hezekiah's army, &c. Now these were extraordinary acts of God's goodness and mercy. Surely they would elicit the most fervent gratitude and praise; yet it is said after all this that Hezekiah did not render, &c. We inquire then,

2. *In what way he did not render again.* We must see this as described, 2 Kings xx. 12. Hearing and witnessing the miracle which had been wrought, they came to visit the honored and distinguished monarch. In this he allowed his heart to be lifted up. With ostentation he showed them his riches, &c. He gave not God the glory of his great goodness, as he might have done, and ought to have done. Hezekiah, who removed the altars from the high

places, &c., yet allowed self for a time to reign. What reason the best have to fear their own hearts! The prophet is sent to proclaim his sin and the punishment it should produce, 2 Kings xx. 16. Hezekiah humbled himself and acknowledged the righteousness and goodness of God's administrations, 2 Kings xx. 19; 2 Chron. xxxii. 27. God's conduct towards Hezekiah in this matter is specified, verse 31. Hezekiah's heart was not perfect; lifted up, and God allowed him to lean upon it, that he might be conscious of it, and be delivered from it; like the nurse and the wayward child. Let us now consider the text,

II. IN REFERENCE TO OURSELVES. Three questions.

1. *What benefits have we received from the Lord?* How shall we describe or number them? Where shall we begin? With our temporal bounties; the good things of this life; food, raiment, dwellings, reason, health, mental enjoyments, religious privileges, sabbaths, sanctuaries, Bibles, ordinances. To the friends of Jesus, I just dwell on two points, for a few moments.

1. *Converting grace.* He has saved you from your natural lost estate. From sin and the power of Satan; from the wrath to come. Brought you into his kingdom, &c. Made you heirs of eternal life.

2. *Preserving mercy.* How great is his mercy towards them, &c. How often forgiven, sustained, blessed, &c. Kept you from the roaring lion; delivered you from innumerable perils, &c. We ask,

2. *What he has expected you to render unto him.*

(1.) Gratitude. Deep, hearty, constantly expressed and exemplified.

(2.) Supreme homage and glory. He did not design you to be lifted up, but rather humbled; he did not wish the glory to be given to his gifts, but to himself; he did not wish you to parade his blessings, but to enjoy them and use them to his glory.

(3.) Imitation of his mercy and goodness. "Be ye followers of God as dear children;" feel as God feels; "Be merciful as your Father," &c. Do good, &c. He has filled your cup to overflowing, but not to be hoarded, nor wasted, but to run in streams of benevolence among the poor and miserable of your fellow-creatures. God puts down all this as done to himself. "I was hungry, and ye fed me," &c. We ask,

3. *Who has not fallen into the sin of Hezekiah?* Not rendered according, &c. "Examine yourselves; prove your own selves," &c. Who is not guilty? He who is clear let him stand up and reproach Hezekiah. Have we not been deficient in gratitude, in humility, in doing good? Then let Hezekiah's repentance be ours. If we feel our guilt, let us confess it. Deplore and seek mercy; trust our hearts less, and seek God's grace more and more. But one word to the unconverted, who never feel grateful, but who have been eagerly sinning against God, against his mercy, his Son, his Spirit, his forbearance. Oh! think how wicked, how base, how ruinous it must be. "There is forgiveness," &c. Seek it now, and through Christ's merits alone.

108

THE CHAFF AND WHEAT CONTRASTED

"What is the chaff to the wheat? saith the Lord."—JEREMIAH xxiii. 28.

FIDELITY in any office is of the utmost importance. It is so in the confidential servant, or steward; it is so in the watchman; it is so in the physician; it is so most of all in the minister, or servant of God. He is a steward of Christ—a watchman on the walls of Zion. He is to direct the sin-sick to the great remedy; he stands forth to show unto men the way of salvation. In every age there have been faithless men who have usurped this office; men who have ministered for hire; who have sought their own profit; have taught for a morsel of bread. Such prophets existed in the time of Jeremiah. Men prophesied whom God had not sent; see verse 21. God affirms his omnipresence, verse 23; he describes the course they adopted, verse 25; then he shows how the true prophets ought to act, verse 28; and then follows the text.

I. WE SHALL APPLY THE TEXT TO THE VALUE AND IMPORTANCE OF THE DIVINE WORD, AS OUR INFALLIBLE DIRECTORY IN MATTERS OF RELIGION. The word of God is indeed the wheat—the grain of life. It is that which he has given to be the food of the soul. As such, it is adapted to our state, sufficient for our necessities; able to save the soul. It never failed when received with reverence, faith, and obedience. Now, every thing else presented to us for this purpose is chaff.

1. *What is reason in the place of the scriptures ?* A telescope in the dark ! With the light of truth, it is incalculably precious ; without it, nothing at all. Go to the rude savage tribes, and they have it ; to the cannibal hordes, and they have it.

2. *What is learning, or science, or philosophy, without the Bible ?* Go to the learned, philosophic Egyptians, who worshipped 3000 animals and plants ; go to the philosophical and scientific Grecians ; see their works of art and science. Their painters and sculptors were chiefly employed in contributing to their idolatrous temples. Go now to the eastern world, where literature both of a metaphysical and poetical character has flourished for ages, and yet the people are without God and hope in the world. If reason or learning would lead men to God and his services, then piety would flourish in the higher classes of our land, &c. ; but the reverse is the case. Beloved, there is one book of light, of legislation, of mercy ; one book to guide you to a better world—it is, *the word of the Lord.*

II. WE SHALL APPLY THE TEXT TO THE ORDINANCES OF GOD AS CONTRASTED WITH THE INSTITUTIONS OF MEN. *God's ordinances* are all founded in his own infinite skill and wisdom ; they never can be improper and unmeaning, because they are God's. *God's ordinances* are clothed with authority ; therefore they are obligatory and binding. *God's ordinances* are ever adapted to edify and do us real good ; not merely ceremonial, but means of profit. A right observance will be productive of spiritual good to every servant of God. *God's ordinances* are all clearly revealed in this book. Nothing is so, if God has not spoken. A divine ordinance must have God's express command. All *human institutions* are chaff ; light, profitless, &c. You may know all such by bringing them to the balances of the sanctuary—to the divine word. They may resemble the true, but they are chaff ; may appear resplendent and attractive, yet chaff ; be very popular, yet chaff ; have the sanction of the learned, still chaff ; regarded by many good men, after all only chaff. Wheat needs no garnishing, no painting, no addition. It is the staff of life, just as God sends it.

III. WE APPLY THE TEXT TO EVERY THING WHICH MEN MAY SUBSTITUTE FOR REAL RELIGION. By real religion, we mean a conversion, a renewed heart, an obedient life, the love of God, &c. ; having the spirit and mind of Christ. How many things persons try to substitute for these :—

1. *Self-righteousness.* A regard to our own supposed excellencies ; a self-complacent trusting to ourselves. Now this, indeed, is chaff ; a covering of filthy rags. The Pharisees boasted of this. Christ said, " Except your righteousness," &c.

2. *Religious profession.* Assuming the name, form, and the speech ; saying, " Lord ! Lord !" regular in attendance on the means, &c. Now, all this is right in itself, but it is not religion. " The kingdom of God is within," &c. " Ye must be born again." This in the place of piety is chaff, mere chaff.

3. *An exact regard to all the Lord's institutions.* We cannot urge this too forcibly ; yet this is only the evidence, and not piety itself. We may depend on these, and look to these, instead of to Christ and his cross ; we may be merely *ceremonial* Christians, without the life and spirit of Christ.

APPLICATION

1. *We urge your attention to the spirit and practice which the divine word exhibits.* Study this as to information, experience, &c.

2. *Urge sinners to obtain the benefits of saving piety.* What are your pleasures ? Chaff ; nothing else. Thousands have proved them so in adversity, sickness, and death. Have not you ? Then give your hearts to God ; set your hearts and souls to seek the Lord, &c.

109

RESPONSIBILITY

" For unto whomsoever much is given, of him shall much be required."—LUKE xii. 48.

OUR subject is that of responsibility, a subject worthy of our very serious consideration. A right apprehension of this is very desirable ; and a feeling sense of it pervading our minds would tend greatly to preserve us from the evils to which we are exposed. To the doctrine of responsibility there are no exceptions but those of idiocy and childhood. Every man of sane mind is responsible, and the consequences involved are solemn and momentous. We ask,

I. FOR WHAT ARE WE RESPONSIBLE?

1. *For our existence.* The means of life are given to us, and we are bound to preserve our lives; not to expose them to unnecessary peril; not to neglect the use of those means by which the providence of God continues our being.

2. *For our natural faculties, and bodily health and vigor.* Every power of the mind was designed for some specific use and wise end: the understanding—the judgment—the memory—the affections, &c. Now, we are responsible for the right use and employment of these. So, also, bodily health is to be cherished, and all lawful solicitude to be exercised respecting it. "Do thyself no harm," is the voice of reason as well as revelation. Hence all persons who injure their bodies, impair their health, and affect their minds by gluttony and intemperance, will not be held guiltless before the Lord.

3. *For our natural and acquired talents.* One has a bright or penetrating genius; another, a discerning judgment; a third, an eloquent tongue; a fourth, a flaming intellect; a fifth, a vivid, fertile imagination. One has acquired extensive knowledge; others are familiar with tongues; while many are intimate with the wonders of nature, or the discoveries of art. For all these we are responsible.

4. *For our wealth.* Riches are only intrusted to men as talents to be laid out for the comfort of themselves, the good of society, and the glory of God. We are responsible as to the way of obtaining it; as to the love we have to it; and as to the manner in which we expend it.

5. *For our influence.* That is, power to affect others; and this is possessed more or less by every human being; the richest and the poorest; the most learned and the most illiterate; the monarch and the peasant; the youth and the sire. All possess the power of doing others good or evil.

6. *For our privileges.* How numerous are these! There is the light of revelation; the preaching of the gospel; the ordinances of religion; the throne of grace; the Christian sabbath; the communion of saints, &c.

7. *For our time.* Next to the blood of Jesus, the most precious blessing we possess. Our seed time; our period of probation; our only day of preparation for the scenes of a solemn eternity. Oh! when we think that on this short span hang everlasting results!

8. *For the activity of life, and all the good or evil we have crowded into it.* We ask,

II. TO WHOM WE ARE RESPONSIBLE?

In some respects we are responsible to conscience, for the voice within demands attention; to an improvement of all our means and blessings; in some sense, also, to one another, according to our stations in life. Magistrates, and civil rulers, are responsible to the public for exercising righteous authority and rule; parents, for an affectionate and faithful discharge of their parental obligations; ministers to their people, for a full and faithful discharge of their ministerial and pastoral duties to their flocks; and thus, too, subjects are responsible to their rulers, children to their masters, and members to those who have the rule over them in the Lord. But we are responsible more especially to God as our Maker; as the bestower of all our blessings; as the Lord of conscience; and as our final judge. Every one must give an account of himself to God. We ask,

III. AS TO THE EXTENT OF OUR RESPONSIBILITY.

This the text affirms will be proportionate. "Where much is given," &c., Now, this accords,

1. *With the eternal principles of equity and righteousness.* Where there is no talent, there is no responsibility; where there are few, the responsibility is according. "Where much is given," &c. From the intellectual more will be demanded than from the illiterate; from the rich more beneficence than from the poor; from professors, more than from the profane; from spiritual persons, more than from the world; from the aged, more than the young. This accords,

2. *With the unvarying testimony of the Holy Scriptures.* This is very clearly presented to us in the history of Cain and Abel; Gen. iv. 7; Ezek. xxxiii. 17; Rom. ii. 11, &c.

3. *With the representations of the judgment-day.* Christ is called the righteous judge, who will judge every man according to his works.

4. *Does not this accord with your conscientious impressions of what is right?* All

earthly legislators act on this principle ; so all masters and parents ; and every man feels that it is right and fitting, that " where much is given," &c.

APPLICATION

We learn,

1. *That each man is accountable to God for himself, &c.* That is, our state and character. We cannot evade it or relinquish it.

2. *That the responsibility of some is much greater than that of others.* What a weight of responsibility rests upon some present !

3. *We should seek to know how much God expects from us.*

4. *Faith in Christ will alone give us the ability necessary to a faithful discharge of the duties, &c., of life, and enable us to stand accepted in the last day.* We must win Christ, and be found in him, &c. " The just shall live by faith," &c.

5. *Unfaithfulness will involve in eternal sorrows.*

110

OBEDIENCE TO GOD

" Then Peter and the other apostles answered and said, We must obey God rather than men."— ACTS v. 29.

THE apostles had been thrust into prison for obedience to their Lord and Master, Jesus Christ. God, however, had sent an angel and delivered them from prison, and had directed them to go forth into the temple, and speak the words of life to the people. In the morning, when they should have appeared before the council, it was discovered, that instead of being in confinement, they were again publishing in the temple the gospel of Jesus Christ. From thence they were brought to answer for their conduct, when the high priest said, " Did not we straitly ?" &c. Then Peter and the other apostles answered and said, " We must obey God," &c. The subject is clearly the obligation of supreme obedience to God. Consider,

I. THE NATURE OF TRUE OBEDIENCE TO GOD. Now, it is obvious that true obedience must,

1. *Be divine in its rule.* Obedience supposes laws—laws published, recognised, and enforced with due authority. Now, there must be a rule for Christian obedience. It is not a vague thing—a matter left to fancy or feeling. This rule is the word of God. The Holy Scriptures contain the mind of God ; they are full, clear, and sufficient. It comprises all that is necessary for present godliness, and for our eternal salvation. True obedience,

2. *Must be universal in its regards.* It must respect all that the Lord hath spoken. If we select a part, so may others, &c. ; thus every commandment of God would be made null and void. All the requirements of God are the emanations of infinite wisdom, holiness, and love. Take the statute-book of any kingdom : a man is not a loyal and good subject, who obeys a few of the laws, and violates the rest. Apply it to forgery, theft, murder ; see James ii. 10. Now. the laws of God are of two kinds— *moral requirements* and *positive institutions.* The moral requirements are found in the ten commandments, and illustrated in Christ's sermon on the mount; positive institutions were numerous under the law, they are few and simple under the gospel. Now of these, the Lord's supper and baptism are the chief. Both of these are expressly enjoined ; they stand prominently in the statute-book of Zion. You would have to erase the gospels, the Acts, and the epistles, before you could erase them. Now, it is often clear that persons who would shudder to violate the moral, yet with the greatest indifference neglect the positive institutions. We ask, in both cases is not the authority the same ? Has not God manifested his severest wrath against those who have violated or neglected his positive institutions ? This was the sin of our *first parents ;* this was the sin of *Lot's wife ;* this was the sin of Uzziah, who invaded the priest's office, and was smitten with leprosy, &c. 2 Chron. xxvi. 16, &c. Unquestionably obedience is the duty of all who profess to be the loyal servants of God.

3. *It must be affectionate and sincere.* Obedience of the affections ; from love and not terror ; to please God more than escape his wrath. " This is the love of God," &c. Sincere in opposition to formal ; obedience of the heart with the body. Both must be united; both make it an acceptable sacrifice.

4. *It must be open and uncompromising* Not secret ; not with policy, &c. This is mean and dishonorable to the sacred

cause. The apostles and martyrs were put to death for "open" obedience. They might have thought and felt as they pleased without persecution; but the love of Christ constrained them, &c. God is to be first; his honor and laws must ever have the pre-eminence; see it in the three Hebrews; in Daniel; in the apostles on this occasion. "Whoso is ashamed of me," &c. We are to testify, to witness, &c.; "living epistles," &c.

5. *It must be constant and persevering.* Not occasional acts, but the habit of the life; the general, the persevering course, even unto death. "He that endureth," &c. "Be faithful," &c.

6. *It must be humble and evangelical.* Our obedience is necessarily that of imperfect beings. After all, unprofitable servants; no room for self-complacency, &c. All must be accepted through Christ; my person, repentance, faith, prayers, and every thing. Consider,

II. OUR OBLIGATION TO TRUE OBEDIENCE. We ought,

1. *From the authority of God.* He has the right to legislate. You do not dispute this. It is our imperative duty, then, to obey. He is the greatest of all beings, infinitely glorious, &c. Disobedience is treason, rebellion, &c.

2. *From grateful feelings to God.* Disobedience is ingratitude. Is it not so in the child? in the servant? in the subject? Think of God, his goodness, love, and mercy. Behold nature, providence, grace. Look at earth, air, sky; especially look at the cross, the scenes of Calvary, &c.

3. *From the present and eternal advantages of obedience.* "His commandments are not grievous." "In keeping of them there is great reward." "Godliness is profitable." Was it not the advantage of the Israelites to look to the brazen serpent? of Naaman, to go and dip in Jordan? of the blind man, to go and wash in Siloam? of the 3000, to repent, believe, and be baptized? It is for our interest, present and eternal, to obey God.

APPLICATION

1. *We ought to obey God rather than men.* However great, learned, pious, or distinguished.

2. *Let our obedience be prompt and immediate.* We should obey him now. Now we can, &c.

3. *Call upon all to repent and believe the gospel.*

111

EZEKIEL'S VISION OF THE VALLEY OF DRY BONES

"The hand of the Lord was upon me, and carried me out in the Spirit of the Lord, and set me down in the midst of the valley which was full of bones," &c.—EZEKIEL xxxvii. 1–10.

EZEKIEL, the writer of the prophecies of this book, was the son of Buzi, and was carried away captive to Babylon by Nebuchadnezzar, in the year of the world 3405, or 598 years before the advent of Christ. He began to prophesy in the fifth year of his captivity, and continued his sacred office for about twenty or twenty-one years. His prophecies are distinguished for their dark parabolical representations, and their highly figurative style. His descriptions are exceedingly bold, and often are wrought up with vehement energy, so as to possess a daring grandeur beyond any other portions of the sacred volume. Not so simple or perspicuous as the other prophets; but in majestic splendor he far excels them, and has no compeer, except in some of the resplendent visions of Isaiah, or the awfully grand predictions of the exiled John in Patmos. The vision we have selected for our present meditation manifestly relates to the restoration of the Jews, and is supposed to include both their return from Babylon, and also their restoration in the latter days to their own land. The former view was realized, when God turned back their captivity, and brought them back to their beloved land; their general restoration is yet to come. They appear at present scattered over the whole region of the valley of our world, without political existence or distinction; having residence everywhere, but citizenship nowhere. Their restoration, however, is matter of glorious certainty. The same hand that scattered will gather them; the same power that dispersed will collect them; and the Jewish stream of existence, which has never commingled with the waters of the common family of man, will return to fertilize and bless the land of Judea. That will be a glorious day, not only for themselves, but for the world. Hear what the apostle says, Rom. xi. 15, xxv. 6. But the vision of the prophet is beautifully applicable to the moral state of our world, and in this respect we shall now consider it. Let us accompany the prophet, and take a survey,

I. OF THE DREARY VALLEY.

II. HEAR THE INSTRUCTIONS GIVEN TO HIM. And,

III. WITNESS THE MARVELLOUS EFFECTS WHICH FOLLOWED. Let us take a survey,

I. OF THE VALLEY OF DRY BONES.

1. *The valley is a fit emblem of our world.* Originally earth was closely allied to heaven. Our world was once the abode of purity, light, and felicity ; now it is fallen, debased ; the region of night, misery, and death. Once the garden of the Lord—the dwelling of the holy—favored by the communications of Jehovah—the presence of angels ; now a waste howling wilderness, the residence of the unbelieving, and the seat of Satan. What mists of darkness encircle it ; what sorrow, and misery, and wo distract it ! it is the region of night, and the shadow of death. And this is the aspect of the whole valley, in all its length and breadth ; in all its extent and circumference. The whole world lieth in the wicked one.

2. *See the condition of its inhabitants.* " A valley of dry bones." One vast graveyard ; one extensive charnel-house. Not covered with the recently deceased remains of humanity, but with dry bones, the scattered fragments of past generations ; heap upon heap, blanched and withered by every wind of heaven. But the question arises, what has produced this scene of desolation ? Has some pestilence wasted ? has famine dried up the reservoirs of existence ? These are the slain of sin ; these are the blighted remains of the pestilence of moral evil ; these have perished in the want and famine which their rebellion and departure from God had produced. Now, in reference to these bones, observe,

(1.) *Their number.* " Many, very many," verse 2. Such is the moral state of the hundreds of myriads of our race. There is no exception to this. All have sinned ; all are dead in trespasses, &c. ; not one righteous, &c.

(2.) *Their peculiar appearance.* " Very dry." Doubtless, there is much difference in the condition of our race. Civilization makes a great difference ; hence contrast the roaming savage and the intellectual Hindoo. The light of the gospel makes a great difference ; hence contrast the Hindoo and European. But yet, as to the want of moral resemblance to God, and a life of holiness, all men are in one state of condemnation and death. Observe,

(3.) *Their hopelessness.* " Can these dry bones live ?" &c., verse 3. Ask the philosopher, and he will confess he has no remedy for such moral dreariness ; ask the naturalist ; he will say there is hope of a tree, &c. ; but here the bones are disembodied ; no flesh, no sinews, and therefore no hope. The prophet in humility referred the subject back to God, " O Lord, thou knowest." Notice,

II. THE INSTRUCTIONS GIVEN TO THE PROPHET. " Prophesy," &c., verse 4. That is, preach. The subject is given, " O ye dry bones, hear the word of the Lord." Now, objectors might say,

(1.) *How unphilosophical !* They cannot hear ; to preach is foolish—out of the question. So might the prophet have replied. Or,

(2.) *It is unnecessary.* If they are raised, God must do it by miracle. Why, therefore, prophesy ? If he will do it, he will do it. He must do all, or none. So say some very sapient persons in reference to preaching the gospel. It is no use, they say, to preach to dead sinners. When God intends to convert them, he will do it, and our calling them is in vain. Shall the wisdom of God or man stand ? The prophet obeyed, and prophesied. Christ sent the apostles to preach the gospel to every creature, and they obeyed. The authority of Christ still extends to the Christian ministry ; and wo, wo, wo to that man who preaches not the gospel of Christ. The prophet, no doubt, cried loudly, earnestly, " Oh ! ye dry bones," &c. Now mark,

III. THE MARVELLOUS EFFECTS WHICH FOLLOWED.

1. *The dry bones heard.* The word of God can open the ears of the deaf, and can awaken the dead. The prophet might have lectured on philosophy, science, civilization, and morality, but they would not have heard. God's word is a hammer and fire ; it is spirit and life. The latent caloric heard it, when he said, " Let there be light." The sea heard it ; the dry land, &c. ; and now the dry bones hear it.

2. *They were excited.* The stillness was disturbed, " There was a shaking," &c., verse 7. How often this has been the case,

when the gospel has exerted its power on the soul! The three thousand on the day of pentecost; the jailer, &c. Fears excited; anxiety produced; prayer offered.

3. *They were brought together.* By the word, men are brought out of the world, and thus to associate together. Thus assemblies are convened, congregations collected. Now they are seen in the sanctuary.

4. *They were clothed with sinews and flesh.* No longer mere bones, dry, &c.; no longer apparently hopeless. Appearances now favorable; begin to look like men; to act, and think, and speak as rational beings; conduct now changed, &c.; habits given up; sins relinquished, &c.; but yet the vitality of religion—spiritual life—is wanting. So the prophet is now to call on the winds, verse 9. And then,

5. *They lived.* By the wind is intended God's Holy Spirit. So often thus likened, "The wind bloweth," &c. Now, the Spirit of God resuscitates; gives newness of life; raises from the dead, &c. "It is the Spirit that quickens."

6. *They appear as an exceeding great army.* Become the soldiers of Christ; fight the battles of the Lord—the good fight; and finally, receive the victorious everlasting crown and reward.

APPLICATION

1. Learn the morally dead state of sinners.

2. The efficacy of the divine word.

3. The importance of gospel prophesying.

4. The ability of sinners to hear and obey.

5. The Spirit's influence in regeneration.

6. The conflicts of the spiritual life.

112

THE SAVIOUR'S VISIT TO OUR WORLD

" Blessed be the Lord God of Israel, for he hath visited and redeemed his people."—LUKE i. 68, 69.

OF all events, that of the advent of the Saviour was the most glorious and interesting; all things connected with it are cal-culated to excite our wonder and command our praise. The glorious person appearing the world from which he came, and the errand which brought him to our earth, are all subjects sublimely important and deserving our studious contemplation. It had been predicted that a herald or harbinger should prepare the way of the Lord. Now the tidings of John's conception were announced to Zechariah, but in consequence of his unbelief he was struck dumb, and it was only when John was to be circumcised according to the law that his mouth was opened, and he spake and blessed God, &c. Notice,

I. THE DECLARATION CONCERNING THE GOD OF ISRAEL. "He hath visited us."

II. THE FIGURATIVE REPRESENTATION OF THE MESSIAH. "Hath raised up a horn."

III. THE PRAISE WHICH WE ARE BOUND TO OFFER IN COMMEMORATING THIS EVENT. " Blessed," &c.

I. THE DECLARATION CONCERNING THE GOD OF ISRAEL. No term so endearing to pious Jews as that of the God of Israel; it reminded them of the covenant he had made, the deliverance he had wrought, and the blessings he had conferred. God had often visited and often redeemed them in a temporal sense; from Egypt and Babylon. Many of these visits had been of a most striking character, as when he appeared to Moses in the bush—on Sinai—in the temple; but chiefly he visited them through the medium of the prophets. God " spake unto the fathers by the prophets;" but there was one visit above all the rest and to crown the whole, that in the person of his Son. Now of this visit of Jesus observe,

1. *It had been long promised and expected.* It was the essence of the first promise, and Eve looked for it and exclaimed, " I have gotten a man from the Lord." Abel had the eye of his faith fixed upon it. So Abraham, he desired to see and did see Christ's day and was glad. To him all the prophets gave witness, and hence a general expectation had been kept up among the pious, to the time of his incarnation. In hope of Israel's Messiah thousands had fallen into the arms of the sleep of death.

(2.) It was a visit which had been *minutely* predicted. As to the miraculous nature of his advent, the place, and the time; at the time that the sceptre departed from Judah, &c.; when Daniel's seventy weeks were accomplished, then did the illustrious visitant appear.

(3.) It was a visit distinguished for a condition of *voluntary abasement*. The Godhead descending to be veiled in flesh, leaving heaven for earth, a throne for a manger, &c.

(4.) It was still a visit of *magnificence* and *glory*. The heavens were illuminated by the star ; the skies resounded with the anthem of praise. Angels descended and proclaimed his birth. " Unto you is born," &c.

(5.) It was a visit of *stupendous love*. " God so loved," &c. " Herein is love," &c. " He sent his Son not to condemn," &c. " He came into the world to save," &c. Hence it was a visit of redeeming power and mercy. " And redeemed." To buy back—to deliver—emancipate.

II. The figurative representation of the Messiah. " Horn of salvation."

(1.) A horn is a symbol of power and strength, see 1 Sam. ii. 1 ; 2 Sam. xxii. 3.

(2.) Or it may refer to the horns of the altar to which criminals fled when in imminent peril, and where, except in case of murder, they found a sanctuary. See the case of Adonijah, 1 Kings i. 50. Now Christ is the horn of salvation to the penitent sinner who is fleeing for mercy. None can be saved elsewhere, and none can perish there.

III. The praise we should offer to God in commemorating this event. " Blessed," &c. " Thanks be to God," &c. Praise may be uttered,

1. By *the lips*. And this is right and proper. Christ must be our song.

2. By the *feelings of the heart*. By thinking, meditating, loving, and delighting in Christ.

3. By the conduct of the *life*. " We are to show forth," &c. Live to Christ, extol him in our conduct, &c. Do his will, carry out his designs.

APPLICATION

1. *This subject condemns those who make these commemorative seasons opportunities of folly and sin*. What would heathens think ?

2. *Let Christians display a spirit and conduct worthy of their profession*.

3. *Receive Christ Jesus into your hearts by personal, living faith*.

113
AN EPITOME OF THE GOSPEL

" This is a faithful saying, and worthy of all acceptation, that Christ Jesus came into the world to save sinners."—1 Timothy i 15.

Our text contains an epitome of the gospel. It is one of those exceedingly rich and comprehensive passages with which the epistles of Paul abound, and yet it may be allowed the pre-eminence of what even that distinguished apostle has penned or left on record for the consolation of the church and the hope of the world. Every word in the text is precious and momentous, and the whole is so comprehensive, that we might with propriety take the text as the basis of a series of discourses on the evidences and blessings of the Christian religion. The apostle had been referring to his own history, and the text is full of the emotion of his heart, see verse 12, &c. Notice,

I. The person to whom the text refers. " Christ Jesus." Now in contemplating the blessed person of the Saviour, we notice,

1. *His deity*. The world's Redeemer is the blessed God. Jehovah of hosts is ever represented in the Old Testament scriptures as the Redeemer of mankind. This divine character Christ also assumed. " He who hath seen me hath seen the Father." " I and the Father are one." " He thought it not robbery," &c.

2. *His humanity*. His existence is clearly intimated before he came into the world. As Deity he existed from everlasting ; when he came into the world he did not appear in the overwhelming *brightness* of his divine *glory ;* he came wrapped in *mortal flesh ;* he tabernacled in human nature ; formerly in the cloud ; now in our nature. He was made of a woman, &c. " God manifest in the flesh," &c. A child born—a son given.

3. *In the union of the two natures*. Godman. Immanuel. Real man—true God. On one occasion the disciples beheld his glory ; saw him ascend the mount as a man ; beheld him transfigured and worshipped as the God of Moses and Elijah ; this is a great mystery ; it is the mystery of godliness.

II. His visit to our world. He came into the world ; this had been long predicted and promised, long believed and expected ; at length the period arrived ; " the fulness of the times." Then he made his advent and paid the visit of his redeeming love, &c. Lived in it for about thirty-three years. Three things connected with the visit.

1. *His holy life.* He exhibited every holy virtue, every grace, every excellency, entire spotlessness. His life, a day without the least cloud of imperfection.

2. *His divine teaching.* He taught men the way to eternal life ; he made known the way of salvation ; he revealed the will of his heavenly Father.

3. *His marvellous sufferings.* Poverty, contempt, hatred, persecution, death, connected with sufferings of soul the most intense ; death the most ignominious and cruel ; death followed by a resurrection the most marvellous.

III. THE GREAT END OF CHRIST'S ADVENT. " To save sinners." Violators of God's law, polluted, wretched, worthless sinners ; sinners without plea or merit ; sinners justly perishing by reason of their own guilt. Now observe,

1. *He came to save from sin and its consequences.* Look at sin. A disease ; death its consequence. Treason ; hell its punishment. Crime ; remorse its punishment. Now his coming did not alter the fact of men being sinners, or render their sins less deserving punishment, or bribe the justice of God so as not to punish ; but he paid the exaction ; he died for the sinner—in his stead—took his place, so that through Christ the sinner may be pardoned. Now God can be just, &c. Now the penalty is withdrawn ; the rebel may live ; no necessity for his eternal death. " God so loved," &c.

2. *Into a state of holiness and its blessed results.* A sinner merely pardoned would immediately sin again, and thus would never be meet for the holy services of a holy world. Christ came into the world to exhibit real purity, and to enforce it ; but more, to obtain it for us ; this he has done by procuring the Holy Spirit, who renews the heart, changes the entire man, and gives power to love and serve God. This is the essence of salvation—to restore the lost image of God ; and this will ensure the bestowment of eternal glory ; made pure in heart, we shall see and enjoy God forever and ever.

IV. THE APOSTLE'S REMARKS CONCERNING THIS GREAT GOSPEL SAYING. He says that it is,

1. *Faithful.* That is, it is true ; it is a verity, not a fable, not an imposition ; that Christ lived, wrought miracles and was crucified, is attested by heathen and Jewish writers as well as Christians. The testimonies of Christians for 300 years, who were put to death by thousands for believing it and professing it. The power and influence of this truth, wherever it has been promulgated by preaching or diffusing the gospel, prove it.

2. *It is worthy of all acceptation.* Worthy of being accepted ; that is, being believed and trusted in ; to accept it, is to give full credit to it, and treat it as true ; to believe it with all our hearts. Now, it is worthy of *all* acceptation, that is, a cordial, decided, and grateful acceptation. With joy and thanksgiving, &c. It is worthy of being accepted *by all.* All classes—learned and illiterate—rich and poor ; all grades, profane and moral ; all ages, young and old.

APPLICATION

1. *But one saying in the world that meets the sinner's case, and it is this concerning Christ.* His cross and gospel, the only ground of hope.

2. *This saying every sinner is heir to.* Gospel has sent it to every creature, even the chief ; the vilest man on earth is but a sinner ; the best man is a sinner too.

3. *Accept it, or it will not, cannot save you.* Do it now. Prove it, &c.

114

JOHN THE BAPTIST
PART 1

" Verily, I say unto you, Among them that are born of women," &c.—MATTHEW xi. 11.

JOHN the Baptist had sent two disciples to inquire into the character of Jesus, and his profession of the Messiahship. It could not be that he thus sent for his own sake, for he had seen and heard the attestation of Christ even at his baptism ; but, doubtless, he did this for the sake of his own disciples, that they might receive him, and cleave to him as the sent of God. The Saviour's account of John is peculiarly forcible and striking. He refers to the plain and powerful characteristics of John's manner, in verses 7 and 8 ; then to his exalted office, verses 9 and 10 ; and thus concludes the description. Our text may refer to his peculiarly holy character—to his powerful and effective ministry ; but we rather think, to the particular office of John as the herald and harbinger of Christ. In this, he was greater than any of the prophets, &c. ; yet in respect of the glory of the gospel dispensation, the least of the apostles of Christ would be greater and more dignified than John. Before we enter on the life of the Baptist, let us just glance at the prophecies which had respect to him ; Isaiah xl. 3, &c. ; Malachi iii. 1. The concluding prophecy, which referred to Christ, also noticed his illustrious harbinger. Observe, then, in reference to the Baptist,

I. His PARENTAGE AND BIRTH. His father, Zacharias, was,

(1.) Priest of the Lord. His mother was a holy woman ; the cousin of the virgin mother of Jesus. Read the description of this godly pair, Luke i. 6.

(2.) He was of the course of Abia. David divided the priests into twenty-four classes, or courses, who performed their duty in the temple week by week. The priests generally resided in cities a little distance from Jerusalem. From these they came to the temple service, and then returned to their dwellings.

(3.) Zacharias was now engaged in his priestly service of offering incense to the Lord. In offering incense, three persons were engaged : one was to remove the ashes of the previous service ; another to bring the pan of burning coals from the altar of burnt sacrifice, and then retire ; the third was to pour the incense on the coals, and while the smoke filled the place, to intercede with Jehovah on behalf of the people. This Zacharias was doing, when he beheld on the right side of the altar, the angel of the Lord. The fears of Zacharias were aroused. Fear is the attendant of sin. The best men feel their sinfulness, and therefore fear.

(4.) The celestial messenger, however, now reveals his errand ; see Luke i. 13, &c. He also reveals his own name— " Gabriel," one of the chief and exalted attendants of God ; he had six hundred years before visited Daniel.

(5.) Observe Zacharias's difficulty of belief, verse 18. Here was the struggle between doubt and faith, " Lord, I believe," &c. God's word enough ; nothing can be really stronger ; he evidently desired a sign. **Observe,**

(6.) The token given, verse 20. A very painful one ; yet, in the midst of deserved wrath, God remembered mercy. Nothing more grievous than unbelief ; it is an insult offered to the veracity of God. He was now the subject of solicitude, as he did not appear at the usual period, &c., verse 21. At length he came forth, but his appearance and manner indicated that something extraordinary had occurred, &c., verse 22. Zacharias, notwithstanding all the events which had taken place, continued his service in the temple, and when his period of ministration was ended, he returned to his own house.

(7.) At length the birth of John took place, amidst the joy and thanksgiving of his friends, verse 58 ; and on the day of his circumcision, they proposed to call him after the name of his father, Zacharias ; but his mother said, " Nay, let him be named John." Zacharias was then appealed to, and he asked for a writing-table, and he wrote his name, " *John,*" and immediately his tongue was loosed, and he spake and praised God, verse 64–66. Let us just glance,

II. AT THE PERSONAL CHARACTER OF JOHN. Now observe,

1. *He was sanctified to the Lord from the womb.* God raised him up for his own special work and glory. The same is also recorded of Jeremiah, i. 5 ; and it was equally so with Samuel.

2. *He was to be a Nazarite in his course of life ;* verse 15. Thus he was not to drink either wine or strong drink. God designed him for an especial work, and demanded great austerity of life. He was to be an example of self-denial and self-government to the people. One inference can be drawn from this : God has connected especial honor with those who avoid intoxicating fluids.

3. *He was to be filled with the Holy Ghost.* Thus in heart and mind, in lip and life, in knowledge, and unction, and power, he was to be a burning and shining light, and a faithful herald of his blessed Lord, &c. Learn,

1. That heads of families should study the graphic exhibition of domestic piety as given in the account of the parents of John, verse 6.

2. While we consider Zacharias and Elizabeth as highly favored of the Lord, yet think on our superior privileges **and**

mercies. "To us a child is born," &c.; the child Jesus; the Lord, the Saviour.

3. To testify of him messengers of mercy have been sent to us. Have we heard, believed, and been brought to a saving knowledge of Jesus?

115

JOHN THE BAPTIST
PART 2

"Verily I say unto you, Among them that are born of women there hath not risen a greater than John the Baptist."—MATTHEW xi. 11.

HAVING previously directed your attention to several leading features in the person of this distinguished servant of God, we now have to contemplate his ministry and public character. A word or two, however, first, respecting his personal appearance and mode of life.

(1.) *His appearance was peculiarly plain.* His garment was made of the coarse camel's hair, bound round him with a leathern girdle—a dress which had often been worn by the Jewish prophets. How great the contrast between his costume and that of some modern preachers of the gospel, who study elegance and finery; whose fingers and persons are often arrayed with rings and jewels; a sad example to the auditories they address.

(2.) *His mode of life was peculiarly austere.* "And his meat was locusts and wild honey." Locusts were only eaten by the poorest of the people; and in this description we are reminded of the humble class of persons with whom he chiefly mixed, and the abstemiousness he observed with regard to his food. Many persons live only to eat and attend to the appetites of the animal man. John only ate to live. He was indifferent to the luxuries of life, and existed to execute his high office and glorify God. In referring to John's public labors, observe,

I. THE SPHERE WHICH HE PRINCIPALLY OCCUPIED. The district called the "wilderness of Judea," was not a dreary, uninhabited part of the land, but one less populated than other regions. It would have been out of character for John to have retired from mankind, when he came expressly to teach them. In this wilderness there were several villages, of which Bethabara was one and the chief. Here, at some distance

from the noisy, busy cities, did he publish the nature of his message, and the truths of his great commission. To the standard of truth John elevated, great numbers resorted; so much so, that in hyperbolical language, "there went out to him Jerusalem, and all Judea;" that is, great numbers of the people. Notice,

II. THE SPIRIT OF JOHN'S MINISTRY. The spirit of John's ministry had been typified in the life and labors of Elijah the prophet, verse 14; Mal. iv. 5. The period when both were called, was one of general declension. In the plainness of their attire they resembled each other; in their holy daring, and lofty, courageous spirit; in their zeal for the glory of God; in faithfully reproving iniquity in exalted places; and as Elijah just went before the prophetical dispensation, and introduced it, so John came to prepare the way for the great Prophet, the heavenly teacher, and the gospel dispensation. Observe,

III. THE NATURE OF HIS MINISTRY. This embraced four things:—

1. *To convince the people of their sins.* There was a spiritual apathy on the people generally; among the Pharisees, a spirit of self-righteousness, and among the Sadducees, a spirit of skepticism and unbelief. He labored to awaken the careless, to strip the Pharisees of their hypocrisy, and to arouse all classes to a sense of religion.

2. *Repentance.* This was John's great doctrine. "Repent." Change your course of life; think differently, feel differently, act differently; he demanded, too, *fruits* of repentance; see Matt. iii. 8, &c.

3. *Baptism.* He was emphatically styled the "Baptist." In the Dutch version he is called the "dipper." He baptized the people in Jordan. On the repentance of the people, he baptized them for the remission of sins. Thus he said, "Forsake your evil doings, confess your faults, be baptized, and expect the Messiah, whose herald I am, and ye shall obtain forgiveness of sin."

4. *Thus his ministry was to prepare a people for the Lord.* Having gone forth for some period doing so, he was then honored by being called to baptize Jesus, his Lord, and introduce the Saviour to the Jewish nation. This he did, his humility being overruled by Christ; for when Jesus had come ninety miles to John, John confessed his unworthiness for the office; but the Re-

deemer said, "Suffer it to be so now, for thus it becometh," &c. It was now that John truly said to his disciples respecting his own ministry, "I must decrease, but he (i. e. Jesus) must increase."

(1.) John's ministry was to a great extent *successful*. Many heard, and feared, and turned to the Lord. His known sanctity, and his holy fidelity, gave him great influence over the people, and his name and virtues were greatly venerated by the Jews.

(2.) His ministry was, however, but of *short duration*. It is probable that John did not begin his work more than a year before Christ's baptism, and considerably before Christ's death it terminated. This will lead us to consider,

IV. THE TRAGICAL DEATH OF THE BAPTIST; Matt. xiv. 1. Herod, the tetrarch, had married his brother Philip's wife, although his brother was still living. This wicked exhibition of adultery and incest, John had faithfully reproved, and had said to Herod, "It is not lawful for thee to have her," &c., verse 4. In this the Baptist exposed his life, for Herod was urged by Herodias to kill him, and would have put him to death but for fear of the people. An occasion, however, is soon found for the removal of this preacher of righteousness, Matt. xiv. 6. Herod's birthday is kept; here was music, and feasting, and dancing; the daughter of Herodias so pleased Herod and the guests, that he said, "Ask of me," &c. Here was a rash and foolish engagement, made under the influence of sensual excitement, and made to a girl on account of her skill and grace in dancing, &c. The daughter consults with the mother, and the mother instructed her as to the nature of her request. Who could have supposed the horrid request, which the sequel of the history presents, would have been made! She asks not for an estate, riches, or glory, but for a head—the head of a living human being; the head of a servant of the living God; the head of John the Baptist!

The king is sorry. Exceedingly so, &c.; yet for his oath's sake, and for his honor with the guests, he consents. Here a wicked vow is still more wickedly kept; the principle the same as the false honor of the duellist and the gambler of our own time; the honor of fiendish spirits; of proud human demons.

The decree is given, for the request is instant. "Give me," says a young, attractive damsel, "*here,* now at this feast, at this time, give me the head of the Baptist in a platter or dish."

The executioner is dispatched. The holy man is secretly beheaded; his head is placed in the horrid dish, and brought to the banquet of wine and revelling; the damsel receives it with the awful distortions of death in the muscles of the countenance, and she gives it to her mother. Here the affecting narrative terminates. History records that the vengeance of God rested upon each of the perpetrators of this atrocious deed. Herod's overthrow soon followed, and he was banished to Lyons, in Gaul. It is said of the impious daughter of Herodias, that as she was crossing a frozen river the ice separated, and she sank to the neck, when two pieces severed her head from the body.

APPLICATION

1. *Learn the mysteriousness of divine providence.* The enemies of God often in purple, in pomp, &c.; John in prison; beheaded. A glance at the judgment, and the eternal state, will reconcile us to the dispensation: "Blessed are the dead who die in the Lord," and especially "for the Lord." Sooner home, sooner glorified.

2. *The snares of unlawful pleasures.* How ruinous has been the banquet! more so than war, or pestilence, or famine. How hardening, &c. Wine is not only a mocker, but often a blood-thirsty demon.

3. *Have we received the Messiah, and the kingdom he came to establish?* This is the great question; personal—individual—universal.

116

THE POOR OF THE STREETS AND LANES INVITED

"Then the master of the house being angry said to his servant, Go out quickly into the streets and lanes of the city, and bring in hither the poor, and the maimed, and the halt, and the blind."— LUKE xiv. 21.

OUR text is part of the parable of the marriage supper, which is designed to exhibit the abundant provision of the gospel, and the sinful rejection of it by unbelieving sinners. Man, by reason of transgression, had involved himself in wretchedness and misery. As a sinful rebel, he had forfeited all claim to the divine goodness and bounty ; here we see then the grace of God in freely providing the means of happiness for his ruined creatures. The blessings of the gospel are likened to a feast, a great supper ; here we have suitable provision ; the richest and most costly provision ; here is an overflowing provision ; an abundance, enough for all ; the invitation issued was of the most free and generous kind, verses 16, 17.

The conduct of the bidden guests was most ungrateful and wicked. " And they all with one consent," &c. It was then that the servants showed these things, &c. ; and he said, " Go out quickly," &c. Notice,

I. THE SPHERE OF MINISTERIAL LABOR. " Streets and lanes of the city." In other passages it is said, " the highways and hedges," &c. Originally God was worshipped in the temple, and in the synagogues about Judea. When John the Baptist, however, came, he went ,abroad into the public places, and cried, " Repent ye," &c. Now Jesus acted upon the same principle. He addressed the people on the sea-shore, on the mountain top, in the highways, &c. The apostles acted in like manner, they went forth preaching the kingdom of the grace of God in the streets of Jerusalem, &c. Our missionaries have to act upon the same plan ; if they were to wait until the heathen came to them, few would hear the word of life ; it is desirable in our own country that this also should be done. Many never think of God or his house ; but if entreated they might be induced to hear : how can this be done ? both by preaching in the streets, &c., and by visiting the families in our benighted neighborhoods, and persuading them to visit the house of God.

II. OBSERVE THE OBJECTS OF MINISTERIAL EFFORT. " The poor, the maimed, the halt, and the blind." If we consider these words literally, then we may consider that the wretched, in general, are to be specially invited, &c. The gospel is emphatically sent to the poor ; it is of the greatest importance to them in this life ; their souls are of incalculable value—of eternal worth; but do we not see that the text is applicable in a spiritual sense to all men ?

1. *All sinners are truly poor.* Poor as it respects the soul and eternity ; as poor as the starving prodigal.

2. *All sinners are maimed and halt* Sin has destroyed the energies of the soul ; they have not the power our holy parents in Paradise had. They are the slaves of the enemy, &c.

3. *All sinners are blind.* In the darkness of moral ignorance—in the darkness of unbelief—in the darkness of condemnation. They see not their own condition—they see not the beauty of religion—they see not the excellency of Christ—they see not the preciousness of the gospel, or the importance of salvation. A poor, maimed, blind creature, in the street, is only a faint type of the true misery of the sinner. To be blind on the verge of eternity ! on the margin of the fathomless lake of fire !

II. THE DIRECTION GIVEN RESPECTING MINISTERIAL EFFORT. It is personal effort. They are to go out. Many duties connected with the ministerial work ; reading, study, &c. ; but all these must be in reference to the work of preaching—of inviting sinners. Now, in going out, three things are important :—

1. *We must go out in Christ's name.* We are his servants ; he commissions us ; all our authority is derived from him.

2. *With his message.* What he has enjoined. Many subjects might amuse, might interest, &c. Wonders of nature—of providence. The earth—the heavens, &c. No, it must be the gospel—the good news of the kingdom ; publishing Christ as the only Saviour. " This is a faithful saying," &c. " The supper is ready," &c. There must be,

3. *Promptitude of action.* "Quickly." Now there are three reasons for this :—

(1.) The work is divine and spiritual : this is the chief thing. Soul and eternity first—God and his glory first.

(2.) Our time of labor is limited. What the minister does, he must do quickly. " I must work," &c. Soon we must give an account.

(3.) Sinners are perishing ; every day —every hour—every moment, they are hurrying into eternity ; every soul thus lost is of eternal value ; then it must be done quickly ; the person enveloped with flames, must be saved quickly ; the shipwrecked mariner must have the life-boat quickly ; the dying sinner must have the balm of life quickly. When the soul and heaven are concerned, every thing must be done quickly.

APPLICATION

1. *You have often been addressed.* Have you obeyed the gospel ? Have you been brought into the favor and family of God ?

2. *Urge it upon all to-night.* We exhort —we entreat—we invite all.

117

THE WEDDING GARMENT

" And when the king came in to see the guests, he saw there a man which had not on a wedding garment; and he saith unto him, Friend, how camest thou in hither not having a wedding garment ? And he was speechless. Then said the king to the servants, Bind him hand and foot, and take him away, and cast him into outer darkness ; there shall be weeping and gnashing of teeth."— MATTHEW xxii. 11–13.

THE gospel minister must declare the whole counsel of God. We must exhibit both the promises and the threatenings ; we must invite by all the greatness and preciousness of the provision, but we must also alarm by exhibiting the terrific consequences of refusing the overtures of life. In the parable of which the text is the conclusion, the embassy of love and mercy had first of all been rejected ; but afterwards, a number had been prevailed upon to comply with the invitation, and the table was furnished with guests ; but there is presented to us the fearful condition of one of the guests. " And when the king came in to see the guests," &c. To realize the force of the picture, imagine the splendid guest-chamber of an eastern monarch, arrayed in all the magnificence of oriental grandeur. The wedding ceremonies of the heir to the throne are to be sumptuously celebrated. The provision is costly and abundant. To add to the effect, and to exhibit the riches and glory of the feast, costly vestments are prepared for all the guests, and in these it is expected they will all appear at the royal banquet. The room is splendidly illuminated ; the guests are all assembled, when the king in majestic state is announced. In looking around, an individual is perceived without the appointed garment ; he is interrogated by the monarch, and it is found that he is an intruder, or one who has treated his king with contempt. He is immediately seized by the servants and borne into the gloomy prison at the base of the palace, where is darkness, and weeping and gnashing of teeth. Such might be considered the literal illustration of the text. Let us reflect on the spiritual import and design of the passage. We must consider what we are to understand,

I. BY THE WEDDING GARMENT. Now it is clear that it is the costume, or spiritual dress, necessary for the enjoyment of heaven. We need not then be in doubt on this subject. The garment is " holiness, without which no man shall see the Lord." It is the complete renewal of the soul in the likeness of the divine image, which consists of knowledge, righteousness, and true holiness. Now this holiness of heart and life is often described as a garment. " I put on righteousness, and it clothed me ; my judgment was as a robe and a diadem," Job xxix. 14. Hence Isaiah says, " He hath clothed me with the garments of salvation, he hath covered me with the robe of righteousness, as a bridegroom decketh himself with ornaments, and as a bride adorneth herself with her jewels," lxi. 10. Hence the church is thus described by the psalmist, " The king's daughter is all glorious within, her clothing is of wrought gold," &c., Psalm xlv. 13. Hence too when the prodigal returned, he was adorned with the best robe. The Laodiceans were exhorted to buy gold, &c. " I counsel thee to buy of me gold tried in the fire, that thou mayest be rich ; and white raiment that thou mayest be clothed," &c. Rev. iii. 18 ; and this agrees with the description of the heavenly company : " And lo ! a great multitude, which no man could number, of all nations, and kindreds, and people, and tongues, stood before the Lamb, clothed with white robes, and palms in their hands," Rev. vii. 9. Mark,

II. THE SOLEMN SCRUTINY. " The king came in," &c. This scrutiny,

1. *Was divine.* The survey was made by that omniscient Being whose eyes are as a flame of fire. Nothing is more dangerous than for mortals to judge one another, " Judge not," &c. It is not likely that even in a future state we shall possess the power of discerning the heart ; but the king immortal, invisible, " whose eyes," &c. He seeth the thoughts afar off. Before him all things are naked, &c. At once he beheld the man without the wedding garment.

2. *This scrutiny was personal.* The guests were not surveyed in masses—not

in nations, sects, or churches, or families; but in their individual character; never was a nation all holy and sacred; nor yet a sect—nor church—nor perhaps an entire family. Religion is a personal concern; it is so from first to last; it will be so in its great and momentous consequences to all eternity.

III. THE AWFUL DETECTION. "He saw there a man," &c. We may form three conjectures as to this robeless character.

1. *It might have resulted from carelessness.* He did not attend to the requirements of the king; he never duly thought and reflected; was never deeply impressed with the dignity and glory for which a sacred preparation was necessary. How many such are now in the presence of God; no deep impression as to the necessity of vital religion, of holiness of heart.

2. *It might have resulted from procrastination.* He had perhaps been aware of the requisite costume, but had deferred the matter until it was too late. How many of such are here this evening? You believe in the doctrine of regeneration, &c.; but you remain the children of nature; spiritual piety is put off; it has been so for years; it may be so until it is too late.

3. *It might have resulted from proud and wicked preference.* Perhaps thought it not essential; had other views; would trust to the mercy of the king, or to his own beautiful habiliments. Are there not some of this class present? You do not like spiritual, internal, evangelical godliness; satisfied without this. Moral, benevolent, nominally Christians. Observe,

IV. THE AWFUL INVESTIGATION. "Friend, how camest thou," &c.

1. *This investigation was public.* Before all the guests. The enemies of Christ will be publicly confounded at the last day; clothed with shame and contempt.

2. *This investigation was reasonable.* It gave an opportunity for the exhibition of righteousness. "How," &c. Give a reason, &c. God will allow the sinner to plead. This investigation,

3. *Was overwhelming.* "He was speechless." He was surprised, detected, ashamed; he had no reason to assign, hence he was confounded. Mark,

V. THE DREADFUL PUNISHMENT. Notice,

1. *The removal.* "Take him away." From a palace to a prison—from a feast to wretchedness—from angels to devils—from heaven to hell.

2. *The sentence.* "Cast him into outer darkness." Regions of darkness—chains of darkness—the blackness of darkness.

3. *The misery.* "There shall be weeping and gnashing," &c. The retrospect shall cause this; a life of folly, of gross infatuation, &c. The present, covered with shame, the gnawing of conscience; the gloomy prospect, no hope of release, or even alleviation. Lost, irreparably lost; lost forever.

APPLICATION

1. *Now all that is necessary for heaven may be obtained, and that by all.*

2. *Let professors examine themselves, &c.* Are you in Christ? Have you put him on? &c.

3. *Let sinners be entreated.* Listen to the voice of the gospel and live.

118

THE WOMAN WITH THE BLOODY ISSUE

"And a certain woman, which had an issue of blood twelve years, and had suffered many things of many physicians," &c.—MARK v. 25, &c.

OUR subject is one of the cures effected by the miraculous power of the Lord Jesus Christ. Numerous and astonishing were the miracles of mercy which he performed; and it is worthy of note, that the diseases he cured were such as were counted hopeless by the ordinary modes of healing. Such was the leper, yet he had but to say, "Be thou clean," &c.; such was natural blindness, yet he opened the eyes of the man born blind; such was established paralysis; but to the most inveterate instance of palsied misery he said, "Arise, take up thy bed," &c. An issue of blood, of twelve years' standing, was a disease evidently of this kind. Let us see in this diseased woman,

I. AN EMBLEM OF THE SINNER'S SPIRITUAL STATE.

II. IN HER MODE OF APPLICATION, AN EXAMPLE WORTHY OF THE SINNER'S IMITATION.

III. IN HER CURE, A PLEDGE OF THE SINNER'S ACCEPTANCE AND SALVATION. In this woman we see,

I. AN EMBLEM OF THE SINNER'S SPIRITUAL CONDITION. Four points: a distressing disease; of long continuance; growing worse and worse ; and incurable by human agency. Observe in this woman,

1. *A distressing disease.* " An issue of blood." The disease was one of Levitical uncleanness ; no doubt a cause of great suffering, and which, according to the Mosaic ritual, excluded her from the society of others. Now, sin is often thus represented. It is the plague of the heart ; it is internal and universal spiritual defilement ; see Isaiah i. 4. This moral pollution excludes the soul from the fellowship of a holy God, and the enjoyment of holy services. With this every sinner is afflicted. This woman's affliction,

2. *Was of long continuance.* " Twelve years." Thus, it was deeply seated and established in the system. The disease of sin is of still longer continuance. Look back to your youth—to your childhood ; the very first actions, thoughts, and words evince that the heart is corrupt, and the soul under the influence of moral disease. Thus for years it has been more and more deeply rooted in the system, and establishing its evil dominion and habits in the inmost recesses of the soul. The affliction of this woman,

3. *Grew worse and worse.* Sin never consumes itself ; never expires of itself ; never heals of itself ; neither is it ever stationary. Like the stream ever flowing ; tree ever growing ; waxing worse and worse ; spreading and extending its power over the whole man.

4. *It was incurable by human instrumentality.* She had felt it, and deplored it, and sought its removal. She had suffered many things, verse 26 ; she had spent all that she had ; she had applied to many physicians. How often do sinners exactly copy her example ; go to a variety of sources for happiness and peace, and find none. Sometimes to the works of the law ; sometimes to nominal religion ; sometimes to penances, fasts, &c. ; sometimes to almsgiving, &c. But all our time, all our energies, are thus employed in vain. None of these can heal or save ; all physicians of no value. Happy for this daughter of affliction that Jesus, the great healer, passed by where she dwelt ; that she heard of him ; and that she presented herself to his compassionate nature.

II. In her mode of application ; an **EXAMPLE WORTHY OF THE SINNER'S IMITATION.** Having heard of Jesus, she,

1. *Exercised faith in his healing power* For she said, " If I may," &c., verse 28. Now this was strong faith, marvellous faith, of which there had been no previous instance. He had spoken and cured diseases ; but she believed that contact with his garment was enough. Thus the sinner must believe. Observe,

2. *Her faith overcame the obstacles in her way to the Saviour.* There was a crowd of persons ; many persons intervened between her and the Messiah ; it required activity, energy, and resolution ; had she waited, or neglected the opportunity, her disease would have remained. There will ever be a crowd of obstacles in the way to the Saviour. Every penitent has so found it ; so that decision and striving are ever necessary.

3. *Her faith brought her to the saving extraction of the Redeemer's virtue.* As she desired, and believed, and hoped, so it was to her. She touched the hem of his garment, and the virtue was drawn out, " and straightway," &c., verse 29. The exercise of faith in Christ is always followed by like results. But this leads us to consider her cure,

III. As a pledge of the sinner's acceptance and salvation. The Saviour knew the effect produced by the going out of the virtue of his healing power. He interrogated her, that the case might be evident, and that he might honor the faith, and confirm the cure. In her case we have a pledge,

1. *He can save and heal the soul, as well as the body.* He came expressly to do this ; the instances are innumerable.

2. *He will save every believing, trusting sinner.* He has engaged to do it ; he loves to do it ; he longs to do it ; it is his reward and joy.

3. *He will save in the same way, and by the same means, and on the same terms.* By his inherent virtue and merits—the efficacy of his atoning blood ; by the same means—the faith of the applicant ; and on the same terms—" without money," &c. Freely, fully, and forever.

APPLICATION

1. *How many are still afflicted with the plague of sin?* Apply to Jesus all of you, and now. He is the only physician ; he alone can save.

2. *How many are anxious to obtain it ?*

Do not let the press keep you back; be resolved; be in earnest. Imitate the spirit and conduct of this woman.

3. *How many are healed?* Oh! exhibit much love and gratitude to Christ, and much compassion for souls. Proclaim this Saviour everywhere, &c.

119

MARTHA'S INORDINATE CAREFULNESS

"But Martha was cumbered about much serving, and came to him, and said, Lord, dost thou not care that my sister hath left me to serve alone? bid her, therefore, that she help me. And Jesus answered and said unto her, Martha, Martha, thou art careful and troubled about many things."— LUKE x. 40, 41.

ALL circumstances and conditions of life have their respective snares and dangers. There are temptations and evils to which all persons are liable; often in danger even from lawful things. Prudence is an important virtue, but often degenerates into selfishness and distrust. Generosity and hospitality have a prominent place in religion; but here we have an instance of their excess being pernicious. Martha and Mary were two Christian sisters, who, with their brother Lazarus, resided at Bethany. They were the object of the Saviour's especial love, and were favored with his gracious visits. Here Jesus was probably often entertained by these beloved female worthies. The text refers to one instance, and shows how, with all her excellencies, Martha evinced a spirit of over-carefulness, so as to call forth the gentle yet pointed admonition of the Redeemer, "Martha, Martha, thou art careful," &c. Observe,

I. THE EVIDENCE OF MARTHA'S CAREFULNESS. Now, three terms are employed in reference to it. Her mind was distracted by,

1. *Multiplicity of objects.* "Was cumbered," &c. The mind is so formed that it cannot actively pursue more than one object at the same time. Our real necessities are few, our imaginary ones numberless. "Much serving" was injurious to Martha, and less serving would have been more acceptable to Christ.

2. *Her mind was tortured with over-solicitude.* "Thou art careful." Carefulness and solicitude are highly proper. Neither reason nor religion requires an improvident recklessness, or thoughtless indif-

ference. A man must employ his reflective powers in providing for his household. There is a becoming care highly proper both as it respects body, soul, reputation, &c. The term often so rendered in our translation, had been better translated, "anxious;" see Matt. vi. 25–34. "Be careful," &c. This anxiety is felt when the mind is tortured and torn by care; when care throws her dark shadows across the mind, and makes it gloomy and fretful. Now, Martha was quite anxious, &c.

3. *She was distracted even to trouble.* "And troubled." Now, this is the necessary result of anxiety. Mind becomes troubled; agitated between hope and fear; perplexed; no calm, no quiet, no enjoyment; the opposite of a placid, peaceful, happy state. We have thus seen the evidences of Martha's carefulness. Consider,

II. THE EVIL OF IT. Jesus evidently designed his remark to be considered in the way of admonition. "Martha, Martha," &c. You will see,

1. *It prevented attention to better things.* Here was the Son of the most high God, the world's Messiah; yet, instead of being an intense listener to his words, she was losing this great opportunity, and distinguished privilege. Is it not so often with you? Does not over-carefulness produce neglect of the Bible? prayer? ordinances? &c.

2. *It led her into censoriousness of spirit,* "My sister hath left me," &c. This was unkind, and an evidence of bitterness of spirit, which ought not to have existed, much less appeared in presence of such an illustrious visitor. Martha is a specimen of all anxious persons; fretful and peevish tempers are often the result.

3. *It caused her to treat the Saviour with apparent disrespect.* No doubt she loved him, and intensely; but Martha ought not to have said, "Lord, dost thou not care?" Had she forgotten the dignity of her guest? Did she not know what it was his meat and drink to do? Now, anxious worldly care is ever in danger of reflecting upon the divine Redeemer, his providence, plans, &c.

4. *It subjected her to the reproof of her divine Lord.* "Martha," &c. Why so anxious? Thou blamest Mary; but I must tell thee "one thing," &c., "and Mary hath," &c. Now, worldly anxiety

is ever displeasing to Christ, and ever injurious to the soul. Let us consider,

III. The remedies by which it may be avoided.

1. *By allowing spiritual things to have the ascendency.* Spiritual food, raiment, health, riches, &c. "Seek ye first," &c.

2. *By cultivating a spirit of moderation in reference to temporal things.* "Let your moderation," &c. Only a little is necessary; only a little can be enjoyed; only wanted for a short time.

3. *By considering the utter inefficiency of worldly care to attain its end.* Your anxiety will produce no beneficial results; nay, it will prevent the enjoyment of what you have. "Who by anxious thought can make one hair?" &c.; see Matt. vi. 24, &c.

4. *By seriously considering the eternity into which we are hastening.* Soon we shall leave all behind—houses, riches, possessions; soon we shall have done with poverty and affliction. Oh! think of heaven and eternity! Why should pilgrims be anxious? citizens of glory!

APPLICATION

1. *Address the moral, and those who admire religion, and are yet strangers to its power.* What is it keeps you back? Are you not careful? &c.

2. *Urge upon all, supreme attention to the salvation of the soul.*

3. *We cannot be too deeply concerned for the riches of glory.* Let us seek to "lay up treasure in heaven," &c.

120

MARY'S HAPPY CHOICE
"But one thing is needful; and Mary hath chosen that good part, which shall not be taken away from her."—Luke x. 42.

We have previously directed your attention to the spirit Martha evinced, and the reproof which Jesus administered on her anxiety about many things. We have now to contemplate the character and spirit of Mary.

(1.) You will observe, that Mary displayed intense attention to the words of Jesus; she heard with eagerness, and with delight, the discourse of the Saviour.

(2.) The humility and reverence of Mary are also stated. "She sat at his feet." The proper place for the pupil, for the disciple. Religion ever commences in this way; attention to the truths of the gospel, and humbleness and docility of mind in the reception of its sacred contents. Our text contains the approbation of the Saviour as to Mary's conduct. "But one thing," &c. Need I say that it is clear Jesus referred to her attention to the soul; giving the preference to spiritual matters—the reception of the words of Christ; in one word, true religion is the "one thing," &c. Observe, the subject directs us,

I. To the unity of true religion. "One thing." It consists in the possession of the grace and Spirit of God, and this is its essential identity. There are not many true religions; never was but one true and acceptable religion. In all ages it has been one; in all climes it is one. The means of religion have varied; dispensations changed; the laws, &c., have been altered; but religion itself has ever been "one thing." True religion is connected with various blessings and privileges, yet is one in character and essence, and one word may express the whole—Love! Love to God, and love to man. Observe,

II. Religion is a voluntary thing. "Mary hath chosen." Reason and revelation establish this:—

(1.) Reason despises force and coercion in all matters of mind. Force may make slaves and hypocrites, but cannot give to the soul the feelings of love and delight.

(2.) Revelation from first to last goes upon this principle. Remember what God said to Cain, "If thou doest well," &c. Joshua to the Israelites, "Behold I have set," &c. God solemnly affirms this by Ezekiel, xxxiii. 10, 11. Paul, although arrested by the supernatural appearance of the Saviour, yet was not coerced, for he says, "I was not disobedient," &c. Jesus, too, when speaking of Mary, says, "She hath chosen," &c. Let no man say he is wicked of necessity; depraved of necessity. Every man may believe and obey the gospel who hears it. "For faith cometh by," &c. "And whosoever calleth," &c. Christ laid the blame upon the will, "Ye will not," &c. Notice,

III. Religion is emphatically a good thing. "That good part." It is good,

1. *In its author and origin.* Every work of God is good. It is his own creation; has his own signet; elevates men to his likeness; tested and tried by the highest standard it is good.

2. *It is good in its adaptation to the soul.* The soul's good. It is the food of the soul; dress, health, and life of the soul.

3. *Good in all its influences.* Breathes good-will to all men; in every circle and sphere. It makes man a blessing to his species, and an ornament to the world.

4. *Good without any admixture.* No evil in it. Like its Author, it is light, and in it is no darkness at all.

IV. RELIGION IS A SURE AND CERTAIN THING. "Shall not be taken away." Here is stability—permanent stability. You cannot say so of any thing else. Who would dare to say it of riches? of honor? of health? of friends? or of life? No; all these are evanescent. We are never sure, &c.; but this is sure. "Shall not?" &c. "God will not," &c. His gifts are without repentance. Satan cannot; the world cannot; the world can neither give it nor take it away. If lost, we must freely abandon it; draw back, &c. It is ever sure and certain. "He who hath begun," &c. "I give unto my sheep," &c.

APPLICATION

1. *What is engaging your chief attention?* Do not trifle away time, opportunities, means, &c.

2. *Now accept the offer of eternal life.* Let this be the turning point. Now bow; now yield yourselves to God.

3. *Believers, thank God, and take courage.* Yours is the approbation of Christ. This is the soul's highest honor, and its sweetest bliss.

121

THE ONE THING NEEDFUL

" One thing is needful "—LUKE x. 42.

WE design on this occasion to press true religion upon you, from its being emphatically the " one thing needful." It is indispensable to the present and eternal well-being of man. Let us ask and answer a few questions, so as to illustrate the sentiment of the text.

I. FROM WHENCE DOES THE NECESSITY OF RELIGION ARISE?

1. *From the constitution of the soul of man.* The soul was formed and designed for religion. True religion implies knowledge—faith—love—righteousness. The faculties of man are capable of these, designed for these. There is light for the understanding, truth for the judgment, motives to influence the will, love for the affections, and peace for the conscience.

2. *From the fallen and wretched state of man.* He is not now in a perfect, happy, and holy state. What can disenthral him? what exalt? what purify? what console? Nothing but religion. Learning and education cannot.

3. *From man's responsible state and character.* Man is accountable to God. Who does not feel this? Every man must give an account to God; be judged, and rewarded or punished in the eternal state. For this in our natural estate we are wholly unfit; cannot shake off our accountability. Religion invests us with a blessed meetness for the judgment-day. It erases the stains of past guilt; it enters our names in the Lamb's book of life; gives a meetness for eternal glory.

II. FOR WHOM IS IT NEEDFUL? One word might answer this; but we must particularize.

1. *It is needful for the young.* "Wherewith shall a young man," &c. It is the unerring pilot of the young; it is the guardian; it is the ornament; it has to do with all their concerns; with health, reputation, subsistence, long life. " Godliness is profitable," &c.; see Prov. iii. 11–26.

2. *It is needful for parents and heads of families.* Most parents are truly anxious to feed, clothe, and educate their children; but if children have souls, they require much more than this. Do they not require a religious training? a consistent example? and fervent prayer with them and for them? What parent can do these things without religion? What a fearful account will prayerless parents have to give at the last day!

3. *It is needful for the aged.* A man never can outlive his evil nature and his sins. The sinner, though he lives a hundred years, yet he shall die accursed. How dreadful for life to be ending, and the great work of life not begun; for spring, for summer, and for harvest to be over, &c. Nothing can make the dim eye bright but this.

4. *It is needful for the rich.*

(1.) Prevents riches from being a curse.

(2.) Does what riches cannot do—gives peace, &c.

(3.) Makes riches a double blessing.

5. *It is needful for the poor.* Bible—the poor man's book ; Christ—the poor man's Saviour ; the gospel—the poor man's portion in life ; the crown of glory—the poor man's reward in heaven. It sanctifies and sweetens poverty, &c.

III. WHEN IS IT NEEDFUL ?

1. *In health and strength.* Even these cannot make the mind really happy without it. Religion is the true health and vigor of the soul.

2. *In times of peril and sickness.* What anxiety is connected with these ! Now, the dissipating scenes of life out of reach. How precious to know that the affliction is administered by our Friend and Father ; that he is the refiner ; that the end is our good ; to be patient, resigned, happy.

3. *In the hour of death.* To illumine ; to sustain ; to save.

APPLICATION

1. *Let me urge all classes to choose religion.*

2. *Do it now.* This day ; this hour.—It will be important,

3. *Through all eternity.*—It is that alone which will produce everlasting felicity in the world to come.

122

THE CALL OF MATTHEW

" And as Jesus passed forth from thence, he saw a man named Matthew, sitting at the receipt of custom ; and he said unto him, Follow me ; and he arose and followed him."—MATTHEW ix. 9.

THE blessed Redeemer was never out of the way of benevolence and mercy ; wherever he went he always found fit objects for the exercise of his grace and compassion. You will perceive in the eighth chapter, that he had been healing a man of that dreadful disease, the leprosy. Restoring the centurion's servant ; then he went out into the coast of the Gadarenes. On the voyage, by his word he stilled the tempest ; when he arrived there he restored two who had been possessed of devils ; and caused the herd of swine to receive the dispossessed spirits, which made them run violently into the sea, where they were drowned. The Gadarenes loved their swine more than the world's Redeemer, so " they besought him to depart out of their coasts." Christ then entered into a ship, and came into his own city, by which we understand Capernaum ; hence it was an ancient saying, " Bethlehem brought him forth, Nazareth brought him up, and Capernaum was his principal dwelling-place." As Jesus was passing forth, " he saw a man named Matthew." Observe,

I. THE PERSON REFERRED TO. " Matthew," &c. Let us notice,

1. *His personal history.* He is generally supposed to have been the son of a sister or cousin of the mother of Jesus, and thus was a distant relative of the Messiah. It seems after his conversion that he was also called Levi. Observe,

2. *His occupation.* He was a publican, or collector of the taxes and customs ; these taxes were levied by the Romans upon the Jews, and were exceedingly grievous to them, as being a visible mark of their subjection to the Roman yoke ; besides, these taxes were sold to the highest bidder, and the collectors of them were noted for their covetousness and rapacity ; in fact they were justly held in abhorrence by the people. You will perceive that for a Jew thus to be employed was degrading in the highest degree, as it was giving countenance to the galling tyranny of the Romans over the Jews. It will be seen then that the occupation of Matthew,

(1.) Was dishonorable to him as a Jew.

(2.) It was associated with great temptations.

(3.) And it was unfavorable to religion and humanity. Let me ask you before I pass on, what is your occupation ? What is your temporal calling ? Is it a righteous one ? Is it such a one as does not injure society ? Can you seek God's blessing upon it ? If so, do you follow it lawfully ? Do not let it engross your chief affections. Do not let it occupy your sabbaths. Do not let it ruin your souls. Notice,

II. THE ADDRESS OF THE SAVIOUR. " And Jesus said unto him, Follow me." Now you will observe,

1. *The conciseness of this address.* Two words embody it. The true nature of religion often may be expressed in a single sentence. Repent and believe the gospel. Give yourselves to God. Be ye reconciled to God. " Turn ye, turn ye," &c.

2. *Its comprehensive meaning.* " Follow me." It implies,

(1.) Renunciation of the world and sin.

We cannot pursue two opposite courses—cannot serve two masters; we cannot be of the world and of Christ; when he says, "Follow me," he says, Leave the world; forsake sin; keep afar off no longer; it implies,

(2.) Deciding for Christ. So soon as the prodigal came to himself, and stood still, he then said, "I will arise," &c. There may be many changes, yet none of them may be effective. We must resolve to be the Lord's. Decide that we will be Christ's, and he shall be ours.

(3.) Practical obedience to Christ. "Follow me." Listening to his words; sitting at his feet; embracing his truth; imbibing his spirit; imitating his conversation; treading in his steps: in one word, becoming Christians; resembling the Saviour; being humble, self-denying, as Christ was; observing all his precepts and ordinances to do them; being benevolent, and merciful, and pitiful as Christ. Notice then,

III. THE CONDUCT OF MATTHEW. "And he arose," &c.

1. *Contrast it with the conduct of many.* Many hear, but hear only; many resolve, but resolve only; many are deeply affected, but are affected only.

2. *Observe the difficulties in the way.*

(1.) He must have been totally indisposed to spiritual things. His habits, pursuits, &c.

(2.) A lucrative employment. He was getting riches; a good business; self-interest at stake.

(3.) The call involved not only the greatest sacrifices, but exposed him to persecution and reproach—to follow Christ into poverty and the hatred of the Jews—to be a disciple of one whom all reviled—to join in his cross and shame—to risk reputation, ease, and life.

3. *Observe how he acted.* "He arose," &c. He resolved, and acted decidedly, and promptly. At once he became a disciple; he conferred not with friends—nor with flesh and blood. He delayed not; he arose, and Matthew the publican became Levi the apostle of Jesus.

4. *See what followed.* He became a disciple of Jesus; a preacher of the gospel; an apostle of the cross; a martyr for the truth. It is supposed he suffered death for his religion, by being pierced with a halbert in Ethiopia, where he had long preached the gospel. In addition, he wrote the gospel which bears his name. We have thus referred you to Matthew who obeyed the call of Jesus, and arose, and followed him.

APPLICATION

1. *Now Christ is passing by.* He is just saying what he said to Matthew. What do you reply? What is it keeps you back? Why delay?

2. *Now arise and follow Christ.* Cannot be too precipitate in this. Why reason? Why study the matter? Christ says, "Follow me." Who will obey? You, young man? &c. You, old man? &c. Shall it be said of any here, "They arose?" &c.

123

THE SYRO-PHENICIAN WOMAN

"Then Jesus went thence, and departed into the coasts of Tyre and Sidon. And, behold, a woman of Canaan came out of the same coasts, and cried unto him, saying, Have mercy on me, O Lord, thou Son of David," &c.—MATTHEW xv. 21–28.

OF the blessed Saviour it is written, that he "went about doing good." He came to bless the world, and wherever he went he realized the truth of this declaration. He was eyes to the blind—ears to the deaf—speech to the dumb—health to the sick—joy to the disconsolate—mercy to the guilty—salvation to the lost—and life to the dead. At the time of the Messiah's sojourn upon earth, Satan seemed to have assumed an immense amount of power, and exercised great and despotical control over the bodies as well as the souls of mankind. Hence Jesus was often called to dispossess those who were under the direct and fearful power of the prince of darkness. One of these cases introduces us to the subject of our present discourse. Let us contemplate,

I. THE DISTRESSED SUFFERER.
II. THE MIGHTY SAVIOUR.
III. THE EFFECTUAL INTERCESSOR.
IV. THE DELIGHTFUL CURE.

I. THE DISTRESSED SUFFERER. "Daughter grievously vexed," &c. Several similar cases are revealed to us. There is the case of a youth, whose father came to Christ; the demoniac; Mary Magdalene. So the daughter in the text; under the direct agency of Satan; impelled by his evil spirit, mind, and body, &c. A young person thus tortured and afflicted; beyond human skill or power to relieve. Let us turn from the sufferer,

II. To THE MIGHTY SAVIOUR. He was sent to destroy the works of the devil; to bruise the head of the serpent; to overthrow the fell usurper; to rescue the world from his iron grasp. He had been typified by Moses, Joshua, Samson, David, &c. Three things favorable to the sufferer:—

1. *That this Saviour was then in the flesh.* She might have lived before Christ's incarnation; before the Shiloh—the Deliverer had come; but the angels had announced, &c.; the Baptist had heralded; the Holy Ghost had descended on him. He had entered on the great work; he had gone forth in all his divine energy, &c.; "mighty to save."

2. *The fame of his power had gone forth.* "Even into the coasts," &c. Four very wondrous cases had been published; the son, who was so torn and cast into the fire, &c.; Mary Magdalene, now a disciple; the restored man, out of whom the legion, &c.; a dumb and blind spirit. Many had come, and by his word the evil spirit had been conquered and dispossessed. The other favorable circumstance was,

3. *That the Saviour was near at hand.* Accessible, verse 21. Entered the coasts of Tyre and Sidon. The promise of the Saviour now ratified; his power and ability tested, and to be near at hand. Oh! happy crisis; important period; golden opportunity; accepted time; "day of salvation."

III. THE EFFECTUAL INTERCESSOR. Here was the afflicted daughter, and the Almighty Saviour. How were they brought together? The mother became the intercessor. Who so suitable? so admirably adapted? What love, what eloquence, what perseverance, and what success, &c. Notice,

1. *The reverence of her address.* She admits him to be the true Messiah; her language involved both his divinity and humanity: "O Lord! thou Son of David."

2. *The petition presented.* "Have mercy upon me." She considered her daughter as herself—her affliction as her own. Who has not felt relative troubles to be more distressing than personal ones? What father? what mother? what friend? &c. "Pity a distressed mother; an afflicted,

almost broken-hearted woman." She cried fervently. Mark! her suit is apparently neglected, verse 23. The disciples unite with her; Jesus now apparently excludes her from hope, "I am not sent," &c., verse 24. "He came to his own," &c.

3. *Her prayer is repeated.* She came, and worshipped, and said, "Lord, help me!" One of another nation—one miserable woman. "Lord, help me!" She gave him divine homage. How interesting the scene—how affecting! He then replied, as if to repulse her altogether, "It is not meet to give the children's bread unto the dogs." The Gentiles were so considered by the Jews. He assumes now the distinction of a Jew.

4. *Her plea is reiterated.* "Truth, Lord." "I know, I feel, I admit my inferiority. I am not one of the highly-favored; not a descendant of the illustrious Abraham; not a daughter of Israel. I claim not equality; I contend not for their dignity and privileges; I am willing even to be considered as a dog; let me have the privilege, and it sufficeth." "Yet the dogs," &c. The kind master does not repulse his dog, but allows it to have the crumbs and pieces that would otherwise be wasted. "Have mercy upon me," and spurn not this poor Gentile dog from thy presence. How amazing must all this have been to his disciples! Here is a poor Gentile—a woman: after silence; after an evident refusal; after being reckoned as only a dog, yet she holds fast; she perseveres; she converts an apparent refusal into an argument; and by humility, vehement earnestness, and faith, she retains the attention of the Saviour. But how and wherefore did Christ seem thus to reject her suit? He knew the state of her heart, and he knew his own purpose and intention of granting her what she sought. In this he might design to try her patience; or to excite her desires still more; or to bring forth brighter evidences of her wondrous faith; or that she might be an example to his own disciples, and to all applicants to the end of the world; or to sweeten and add to the preciousness of the boon bestowed. It was not coldness, neglect, or indifference on the part of Christ. Her heart moved not with more earnest desire towards him, than his compassion moved towards her. At length, he allows her to conquer, and to secure her point. Here notice,

IV. THE CURE OBTAINED. "Oh, woman! great is thy faith; be it unto thee," &c. Observe,

1. *He extols the successful pleader.* "Great is thy faith." It does not first appear that this was the reigning, triumphant grace. Might he not have said, Marvellous is thy self-abasement, thy humility, thy fervency, thy firmness and perseverance, thy love to thy child, thy resolve not to depart without the blessing? But in all this faith was the root, the main-spring, the active vital power of her soul. This brought her to Christ; this caused her to honor and worship Christ; to plead—to parry the thrusts—to put up with the silence—to argue the whole matter. "Faith, mighty faith, the promise sees," &c.

2. *He grants all that she sought.* "Be it unto thee as thou wilt." Faith takes hold of Christ's strength; faith restrains the wrath of God. Thus he cried to Moses, "Let me alone." It holds him fast, so that he cannot go till the blessing is given. Faith brings virtue out of Christ, though it touches but the hem of his garment. "All things are possible," &c. Her daughter was healed—the devil was ejected—and she was perfectly restored. Oh, happy child! Oh, wonderful mother! Oh, almighty and gracious Saviour! This subject addresses,

(1.) Parents and heads of families—on the duty they owe to the children under their charge.

(2.) The Christian church—on the solicitude they should evince for the religious instruction and welfare of the rising generation.

(3.) Sabbath school teachers—on the importance of leading those whom they instruct to a knowledge of the Lord Jesus Christ, the only source of spiritual health and salvation.

124

BETHESDA

"Now there is at Jerusalem by the sheep market a pool, which is called in the Hebrew tongue Bethesda, having five porches."—JOHN v. 2.

OUR text contains the name of a very interesting place in Jerusalem; a place of very great celebrity and importance to the afflicted inhabitants of that city; a place which would live in the associations and recollections of the multitude who had there found healing and temporal happiness; and a place of much anxiety to the infirm and afflicted. Every particular is given by the evangelist in the brief paragraph of which the text forms a part; read verses 2 to 4. Then there is given the history of an afflicted person, who had long been waiting to enjoy its marvellous influences; see verses 5 to 7. On him Christ had compassion, verse 8; an instantaneous cure was wrought, verse 9. We desire at this time to call your attention to a three-fold view of Bethesda :—

I. AS EXHIBITING A STRIKING REPRESENTATION OF THE LEVITICAL ECONOMY.

II. AS BEING TOTALLY SUPERSEDED BY THE GLORIOUS DISPENSATION OF THE GOSPEL.

III. AS BEING PECULIARLY APPROPRIATE TO THE PRESENT OCCASION.

I. AS EXHIBITING A STRIKING REPRESENTATION OF THE LEVITICAL ECONOMY. Observe, Bethesda was really worthy of the title it possessed. It was, indeed, a house of mercy; the removal of the infirmities of the body. The features of resemblance between Bethesda and the Levitical economy are chiefly these :—

1. *It was local.* The Levitical economy was the religion of Judea; it was associated especially with Palestine, and more immediately still with Jerusalem. Its worship, its priesthood, and its rites were designed for one circumscribed locality. This Bethesda—the house of mercy—was one small pool, limited to one locality in Jerusalem.

2. *It was limited as well as local.* At Bethesda only the first of the multitudes waiting was healed; so the benefits of Judaism were limited to one nation, including a few proselytes of other countries. The wide world was without the range; myriads of mankind strangers to its light and blessings.

3. *Its privileges and blessings were only occasional.* "At certain seasons." Numerous and long intervals between; just so that dispensation. Its ordinances were numerous, but its great rites and chief festivals were very occasional. Its great feasts three times a year; grand jubilee only every fifty years; a minor one, or sabbatical year, every seven; only one day of national expiation; one annual sacrifice.

4. *It was connected with waiting and expectation.* Here numbers were collected, and they had to look forward to, and wait for, the troubling of the waters, &c. Just such was the Levitical economy. It was one of waiting and expectation. Prophecies were given, but they had to wait for their realization ; promises made, but their fulfilment was future. They had many offerings, and ceremonial institutions, but their sacrifices could not wash away sin.

" Not all the blood of beasts
 On Jewish altars slain,
Could give the guilty conscience peace,
 Or wash away the stain."

Thus the patriarchs and prophets looked and longed for the gospel day, but died in faith, and without the actual sight.

5. *It was not distinguished for pre-eminent benevolence.* Here was a helpless, friendless person ; but no one felt sufficient interest to give him a place during the troubling of the waters. We do not say that goodness and mercy had no place in the old economy ; assuredly they had, but they were not the chief and prominent glories of that dispensation. It was more an economy of law and justice than of compassion and mercy. Such are the features of resemblance. Notice, then,

II. The Jewish Bethesda, as being totally superseded by the glorious dispensation of the gospel. Christ appeared, and dispensed with the pool. The Church of Christ may well and appositely be styled the House of Mercy. It is so in the truest and most exalted sense of the term. It is associated with a *fountain* which has been opened for sin, &c. Now, the healing fountain of divine grace totally eclipses the glory of the ancient Levitical economy, as well as supersedes the Jerusalem Bethesda. Observe, this is,

1. *Universal, not local.* Not confined to Jerusalem, or Palestine, or the Jews. It exists everywhere, where the gospel is preached. It is acceptable to the whole world, and to every creature.

" Its streams the whole creation reach,
 So plenteous is the store ;
Enough for all, enough for each,
 Enough for evermore."

2. *Its blessings are ever accessible, and not occasional.* Every year a jubilee ; every day a sabbath ; every moment one of expiation ; every instant one of mercy.

3. *Its blessings are present, and not in prospect.* There are, indeed, blessings in prospect ; but pardon,—remission of sin,—justification,—holiness, —peace,—adoption, are all now presented. " This is the acceptable time,"&c. " The word is nigh thee," &c.

4. *It is emphatically a dispensation of love and mercy.* Grace and truth, love and embodied goodness, came by Jesus Christ, fully, gloriously, universally ; and these it teaches. The disciples of Christ are constrained by this love to love the souls of those around. Such then, brethren, are some of the glories of the gospel dispensation, which entirely supersedes the Mosaical economy, and the Bethesda at Jerusalem. But there is,

III. Another application of the text peculiarly appropriate to the present occasion. May not every house erected for the preaching of the gospel, and the celebration of the ordinances of Christ, be styled " Bethesda," the House of Mercy ? We ask,

1. *For whom, and to whom, is this house erected and consecrated ?* To the God of mercy ; to him who delighteth in mercy. Here you record his name—celebrate his praise—proclaim his glory—and here he will surely come and bless you. Here his glory shall be seen. Hearken ! " The Lord loveth the gates of Zion better than all," &c.

2. *For what great purpose is this house to be devoted ?* The proclamation of mercy ; the rich, universal mercy of God, as flowing in the streams of the gospel ; mercy to the guilty, wretched outcasts of mankind ; mercy to all who need it ; mercy to all who will receive it.

3. *May we not hopefully anticipate that here effusions of mercy will be enjoyed ?* Who can tell how many sinners shall enjoy that promise, " Let the wicked," &c. How many penitents shall here meet the mercy promised to their fathers ? How many backsliders shall here feel the application of restoring mercy ? When the Lord shall say, " I will heal your backslidings ; I will love you freely ; for my anger is turned away." How many of the people of God shall come here, that with boldness they may approach the throne of grace ?

4. *Shall not the monuments of mercy here celebrate the riches of mercy from time to time ?* Oh ! how delightful to contemplate brands plucked from the fire ; rebels soft-

ened by divine love ; prodigals accepted of their father ; all meeting, and all uniting. " O Lord ! we will praise thee ; for, though thou wast angry," &c.

5. *I ask, finally, shall not a spirit of mercy distinguish the friends of Jesus who dwell within these walls ?* As the elect of God, will not they possess bowels of mercy ? Will they not exhibit the mercifulness of Jesus in their spirit, and conversation, and conduct ? Will they not manifest the fruits of mercy in their lives, and thus "show forth the praises of him," &c. How desirable that at the opening services,

1. That divine mercy might be experienced by some soul as a token for good—as a kind of first-fruit. Who will be the person ? Who feels his need ? Who will seek, and ask, and believe ?

2. Let the mercy of the Lord be the song of his redeemed people. " Oh ! magnify the Lord," &c.

3. Let your generosity evince that you are deeply sensible of your obligations to the mercy of God, and that you long for his mercy to be enjoyed by others.

125

THE RESTORED DEMONIAC

" Now the man out of whom the devils were departed besought him that he might be with him : but Jesus sent him away, saying, Return to thine own house, and show how great things God hath done unto thee. And he went his way, and published throughout the whole city how great things Jesus had done unto him."—LUKE viii. 38, 39.

OUR text relates to the man who had been rescued from the legion of devils. His condition was now totally reversed ; restored to reason and happiness, we are called to see him at the feet of the Saviour, &c. After this we are referred to two prayers offered up to Jesus ; the one by the Gadarenes, a most awful instance of ignorance, selfishness, and infatuation, " that Christ would depart from them," &c. This prayer Christ answered by immediately retiring from their coast ; then there is the prayer of the recovered demoniac, a prayer exceedingly proper and interesting, &c. How different to the other, " Now the man out of whom," &c. In the text we have,

I. AN INTERESTING PRAYER, WHICH NOTWITHSTANDING WAS REJECTED. Now look,

1. *At the prayer itself.* " To be with Christ." Was not this the end of Christ's

mission, that he might collect souls to himself ? Gather them out of the world, &c. Had he not taught, " If any man will be my disciple," &c. It seems evidently a wise and proper prayer ; a pious prayer, the sign of a gracious state of soul. Consider,

2. *The probable reasons by which this prayer was dictated.* It might be the result,

(1.) Of holy cautiousness and fear. He had just been dispossessed of a legion of spirits. " A stronger than they," &c. But might they not again overcome him ? &c. How natural and proper then to fear ; how proper to desire to be near the deliverer, &c.

(2.) It might arise also from grateful love to Jesus ; his position how interesting, at Christ's feet ; he would cling to that spot ; his heart was entwined around that of the Saviour ; he knew not how to express his love and gratitude to Jesus.

(3.) It might arise from a desire to know more of Christ ; he could not be satisfied with a few minutes, he wished to be his pupil, his personal adherent, his disciple and follower. Notice,

3. *The refusal of this request.* " But Christ sent him away." However wise, and proper, and pious the man's petition appears, Jesus determined and directed otherwise ; his suit could not be granted. Now, here let us pause, and learn,

(1.) How necessary to be taught rightly to pray. We know not what we should pray for ; Peter prayed on the mountain of transfiguration, that they might build tabernacles, &c. James and John that they might sit, one on the right hand and the other on the left. Paul prayed thrice that the thorn in the flesh, &c. Lord, teach us how to pray ! When we have not express direction and promise we must refer all to the will of God.

(2.) We should learn to be satisfied with the Lord's good pleasure, whether he grants our requests or not. " He is too wise to err, too good to be unkind." He loves us too well to neglect our best interests, our real welfare. Observe,

II. AN IMPORTANT COMMAND WHICH WAS PIOUSLY OBEYED. " Jesus sent him," &c.

1. *Let us look at the nature of the command.* To return to his own house and show, &c. He was to be a personal witness for Christ ; a monument of Christ's power and Christ's compassion. He could testify,

(1.) To the enthronement of reason. He had been beside himself, irrational; now he was intelligent, cool, reflecting.

(2.) To emancipation from the thraldom of evil spirits; released from the power of the devil.

(3.) To restoration to happiness. No longer cutting himself, a wretched outcast, but clothed and happy, &c. Then, in testifying he would have to refer,

(4.) To the author of his deliverance. "Jesus." The compassion and power of Christ. Now, let the happy saved believer apply the remarks to himself; you can testify in like manner, and to the same things. Observe,

2. *The obedience which was rendered.* "And he went his way," &c.

(1.) It was prompt and immediate. He did not cavil, nor reason, nor refuse.

(2.) It was decided and public. "Wherever he went," &c. "How great things," &c. Not afraid, nor ashamed.

APPLICATION

1. *The end of our conversion is more than our own salvation.*

(1.) We must testify to and for the benefit of others.

(2.) We must glorify Christ. Show forth his praises, his compassion and power.

2. *The converted should not consult merely their own comfort.* But deny themselves for Christ's sake; not to be indifferent to ourselves, yet to take up our cross, &c.

3. *Christian obedience is unquestioning and exact.* To do as the Lord enjoins; just in the Lord's way. Soul entirely submissive to God.

4. *The heart's desires of the saints shall be granted in a future state.* Be with Jesus forever, &c.

126

THE RECOVERED LEPER

"And, behold, there came a leper and worshipped him, saying, Lord, if thou wilt, thou canst make me clean. And Jesus put forth his hand, and touched him, saying, I will, be thou clean. And immediately his leprosy was cleansed. And Jesus saith unto him, See thou tell no man; but go thy way, show thyself to the priest, and offer the gift that Moses commanded, for a testimony unto them."—MATTHEW viii. 2–4.

ONE of the results of sin is the fearful catalogue of bodily diseases which it has introduced. Man was formed free from affliction, sorrow, and pain; neither was he liable to death; but sin has filled the world with sickness and misery. Hence,

" Fierce diseases wait around,
To hurry mortals home."

Every part of the body is alike vulnerable, alike in danger, alike susceptible of affliction and agony; some are tedious in their progress, and men groan beneath them for years; others are rapid in their course, and speedily cast their victims into the gloomy grave; some are curable, while others defy the physician's art, and medicine's power. During Christ's mission on earth he employed his benevolent power in healing the diseases both of body and mind. Our text refers to one delightful instance, to which we invite your attention on the present occasion. Consider,

I. THE INDIVIDUAL REFERRED TO. "A leper." Perhaps no condition was more truly awful and distressing; leprosy was common in Palestine, and is so still in various parts of the east; at present we shall consider it as exhibiting a striking representation of sin, the leprosy of the soul. Now leprosy,

1. *Was generally hereditary.* Thus from Adam and Eve, sin has spread into every country, and down through every generation. Men are not only born under the effects of the guilt of sin, but under its depraving and defiling power.

2. *It was small in its first appearance.* A small spot on the countenance of an inflamed red character was the first sign; those unacquainted with it might suspect no danger. Now sin is little in its beginning; look at children in their tempers, &c.; look at individuals who at one period were amiable, and have become thoroughly vile.

3. *It was deep-seated and inveterate in its nature.* The heart and blood are under its influence: so with sin, the heart is the seat, the soul is the spring and root of all the evil.

4. *It was universal in its prevalence.* All the man affected. From the head through all the extremities. No part of a leper clean; so with sin and the sinner, "the whole head," &c. All the faculties of the soul; all the senses of the body, &c.

5. *It was very loathsome in its appearance.* The eyes and countenance assumed a horrid and disgusting appearance, painful, and it rendered the person a burden to

himself, and life itself a curse : such also is sin ; it renders man abominable to God and holy angels, and fills him with anguish and misery.

6. *It excluded from society, and rendered them objects of terror to all around.* However united by the ties of kindredness, their breath was dreaded, it was the breath of disease, to touch them was to receive their malady ; not allowed to mix with the healthy, or to go into the congregation of the Lord. Travellers feared to meet them, &c. : so sin infests and excludes from the family and presence of God.

7. *It was incurable by human power, and generally produced a most awful death.* It raged until the whole person became one mass of foulness and pollution ; then the vital organs being powerfully attacked, death terminated the career of suffering : such also is the leprosy of the soul ; no man can recover himself from it ; no created power can restore ; it never cures itself. " Sin when it is finished bringeth forth death." Such was the condition of the man who applied to Christ. Notice,

II. HIS ADDRESS TO THE REDEEMER. " Lord, if thou wilt," &c.

1. *It was an address of humble respect.* " Lord." He acknowledged him as a dignified person ; received him as the Messiah, worshipped, &c.

2. *It was associated with faith.* " Thou canst." Not ordinary faith. He would not have said so to any other person on earth. Christ had the power, and this was the power of God.

3. *It contained an affecting reference to his own misery and Christ's goodness.* " If thou wilt thou canst make me clean." Nothing so important to him as this ; this was his heart's desire ; he appealed to Christ's disposition. " If thou wilt," &c.

III. THE CONDUCT OF THE SAVIOUR.

1. *Christ responded to his appeal.* And said, " I will." " His love is as great as his power," &c. Christ's willingness is established on the most immoveable truths and facts.

2. *His word was omnipotent, and conveyed the healing power.* He might have willed it, and effected it silently, but he spake, &c. ; so he did in creation, so in all his miracles. At the grave of Lazarus— to the devils who possessed the demoniac— to the raging sea, &c.

3. *He put forth his hand to testify to his*

cleanness. A touch would infect, and in any case ceremonially defile ; but Jesus now touched him to show that the foul disease was gone. What a cure ! How complete ! How instantaneous ! How free ! How precious !

4. *He sent him to the priest that his recovery might be duly attested.* The priest was appointed of God to testify when a person was cleansed and fit for society. Now this case might have been disputed, &c. He was to go at once for fear the priest might hear, and through prejudice refuse to attest, &c.

5. *He was to present a gift unto the Lord.* See Levit. xiv. 10, and if poor, verse 21. Now Christ enforced this to show that he came to fulfil all the law, &c. ; and to elicit a grateful spirit from the leper. Now let me turn to the leprous sinner.

1. *See how you are to obtain healing and purity.* From Christ ; by personal, humble, and believing application to him.

2. *See the way in which Christ will receive you.* He will freely and graciously deliver ; he desires to do this, &c. He can do it now, &c.

3. *See what Christ expects from those he has healed.* Dedication of yourselves and all you have to the Lord.

APPLICATION

1. Bless God for health of body.

2. Especially be anxious for health of soul.

3. Praise God for the Almighty Saviour and the means of spiritual health and felicity.

4. We now invite all to be healed.

127

FAITH, THE ANTIDOTE TO FEAR

" Be not afraid, only believe."—MARK v. 36.

OUR text is connected with one of the Saviour's most resplendent miracles. The ruler's daughter was sick ; her father, full of anguish, applies to Jesus. His application was reverential, " for he fell at Christ's feet," &c., verse 22 ; his application was most importunate, " And besought him greatly," verse 23 ; his application evinced great parental tenderness, " My little daughter lieth at the point of death ;" his application was connected with strong faith, " Come and lay thy hands, &c., and she shall live," verse 23. Before Jesus arrived, word came from the ruler's house saying his daughter was dead, verse 35. It was then that Christ addressed to him the words of our text; the sequel is well known. He exerted his mighty power, and brought her back into the land of the living. A more difficult case could not be well conceived of; yet living faith and the power of Christ were adequate to it—and to every possible exigency they are equally adapted. Let us look at some cases wherein the text may be appropriately applied. Observe its applicability to the anxious inquirer; to the conflicting believer; to tried Christians; to the spiritual laborer; to the dying saint. We apply the text,

I. To THE ANXIOUS INQUIRER. To the individual convinced of sin—alarmed with apprehensions of wrath—trembling for fear of the devouring wrath of Deity. It may be that the sins of the convicted penitent have been enormous; aggravated; of long continuance; red as scarlet; or deeply stained as crimson. Such may see how ordinary transgressors may be saved; but they view their own state as extreme, desperate, and perhaps hopeless. Now, what shall I say to such a one? what instance present? what direction afford? Shall we refer to some preparatory work? shall we keep them back for a time from the grand remedy? shall we urge a series of external reformations? Oh! no; the deeper the guilt and misery, and the more necessitous the case, the more eager we should be to bring it at once to the great remedy. The fears of such may be most terrific; but we exclaim with all possible earnestness, "Be not afraid, only believe." Believe the incomprehensible vastness of the divine love and mercy, "As the heavens are higher," &c. Believe the readiness of God to save the greatest of transgressors, "As I live," &c. "Come, and let us reason," &c. Believe the infinite efficacy of the sacrifice of Christ, "The blood of Jesus Christ," &c. "This is a faithful saying," &c. Believe that your salvation is to be a matter of entire grace, the free gift of God, "Not by works of righteousness," &c. Believe that God is waiting, &c., solicitous to save you, "For whosoever will come," &c. "Him that cometh," &c. "O that thou, even thou, hadst known,"

&c. Believe, and all the gracious promises of God become your own; believe, and all the virtue of Christ's merit and power will be exerted for your benefit:

"Believe, and all your sin's forgiven;
Only believe, and yours is heaven."

We apply the text,

II. To THE CONFLICTING BELIEVER. The life of the believer is a state of conflict; it is a course of moral wrestling, "We wrestle not," &c.; it is a course of contention, "Contend earnestly," &c.; a warfare, "War a good warfare," &c. Now, in this conflicting state, our enemies are very numerous, malevolent, and persevering in their assaults. We read of the "fiery darts of the devil." To be harassed with these foes incessantly, may damp the ardor and chill the enjoyments of the believer. He may be discouraged on account of the way, &c. Now, what is our advice to the conflicting believer? Philosophize—reason— be resolute—rely on the goodness of your cause? &c. No; it is, "only believe." Faith is your shield; by it you will quench all the fiery darts, &c. Faith will enable you to wield the sword of the Spirit, &c.; faith kept in lively exercise, and devils will fear and tremble; a believing application of God's word, and we successfully overcome the army of the aliens. We apply the text,

III. To THE TRIED CHRISTIAN. This is a state of probationary trial; sorrows and troubles form a great portion of our inventory; in the world, we shall, we must have tribulation. Now, what shall we do in these trials? Murmur, repine, become dispirited; or sink into inactivity and gloom? Oh! no; our text is the antidote, "Only believe." Hear David—"I had fainted unless I had believed," &c. Hearken to Jesus—"Let not your hearts be troubled," &c. Paul—"I know whom," &c. Believe these troubles are under divine direction or control; believe they are not tokens of wrath, but of love; believe that they are really light and transitory; believe they will conform to Christ, and enhance future blessedness; only believe, and then you may truly sing, "In darkest shades, if he appear," &c. We apply the text,

IV. To THE SPIRITUAL LABORER. You are anxious to please and serve God, by the practical dedication of your power and talents to his glory. In the school, training up the young, you are discouraged ; but believe what God has spoken, and obey his word. " In the morning sow thy seed." In laboring to save your neighbors, &c., but so thoughtless, &c. Believe that your labor cannot be in vain ; how many have succeeded. Let faith nerve you afresh. Believe in the wisdom and goodness of these efforts, " He that winneth souls," &c. " He that converteth a sinner," &c. In training up your families : perhaps some of your children " sons of Belial ;" all dark and gloomy ; no signs of grace. Let faith lead you to enforce scriptural tuition and discipline, and rest on that word, " Train up a child," &c. In working in the church you do not see any good arise ; nor your ability to increase it ; feel as cumberers of the ground, &c. Have you fervently prayed ? have you pleaded with God ? are you deeply anxious for the revival of religion ? You cannot tell but God's blessing may have rested on the minister— on his word, &c., through your faith. Be not dispirited, use the means, and " only believe." We apply the text,

V. To THE DYING SAINT. That solemn crisis of death must be personally known by every one. To a dying saint, we would not say, " Remember your past excellent life, your long profession of religion, your rich and mellowed experience." Oh ! no ; we say even now, as at first, your salvation is of faith. To die safely, happily, triumphantly, you must die in faith. " Only believe." Believe in the fidelity of your God ; believe in the presence of your Saviour ; believe that sin is atoned for ; that death is subdued ; that the grave has been hallowed ; that the gates of paradise have been flung wide open ; that Christ has prepared mansions of blessedness for you ; waits to receive you to himself, &c. Believe, and pass confidently through the valley, &c. ; believe, and plunge into the swellings of Jordan ; believe, and grapple with your last enemy. Hark ! the conflict is over ; the saint is victorious. He exclaims, " O death ! where is thy sting ?" &c.

OBSERVATIONS

1. *See the reason why we are counselled only to believe.*

(1.) Faith is the first great exercise of the soul ; that which unites us to God ; that which builds on the good foundation.

(2.) Faith is ever accompanied by the other graces of the Spirit. It works by love ; it inspires hope ; it produces Christian diligence. " The work of faith."

(3.) Faith makes all that is in God ours —the Father, Son, and Spirit. It appropriates the whole Deity ; it interests us in the entire Godhead ; and honors all his persons and attributes.

2. *Observe the general and perpetual appropriation of the text.* To all states and circumstances in life. It is never out of place ; never unseasonable ; ever proper, right, necessary, and efficacious.

3. *Ascertain if this faith is exemplified in your experience.*

128

THE CENTURION AND HIS SERVANT

" And when Jesus was entered into Capernaum, there came untu him a centurion, beseeching him," &c.—MATTHEW viii. 5-10.

HERE we are presented with an account of one of Christ's illustrious and gracious miracles ; one of those signs of goodness and power, which compelled Nicodemus to exclaim, " Rabbi, we know," &c. One astounding miracle he had just wrought, in cleansing the poor miserable leper, and then he entered into Capernaum, when he was addressed by a centurion, who came, and beseeching him, said, " Lord, my servant," &c. Notice,

I. THE APPLICANT. He was a centurion ; that is, an officer having the command of one hundred soldiers. In many respects, we may be justly astonished that such an individual should be found drawing near to the Saviour. Let us glance at some of these particulars.

1. *He was a Gentile, and not of the house of Israel.* In this respect, he had not possessed the national privileges of the Jews ; he had originally been involved in the darkness of paganism ; his first impressions had been unfavorable to religion. Our education, the national and family privileges are of the greatest worth, and deserve our gratitude ; we are also responsible for them.

2. *His profession was unfavorable to piety.* He was a military man. Few positions in life are more unfriendly to godliness. It is eminently a worldly profession ; it is based on ambition and worldly glory ; it is opposed to humanity and goodness ;

there is little time for reflection. Now, it appears that this centurion had become attached to the Jewish religion, and most likely was a proselyte to their faith; for it is said, Luke vii. 5, "that he loved their nation, and had built for them a synagogue." Such was the applicant. Notice,

II. THE SUIT HE PRESENTED. Several things in this deserve our attention.

1. *The object of his suit.* "His servant." Many had applied to Christ on their own account; some on behalf of their relatives; as the ruler's daughter; father for his son; Peter's wife's mother, &c.; but here is a master seeking the restoration of his servant. Piety renders every station in life a blessing. It makes good parents, good children, good masters, good servants. It is highly probable that his servant had been a faithful, devoted one; thus he had secured the esteem and affection of his master. We read of several distinguished servants in the word of God. There was the excellent servant of Abraham, and the servants of Naaman, &c. What an example to masters and mistresses; what a contrast to the condition of many! How benevolent, and tender, and solicitous!

2. *The way in which he presented it.*

(1.) There was personal exertion. He came to Jesus; he employed his time and personal influence.

(2.) He was earnest in his application. "Beseeching him." Not cold and formal, but with anxious earnestness and ardor.

(3.) He displayed great reverence and humility, "Lord," &c. He assumed nothing on account of his station. When Christ complied, he answered, "I am not worthy," &c. What self-abasement! What exalted views of Christ! What a pattern!

(4.) He manifested extraordinary faith. He said, "Thy journey is not necessary," "but speak the word," &c. Thy mandate is enough; thou art Lord of all; a word will answer the mighty end, &c. He illustrated it himself by referring to his authority, verse 9. Notice,

III. THE SUCCESS HE EXPERIENCED.

1. *He was honored by the Saviour.* "When Jesus heard it, he marvelled," &c. What a contrast to the conduct of the scribes and Pharisees; to the Jews in general. Even to his own disciples, Christ pronounced this honorable distinction, "I say unto you," &c. Here confession was praised, humility exalted, and faith applauded, by the Son of God.

2. *His servant was healed;* Luke vii. 10. Here we see the result of pious, benevolent influence. The master a blessing to the servant, &c.; one the channel of good to the other, "I will bless thee and make thee a blessing."

APPLICATION

1. *Admire this example of human excellency.* Christ did so, and honored it. Let us do so, and imitate it.

2. *See the grace and power of the Saviour.* How all-sufficient and infinitely merciful. His word is enough.

3. *Let all believers exert their influence for the good of others.* You have influence as well as the centurion. Prayer—faith—access to Christ; exert it. Have you not relatives? servants? neighbors? It is your duty, and your real advantage to do so. Do it in the closet; do it in the family; do it in the congregation of the saints. Let us all admire and feel as the centurion did, and go and do likewise.

129

THE PRODIGAL SON
PART I

"And he said, A certain man had two sons; and the younger of them said to his father, Father, give me the portion of goods that falleth to me. And he divided unto them his living," &c.
—LUKE xv. 11, &c.

THIS is one of the Saviour's beautiful and interesting parables. It is impossible to read it without being struck with the true picture it draws, the graphic imagery with which it abounds, and the nervous, yet simple language in which it is written. The occasion of the parable is found in the first and second verses of the chapter. Two minor parables precede and appropriately introduce it—the lost sheep, and the piece of money. It is not the design of the Spirit that the filling up of the parable should, of necessity, be spiritualized, and made to support the great end the parable was to answer. Three great lessons are evidently taught;—the depravity of the sinner and its results; the hardening and lamentable consequences of a sinful life; and the nature of true repentance, with its happy effects. At present we shall dwell on the first of these, and by a series of propositions grounded on the text endeavor to present the subject clearly to your minds.

I. ONE OF THE EVIDENCES OF A DEPRAVED AND SINFUL STATE, IS TO THROW OFF THE DIVINE AUTHORITY AND RESTRAINT. Sin thus commenced in our world. Our first parents desired to be as gods, and broke through the restrictions in reference to the tree of the knowledge of good and evil. Thus the prodigal is described as impatient —restless and anxious to escape his father's cognizance—to leave the paternal roof; to think, and choose, and act as he pleased. Thus to feel and act is the essence of sin. A loyal subject does not desire to conduct himself without respect to the constitution and laws of the land. A good child does not despise parental authority. A faithful servant desires not to act according to his own pleasure. Holy spirits do the will of God, and they are perfectly happy to be regulated by Deity. But sin rejects God's authority, bursts through his restraints, and sets up the rebel desires of the soul against God and his word.

II. GOD GIVES A PORTION OF HIS BOUNTIES EVEN TO THE WICKED AND UNGODLY. "Give me the portion," &c. Every created thing has its portion from God. Men, as the creatures of God, enjoy many blessings from the Most High. There is life with all its privileges; health, and physical comfort; reason and mental endowments; natural gifts, and talents; to some riches and influence; many privileges and opportunities of improvement, &c. A portion full of goodness and mercy.

III. A STATE OF SIN IS ONE OF DEPARTURE FROM GOD. He took his journey. Sin is forsaking God, departing from his ways. Sin creates moral distance between the soul and Jehovah. It does so as it respects his *favor*. He cannot approve, &c. His face is against the wicked. Angry, &c. His *image*,—it effaces it, &c. Every faculty suffers, — understanding, — judgment, — conscience,—affections,—desires, &c. His *family*. It excludes—drives out—separates from his holy dwelling. Sin is travelling from, not towards heaven. Wandering towards the blackness, &c., of hell. It is the way of death. By a course of sin, this state of distance is constantly increasing, widening, &c. The Christian is daily journeying nearer and nearer towards heaven: the sinner, &c., towards the abodes of eternal despair.

IV. THE PRACTICE OF SIN IS ONE OF PERVERSION AND WASTE OF THE BLESSINGS OF HEAVEN. "Wasted," &c. Sin seeketh the sacrifice of all. Health and strength, &c. The sinner wastes—wealth, and influence. The one sin of drunkenness costs this country fifty million pounds sterling of our national means. Faculties—talents, &c.—life itself, and the solemn capabilities of the soul. Sin often destroys all; ruins the whole.

V. SIN IS PECULIARLY DEBASING TO ITS VICTIMS. The son now a slave. The rich son now poor. The son of a noble family now a swineherd. How it degrades! how it sinks its possessors! It casts the crown of excellency from the head. It takes the robe of beauty, &c. It often affects the countenance—the face divine, and stamps the features with infamy and degradation. How many has it shut up in prison—the penal settlements. The great majority of criminals are the dissipated; abandoned, young.

VI. SIN IS OFTEN PRODUCTIVE OF UTTER WRETCHEDNESS TO BOTH BODY AND MIND. Hear the prodigal—his exclamation, "I perish with hunger." He fain would have filled himself with the husks, "the fruit of the carib tree," in shape resembling the large scarlet bean. His remuneration was not sufficient to satisfy his hunger, &c. And the swine were better fed than he. How truly is this often experienced in the circumstances that sin produces! The evils of its effects are truly legion, for they are many—temporal—domestic—mental—and those of the conscience and spirit.

VII. SINNERS IN THEIR MISERY ARE SELDOM BEFRIENDED BY THOSE AROUND THEM. No man gave the prodigal "husks." Where are his companions who assisted him to spend his portion? See the gambler, the pleasure-taker, the drunkard. How they all become friendless in their adversity, sickness, &c. Self seeks its own, and fawns and flatters in prosperity, but frowns and forsakes in adversity.

APPLICATION

1. Many can read their own experience in the text.

2. Let the young ponder it well.

3. It may instruct and admonish all. The condition described is wretched, indeed, but not hopeless. Light will break forth on our next subject.

130
THE PRODIGAL SON
PART 2

" And he said, A certain man had two sons: and the younger of them said to his father, Father, give me," &c.—LUKE xv. 11, &c.

IN our last discourse we contemplated the prodigal throwing off the paternal authority and restraint, claiming his share of the family portion, leaving his home and departing into a far country, spending all he had in profligacy and riotous living, reduced to a situation the most degrading and wretched, forsaken by all, and ready to die of want. Our present subject leads us to consider,

I. THAT A SINFUL CONDITION IS ONE OF INFATUATION AND MADNESS. " When he came to himself." That is, when he paused, considered, reflected, acted as a rational creature. One chief cause of continued sin, is inconsideration. Men will not know—do not consider. Passion reigns and rules. Would a man exchange home for exile—plenty for famine—a robe for rags—dignity for servile degradation—comfort for wretchedness? Yet all sinners act thus. They give gold for tinsel—bread for husks—gratifying the body at the expense of the soul. The moment of pleasure is preferred to the realities of eternity. Madness is want of judgment; and is not sin? Madness is rashness; and is not sin? Madness is acting without regard to reason, and not consulting the proper end of existence, &c. Look at the superiority of the mere animal creatures as answering the end of their existence, Isa. i. 3; Jer. viii. 6, 7.

II. THAT AFFLICTION IS SOMETIMES THE MEANS OF PRODUCING SERIOUSNESS AND REFLECTION. Just perishing! The exclamation showed his state. " I perish with hunger." We say affliction *sometimes* is the means of conversion, not always. Many leave the furnace harder and more reprobate. Many curse God and die. But there are instances of the reverse—similar to that of the prodigal. There was the wicked, blood-thirsty Manasseh, 2 Chron. xxxiii. 12. The proud, imperious Nebuchadnezzar, Dan. iv. 33, 34. Happy is it when adversity and affliction lead to consideration and repentance. No doubt there are some instances of this kind here. Some have lost a child—a parent—a friend—have been brought to the verge of the tomb, &c., and thus led to humiliation, and penitency, and prayer.

III. GENUINE REPENTANCE IS RETRACING OUR STEPS TO THE GOD WHOM WE HAVE FORSAKEN. Repentance signifies change of mind. " I think differently, I feel differently, I will act differently. I thought it best to be without restraint; not so now. I thought it best to leave my home, &c., to be the companion of profligates, to give myself to rioting. My mind is entirely altered —changed. My course shall now be the reverse. I will go back—cease to do evil, learn to do well." This is repentance, and nothing else. It always changes the conduct—changes the life. " Let the wicked man forsake his wickedness," &c. It will ever be accompanied with shame. " What fruit had ye," &c. Sorrow, keen regret, a sense of self-condemnation. The repenting sinner needs none to condemn him. He writes by far the most bitter things against himself. Overwhelmed with a sense of his ingratitude, he feels sin has injured himself—society—and offended his God. He beholds what he has forfeited, verse 17.

IV. THAT DETERMINATE RESOLUTION IS NECESSARY TO GENUINE REPENTANCE. He considers, reflects, perceives the only alternative, and then he resolves; " I will arise and go," &c. Many desire, many purpose, but yet do not *resolve*. There must be decision, determination;—this is indispensable. But it is not every resolution that is effectual.

1. *It must arise as much from a sense of the evil of sin as a fear of its punishment.* The one feeling is entirely selfish and carnal. I dread the death, but do not hate the crime, &c. But the prodigal felt that he had " sinned," that he was unworthy, &c.

2. *It must be made with a full conviction of our own weakness, and relying on God's aid.* Many have resolved presumptuously, self-righteously, and have failed. These must fail. To know our helplessness is essential;—that we can do nothing, and then God will be trusted, relied on: we must rest all *here*, " Thy grace is sufficient," &c. The Lord's help, &c.

3. *Hence it must be accompanied by earnest prayer.* God's aid must be implored, and that fervently; with all the intensity of a person in deep distress.

> " Beware of Peter's word,
> Nor confidently say,
> I never will deny thee, Lord,
> But grant I never may."

4. *The best resolutions must be promptly acted upon.* Carried out; and immediately. If we delay, the impression will vanish; if we delay, the ardor will subside, the enemy gain strength. It must be brought to the present tense; now, this day, this season, this evening, this moment.

> "I must this instant now begin
> Out of my sin t'awake;
> And turn to God, and every sin
> Continually forsake."

Thus acted the prodigal, and thus must we act, to enjoy God's favor, and obtain salvation. Now, by how many reasons may this be enforced on all unconverted sinners present! We shall confine ourselves to the following.

(1.) Have we not sufficiently felt the misery of our present state to desire deliverance? Is not a sinful state wretched, degrading, perilous? We cannot doubt the necessity of immediate extrication.

(2.) Is there not ample provision, even for prodigals, in their Father's house, if they repent? The least and the lowliest in Christ's family is infinitely better off than we are. "Better be a door-keeper," &c. "Hired servants," &c. Better be a dog to have the falling crumbs, &c.

(3.) There is but one way of access to that home. By repentance; by going and casting ourselves on his mercy; by venturing on his goodness and compassion.

(4.) No time so suitable or so sure as the present. Who then will arise? who will take the first step to-night? Is there not some young person? some head of a family or aged person? We entreat you to weigh, ponder, and now resolve. The prodigal is now on his way back. His reception and restoration we must postpone until our next discourse.

131

THE PRODIGAL SON
PART 3

"A certain man had two sons: and the younger of them said to his father, Father, give me," &c. —Luke xv. 11, &c.

We have previously contemplated the prodigal leaving his father's house; spending his portion in riotous living; reduced to want, degradation, and misery. We have also witnessed the happy change which took place in his mind; the impor-tant pause; the noble resolve; the feelings of repentance and genuine sorrow which he experienced; and the prompt manner in which he began to retrace his steps. At this part of the parable, we must recommence our observations, "And he arose," &c.

I. Observe the aspect of the repenting sinner. He is now moving towards his father's house. How different his appearance.

1. *To what it was when he abandoned his home.* Then, invested with the riches of his portion; clothed in the costume belonging to his rank; a retinue of servants; a host of professed friends. Now poor—in rags—alone—ready to perish. Yet how different,

2. *To that part of his history, when he was wasting his substance.* Look at his recklessness, profligacy; look at his company; hear the mad mirth; witness the scenes of dissipation. But, alas! it was the way of ruin—the carnival of death; the victim was fitting for the slaughter. But now he is alone—thoughtful—reflecting —serious—journeying homeward; and, notwithstanding his wretched condition, he is in the way of life and salvation. We observe, that such a difference will always be seen where genuine repentance is experienced. No conversion without such an entire change. We remark,

II. God sees repenting sinners in the first movements of their hearts and lives towards him; verse 20. "When he was a great way off," &c. Yes; as if he had been looking out for his return. He beheld him at a great distance, and knew him. The first gracious motions of the heart are known by the Lord. That serious thought; that keen pang of regret; that contrite groan; that resolution of amendment; that sigh for happiness. He is in a merciful position, seeking the return of the sinful, wandering soul.

III. God hastens to meet the contrite penitent. He saw, had compassion, and "ran," &c. Observe these three points:—

1. *He beheld our misery*—our return from the way of rebellion, and did not feel the spirit of stern, inflexible righteousness, but the movings of love and pity.

2. *His compassion prevailed.* "Had compassion." Nothing else would serve the sinner, for he had no claim—no merit—nothing to deserve—every thing to con-

demn; but God felt the movings of compassion.

3. *Compassion brought him speedily towards his returning child.* The prodigal moves slowly; his sins are heavy; his grief oppressive; his fears numerous; but the father " runs"—hastens to meet him.

IV. GOD DISPLAYS THE UTMOST MERCY, AND THE SOFTEST TENDERNESS TOWARDS HIS PENITENT CHILDREN. " He fell on his neck, and kissed him," &c. How beautiful this scene! The father who had been disobeyed—offended; yet he exhibits the greatest love, the most intense affection. He passes by the sin—there is no upbraiding; he passes by the pollution of the sinner, and even embraces him; he prevents his self-reproaches—his confessions, &c.; gives him the most tender token of his forgiving love; " kisses him;" is at once reconciled, &c. How surprising! Yet thus does God receive sinners, yea, the vilest of them; yea, thus he will receive you—every one of you, " Come, and let us reason," &c. He receives them graciously; forgives them freely.

V. THE RICHNESS OF THE DIVINE MERCY WILL NOT PREVENT THE HUMBLED CONFESSIONS OF THE TRUE PENITENT. This conduct of the father does not cause the son to think less of his sins—his wanderings. Oh! no, but more. This makes him feel his guilt the more deeply. He must unbosom his soul by confession. His own heart requires this; his peace; especially his father's compassion. Oh! how the tears flowed; how difficult was utterance! his soul melted within him, and he said, " Father, I have sinned," &c., verse 21. Every word would bear emphasis.

VI. THE STATE OF THE SINNER IS COMPLETELY TRANSFORMED IN THE DAY OF CONVERSION. What is the reply of the father? He turns from the son, and addresses the servants. The misery and wretchedness of the son must be relieved.

1. " *Bring hither the best robe.*" The rags are cast aside forever. The best—the choicest—the most expensive—the most ornamental—the most dignified is brought. What is this but the garment of salvation; the robe of righteousness; that in which God clothes the contrite sinner; the garment of praise instead of the sackcloth of mourning.

2. *The ring is put on his finger.* The token of the father's reconciliation; the

sign of the son's elevation to his former rank; that which ratifies the gracious reception. This is the Holy Spirit. " Because ye are sons," &c. " The Spirit itself beareth witness," &c. " Ye have not received the spirit of fear, but adoption," &c.

3. *Shoes on his feet.* The shoes of the preparation of the gospel of peace, so that he shall now walk in the ways of peace and holiness, having the spirit of a holy, affectionate child. " He shall run in the way of his commandments to do them."

4. *The feast is provided.* " The fatted calf" is killed, and made ready, &c. He was dying of hunger—now abundance is prepared for him. Not only hunger alleviated, but a sumptuous repast, worthy of the father's riches, and of his still richer love. This is that supper revealed and tendered in the gospel; the provision of mercy—the feast of fat things—the banquet of love, wherein all things are ready. Christ's flesh is the food of the believer. He is the Lamb slain for the life of his people. We live by faith in the Son of God.

VII. JOY AND FESTIVITY CELEBRATE THE SINNER'S RETURN AND ACCEPTANCE OF GOD. " They began to be merry." Others entered into the father's joy, and rejoiced with him; sadness and sorrow were put away; music, and songs, and gladness were heard. What overflowing, rich, unspeakable mercy! Yet this is all true on the sinner's conversion to God. " I say unto you, there is joy in the presence of the angels of God," &c. What an association of joy! The father—the servants—the son—God—angels—glorified spirits—the saints on earth—the accepted sinner. " I will praise thee," &c.

VIII. NONE BUT THE ENVIOUS AND WICKED WILL MURMUR WHEN THE VILEST ARE RECEIVED INTO THE DIVINE FAMILY. As the elder brother, &c.; the Pharisees of old. " This man receiveth sinners," &c. Surely he came for this purpose. But is not the joy reasonable and proper, yea, indispensable? Is it not meet? &c.

APPLICATION

1. *What a subject for grateful retrospection to the Christian!* How all this is familiar and delightful!

2. *What encouragement for the penitent!*

3. *What hope for all!*

132

CHRIST EXALTED BY THE MULTITUDE

" And when he was come nigh, even now at the descent of the Mount of Olives, the whole multitude of the disciples began to rejoice and praise God with a loud voice, for all the mighty works that they had seen ; saying, Blessed be the King that cometh in the name of the Lord ; peace in heaven and glory in the highest. And some of the Pharisees from among the multitude said unto him, Master, rebuke thy disciples. And he answered and said unto them, I tell you that, if these should hold their peace, the stones would immediately cry out."—LUKE xix. 37–40.

THE passage we have selected for our present meditation is one of those striking fulfilments of prophecy in which the New Testament so amply abounds. Read the 9th verse of the 9th chapter of Zechariah. A similar prediction had been uttered by Isaiah, lxii. 11. One of these prophecies had been uttered nearly 700, and the other nearly 600 years before ; here they are literally accomplished. Every sentence is adapted to elevate the true Christian, and excite in his soul more ardent praise to the blessed Saviour. Observe from the text,

I. THAT JESUS THE SAVIOUR IS WORTHY OF THE LOFTIEST PRAISE.

II. THAT THE GODLY OF ALL AGES HAVE SUNG HIS PRAISES.

III. THAT MANY WOULD SUPPRESS THE PRAISES OF CHRIST.

IV. THAT GOD WILL EVER SECURE THE LAUDATORY EXALTATION OF HIS SON.

I. THAT JESUS THE SAVIOUR IS WORTHY OF THE LOFTIEST PRAISE. Praise is awarded to men on earth on many and varied accounts : lofty genius ; literary attainments ; distinguished heroism ; expansive benevolence ; mighty achievements. The divine Saviour should be praised,

1. *For his personal excellencies.* " He is fairer," &c. The desire of all nations. In Christ dwells infinite knowledge—spotless purity—unrivalled dignity—unlimited goodness—and every feature of humanity, tenderness, and grace ; a body without sinful weakness ; a mind without error or obscuration ; a soul reflecting all the moral glories of the Father.

2. *For his unsearchable grace.* The favor of his heart, which he manifested to a lost world ; favor that surmounted every obstacle in the way of our recovery ; favor that paid the severest price for our ransom. " Ye know the grace of our Lord Jesus Christ." " Greater love," &c. No wonder this is part of heaven's anthem, " Worthy is the Lamb that was slain."

3. *For his wonderful achievements.* To note all these, we must give you the history of redemption. What has he achieved ? The emancipation of the world from Satanic ignorance and vassalage ; the bestowment of divine love through the channel of his own sufferings ; the opening of the kingdom of heaven to all believers ; the sure and certain exaltation both of the bodies and souls of his people to his eternal kingdom and glory, " Father, I will that those whom thou hast given," &c. Observe,

II. THE GODLY IN ALL AGES HAVE SUNG HIS PRAISES. Abraham, the representative of the patriarchal age, looked forward to his day, and saw it, and was glad ; his heart praised the promised seed. Jacob, in his dying predictions, sang of the Shiloh, and ended his life exulting, " I have waited for thy salvation," &c. Moses chose as the subject of his eulogy, the prophet like unto himself, unto whom the people should hearken. David referred, in exalted strains, both to his character and work—his sufferings and triumph—his kingdom and glory ; he died exulting, " Blessed be the Lord God of Israel," &c. Think of the songs of all the prophets ; how they exult in Zion's delivery, and Judah's glorious king. At his birth, angels, and shepherds, and sages, all exulted in his advent. Wherever he went the mourners were made happy, the sick healed, and the lame danced for joy. On the occasion to which the text refers, the praise was public and loud, and expressive of the highest joy and exultation. The early Christians in all their assemblies sang a hymn of praise to Christ ; so now, whenever Christian assemblies meet, one great design is to bless and laud the Saviour's name. It is delightful to contemplate, that the sun never sets on those who sing the hosannas of Christ— east and west, north and south. In the torrid and frigid zones ; on eastern sultry sands, and mid polar snows, the glories of Christ are celebrated in strains of highest praise. He is praised in the happy musings of the Christian's retirement ; he is praised at the family altar ; he is praised by the rising generation of the sabbath school ; in the social prayer-meeting, and in the great congregations of his people. We notice,

III. THAT MANY WOULD SUPPRESS THE PRAISES OF CHRIST. In the text the Pharisees labored to do so.

1. *The skeptical and unbelieving would confine our praises to the works of nature.* They refer us to the landscape, the ocean, the firmament, &c. Or they would have us extol reason, and science, and philosophy, &c. ; but would not give one line to Jesus.

2. *The profligate would have us sing of wine, and feasting, and sensuality.*

3. *The sanguinary would have us sing of war, and victories, and warriors, and conquests.*

4. *The self-righteous would have all praise to elevate their own goodness and superiority.*

5. *The formal and supine think it unnecessary or superfluous.* Now, all and each of these subjects are opposed to the praise of Christ, as much so as the odes which exalt Mohammed, or the songs sung to the honor of the idols of the heathen. The heart cannot give its highest emotions to these and to Christ. It must be Christ and not these, or these and not Christ. We observe,

IV. THAT GOD WILL EVER SECURE THE LAUDATORY EXALTATION OF THE SAVIOUR. He secured this at the birth of Christ, by giving the mandate, " Let all the angels of God," &c. Also at his ascension, " He went up with a shout," &c. He secures this in all saints by his Holy Spirit that dwells in them. It is a spirit full of love to him, and of praise and hosanna to Christ ; it is his declared will, that Christ is to have equal honor and glory with himself. This is one of the characteristics of the Christian, he rejoices in Christ Jesus. He will secure this in heaven by the universal acclamations of angels and redeemed spirits, Rev. v. 11, &c.

APPLICATION

1. *Are you amongst those who praise the Saviour ?* Do you exult, boast, glory, extol, celebrate the praises of Christ ?

> " When he's the subject of the song,
> Who can refuse to sing ?"

I tell you who should not : those he has not compassionated—those whose nature he has not assumed—those for whom he has not

died—those against whom his heart is closed—those he cannot or will not save ; but of such there is not one in this congregation, nor yet in the wide world itself.

2. *Neglect of this duty by the Christian would be criminal indeed.* " The very stones," &c. The gay, the licentious, the frivolous, all would condemn you. Let your hosanna be the hosanna of the heart, of the profession, of the life. " In all things show forth," &c.

3. *The advantages of praising Christ.* Elevates the mind, refreshes the spirit, assimilates to the beatified. It dispels clouds, banishes night, brings day. What endless matter of praise in Christ !

133

THE TEN VIRGINS

PART 1

" Then shall the kingdom of heaven be likened unto ten virgins, which took their lamps, and went forth to meet the bridegroom," &c.—MATT. xxv. 1, &c.

THIS is one of Christ's most striking and impressive parables. It has to do with events of the most momentous character. It refers to the glory of the Saviour, the necessity of vital piety, the second advent of the Messiah, the glorification of believers, and the rejection, the everlasting rejection, of those not prepared for the heavenly state. It may be necessary, and, perhaps, most edifying, that we should,

1. REVIEW THE PARABLE IN ITS LITERAL SIGNIFICATION. The event described is that of an eastern marriage procession. The bride is brought to the house of the bridegroom with great pomp and splendor. The friends of the bridegroom and bride are invited to join in the procession, and to partake of the banquet with which it would be followed. The procession was generally delayed till evening, sometimes till midnight. Those who were to grace the train must have lighted torches, or flambeaux ; and to keep these burning, they provided vessels of oil, into which they were dipped, or which they poured upon them. In the present instance the bridegroom delayed his appearance until midnight, and in the interval the virgins all slumbered and slept. At length the cry is heard, " Behold, the bridegroom cometh," &c. Then they all arise to get their torches ready, that they may go forth to meet him. Part, however,

of the company had neglected a provision of oil for the future, and they exclaimed, "Our lamps are gone out." They sought assistance from the other persons in attendance, but their stock was only adequate to their own necessity. And while they labor to supply the deficiency, the bridegroom appears, and they who are ready, go forth to the honors and enjoyments of the marriage feast. The others now try to gain admission, but they are rejected, with the solemn announcement, "Verily I say unto you, I know you not." Let us now consider,

II. Its spiritual application.

1. *The Bridegroom is Jesus.* This is one of the general scriptural representations of the Saviour, and there is one passage in the Psalms which is almost identified in spirit with this parable, Ps. xlv. 10, &c. The prophet Isaiah, xliv. 5, also. The Saviour gave the same representation of himself in his parable of the marriage feast, Matt. xxii. 1, 2. So also when asked wherefore his disciples did not fast, as those of John, Jesus replied, "Can the children of the bridechamber mourn, as long as the bridegroom is with them," &c., Matt. ix. 15. So John the Baptist testified of Christ, John iv. 29, "He that hath the bride is the bridegroom," &c.

III. The object of the bridegroom's affection is the church. Thus the apostle writes to the Corinthian church. "For I am jealous over you," &c., 2 Cor. xi. 2, &c. See also Eph. v. 25. Now to render a union possible between Christ and mankind,

1. *They must have one nature.* Hence Christ took our nature upon himself, he dwelt in our flesh, became a man, made of a woman, &c. And he provided the means for restoring the sinner to the divine nature. For the renewal of his heart and life. See Titus ii. 14, and iii. 4.

2. *They must have one mind.* In our natural state, we are alienated, at enmity, &c. Now Christ, by the exhibition of his love in the gospel, overcomes this. By the power of his truth he melts the soul. By the exhibition of his own bleeding side he allures to himself, draws the soul to him; the rebel throws down his weapons, and exclaims, "I yield, I yield," &c.

3. *In conversion the soul is espoused to Christ.* Thus the apostle said, "I have espoused you to Christ," a promise and en-

gagement of marriage. Jehovah very affectionately reminded Israel of his espousal to that people, Jer. ii. 2.

4. *The marriage celebration is reserved for his second advent.* To this John refers us in one of his visions. "Let us be glad and rejoice, for the marriage of the Lamb is come, and his wife hath made herself ready," Rev. xix. 7. With that event will conclude all the arrangements of grace, and will begin all the dignity and bliss of perfected glory to his church. The whole church of Jesus will stand thus related to Christ forever and ever. So John thus again describes the splendors of this glorious consummation, Rev. xxi. 2, &c. Now let us conclude by placing Jesus as the dignified bridegroom before you. We remind you that,

(1.) *His glory is supreme.*

(2.) *His riches are infinite.*

(3.) *His beauty unrivalled.*

(4.) *His love unspeakable, and passing understanding.*

(5.) *Are not his claims, then, irresistible?* Notice also as to the character of true Christians; represented as virgins in this parable. As such they are,

(1.) To be separated from the world.

(2.) To be distinguished for their purity of heart and life.

(3.) To live in the enjoyment of love to Christ, and hope of union with him forever and ever. We offer Jesus to you all. Reject him not, &c. We congratulate believers on their choice and portion. We expostulate with those who have forsaken him. Oh return, &c.

134

THE TEN VIRGINS
PART 2

"Then shall the kingdom of heaven be likened unto ten virgins, which took their lamps, and went forth to meet the bridegroom," &c.—Matt. xxv. 1, &c.

We previously considered the former part of this parable, and also the general spirit of the whole, as applied to an eastern marriage ceremony. We noticed the character of Christ as a bridegroom; believers as virgins, &c. We now have to consider the virgins,

I. In their professional probationary condition. "Who took their lamps."

Now in this, the profession of Christianity is exhibited. The people of God are not in darkness, but they are light in the Lord; and they are to shine as lights in the world. Religion is to be seen, to be manifest. "City set on a hill," &c. Now the virgins are described as "taking their lamps, and going forth," &c. This profession of discipleship and friendship to Christ,

1. *Should arise from love to Christ.* In the early ages of Christianity, no fear of any other motive. Now, it is respectable; in some cases profitable. The love of Christ is the only right constraining principle. " I am crucified with Christ," &c.

2. *Must be public and open before men.* "Follow me," &c. "Let your light, &c., *before* men." "Went forth."

3. *Must be constant and continued.* Every day, place, and circumstance. In good report, and evil report, &c. Must be maintained, held fast, &c.

4. *It must be sustained by divine grace.* Grace is the "oil." This will give the profession the right tone. Beautify us; make us to be firm and persevering. Now a profession without the grace of God in the soul, will,

(1.) Be joyless; no real bliss; no real peace; no solid hope. Mechanical; no experience; no feeling in it.

(2.) It is promiseless. The promises are given to the true Christian; to the sincere follower of Christ.

(3.) It is often transitory. No root; soon given up; soon cast off. How necessary, then, the oil of divine grace! Doing all in Christ's name, and in the sufficiency of his grace. We now proceed to notice,

II. The delay of the bridegroom, and the virgins in their sleeping state. "The bridegroom tarried." The early Christians expected his second advent in their time. So in many ages since. But as to that period it is not revealed, except that it will be in the end of the world. Now, in the interval, one generation after another passeth away. Of the virgins it is said, "They all slumbered and slept." This evidently refers to death. Death to the godly, is falling asleep; sleeping in Jesus. Now let it be observed, that up to this period, there are no obvious distinctions between the two classes of virgins. They all have the same title; all have lamps; all are burning for a time, and they all fall asleep, waiting for the bridegroom. But

this is the grand and awful difference: the wise have prepared for the future; " the prudent man foreseeth the evil," &c. The others have been satisfied with the present; have no supply for the coming exigency. See 1 Tim. vi. 19. We notice,

III. The solemn announcement. "Behold the bridegroom cometh," &c.

1. *The period of this announcement is midnight.* At the end of our world's day. Not literal: it cannot be so to all the world.

2. *The pomp and magnificence of his coming.* The event is most momentous, and the scene truly sublime. All beings in all worlds will be interested in it. The Father now sees the end of his gracious administration to a world of sinners. Jesus now has the full crown of his joy, his promised reward. Believers now hail the day of their full and eternal redemption, the coronation of the saints. Angels now grace the train of the descending Judge, the glorified Messiah. Devils and lost spirits now tremble, as they wait for the passing of their final sentence and their irrevocable doom. The dead, small and great, hear the trumpet's loud, shrill blast; and the graves, and the sea, and death, and hades, give up their dead. " Behold the bridegroom cometh," is heard by each and every human being. " Then all those virgins," &c. And now we notice,

IV. The awful deficiency of the foolish virgins is discovered. And the foolish said, " Give us," &c. What a discovery! Lamps gone out! and gone out when most needed. What shall they do? They apply to the wise virgins. " Give us of your oil;" but the wise reply, " Not so," &c., verse 9. In this life we cannot give grace to each other. How much less then! Let me suppose a few cases which this passage suggests. Parents and children;— and the former have only had the provision of oil, and for the son to say to his father, Give me of your oil; the daughter to her mother, &c. Wives and husbands;—and the latter have not had the store of oil, and shall say, " Give me," &c. The pastor and people, and they shall say to him, " O give us," &c. Not a saint will have more than his own state will require. Will any in this assembly put the request? or will any have to give the refusal? Notice,

V. The conclusion of the ceremony, and the consummation of the feast. The wise join in the train and are acknowledged as the friends of the bridegroom, and they go into the marriage. Their hopes are now realized; their desires now fulfilled; their joys now complete; their salvation now perfected, and that forever. The bliss, the glory, are unutterable. But the foolish virgins labor to supply the deficiency in seeking oil. But "the door is shut." What a solemn sentence!

(1.) The door of opportunities and means now shut. Not a messenger, not a sanctuary, not a sermon; the season of means all passed forever.

(2.) The door of mercy, which had been open to all for thousands of years, now shut. The king has laid aside the golden sceptre.

(3.) The door of hope;—only one in the universe, and that closed: everywhere else black despair.

(4.) The door of heaven which Christ opened, as our sacrifice and priest. But now he has retired from the intercessory, and has given the keys of authority to the Father, that God may be all and in all. And the exclusion is absolute;—urgent entreaty avails not. They knock, and cry "Lord, Lord," &c. But the solemn sentence concludes the fearful scene. "Verily, I say unto you," &c.

APPLICATION

1. Let the subject lead to solemn examination. Are we Christ's real disciples? Have we the oil of grace in our hearts— laid up? Do we wait for Christ's coming? Is this the end of our lives? the one grand object ever in view?

2. Exhortation to earnestness and diligence. This is the one thing needful, &c. Be steadfast and immoveable. Be diligent, that ye may be found, &c.

3. It inculcates vigilance on all. "Watch," &c.. In one sense Christ comes at death. At least our probationary opportunities then end. Oh then, let us live, and pray, and watch. "Hold fast that which thou hast," &c.

135

THE GOOD SAMARITAN

"Which now of these three, thinkest thou, was neighbor unto him that fell among the thieves," &c.—LUKE x. 36, 37.

IT is somewhat doubtful whether this is a parable or a narrative of facts which had come under the notice of the Redeemer; yet we admit that some of the chief instructions of Jesus were delivered in parables. When he wished to set forth the readiness of God to receive humble, repenting sinners, he delivered the series of parables connected with the lost sheep, lost piece of silver, and the prodigal son; when he wished to exhibit the importance of humility and the abominableness of pride and self-righteousness, he delivered the parable of the Pharisee and the publican. When he wished to show the various results arising from hearing the gospel, he delivered the parable of the sower and the seed. When he wished to show the eternal advantages of righteous poverty over worldly pomp and splendor, he discoursed on the rich man and Lazarus. When he desires to show the extent of the benevolent law of God, which says, "Thou shalt love thy neighbor as thyself," he presents before them the scene connected with the text. We are called to contemplate,

I. A FELLOW-BEING IN IMMINENT PERIL AND DISTRESS, verse 30. "A certain man," &c. Part of the way from Jerusalem to Jericho lay through a desert, which was so infested with robbers as to be termed the bloody way; for greater safety, persons generally travelled in company; but here is a poor lonely traveller who falls into the hands of the robbers, who is stripped of his garments, wounded, and left half dead. The miseries of our world seem chiefly to be reducible to three kinds.

1. *Self-procured.* There is an inseparable connection between certain courses of conduct and suffering; some of the ways of men lead to penury, disease, and death. "The way of transgressors is hard." Even in this life it is often ill with the wicked. The way of sin, shame, and ruin.

2. *Some of the miseries of life are clearly sent from God.* How often the wise, and good, and prudent, suffer. Behold the patriarch Jacob; look at Job; "Shall we receive good at the hand of the Lord," &c. But observe,

3. *A great amount of our suffering is from our fellow-men.* Behold those children covered with shame and misery! whence is it? From their wicked parents. See those parents heart-broken! how is it? Their children are vile, irreverent, without natural affection. See that man ruined in his reputation and property. How is it? He has

been swindled out of his property, &c. Sin ripens men for every crime ; hence, daily the possessions and lives of men are taken by beasts of prey, in the shape and form of men. Here is a poor man! They have taken his money and his clothes, and wounded him ; left him weltering in his gore, "half dead." "The tender mercies of the wicked are cruel." We are called to witness,

II. Two OFFICIAL RELIGIONISTS EXHIBITING A TOTAL WANT OF HUMANITY. One of them is a priest, the other a Levite, individuals closely connected with the rites of a divine religion. No doubt the hopes of the man would be revived as he saw two travellers, especially when he beheld their priestly apparel ; the priest, however, went at once on the other side, as if he had not seen him, or were intent on some more important business. The other stood opposite and looked, and then he too, whatever he might feel, passed by, &c. Perhaps he pitied, but he helped not. Observe, they trampled upon the principles of humanity, patriotism, and religion ; that religion is hypocritical and totally false, which does not produce works of goodness and mercy. What avails religious knowledge ? What avails religious profession ? What avails assumed sanctity of life ? " God is love." " Jesus went about," &c. " Pure religion," &c. " To do good," &c. We are called to witness,

III. A MANIFESTATION OF MERCY WHERE IT MIGHT HAVE BEEN LEAST EXPECTED, verse 33. " But a certain Samaritan," &c.

(1.) He was arrested in his course. "Came where he was." Easy to have evaded, &c.

(2.) He examined into his condition.

(3.) He had compassion ; his heart melted, and it was not merely sentimental.

(4.) He entered on a course of kindness, &c. " Bound up his wounds," lest he should bleed to death ; poured in wine as an astringent to cleanse, &c.; oil as an emollient to heal ; did not leave him to his fate ; set him on his beast, &c. ; took him to the inn, gave him two denarii, and engaged to pay the remainder. Here was *generous, practical,* and *continued goodness.* Think of the excuses he might have made, " I am a Samaritan, I hate him, and if he had seen me thus he would not have helped me. Let his own people help. I am on a journey," &c. Consider,

IV. CHRIST'S PRACTICAL APPLICATION OF THIS PARABLE. " Go and do likewise." When you see human misery do not neglect it. According to your means and opportunity do good.

(1.) Such a course will be exceedingly pleasing to God.

(2.) Have a happy influence on your own hearts.

(3.) Will secure you an interest in the benign providence of God, Psalm xli. 1, &c.

(4.) Will not go unrewarded at the last day, Matthew xxv. 35, &c.

APPLICATION

1. *The subject has been considered by some as representing the character and work of Christ.*

(1.) Man's condition, &c.

(2.) The inefficiency of the law and sacrifices to help.

(3.) The gracious visitation of Christ to our world.

(4.) His provision ; wine and oil ; his precious blood, and divine Spirit.

(5.) His taking him to the banqueting house of his church, &c. Christ is now passing. We learn,

2. *True mercy embraces both the bodies and souls of men.* Christian benevolence is universal ; it extends to all objects ; not a mere relative or domestic feeling ; not local—not national. Wherever there is a human being in misery, whether of body or soul, we are bound to show compassion and help.

136

THE PHARISEE AND PUBLICAN

" Two men went up into the temple to pray the one a Pharisee and the other a publican," &c.— LUKE xviii. 10–14.

PRAYER forms a leading exercise in every system of religion under heaven ; it was one of the evidences of patriarchal piety ; it was one of the frequent services of the tabernacle, and afterwards of the temple. Mohammedanism is distinguished for its numerous prayers. Pagans of every grade and age have performed their devotional services to their imaginary deities. The worshippers of Baal cried from morning to evening to their senseless idol. How important then that Christians should not allow ignorant pagans to rise in condemnation against them at the last day ; but it is not every thing which men present, that God will regard or acknowledge as prayer; to this end is the scope and design of the parable before us. Let us,

I. CONSIDER THE CHARACTER AND PRAYER OF THE PHARISEE, AND HIS REJECTION OF THE LORD.

1. *The person.* A Pharisee, of the strictest sect of the Jews.. Persons who made pretences to very superior piety, but who generally were filled with the spirit of self-righteousness and spiritual pride. Men who sought their own glory rather than the glory of God.

2. *The place to which he repaired.* "The temple." Building erected for God's worship and glory. Here the sacrifices were presented, the law read, and prayer offered to God; it was emphatically to be a house of prayer for all nations. One of the leading designs of worship is, to make prayer and supplication to God.

3. *The service he offered.* I cannot call it prayer, for not one word of petition, or supplication, or intercession is found in it. There was, however, apparent *thanksgiving,* and that is part of prayer, but even that, while it professed to honor God, was a mere exaltation of self. What he said was in commendation of himself under the mask of thanking God. He thanked God because he was,

(1.) *Not as other men.* Not so vile as the vilest; but probably he might owe much of this to his education, to parental restraints, and the more favorable circumstances in which the providence of God had placed him. What would you think of a man, even in the presence of his fellow-mortals, praising himself because he was not a savage, or an assassin, because some of his fellow-men were such!

(2.) But he refers to his *good deeds.* "I fast," &c. These he thinks render God under obligations to him, or at any rate, give him a right to God's peculiar regards.

(3.) *But he contrasts himself with his fellow-worshipper.* How odious! "Or even as this publican." Instead of feeling pity or compassion for him, instead of giving him a place in his prayers, he tries to exalt himself by abasing his fellow. Yet how often are we thus guilty! How often do we hear for others! How often institute invidious comparisons! This was his service, but where was the prayer? Where the confession of sin—the contrition

—the supplication? He asks no favor, seeks no pardon, entreats no grace. Self possessed the throne, and he was totally ignorant of his own heart, of the purity of God's character and law.

(4.) Let us notice the *result.* God was not honored nor pleased. God beheld him afar off; his only reward was the delusion of his own heart, the infatuated self-complacency of his own soul. Observe,

II. THE CHARACTER AND PRAYER OF THE PUBLICAN WITH HIS ACCEPTANCE OF GOD.

1. *He worships in the same place, but feels unworthy of the privilege.* Stands afar off, considers it holy ground, fears to draw near: how slow his approach, how reverent!

2. *He would not look towards God's holy place.* "Would not lift," &c. Why would he not look up? He thought of its purity, and felt his vileness; he thought of its goodness and his ingratitude; he thought of its holiness and his guilt with its desert, and therefore lifted not his eyes, &c.

3. *He smote upon his breast.* He was inwardly smitten—his conscience condemned; he felt his guilt, his worthlessness, and smote upon his breast. Ah! that treacherous heart—that ungrateful, wicked heart.

4. *He prayed fervently for mercy.* In this prayer,

(1.) *The object was right.* "God" the only object of prayer. Who hears and answers prayer.

(2.) *The confession was appropriate.* God demands confession. There are promises given to it. Is it not proper? If God would dispense with it, the ingenuous penitent could not. "A sinner." He extenuates not—he mentions not one righteous act. A sinner—nothing else, nothing better.

(3.) *His request was suitable.* He asks for mercy, not justice, but mercy, compassion, to the unworthy; kindness to the miserable. Every sinner needs this; nothing else will save.

(4.) *His suit was granted.* He went down "justified." "Rather," is in italics. God was glorified, God's justice and mercy; God heard, approved, and accepted the suppliant, and granted his request. God was propitious, and he received mercy. From the whole we learn,

1. *How liable are we to be deceived as to our true state!* Do not err in this; be not the victims of infatuation, especially as to self-righteousness.

2. *How necessary is self-abasement!* Grace always humbles, always prostrates. If we are not abased we are strangers to God's grace; no exception to this; nothing will supply its place.

3. *What encouragement to the contrite!* "To that man will I look," &c. "A broken and contrite heart," &c. How many of you have felt thus? Prayed thus, &c. If not, do so now. God is seated on a throne of grace; draw near and look to the sacrifice God has provided; utter this fervently, and you shall not, you cannot pray in vain, &c.

137
THE PENITENT MALEFACTOR

"And he said unto Jesus, Lord, remember me when thou comest into thy kingdom," &c.—LUKE xxiii. 42, 43.

THE circumstances attending the death of Jesus were of the most wonderful kind. The blessed Messiah had for three years been traversing the land of Judea, illumining the benighted, healing the sick, and making the miserable and desponding happy. No teacher had ever delivered such discourses; no one had ever wrought such miracles; no one had ever exhibited such piety, benignity, and love; yet, by the malice of his own countrymen, he is persecuted even to death, and we are called to witness him enduring all the painful agonies attending crucifixion. He is now dying the ignominious death of the cross; but his death, like every other part of his wonderful history, is distinguished by scenes of the most wonderful character. The rocks rend —the earth quakes—the sun is darkened —and the veil of the temple is rent in twain. During these amazing phenomena, we are called to witness the conduct of those robbers who were suffering with Christ. One of them joined in the unbelieving railing of the surrounding mob, and said, "If thou be the Christ," verse 39. "But the other," verse 40, and text. There are two leading divisions.

I. THE PRAYER HE PRESENTED.
II. THE ANSWER HE RECEIVED.

I. THE PRAYER HE PRESENTED. Two things must be noticed before we enter upon his prayer.

(1.) *The character of the suppliant.* He is denominated a thief and malefactor. It is probable that he had been a public robber—a daring outlaw; and not improbable that they had been confederates in crime; doubtless one of the most debased and abandoned of criminals, for only such were condemned to crucifixion.

(2.) *The situation in which he was placed.* Suffering the extreme sentence of the law; enduring the horrible death of crucifixion; a situation of extreme debasement and agony. Life was just ebbing out; on the verge of the eternal state; the world and time receding; his day of probation just expiring. Observe, then, his prayer.

1. *Short, yet comprehensive.* A few words embody all his requests; but in those words what an immensity of meaning!

2. *It was spiritual in its object.* It referred not to the body; not to ease or mitigation; or to his life. It all had respect to the soul and a future world.

3. *It was a prayer of mighty faith.* Faith in the *soul's immortality;* faith in a future state, &c., of rewards; it was faith in Jesus Christ. Observe, he addresses him as *Lord;* but where were the signs of his dignity and power? Yet he honored him as the Messiah—as having an invisible kingdom. "Thy kingdom;" and herein he recognised the Godhead of Christ, as the Lord of the invisible world. He acknowledged his *prerogative* to dispense future rewards, "Remember me," &c.; but it was also *mighty, wondrous* faith. Consider his character; his condition in life; his unfavorable position as to means. Contrast his state with the worthies of the Old Testament, or the disciples of the New. Moses believed; but then God addressed him, and showed him the symbol of his presence in the burning bush. Abraham believed; but then he had many precious promises. Isaiah believed; but he saw his glory. John the Baptist believed; but he saw the heavens opened, &c. The disciples believed; but they beheld his mighty works, &c.; they saw his miracles, &c.; transfiguration, &c.; even Saul of Tarsus was surrounded by his resplendent glory; but the dying malefactor beheld Christ in the depths of his sorrows; in the period of his abasement; reviled and crucified as an enemy to God and man; and yet through the whole his faith penetrated, and he recognised in that sufferer the Lord of the universe, and the only Saviour of the world; yet he so believed in Christ as to rest his

soul upon him, and depended upon his mercy for eternal life. He saw no sceptre—beheld no crown—had no prospect of a kingdom—that is, to the eye of sense, yet he recognised all these as rightly belonging to Jesus the Messiah, and as such he prayed, " Lord, remember," &c.

4. *This prayer was associated with the genuine fruits of repentance.* Saving faith and repentance are ever joined together. We do not add repentance as if it followed faith ; generally it goes before ; but in all cases it is connected with it. He confesses his own guilt, " We indeed suffer justly," &c., verse 41 ; he rebukes the impiety of his suffering fellow-malefactor, " Dost thou not fear God ?" &c., verse 40 ; he affirms the innocency and the holiness of Christ, " But this man hath done nothing amiss," verse 41. Thus, his last moments were spent in confession of sin, in reproof of wickedness, and in vindicating the Redeemer.

5. *His prayer was effectual.* He did not pray in vain ; and who ever did ? Jesus was not so much absorbed in his own agonies as to neglect the suppliant by his side. He listened to his petition ; he entertained his request ; and richly exhibited towards him the fulness of his grace. Christ came into the world to save sinners, and his last act was to deliver one of the chief of them from guilt and eternal death. Notice,

II. THE ANSWER HE RECEIVED. " And Jesus said, Verily, I say," &c. Now, let us look at the various features this answer exhibited.

1. *It was immediate.* He did not defer, or put off his suit. On some occasions Christ tried the faith of the applicants, as the Syro-Phenician woman ; but this was a desperate matter. Here life was expiring; and therefore at once Jesus mercifully replied to his petition.

2. *It was compassionate and merciful.* He had no claim ; no right. Natural death was a penalty of his crimes against man, and eternal death the penalty for his sins against God. But the compassion of Jesus was affected. He saw him ready to perish, and therefore beheld a fit object on whom to bestow the last blessing of his mission to our world. He came unto Christ, and Christ opened his heart to receive him ; he believed in him, and Jesus gave him the desire of his trembling spirit.

3. *The answer was peculiarly strong and* **positive.** Christ might have said, " I will

not forget thy prayer, but will show thee mercy." But Jesus resolved to fill him with ecstasy and joy, by the most solemn assurance that his prayer was successful, " Verily," &c. " I pledge my name, and honor, and truth, and faithfulness, that this petition shall be granted."

4. *It was superabundant.* He prayed to be remembered, but Christ treats with him richly, most munificently. He gave unto him a splendid promise—a blissful assurance of a place and portion with him in glory, " To-day thou shalt," &c. Here are three things :

(1.) The place—*Paradise.* This word is of Persian origin, and signifies a garden of pleasure—a figurative description of heaven. It is used in reference to the garden of Eden ; but Paul in his holy vision when caught up to heaven, calls it paradise, 2 Cor. xii. 4. John, also, in Revelation ii. 7, says, " To him that overcometh will I give to eat of the tree of life, which is in the midst of the paradise of God."

(2.) In paradise he was to be *with Christ.* It is Christ's presence that constitutes the light and bliss of glory. The richest assurance he ever gave was this, " Where I am, there ye shall be also."

> " There we shall see his face,
> And never, never sin," &c.

(3.) He was to be with Christ in paradise *that day.* " To-day." " Before the sun sets thou shalt enjoy the light and glory of heaven. As a trophy of my grace, I will present thee this day to my Father, ' before angels, and the spirits of just men made perfect.' "

APPLICATION

1. *Learn the richness and freeness of the grace of Christ.* The dying malefactor stands out on the page of the gospel that no sinner may despair. Here we see what grace can do—forgive, and cleanse, and glorify in a few hours.

2. *No encouragement for the presumptuous.* Only this case. Only one to prevent the abuse of God's long-suffering. A peculiar case altogether.

3. *The way of salvation.* Application to Christ.

4. *Death at once conveys to glory.* To die in Christ is instant, inexpressible, **and** eternal gain.

138

SATAN'S PALACE

" When a strong man armed keepeth his palace, his goods are in peace," &c.—LUKE xi. 21, 22.

NOTHING so completely blinds the mind and hardens the heart as envy. It is one of those evil principles which completely poison the soul, render it totally callous, and prepare it for every evil work. It was this that led Cain to become a fratricide, and slay his own brother; this that led the sons of Jacob to devise the death of Joseph; this that caused Haman to attempt the destruction of all the Jews in the kingdom of Persia; it was this that led the Pharisees to treat Jesus with such scorn and unbelief. As often as possible they denied his miracles; and when they could not do that, they wickedly said that he cast out devils by the power of the prince of devils. To this the Saviour thus replies, verse 17. He then illustrates his power in casting out devils by the figurative language of the text. Notice,

I. THE STRIKING REPRESENTATION OF SATAN.

II. THE TRUE DESCRIPTION OF HIS PALACE.

III. THE MANNER IN WHICH HE KEEPETH POSSESSION. And,

IV. HOW IT IS BESIEGED, AND SATAN DISPOSSESSED. Observe,

I. A STRIKING REPRESENTATION OF SATAN. He is described in verses 18 and 19 as Beelzebub; that is, the prince of the devils. He is the head and leader of the fallen angels, Rev. ix. 11. He is called Apollyon; i. e. a destroyer. He is also styled the old dragon; the serpent; the adversary; the deceiver; Lucifer, the fallen bright one; Belial; accuser; and devil, or diabolus, signifying the slanderer. Now, the reality of such a being,

1. *Is fully established by the sacred scriptures.* By some who profess to believe the Bible it is said that the name simply refers to the principle of evil, and not to any living spirit. But the word of God as clearly teaches the existence of a Devil as the existence of God, and employs such terms as cannot apply to a mere principle. As a real spirit, he conversed with Eve; persuaded her to believe his lies rather than God's truth; and hence he is called the father of lies. As such, he accused Job, and thirsted for his destruction; as such, he tempteo Jesus; as such, he is said to go up and down as a roaring lion; as such, Christ said he desired to have Peter, &c. We are exhorted to be vigilant, and resist the devil. It is said, too, that the devil and his fallen compeers are reserved for the judgment of the great day; see Jude 6; Rev. xx. 10.

2. *The text refers to his power.* He is described as a "strong man." Angels are said to excel in strength. We do not imagine this was impaired by their apostacy. His power may denote,

(1.) His authority. And he is a prince; the god of this world; the ruler of the powers of disobedience. It may denote,

(2.) His dominions. How vast and extensive! He usurped God's earth, and here he has his kingdom of darkness. In it are countless myriads of subjects—of men and women prostrate beneath his hellish and cruel yoke.

(3.) See the effects of his control. In Christ's day many human bodies were possessed. Look at the demoniac; look at the child possessed; look at the mental and moral effects of his influence on the souls of mankind.

(4.) Consider how he has maintained his possessions. For thousands of years. Learning, science, philosophy, and a thousand systems for effecting human happiness, have been vain and fruitless, and he has even resisted the reign of God extensively to this hour. Notice,

II. THE TRUE DESCRIPTION OF HIS PALACE. That is, the human heart; the soul of man. As his palace,

1. *Here he dwells.* This is his residence. As the Spirit of God dwells in the Christian, so the spirit of Satan dwells in the unrenewed soul. The various faculties and powers of the soul are the apartments of this palace, and these are all occupied by the prince of darkness. He surrounds the understanding with the curtains of delusion; he debases the judgment with diabolical perverseness; he decorates the imagination with pictures of uncleanness; he fills the affections with earthly things. Worldliness, vanity, or pride, furnishes the residence of the god of this world. As his palace,

2. *Here he has his throne.* God is not the Lord of the unrenewed heart. Here Satan is exalted and served; here he receives the homage of the intellect, and the willing service of the heart and life. Over the mind, and heart, and life, he sways his

sceptre, and has unlimited and incessant obedience. He says to one, ' Go ! and he goes ;' and to another, ' Come ! he comes.' Observe,

III. THE MANNER IN WHICH HE KEEPETH POSSESSION. It is said he keepeth his palace, and thus his goods are in peace. Now, he keepeth his palace by his wiles and stratagems ; by the subtlety and deceit he exercises. He does this,

1. *By keeping it in darkness.* Darkness is the element suited to his designs. He labors to keep men in ignorance of themselves, of God, of their responsibility, &c.; see 2 Cor. iv. 4.

2. *He keepeth it, under the influence of sense.* Sense has only to do with the palpable things of the present, " What shall I eat," &c. The body absorbs all the anxieties. Time present is every thing, &c. He urges men to seek present wealth, pleasures, &c. ; he keeps this world first and uppermost, &c.

3. *He keepeth it, by the influence of procrastination.* He says there is plenty of time ; ample means ; lengthened opportunities ; no need for present reflection; death is a great way off; and thus to invitations and warnings the soul replies, " When I have a convenient season," &c.

4. *He keepeth it, by producing lethargy and torpor of spirit.* Hardens the heart ; petrifies the feeling ; stupifies the conscience ; gives an opiate to the powers of reflection, &c.; so that insensibility is produced, and consideration and anxiety annihilated. Such persons are like a man sleeping on the top of a mast; or a person walking heedlessly on the very verge of a burning crater ; or blindfolded, rushing onward on the margin of a fearful chasm. He sometimes keeps it,

5. *By clothing the spirit in the habiliments of despair.* What a fearful sight is this ! Hope extinguished ; the fell mists of despair surrounding the mind. He then says, " Means are useless ; the distance from heaven is too great ; guilt too heavy ; disease incurable." He fills the soul with the affecting language, " The harvest is past," &c.

IV. How IT IS BESIEGED, AND SATAN DISPOSSESSED.

1. *The glorious personage by whom this is effected.* " Stronger." Almighty ; allpowerful. His word effected wonders.

2. *The means employed are the gospel, and the Spirit of Christ.* The gospel is the power of God, &c. The truth makes free. It proclaims liberty, &c.; opens the eyes ; awakens, excites, and draws the victims from the way of death.

3. *The change effected is wondrous and delightful.* Satan's power destroyed, and himself expelled. The soul becomes the palace of Christ. " Christ in you the hope of glory."

APPLICATION

1. Believers, bless your deliverer.
2. Sinners, call on Christ to save you.
3. The victims of Satan's power must share his final doom.

139

VESSELS OF WRATH
" The vessels of wrath fitted to destruction."— ROMANS ix. 22.

" How readest thou ?" is an important and necessary question to every diligent student of the divine word. If persons could read without having their views affected by preconceived opinions, then, generally, they would arrive at the meaning of the Holy Spirit. But it is too common to read the Bible, that we may establish our own opinions from its divine pages. It should be our desire that our opinions and judgment should be guided entirely by its hallowed truths. Men in law have to read with exactness, to know the spirit of the statute they are consulting. Chemists and apothecaries have to read carefully, that they may compound the medicines with accuracy and precision. Men of science have to exercise great attention, to understand the various laws of mechanism. Surely much more care is necessary to understand the truths of revelation,—truths which relate to immortality and eternal life. Negligent Bible reading, and reading with a mind under a sectarian bias, have been productive of the most awful mistakes and perversions of the divine word. This is especially true of this epistle, and more especially as to this chapter. The scope and tendency of the seventh, eighth, ninth, tenth, and eleventh chapters, are evident ; —the sovereign right of God to cast off the Jews, and elect the Gentiles to the privileges of the gospel ;—and to establish and illustrate this, is the one great design of the apostle. The doctrines usually deduced, are the unconditional election of some persons, and the unconditional reprobation or rejection of others, as an act of divine sovereignty. Let us at this time consider the immediate language of the text. We ask,

I. WHO ARE THE CHARACTERS ?
II. WHAT ARE THE EVIDENCES OF THAT CHARACTER ? And,
III. THEIR FINAL END. We ask,

I. WHO ARE THE CHARACTERS ? We might expatiate on the diversity of character specified in God's word. We might refer to the skeptic, the scoffer, the blasphemer, the sensualist, the proud, the worldly, the trifler, &c. There is one scriptural expression including the whole, " He that believeth not," &c. John iii. 36. All despisers and rejecters of the gospel of Christ, however profane, or however externally moral, are included. It is a fearfully wide range. How many are within it ! Now, it may be noted that such fit themselves for destruction. God does not. He is the fountain of holiness and goodness. Satan alone cannot ; he aids. It is his work to allure and deceive, but the sinner must co-operate,—be his willing slave. Men cannot make others such, except in the same sense in which Satan does so. It is the sinner's personal act. " O Israel, thou hast destroyed thyself,"—self-destroyed. Sin destroys, as disease destroys the body. As rust destroys the iron ; or the moth, the garment ; or poison, life ; or crime brings to an ignominious end. Unbelief destroys, as it neglects the remedy, puts away the Saviour, and rejects the intervention of God's mercy. Every sinner, therefore, fits himself as a vessel of wrath.

II. WHAT ARE THE EVIDENCES OF THAT CHARACTER ? Two kinds of evidence.
1. *Internal.* Known only to the individual and God. Without any love to God, any delight in holiness, any internal trust and reliance on Jesus Christ ; where the heart is indisposed to spiritual things.
2. *External.*
(1.) Indifference to God's holy word. A man must love and delight in it if he would be saved.
(2.) Neglect of the means of grace, especially prayer and hearing the gospel. These are essential to salvation.

(3.) Worldliness of spirit. " If any man love the world," &c.
(4.) Disregard of God's authority ; living in sin ; doing the work of the evil one. We need not add more signs of those who are vessels fitted for destruction. Consider then,

III. THEIR FEARFUL END. " Destruction." This does not mean annihilation. It is evident that the wicked, as well as the righteous, will exist forever. But it signifies the infliction of that wrath which their sin deserved. The psalmist has in view the metaphor of the text, Ps. ii. 10, 12. " Upon the wicked God will rain fire," &c. " The wicked shall be turned," &c. " These," it affirms, " shall go away into everlasting punishment," &c. Now this may be called destruction,

1. *As it will be the annihilation of all hope.* An indefinite kind of hope sustains men here ;—a vague, uncertain idea that they will not eventually perish. This is sometimes based on God's mercy ; on his indifference to the actions of mankind ; on the certainty of all men being saved at last, through Christ ; or on the exercise of repentance at the last hour. But now the candle of the wicked will be put out, and not one ray of hope irradiate the horizon of their prison forever.
2. *The utter cessation of all enjoyment.* What is existence without enjoyment ? Destruction involves this, that they shall have no peace, no pleasure, no bliss, forever. The ordinary enjoyments of time are passed away ; the sinful enjoyments of sense, &c. Not one stream of enjoyment left. The rich man requested a *drop of water,* but in vain.
3. *The righteous infliction of God's displeasure.* Imprisoned in hell ; shut up in utter darkness ; cast into the fiery lake ; the companion of the devil and his angels. The preying of the worm of conscience ; probably in sight of heaven, within hearing of its melody ; yet excluded, and totally unfit for the felicity of glory.

APPLICATION

Learn,
1. *It is the wickedness of sinners that ruins their souls.* Charge it not on some eternal decree ; it is the inward resolving of the soul to live in iniquity. Charge not the unmercifulness of God ; it is the want of compassion in your own souls. Say not

it is necessity ; it is the necessity of your own will. God says, " As I live," &c. ; Jesus says, " Ye will not," &c. ; the Holy Spirit says, "If ye will hear my voice," &c.

2. *Vessels of destruction may be changed into vessels of mercy.* " If the wicked will turn from his wickedness," &c. " Hear, and your souls shall live," &c. " Unto you is the word of this salvation sent," &c. " He that believeth shall be saved," &c. Do you want instances ? There is Manasseh ; there is the woman that was a sinner ; the extortionate Zaccheus ; the dying thief; Saul of Tarsus ; many in this congregation. May you be enrolled in the same record of salvation and mercy.

140

VESSELS OF MERCY

" Vessels of mercy, which he had afore prepared unto glory."—Rom. ix. 23.

THERE are two great cardinal truths of our holy religion : that the misery and ruin of the sinner is of himself, and that the happiness and salvation of the Christian is of God. These truths are equally true and important. To lay the sinner's ruin at the door of God, is an attack upon his goodness and mercy, and giving falsity to his own asseveration, that he has no pleasure in the death of him that dieth. To ascribe the salvation of the righteous to themselves, would be to rob God of his glory, and destroy the gospel system of grace altogether. There are three important questions which arise from the text.

I. WHO ARE THE VESSELS OF MERCY ?
II. HOW DO THEY BECOME SUCH ?
III. WHAT IS THEIR FINAL DESTINATION ?

I. WHO ARE THE VESSELS OF MERCY ? Now the scriptures affirm all men to be *objects* of mercy. " God is good to all, and his tender mercies," &c. But an object and a vessel are very different. A vessel of mercy, is one receiving and containing within it the saving mercy of God. Observe the vessels of mercy,

1. *Heard the gospel of mercy.* " This is a faithful saying," &c. Heard of the mercy promised to the guilty ; had the overtures of mercy made to them ; were urged to receive it—to accept it.

2. *Such have received the revelation of mercy made to them.* Paul did so, and was not disobedient to the heavenly vision. The three thousand on the day of Pentecost did so, and received the gift of the Holy Ghost. The jailer did so, and confessed his faith in the Lord Jesus. So also have the saints afar off; they heard the invitation, and drew nigh. Enemies, they accepted the terms of amnesty ; guilty, received the pardon through the blood of Christ, in which they had redemption, &c.

3. *Such give evidence of their changed and saved condition.* Delight in the God of mercy ; rejoice in the merciful Saviour ; glory in his cross ; exhibit the spirit of mercy, by living in peace, and exercising compassion to those around them. They live as those redeemed and raised from sin, and misery, and death.

II. How DO THEY BECOME SUCH ? Not by lineage, as the children of Abraham ; or of pious ancestry. Not by education, or the power of religious example. Not by acts of self-righteousness, &c.

1. *By the exercise of free grace on the part of God.* The grace of God bringeth salvation, &c. Salvation is traceable to this source, and no other. " Not by works of righteousness," &c. He has mercy because he will ; because he delights in mercy ; because it is rich, free, boundless, everlasting.

2. *Through the merits of the Lord Jesus Christ.* Gift of God, &c., through Christ. His obedience ; his spotless purity ; his sacrificial death. " He loved us, and gave himself," &c. " Though he was rich," &c. " He suffered, the just," &c. " Himself bare," &c. " With his stripes," &c.

" 'Tis all our hope, and all our plea,
  For us the Saviour died."

3. *By simple and meritless faith on the part of the sinner.* Pardon is presented, the sinner receives it, and it becomes his own. He hears by faith and lives. He looks, and is saved. He runs into the refuge, and is delivered. He opens his mouth in prayer, and God fills his soul with the saving influences of the Holy Spirit. In this there is no merit, unless accepting a pardon by a culprit is such. I would just add, that all the saints are vessels of mercy, and become such, by this one simple, saving process.

III. WHAT IS THIER FINAL DESTINATION ? " Afore prepared unto glory." I doubt if these words literally refer to the Christian's eternal destination; see Rom. viii. 30. There is a glory which pertains to all saints here. "All we with open face beholding," &c. There are glorious titles, glorious privileges, glorious promises, here. But let us look to the final destiny of the vessels of mercy. They are destined,

1. *To a world of glory.* Called to God's eternal kingdom of glory, they shall dwell forever in the blissful regions of immortality. Born again, to an inheritance, &c. To be the associates of angels, and to dwell with Abraham and Isaac, &c., in the kingdom of their Father forever.

2. *To a glorious condition of both soul and body.* The *soul* made intellectual, and perfect in holiness; invested with power to enjoy the blaze of eternal light, emanating from the face of God and the Lamb. The *body* to be raised in the likeness of Christ's glorious body; to be free from all the weakness, frailties, and pollutions of the flesh, and made holy in their degree, as God himself is holy.

3. *To a glorious reward.* To sit on a throne of dominion and power; to wear a crown of glory; to enjoy all the love of God, and all the bliss of the divine presence; to drink of the streams of pleasure; to partake of the fruit of the tree of life; in one word, to be "forever with the Lord." "In thy presence is fulness of joy," &c.

APPLICATION

1. *Learn the true title of every Christian.* A vessel of mercy, not of merit, or excellency. Of mercy, first and last, and always.

"I the chief of sinners am,
But Jesus died for me."

2. *The Christian's present state.* One of preparation; of spiritual growth; of increasing grace; spiritual advancement. Let us not forget this. Be this our one great concern, to "work out our own salvation," &c.

3. *God waits to be gracious to every sinner.* You may all become vessels of mercy, and *now.* "For, behold, now is the accepted time," &c.

141

THE CONQUERING REDEEMER

"And I saw, and behold a white horse: and he that sat on him had a bow; and a crown was given unto him: and he went forth conquering, and to conquer."—REVELATION vi. 2.

THE prophecies of Ezekiel and the visions of John contain figurative representations of the most sublime description; this kind of writing is common to all oriental authors, especially to the poets. It must necessarily follow that such portions of the holy scriptures are difficult of interpretation. Commentators have been exceedingly divided on the meaning of many of the prophecies of the apocalyptic vision. Some writers of critical eminence have applied the text to the victories of Titus and Vespasian, who came from the east and obtained complete dominion over Judea, destroyed Jerusalem, and carried the Jews captive into all lands. Others have referred the passage to the reign of Constantine. I think the very reading of the text impresses the mind, that however celebrated Titus and Vespasian might be, a greater than they were is here; neither should we be warranted in applying it to Constantine, seeing that the reign of Constantine began the era of the corruption of Christianity, and did more mischief to the interests of true religion than all the fires which persecution ever kindled. Scripture is often the safest interpreter of scripture. For an explanation of this passage of this book, I refer you then to the 19th chapter and 11th verse. Our text, doubtless, refers to the glorious achievements of the Lord Jesus Christ. Let us notice,

I. THE SUBLIME REPRESENTATION GIVEN OF THE REDEEMER. And,

II. THE CHARACTER OF HIS GLORIOUS ACHIEVEMENTS. Notice,

I. THE SUBLIME REPRESENTATION GIVEN OF THE REDEEMER. Observe,

1. *His martial appearance.* Seated on a horse of war. Here we interpret the symbol as expressive of the *power* of Christ. "All power is given," &c. Bozrah's conqueror, &c., "mighty to save," &c. Of the *dignity* of Christ, see Psalm ii. 1. Of the *courage* of Jesus. He united meekness with the most undaunted intrepidity and courage; he appeared single-handed; he thirsted for the conflict; he trod the winepress, &c. See the description of the war horse, Job xxxix. 19. Notice,

2. *The description of the horse on which the Redeemer goes forth.* "White," not

black, or pale, or red. Though Zechariah saw him upon a *red* horse, and though Isaiah speaks of his being red in his appearance, they referred to his personal conflicts in obtaining our redemption. "White horses," were reserved for generals, captains, and commanders. *Joshua* had a conversation with Jesus, as captain, when he stood over against Jericho. *Paul* represents Jesus as the captain of our salvation, &c. Now, the "white horse" seems symbolical,

(1.) Of the purity of Christ's person. Warriors were often the very basest of mankind; avaricious, proud, cruel, desperate. Jesus, essential holiness, purity embodied, heart of love, a life of truth and benevolence.

(2.) Of the righteousness of his claims. The spoiler and oppressor may ride upon horses of a crimson hue, as characteristic of their injustice and their oppressions. War is generally based on unrighteousness; often on no other principle but power; no object but ambition; no end but gain. Christ's warfare is one of eternal righteousness, equity, &c. He designs to regain his revolted dominions. Satan has usurped the dominion of this world, though made by Christ, and for Christ; filled it with terror and misery. Jesus contemplates its restoration to its original allegiance, purity, and glory. He is heir of the world, &c.; heir of all things; he has a right to reign, &c.

(3.) Of the felicity of his administration. Desolation and wo attend the footsteps of earthly warriors—countries ravaged, cities burned, families ruined, streams of blood flowing; often followed by famine and pestilence; how delightful the contrast! Jesus's conquests obliterate wo and misery. The desert rejoices, and the wilderness blossoms as the rose; justice and benevolence ever accompany his steps. One song is heard, "Glory to God," &c.

> " Blessings abound where'er he reigns;
> The prisoner leaps to lose his chains:
> The weary find eternal rest,
> And all the sons of want are blest."

Observe,

3. *The warlike instrument which Jesus bears.* "He had given him a bow," one of the most ancient and universally used instruments; now this bow is, *The truth of his blessed gospel.* All Christ's victories are to be obtained by this; this in the hands of the Holy Spirit is to evangelize the world, see John xvi. 7–14. He gained the personal victory over Satan by this— he sent out his servants with this—he frees men, he regenerates, he sanctifies by this. His word is likened to the hammer, fire, &c. "Our gospel," &c. "I am not ashamed," &c. "We preach Christ crucified," &c. See Psalm xlv. 5. Notice,

4. *His regal dignity.* "Crown." Not the essential crown of his Godhead, but his mediatorial one. Given him as king of Zion—the Head of his church. Now of this crown we notice it is,

(1.) A crown for which he covenanted and suffered, Isaiah liii. 6; Phil. ii. 6.

(2.) A crown which as our exalted king he now wears in heaven, Acts v. 30; Heb. ii. 9; Rev. v. 6. Observe,

II. THE CHARACTER OF HIS GLORIOUS ACHIEVEMENTS. "He went forth," &c. Now here we must glance,

1. *At the enemies he had to encounter.* Powers of earth and hell. Satan and the world allied. Judaism, Paganism, Mohammedanism, papacy, infidelity, and sin of every class. Observe,

2. *The conquests he gained.* He went forth "conquering." He conquered by his personal prowess in the *desert*, by miracles, on the cross, in the grave, from thence by his gospel. When John saw him he had obtained the great first general victory in the city of his death. Where was Pilate, the Jewish Sanhedrim, Calvary? &c. A victory over 3000 souls, and soon increased to 5000; from thence went from conquering to conquer in Samaria, Athens, Corinth, Rome, &c. In the first ages he went forth, till Paul thus writes, Col. i. 16.

3. *He is still going forth, and there are immense triumphs for Jesus to gain.* Hence he goes forth from conquering to conquer. The world yet lieth in the arms of the wicked one. Six hundred millions yet in battle array against God, and against his Anointed. He is going forth now, in the east and west, north and south. " And this gospel," &c. "The stone cut out," &c. "Christ's conquering car," &c. Isaiah lx. 1–5, 21, 22. O yes! he must reign, and he must conquer, until the song of the world's jubilee is heard from every hill and vale, "Hallelujah! Hallelujah! for the Lord God Omnipotent reigneth!"

APPLICATION

1. *Let the subject be applied personally.*
Are you numbered among the conquests of
Christ ? Have you ceased to rebel and
fight ? Have you sued for peace ? Have
his arrows stuck fast ? Are you enrolled
among his friends ? Are you the soldiers
of the cross ? If so, rejoice ! Happy are ye,
&c. If not, reflect upon your state ; it is
one of wretchedness, one of hopelessness,
and one of certain ruin. Christ will break
his enemies in pieces as a potter's vessel.
" Wo unto him," &c. " Kiss the son, lest
he be angry with thee, and thou perish
from the way, when his anger is kindled
but a little." " Agree with thine adversary whilst thou art in the way with him,"
&c.

2. *Remember you cannot aid Jesus unless
you are enlisted under his banner.* Your
gold, &c., he will scorn, if your heart be
with his enemies. He demands first yourselves, then what you have.

3. *The friends of Jesus are deeply interested in the triumphs of the cross.* You are
on one side of the mighty contest ; your
prayers must be there then ; your personal
efforts must be there ; your pecuniary
aid must be there also. Think of the
territories yet unoccupied ; think of the sin
which yet abounds ; think of the myriads
and millions who are still perishing for lack
of knowledge ; think of the claims of humanity ; think of Christ ; and oh ! think of
the day of the Lord, when the Saviour shall
be revealed in flaming fire, &c.

142

ALL THINGS FOR THE CHRISTIAN'S GOOD

" And we know that all things work together
for good to them that love God, to them who are
the called according to his purpose."—ROMANS
viii. 28.

ALL scripture was given by inspiration,
and all scripture is profitable, &c.; but
there is infinite variety in the portions of
the divine word. The word of God may
resemble the heavenly firmament, but some
portions are more radiant and bright than
others. Some passages of the word resemble the milky way in the heavens ;
some texts shine forth with unusual brightness and celestial lustre. The chapter in
which our text is found is like the brightest
portion of the heavens, and our text is the
most resplendent star of that radiant galaxy.
I doubt if any passage of the holy word has
been more generally useful to the Christian
church, or more especially consoling to the
believer in trouble. Let us, then, examine
it, and see what counsel and consolation
may be deduced from it. Let us,

I. EXPLAIN THE CHARACTER PRESENTED
TO US. " Them that love God," &c. Now,
here are three things :—

1. *The divine purpose.* Now, by this
purpose we understand God's pre-determi-
nation to offer to mankind the blessings of
salvation in Christ Jesus ; and it was God's
purpose that the Jews first of all should receive this offer, Romans i. 16 ; Luke xxiv.
46, 47. Now, the gospel was first published to the Jews, and then, according to
God's purpose, afterwards to the Gentiles,
Ephesians i. 7–11. Observe,

2. *The divine calling.* To call, is to invite, to entreat, &c. Now, it was God's
purpose that in this order—the Jew first,
and then the Gentile—should be called by
the messages of truth to participate in all
the blessings of the gospel. Thus the provision of the gospel is likened to a feast,
and men are to be called to come in and
enjoy the banquet. Jesus Christ called in
the days of his ministry sinners to repentance ; the apostles and disciples thus called
men to repent and believe the gospel. Thus
the believers at Rome had been called according to God's gracious purpose.

3. *The divine principle.* " Love God."
Those who had thus been called, and who
had obeyed the call, became the subjects
of God's mercy and favor. Such had been
chosen of God to be his people, his sons and
daughters, and the love of God had been
shed abroad in their hearts by the Holy Ghost
given unto them. Now, this divine principle imparted to them is evinced in loving
God, " We love him because he first loved
us." All who have believingly obeyed the
call of the gospel, love God. They love
him as their creator, preserver, but especially as their redeemer. They love his
name, his word, his people, his ordinances ;
they love God truly and fervently in spirit ;
they love to meditate on God—to commune
with God—to hold converse with him ; and
they earnestly desire to love him more, and
to serve him better. Let us,

II. ILLUSTRATE THE TRUTH AFFIRMED.
" All things work together for good." Now,

a few preliminary things must be noticed. The term, "all things," must in one thing be limited; sin must not be included, for sin is evil in its nature, influence, and tendency; and if sin could be included, then with propriety we might say, "Let us sin that grace may abound." But the apostle says to this, "God forbid." Then when it is said, "all things work together for good," we must take the word "good" in its highest acceptation; not present enjoyment, but final well-being. The soul in its moral advantages, and eternity in its final decisions, must both be taken into consideration. Limit your views to the present, and think only of immediate happiness, and the text would be inexplicable. Notice then, with this prefatory explanation,

1. *The extent of the thing specified.* "All things." All things in heaven; the blessed God, the Father, Son, and Spirit, angels, &c., spirits of the just made perfect. All on earth; all men; good men, by their prayers and love; and bad men, by their hatred and opposition. All events; prosperous and adverse—joyous and grievous—health and sickness—prosperity and adversity—life and death. All things in hell; Satan and his agents, by their frowns and temptations, though not joyous but grievous, yet afterwards is yielded the peaceable fruits, &c. All things in nature, providence, and grace.

2. *The operation stated.* "All things *work.*" There is nothing in the mental or moral department of the universe entirely quiescent. "All things work;" thoughts, desires, imaginations, all work and produce their kind. All events and occurrences tend to some end. As in nature, so in the mental kingdom; as wind, light, rain, dew, calms, and tempests, all operate to some end; so all things in providence and grace work, and have a tendency to produce some effect. Notice,

3. *The universal harmony declared.* "All things work *together.*" There is diversity of element, but the operation and the end are harmonious. Look at that musical instrument; all the notes and sounds are different, yet they all produce harmonious melody. Look at that most beautiful creature, light: there are seven prismatic colors, quite distinct and dissimilar; through a prism you perceive them separately, but they all unite together, and form that soft and radiant emblem of the Creator. Look at that scene in nature: there is the moun tain with its craggy summit; the verdant valley, the flowing stream, and the roaring cataract; how diverse are the various parts, yet how harmoniously they unite to form the landscape and please the eye. Look at that piece of mechanism: see the various parts, in their action how opposite; wheels within wheels are moving in one direction, and a second in another, yet they all work together, and accomplish the design of the inventor. Look at the human body: what variety of parts and operations; some parts receiving nutrition, others throwing various elements out of the system; inspiring the air to supply the lungs, and respiring air again from the lungs, as it were, living and dying by rotation; and yet all these work together to sustain life and prolong our existence.

4. *The final end affirmed.* "All things work together for good." Separately, some things appear to work for good, and others for evil; but conjointly, they all tend to one blessed end, the real and eternal good of them that love God, &c. Now, let us establish this, for the apostle says, "We know," &c.

(1.) I appeal to scripture declarations. And in reference to positive and manifest blessings proof is unnecessary; so we will confine our attention to afflictions, sorrows, &c. Hebrews xii. 11; Romans v. 5, &c.; James i. 2, &c., "For our light afflictions," &c.

(2.) I appeal to scripture facts. There was Jacob and his final good in the time of famine, &c. See how "all things work:" even the envy of his sons is overruled, &c.; Joseph sold, &c.; Simeon, &c.; Benjamin demanded, &c. "All these things are against me," &c. Oh! no; they are all working together, &c. There was Moses, his final good, and the good of Israel; but see the events of his career: edict; exposed in the fragile ark—yet how all things worked. There was the blessed Jesus; his final exaltation; and the salvation of myriads, &c. But behold his birth, life, sufferings, and death; but they all worked, &c., Acts ii. 23.

(3.) I appeal to scripture, as exemplified in your experience. Have you not proved the truth of the text in many cases? You thought that severe loss would have ruined you—that bereavement crushed, that sickness destroyed you; but now you observe how necessary they were ; that they all worked together, &c.

APPLICATION

1. *Are you the characters described ?*
2. *Rejoice in God's good providence.* In his universal, benignant reign.
3. *Cultivate the grace of contentment.* Be not murmurers ; or anxious ; or in haste.
4. *Look to the termination.* The soldier —the traveller—the mariner does this. Oh ! cherish the spirit of the text, &c.

143

THE DEATH OF THE RIGHTEOUS

" Let me die the death of the righteous, and let my last end be like his !"—NUMBERS xxiii. 10.

OUR text contains the expressed desire of the wicked Balaam, and it has doubtless been the desire of thousands equally estranged from holiness and God. Even the wicked know that they must die, and it is well that they should think and reflect upon it. But, like innumerable other vanities of the imagination, this wish will be fruitless in its results, to all who continue alienated from purity and God. The end of Balaam was what may reasonably be expected to be that of all who live a life like his. The text refers to a character that we must define, an event that we must illustrate, and a desire that must be regulated.

I. A CHARACTER THAT WE MUST DEFINE. " The righteous." None are such by nature ; none are such by mere education or parental discipline; none are such by self-exertion. This character is divine, and therefore of God. It includes,

1. *Justification.* By which, through faith in the Lord Jesus, we are constituted righteous, and dealt with as such. Isa. xlv. 25 ; Rom. iii. 16.

2. *Regeneration.* Born from above; born of God ; partakers of the divine nature. This is the new man ; the holy nature which the children of God possess. John iii. 3, &c. ; Col. iii. 10.

3. *Sanctification.* Or the progress of the new man in holiness ; the spiritual growth, and advancement in the divine life. This includes also the consecration of the heart to the service and glory of God. An increasing conformity to the holy image of the blessed God, 2 Cor. iii. 18.

4. *Practical obedience ;* or righteousness of life. This is the great evidence of righteousness of heart. The fruit testifies that the tree is made good ; that the fountain has become pure. He only is righteous who doeth righteousness. Those who have received Christ Jesus the Lord, walk in him ; following his example, treading in his imitable steps. " Being made free from sin," &c. Rom. vi. 22.

II. AN EVENT THAT WE MUST ILLUSTRATE. " The death of the righteous." Even the righteous must die. The righteous of all ages, except Enoch and Elijah, have died. The righteous patriarchs, prophets, apostles, and fathers, have all died. " It is appointed unto men once to die," &c. But the righteous die,

1. *Under the immediate direction of God.* The wicked often die prematurely. By their own hands ; by the hands of the executioner ; by the power of sin producing disease ; by the judgments of God. But the righteous, in life, in sickness, and in old age, are the especial objects of the divine care. They are in his hand, " and precious in his sight is the death of his saints." When their work is done he calls them home. When they are meet for glory, he receives them to himself. The righteous die,

2. *In a state of gracious security.* They die in covenant with God ; with an interest in Christ ; the subjects of the indwelling Spirit ; heirs of glory. " Die in the Lord." " Death is theirs." Not an enemy to destroy, but a messenger to conduct them to their better home. Death cannot separate the saint from Jesus. The righteous often die,

3. *In ecstasy and triumph.* " Have an abundant entrance ministered unto them," &c. Thus died Stephen, with the vision of glory before his eyes. Hearken to the apostle, " I have fought the good fight," &c. So thousands and myriads. Death has been victory. " O death, where is thy sting !" &c. Thus Payson : " The battle is fought, and the victory is won." The righteous always at death,

4. *Enter upon a life of immortality.* They are intimately present with the Lord. Ascend to the Saviour's God, and to their God, &c. To die is gain, immediate, consummate, eternal gain. " Blessed are the dead who die in the Lord," &c. Then it is that Christ receives them to himself, &c.

Death is the gate of life—the vestibule of glory. Our text contains,

III. A DESIRE THAT MUST BE REGULATED. "Let me," &c. It is a very proper desire. Should be the desire of every human being. But it will be fruitless unless it is regulated,

1. *By a personal regard to the character of the righteous.* The character and the death are united; they cannot be separated. We cannot die their death if we are wicked, impenitent, or merely moral, or only professors of righteousness. We must attain the spirit and principle of the righteous. It must be regulated,

2. *By a preparation for dying.* This, by the righteous, cannot be forgotten. He, therefore, acts, and prays, and believes, in reference to this solemn event. He is anxious to be ready for the coming of the Son of Man; to have the robe and the Spirit; the lamp and the oil; the title and the meetness. This is the only desire of any value. It must be regulated,

3. *By a constant deference to the divine will.* The righteous cannot suggest any thing as to the mode, the place, or the circumstances of dying. They say, "My times are in thy hand." They regard present duties and privileges, and leave all that concerns the act of dying in the Lord's hands. "I will wait all the days," &c. With God are the issues both of death and life.

APPLICATION

1. *The subject of the text is solemn.* Dying is always an awful, momentous thing; the great crisis in man's history; the point on which hang the everlasting destinies of the soul. And, remember, all must die Oh yes! there will be no discharge from this war.

2. *What is your prospect respecting death?* I ask not what you wish or imagine; but what is the well-grounded prospect? Oh, appeal to your heart, conscience, life, and see if they refer to a safe and happy death-bed.

3. *How different is the death of the wicked from that of the righteous!* Dark, dreary, hopeless; the beginning of sorrows; the prelude to everlasting woes. Oh! avoid this. Deprecate this.

144

MESSIAH'S FINAL TRIUMPH

"I will overturn, overturn, overturn it; and it shall be no more, until he come whose right it is; and I will give it him."—*Ezek.* xxi. 27.

THE prophecy of the text has reference to the removal of the crown from the head of Zedekiah, and the vacancy in the royal line of David, which should not be filled up until the sceptre should be given into Christ's hands, whose true right it should be to reign. Now, all this was literally fulfilled, for the kingdom of Judah ceased not until Christ appeared, who was the root and offspring of David, and King of kings and Lord of lords. But there is another version of the text which may be taken, and which is in perfect unison with the spirit of prophecy—that Jehovah has given universal empire to Jesus, that it is Christ's right to reign, and that God will overturn every obstacle and impediment until it be accomplished. Let these three topics, then, now engage our attention.

I. *Jehovah has given universal empire to Jesus.*

A few citations from the oracles of truth will establish this. Ps. lxxii. 1–11, ii. 8, lxxxix. 27; Dan. vii. 14; Zech. ix. 10; Phil. ii. 10; Acts ii. 32, &c. It is evident from these truths that Christ's dominion is to embrace the whole world—every empire, kingdom, continent, and island. All people of every language, and color, and tongue. His kingdom is to swallow up every other; and the kingdom that will not serve him is to utterly perish. This blissful consummation was beheld in prophetic vision by John, Rev. xi. 15. With this state of things will be associated universal righteousness, universal knowledge, universal peace, universal bliss. We notice,

II. *That it is Christ's right thus to reign.* "Whose right it is." Now, this right of Jesus to reign supremely and universally, is founded,

1. *On his creative property in all things.* The apostle says, Col. i. 16, "All things were made by him and for him." By his power, and for his glory. Satan is a usurper—the world is alienated from its rightful

Lord. But the right of Christ remains un-affected, and that right he will demand and obtain.

2. *On his supreme authority as universal Lord.*

He is Lord of all, King of kings, &c. His majesty and glory fill the heavens. His claims are as great as the universe. As such, he has a right surely to the earth—to the whole earth. This authority is seen in controlling all events, in upholding all things, &c. In his infinite out-goings of benevo-lence and love.

3. *He has a redeeming right.*

He became incarnate, he descended into the world, he brought the light of heaven into it, he gave his own life for it, he is the proprietor, &c. Here then is a right, ratified with his precious blood. And he redeemed it expressly that he might reign over it. That he might be King, and King alone, that the diadem might encircle his own brow. And thus in the extension of his kingdom he is receiving his joy and reward. He was willingly lifted up that he " might draw all men unto him."

III. *God will overturn every obstacle until this be effected.*

" I will overturn," &c. Now, in effecting this glorious purpose the works of the devil must be destroyed, and the empire of sin totally overthrown. Ignorance must give place to light, error to truth, sin to holiness. Satan must be driven from his strongholds, and thus Jesus will enlarge his empire, and extend his domains. There are, however, four mighty impediments, which must be overthrown, entirely overturned.

1. *Paganism, and all its multifarious rites.*

The idolatry of paganism, the supersti-tions of paganism, the cruelty of paganism. The very atmosphere of paganism is the smoke of the bottomless pit. Paganism, whether of the intellectual and metaphysi-cal kind of the Hindoos, or of the rude and illiterate kind of the untutored tribes, must be overturned. Every pagan idol must be cast to the moles and the bats, &c. Every altar razed, and every temple desolated, Isa. ii. 18.

2. *Mohammedanism in all its earthly gratifications.*

Mohammedanism is a splendid admixture of adulterated truth and vulgar error. Now this must be overturned. The false prophet must be denounced and forsaken, the cres-cent must wane and retire into oblivion be-fore the power of the cross.

3. *Judaism, with its obsolete rights.*

A system originally of God, but which consisted of types and shadows, which have long ago been ratified in Jesus, the great substitute and antitype. Eighteen hundred years ago that system lost its vitality ; and Ichabod has been for ages written upon its rites, and services, and people—the glory has departed. The Jews are like persons who at eventide are looking for the rising of the sun ; but every vestige of that shadowy economy must pass away, and all the relics of the scattered tribes be collected into the fold of the Nazarene, Rom. xi. 25.

4. *Antichristian Rome.*

The papal hierarchy is evidently that Man of Sin to which the apostle alludes, who must be destroyed. This is evidently the mystical Babylon, whose overthrow is cer-tain. This is to be as a millstone thrown into the depths of the sea, Rev. xviii. 20. Every thing that exalteth itself against God, or attempts the division of Christ's merits, must be consumed before the brightness of Messiah's countenance, and the power of his truth. But you ask, How will God over-turn, &c. ? Doubtless his providence will subserve the purposes of his grace. He may cause science and commerce to open a passage for the message of truth. He may even overrule war, and may allow the mili-tary hero to pioneer the ambassador of peace. But he will do it by the power of the gos-pel of truth. The doctrines of the cross are to effect it. " We preach Christ cruci-fied," &c. " Not by might, nor by power," &c. The spiritual sword is the word of God. He did this by the gospel in primitive times. In bigoted Jerusalem, in idolatrous Athens, in lascivious Corinth, in imperial Rome, and in these, then rude islands of the sea. He is doing so now. Look at the isl-ands of the South Sea, look at Central Af-rica, look on the shores of continental India, look into the interior of Burmah ; in one word, that which converts a blaspheming Briton will save a Hindoo idolater, or savage American Indian.

APPLICATION

1. Are your sympathies and affections on the side of Jesus ? Does the subject inspire, inspirit you ? Has it your affections, pray-ers, influence, and help ?

2. How necessary is devoted, concentra-

ted effort. What has to be achieved? make the calculation. We spoke of Pagans—write down 482 millions; Mohammedans, 140 millions; Jews, 3 millions; then add, as disciples of Papal Rome, 80 millions; total, 705 millions. Is it not hopeless? No—read the text. God has spoken it.

3. Secure a personal interest in the gracious administration of Jesus.

145

THE ENEMIES AND FRIENDS OF JEHOVAH

"So let all thine enemies perish, O Lord; but let them that love him be as the sun, when he goeth forth in his might."—*Judges v.* 31.

God has often employed holy and devout women to effect his purposes, and carry on his cause. The Scriptures contain many biographical sketches of female piety and excellency. The name of Sarah is mentioned, and Ruth, Manoah's wife the mother of Samson, and Hannah; Esther was not half so illustrious in all her royal splendor, as when we view her pleading for her countrymen, and risking her life to save them from the Persian edict. In the New Testament we have a galaxy of pious women, who shone in the hemisphere of the church with bright effulgency, as the milky way in the midst of the heavens. There was Anna, the prophetess; Elizabeth, the mother of the Baptist; the amiable sisters of Bethany; Dorcas, the friend of the poor; Lydia, the first European convert; and, at the head of the illustrious list, the virgin mother of Jesus, of whom it was properly said, "Blessed is the womb," &c. But we must refer for a moment to the writer of the celebrated song, of which the text is the sublime conclusion. Deborah, the wife of Lapidoth, was raised up as a prophetess, and to be a judge in Israel. In connection with Barak, she roused the armies of Israel, encountered the powerful hosts of Sisera, and the Lord made them victorious; and she then recounts the whole in this song of triumph, and concludes, "So let all," &c. We may appropriately apply the text to the cause of Jesus, the Bozrah conqueror, who is going forth from conquering to conquer. Similar passage to the first clause, Ps. lxviii. 1, "Let God arise, let his enemies be scattered," &c. Let us rather read them as predictory declarations. Thus we shall consider the text,

I. *As descriptive of the true character and certain doom of the ungodly.* And,

II. *As giving an illustrious representation of the friends of Jesus.*

I. *As descriptive of the true character and certain doom of the ungodly.*

The term "enemies" will apply to all the unrenewed portions of mankind. The heart is positively hostile, &c. "Carnal mind is enmity against God," &c. Christ died for us when we were enemies. Not all enemies in the same way, or to the same degree.

1. *There are the daring enemies of God.*

Who skeptically treat his revelation, yea, deny his being. "The fool, who says in his heart, There is no God." They attack his rule—despise his word—rail at his servants—try to subvert his cause.

2. *There are the profane and reckless enemies of God.*

Who defy, contemn the Most High—Pharaoh, Belshazzar, Herod.

3. *There are those who are wickedly neutral, and who temporize in religion.*

Not professedly on the side of Satan. They admire, consent, are considerate, yet they are not decided, not changed, &c., see Matt. xii. 30. "He that is not with me is against me," &c. Now as to the doom of the enemies of God, they will all perish, except they repent; all have one condemnation, sentence, woeful abode. It will include,

(1.) *Utter shame and confusion.*

Now they boast and exalt themselves. Now they scoff, &c. Then they will be abased, and howl, and weep. "Many shall awake," &c. "Speechless," &c. "So will all," &c.

(2.) *Total wretchedness and misery.*

Now occasionally miserable, but have many subterfuges. Many awful statements. "Thou shalt break them," &c., Ps. xi. 6. "Upon the wicked he shall rain snares, fire, and brimstone, and a horrible tempest; this shall be the portion of their cup." He shall say, "Take these mine enemies," &c.

(3.) *Eternal ruin and despair.*

They shall perish irreparably. Beyond the reach of mercy, all felicity and hope expire, all misery concentrated. "So will all thine," &c. Let us now turn to the bright and glorious side of the text, and notice,

II. *The illustrious representation given of the friends of Jesus.*

"Them that love him." In the enemy we look for hate; in the friend, love. Now love to Jesus is,

1. *A divine principle.*

It is of God, and from God. The result of regeneration. "Love of God shed abroad in our hearts."

2. *It is a pre-eminent principle.*

Not inconsistent with other love, &c. But above all, it has the centre, it reigns, it subordinates, &c. "Lovest thou me more than these?"

3. *It is manifest.*

Not hidden. It lives, and breathes, and speaks, and acts. It moves all the springs of the heart. Affects all the machinery of the life. It loosens the tongue, employs the hands and feet. Now this is the character. Mark the representation—"Let them that love him be as the sun," &c. Now the metaphor will apply,

(1.) *To the exalted station which they occupy.*

Sin debases, sinks, &c. Religion exalts, raises the slave to be a prince, &c. "He shall dwell on high."

(2.) *To the spiritual rays they diffuse abroad.*

"Ye were once darkness," &c. Now lights, &c. "Arise, shine," &c. "Ye are the lights of the world," &c.

(3.) *As fertilizing and beautifying all around.*

When summer rays are gone, nature languishes, sterility reigns, &c. But as these rays return, every thing is softened and mellowed, the wilderness is gladdened. His rays, as the source of beauty, impart to every plant and flower its various hues and shades. Now believers shed moral beauty all around. Holy virtues, heavenly graces, Christ-like feelings, all tend to expel the winter of moral evil and misery, like the sun.

(4.) *Irresistibly advancing in their glorious career.*

Numerous foes and difficulties; but these cannot impede their course. Hell may be moved from beneath, tempests roar, &c. "Yet if God," &c. "In all these things," &c. "The path of the just shines brighter and brighter, until the perfect day." All efforts fruitless to subvert the cause of God. Those who have loved him have been as the sun, &c.

(5.) *Like the sun setting in celestial radiance, and moral splendor.*

However bright the career, it must cease on earth. See the young convert, as the rising orb. See the matured Christian shining in his meridian glory. See the aged Christian declining, &c.; at last it sets—but watch the scene. No stormy sky, no threatening tempest, no cloud; all still, and tranquil, and clear; the whole horizon mellowed with the golden glory. No wonder that Balaam exclaimed, "Let me die the death of the righteous," &c. "Mark the perfect man, and behold the upright; the end of that man is peace."

(6.) *As the sun rising in another hemisphere, and shining in fairer worlds.*

Is that setting sun annihilated? Is he no more? He rises in another land, as he sets in this. He exists and shines, &c. So with those who once shone here, &c. They are lost to us, but they still live, and are more radiant, shine brighter, &c. They now indeed shine forth in the kingdom of their Father, as the brightness of the sun, &c.

APPLICATION

1. Let the subject be the test of character. Are we enemies, &c.

2. Learn the supreme excellence of true religion. Godliness leads to honor, usefulness, blessedness, and glory.

3. Let the enemies of God consider. Now pause, reflect, weigh the matter. Read the history of the enemies of God. Think of your adversary. What will you do? Now trembling, draw near, Christ is the way to God's favor. He is ready to pardon. "Let the wicked man turn from his wickedness." "Kiss the Son, lest he be angry," &c.

4. Let the professed friends of Jesus exemplify their principles. You are to diffuse knowledge, to communicate the warm beams of benevolence and mercy.

146

PERPETUITY OF CHRIST'S NAME AND PRAISE

"I will make thy name to be remembered in all generations : therefore shall the people praise thee forever and ever."—*Ps.* xlv. 17.

WHATEVER original reference there may be in this psalm to David's son and successor, it is clear to the spiritually-minded reader that a greater than Solomon is here. The psalm contains a chain of clear and beautiful predictions of the Messiah and his kingdom. The text is the climax of the passage, and contains the declaration of Jehovah, that the name of the Redeemer shall be handed down to the latest posterity. "I will make," &c. Observe,

I. *The nature of the prediction.*
II. *The certainty of its realization.* And,
III. *The means of its accomplishment.*

I. *The nature of the prediction.*

The prediction consists of two parts—the perpetuation of the Saviour's name, and the celebration of his praise. Observe, then,

1. *The perpetuation of the Redeemer's name.* "I will make thy name," &c. The name.

(1.) It is said of Christ that he had on his head many crowns, so he is distinguished by many titles. Like the stars of the firmament they bestud the oracles of truth : Jacob spake of him as the Shiloh ; Job as the Redeemer ; Isaiah as the child born, Immanuel. But the especial and pre-eminent name of the Redeemer is *Jesus*—"They shall call his name *Jesus*," &c. In connection with this "Christ" the anointed. The anointed Jesus. Now as the anointed Saviour he stands pre-eminent. His name belongs especially to his person and work. A name above every name ; sweeter and more precious than any other. A name which God put upon him, and in which he delights. A name which angels adore and worship. A name full of consolation to a lost world. A name before which *devils* fear and tremble. A name to be identified with all the interesting events of time, and to be remembered in all generations.

(2.) The remembrance of this name. It is not to be blotted out. It is not to be lost in the vast assemblage of great and distinguished names. Not as a star in the milky way, but as the sun, the orb of day, he is to stand forth, above every other, moving in his own glorious orbit, in all things having the supremacy. But few names live through posterity. Few are the subjects of general remembrance, and among these some are remembered on account of wicked and monstrous crimes, as Nero. Some on account of warlike achievements, as Alexander and Hannibal, Napoleon, &c. Some on account of their discoveries in science or art. Some on account of their literary productions, or their philosophy, &c. Some on account of their virtues. And some few on account of their goodness and philanthropy. Christ will be remembered on account of his personal purity—his holy doctrines—his astonishing miracles—his unbounded love—his unexampled sufferings—his mysterious passion—his marvellous death—his glorious

triumphs over men and devils, over earth and hell. He will be remembered as the Great Teacher—the priest of the universe—the founder of Christianity—and the Redeemer of the world. Observe,

(3.) This remembrance of the Redeemer's name is to be to the latest posterity, "through all generations." See a parallel passage, Ps. lxxii. 17. The last generation of human probationers shall remember it. It shall not perish with the conflagration of the earth, for it shall be the glory of the new heavens and of the new earth, wherein dwelleth righteousness. And it shall be the burden of the song of all the hosts of glory, through the rolling ages of eternity. But we are anticipating the prediction, for it also refers,

2. *To the celebration of his praise.*

"The people shall praise thee," &c. Now the idea is clearly this, that all the people shall praise him. That "all nations shall call him blessed." They shall praise him from the rising to the setting of the sun. Now although Christ has been remembered in all ages, yet the people, the majority, have not known his name. Myriads have never heard it. Myriads of Mohammedans degrade it. Myriads of Jews hate and blaspheme it. Myriads of skeptics revile it, and myriads care nothing about it. But then all people, of all climes, and colors, and tongues, shall know it, and love it, and adoring, present their incense of praise unto it. What a delightful period, when Christ's name shall be sung in every nation, on every hill, in every vale, on the mountain-top, and on the sea-shore, and when those who go in ships shall bear it across the waves of the ocean, when earth, and sea, and skies will resound with Immanuel's praise. Such, brethren, is the prediction. Let us consider,

II. *The certainty of its realization.*

It is not a doubtful matter. It is written in the volume of inviolable and eternal truth, of which not one jot or tittle can possibly fail. This certainty rests not only on its being a portion of the word of truth, but we may conclude as to its realization,

1. *From the claims of Christ.*

In the covenant made with the Saviour, it was stipulated that he should be rewarded for his toils, and be amply recompensed for all his sufferings and shame. This is beautifully and fully expressed by the prophet Isaiah, see liii. 10. Christ's prayer referred to the same subject, John xvii. 45 The apostle, too, refers to it, Phil. ii. 6, &c.

Now, shall the claims of Christ be disregarded? Assuredly not. He has entered upon his reward. He is receiving the joy. He is extending his kingdom, and assuredly "He shall reign until," &c. "His name shall," &c.

2. *From the ability of the Father.*

It is the engagement of the Father. Jehovah says, "I will," and upon what principle shall it fail? He is not fallible. He does not change. He will not break his word. He will not disregard his son's hard-earned claims. His power is sufficient. His resources exhaustless. His means ample. He hath said, and it must come to pass. Heaven and earth may pass away, but not one word of his can ever fail.

3. *The history of the past, and the survey of the present, clearly indicate the certainty of its realization.*

Before Messiah's advent his name and work were the subject of grateful contemplation through all generations. As the seed of the woman he was received by our first parents. As the Shiloh, &c., by the patriarchs. Abraham desired to see his day, &c.; the prophets all testified of Christ, of the sufferings he should endure, and the glory which should follow. The Baptist acted as his herald. Good old Simeon clasped him to his bosom. And the apostles and disciples preached him through the then known kingdoms of the world, &c. Even one apostle, Paul, preached him from Jerusalem to Illyricum. And from that period to the present, his name has been remembered. Then remember that earth and hell have conspired to blot out his name. The kings and rulers have covenanted against him. Learning and philosophy, power and wealth, influence and arms, have all been employed, but all in vain. His name has been perpetuated, and is still celebrated in the praises of countless thousands. And who, that surveys the present influence and extent of Christianity, can doubt its being continued to the latest posterity? Who can doubt its final triumphs and universal diffusion? It has lived in all ages, and in all countries, and now the sun never sets upon the disciples of the Lamb. But let us glance,

III. *At the means of its accomplishment.*

The dispensation is a dispensation of means. Christ's name is to be perpetuated by means.

1. *There must be the diffusion of the scriptures.*

As long as the Bible lasts, Christ's name will endure. Wherever that book is received, Christ's name will be prized and praised.

2. *The gospel must be proclaimed.*

It is the gospel of Christ. To preach the gospel is to exalt Christ. It is the express work of the ministers of the gospel.

"'Tis all their business here below,
   To cry, Behold the Lamb!"

3. *The ordinances of religion must be maintained.*

Where Christian worship is celebrated, and the ordinances administered, Christ's name must be remembered. Look at a Christian congregation. The place is palpably a Christian erection. The people are professed Christians. The word read is Christ's word. The gospel is the gospel of Christ. The prayer is based upon his merit, and presented in his name. The praise is to Christ. He is the subject of our songs. The church is Christ's. Baptism is being baptized into his death. The sacrament is the Lord's supper. The life of the Christian is to magnify Christ; and the death of the Christian glorifies the Lord. Now these are the means, and shall I ask, by way of

APPLICATION

1. *Are not we responsible for their employment?*

Oh yes, it devolves on me, on you, on every Christian in the world.

2. *Should we not feel intensely interested in them?*

Shall we not identify ourselves? And,

3. *Let our profession be embodied.*

Let the love of Christ constrain us.

4. *Oh, that Christ might be precious to some waiting soul for the first time.*

What think ye of Christ? Oh, receive him. Let his name be engraven on your hearts.

5. *Christ's name shall be remembered.*

It must be. Nothing can prevent it. Think what it would require to erase it. Every Bible annihilated—every meeting-house thrown down—every Christian martyred—and all the angels must be silenced. Nay, more—the sceptre must be wrested from Jehovah's grasp, and his exalted throne levelled with the dust. Oh, rejoice, rejoice! "Christ's name shall be remembered in all generations, and the people shall praise him forever and ever!"

"Let every kindred, every tribe,
On this terrestrial ball,
To him all majesty ascribe,
And crown him Lord of all."

147

THE SIX MORNINGS

"The morning cometh."—*Isa.* xxi. 12.

THE various portions of the day are often employed in the way of figure by the sacred writers. Day is the emblem of joy and gladness; night, of sorrow and trouble. Thus, too, evening is the sign of approaching distress or affliction, and morning is the token of happiness and prosperity. There are two or three things necessarily connected with morning. Night must precede, and day must follow. A few hours have passed away since darkness overcast the whole of our horizon; and now, since morning has shed its cheering beams, we are enjoying the gladsome light of day. How right and proper that every morning should bear witness to our gratitude to God for the mercies of the night, and our supplications for the needful blessings of the succeeding day. Every pious heart knows experimentally the meaning of these words, "My voice shalt thou hear in the morning." Our subject is the morning, and we design to lead your contemplations,

I. *To the morning of our world's existence.*

Ere that morning arose the earth was without form, and void; one dark, chaotic mass presented itself before the mind of the Eternal. Silent darkness reigned undisturbed. The Son of God had long anticipated the formation of our world. He had fixed his delights upon it before the mountains were settled, before the hills were brought forth, yea, long before the depths of the sea were formed, or its boundaries decreed. He was rejoicing in the habitable parts of the earth, and his delights were with the sons of men. At length the day of our world's existence dawned. The great Fountain of light, by his only-begotten Son, formed the worlds. The slumbers of night were broken by the voice of God. His spirit brooded o'er the mighty void; and he said, "Let there be light, and there was light." That was the first morning our world ever beheld—a morning which exhibited the almighty power of Jehovah, and gave a transcendently glorious manifestation of his

benevolence and love. Now "the morning stars sang together," &c. The day which followed was one of purity and bliss. Every thing displayed the wisdom and goodness of the great Artificer; and God smiled with infinite complacency when he took a survey of the whole, and pronounced it very good. Eden was the sphere of man's labors, dominion, and enjoyment. But mark, the heavens darken, nature is convulsed, tempestuous clouds of an awfully threatening character streak the horizon. Sin has entered our world; pollution has defiled the noblest workmanship of God; hell has triumphed over wretched, apostate man; night, darkness, and death, in all their sable blackness, now surround our world. Mercy intervenes, compassion triumphs, and a ray of light indicates the coming of another day. Stars now irradiate the heavens; types, sacrifices, and promises lead Old Testament believers to expect the dawning of the day of mercy and salvation. Notice, then,

II. *The morning of our world's redemption.*

Before the breaking of the day the darkness is more dense and palpable. So before this day prophecy had ceased, and the oracles of heaven had been silent for ages. But at length the glad jubal morning arrived, the typical stars disappear, sacrificial mists pass away, and the Son of God appears in our world, and is manifest in our flesh. Angels introduced this morning with songs, as they did the morning of the world's existence—the anthem falls on the ears of the astonished shepherds, "Glory to God in the highest, peace on earth, and good-will to men." This morning was followed by the day of Christ's tabernacling among us. A day "when life and immortality were brought to light," &c. A day of mercy to the wretched and sinful of our race. Jesus went forth as the Sun of Righteousness, with healing beneath his wings. He stood as the sun in his lofty orbit, and exclaimed, "I am the light of the world." But this day ended in the night of Christ's sufferings and death. By the persecution of the Son of God, his rejection by his own people, by conspiracy, by cruel arrest, by Gethsemane's woes, and the ignominious death of the cross. That Sun, which rose in such beautiful and heavenly radiance in Bethlehem, now set in blood, on the summit of Calvary. There was the burial, and the silent darkness of the sepulchre. But this was a short night—it soon passed away; for behold, "the morning cometh."

III. *The morning of Christ's glorious resurrection.* .

With this morning revived the hopes of the disciples of Christ. The salvation of the world seemed to be the sepulchred with him. With this morning the hopes of the deathless myriads of our race were placed on a glorious and sure foundation. His resurrection declared him to be the Son of God, with power; it became the key-stone to the whole edifice of his church, and one of the leading doctrines of his blessed gospel.

> " Welcome, sweet day of rest,
>   That saw the Lord arise,
>   Welcome to this reviving breast,
>   And these rejoicing eyes."

Yes, every Lord's day should remind us of this morning. The resurrection of Christ was the morning of the Christian's day of holy rest, and spiritual communion. At the close of the week it ought to gladden us that the morning cometh; and it ought to be introduced with the joyful lines of the poet—

> " Another six days' work is done,
>   Another Sabbath is begun," &c.

And this introduced the gospel day—the day of Christ's spiritual reign on earth. In his day the kingdom of heaven was at hand; but he must suffer and rise again before its foundation could be laid. His spiritual empire was introduced on the day of pentecost, when the Spirit was poured out from on high. This was the beginning of the reign of the Holy Spirit of God, that to which Christ referred when he said, "If I go away, the Comforter will come," and to this he directed the attention of his disciples, just before he left them, Acts i. 4, &c. See its realization, Acts ii. 1, &c. Now began the progress of light and truth, the diffusion of the gospel, and the commencement of the New Testament dispensation among men. Observe,

IV. *The morning of the soul's conversion to God.*

It is darkness and night with all unbelievers. But when the gospel comes, light comes; and if received, the soul is illumined, and the beams of a holy morning dawn upon the soul—the life of the Christian is the day—a season of light, and joy, and holiness. His path begins with the morning, and "shines more and more unto the perfect day." Happy that soul on whom the Sun

of Righteousness has arisen! But this must be followed by the night of death. There is yet another day before the church of God.

V. *The morning of Christ's millennial kingdom and glory.*

Then will Christ shine forth in all his meridian brightness; his appearance will usher in his heavenly administration. Then will be the days of heaven upon earth. Then will God's tabernacle be with men, &c. Then Zion will arise and shine, her light having come, &c. The light of the moon will then be as the light of the sun, &c. "The Gentiles shall come to their light, and kings to the brightness of their rising." Behold the enrapturing vision, as beheld through the medium of prophecy, Isa. lx. 18 to end.

VI. *The morning of a glorious eternity.*

The saints shall now have dominion and glory—dwell in regions of celestial light. Jesus the Sun of the eternal world. No night to succeed this. One day of effulgent brightness and everlasting blessedness, Rev. xxi. 22. Now observe,

1. *Christ is essentially connected with each of these mornings.*

Creation, redemption, resurrection, spiritual reign, conversion, millennium.

2. *Each morning is identified with the happiness of man.* Look at his primeval dignity—redemption; raised in his resurrection; means for his transformation in the gift of the Spirit. Personally saved in the morning of conversion. That salvation consummated in the day of Christ's personal reign and glory.

3. *How many are the children of the morning of the day?*

If believers, "ye are not of the night, and of darkness." "Light is sown for the righteous, and joy for the upright."

4. *To the unbelieving, we observe, the night also is coming.*

Of death, and eternal misery.

148

THE GOSPEL STANDARD

" Lift up a standard for the people."—*Isa.* lxii. 10.

THE text forms a part of a prediction supposed to refer primarily to the deliverance of the Jews from Babylon, but a part of the prophecy clearly points to the Messiah, to the proclamation of his gospel, and the diffusion of his glory. It is in this evangelical sense that we consider that portion we have selected for our present meditation. Let us then consider,

I. *The state of the people.*

II. *The standard which must be elevated.*

III. *The duty of the Church, to lift the standard up.*

1. *The state of the people.*

By the people we must include the great mass of human beings. All nations, climes, colors, kindred, and tongues; Jews and Gentiles, barbarian and Scythian, bond and free. But more especially let us consider the state of the people without God, and ignorant of the gospel of his Son. In this light, there are four views in which the people may be contemplated.

1. *As wandering in the regions of ignorance and superstition.*

The pagan world is the valley and shadow of death. "Darkness hath covered," &c. The people dwell in darkness. Dark as to their nature and state; as to the supreme God; as to the blessed Messiah, and the way of life; as to heaven, eternity, and hell. Superstitious as they are ignorant. Gloomy shadows overspread their path. Horrific fears haunt their spirits.

2. *As the victims of Satanic vassalage.*

They are the captives of Satan. Enfettered with chains of guilt. Degraded and enslaved, he drags them at his infernal chariot wheels. Their vassalage is that of the soul. It is mental as well as bodily. It is a vassalage in which all is sunken and debased.

3. *As in a state of utter defilement.*

We say nothing of the common evidences of depravity. Their vice is that which has become more deep through the habits and customs of ages upon ages. Vice where the whole person is leprous—which enters into all their movements—which pollutes their literature—which infects their recreations—which spoils their domestic comforts—which is the glory of their religion, and perpetuated in the presence and under the patronage of their gods. Pollution stalking abroad—improved by the artist—composed in their poetry—sung in their songs—and identified with their being.

4. *As strangers to solid happiness.*

How can they be happy? Nature deranged and diseased throughout—without God—without hope—without peace. Their horrid rites tell you they are not happy, &c. And with all their guilt and depravity, are they meet for happiness in the world to come? Observe,

II. *The standard which must be elevated.*

Now this standard is that of the gospel. A standard bearing on it the form of the cross, on which is written in characters of blood, "Behold the Lamb of God," &c. See ver. 11. Now in the elevation of this standard we have a full and perfect remedy for the perishing condition of the people. The gospel standard,

1. *Communicates light.*

It reveals the knowledge, for the lack of which the people perish; it publishes the great salvation which they need—brings life and immortality to light—it is the harbinger of day to the people: and when it comes, "the people which sat in darkness," &c. The gospel standard is connected,

2. *With the publication of freedom.*

It gives "liberty to the captives, and the opening of the prison," &c.; it attacks and beats down the bulwarks of Satan's empire; it pulls to the dust his strongholds; it combats and overthrows the despotical powers of darkness, and opens a way of escape for the redeemed prisoners of hope. The people know the gospel truth, and it makes them free.

3. *It presents a remedy for human pollution.*

"It is a fountain open for sin," &c.; the grand catholicon remedy for all the moral maladies of the soul; nothing too complicated, too inveterate, &c. It can bring down to the humility of the child, the proud metaphysician, self-deified Brahmin. It even tames the savage—it turns the raven, &c.

4. *It imparts abiding peace to the miserable and perishing.*

Gives the favor of God to men—implants his kindness in the soul—gives the spirit the chief good, attracts it to the centre of bliss, and causes it to revolve in the light of purity and blessedness forever and ever. "Standard of salvation," the power of God to the eternal life of all who behold it.

III. *The duty of the Church to lift the standard up.*

We shall now speak to the members of the Church of Christ, and of the Church in her collective character.

1. *The standard is in our possession.* It

is intrusted to us—we must therefore be responsible; we have it not for monopoly, but diffusion; the people need it, and will die without it—and we have it. Christ expects us to lift it up to the people in the regions far off. The very spirit of

2. *Our religion involves this great principle.*

Our religion is love—it is having Christ's spirit—zealous for Christ's glory—to be Christ's conscientious property. Then that religion will inspire the missionary spirit, and consecrate us to the missionary cause.

3. *The grand commission requires it.*

Two views. At any rate, the gospel must be proposed to all. " If I be lifted up," &c. If we do not, God will give it others who will, &c.

APPLICATION

1. Have you all been savingly interested in the standard of the gospel? You must look, and feel, and live. Be drawn and united.

2. The standard-bearers must be supported. By prayer, and help.

3. More laborers must be sent forth. "The harvest is great," &c.

149

LIGHT AND DARKNESS, OR THE CHURCH AND THE WORLD

" And there was a thick darkness in all the land of Egypt three days: they saw not one another, neither rose any from his place for three days; but all the children of Israel had light in their dwellings."—*Exod.* x. 22, 23.

Nothing affects so much as contrast, and much of divine truth is presented to us in this form. In this way we are deeply struck with the condition of our first parents, before and after the fall, in the enjoyment and loss of paradise. Thus, too, the different characters of the righteous and wicked are more striking. See Cain and Abel: a murderer and a martyr: a child of Beelzebub and an heir of glory. Look, too, at Jacob and Esau. One ardently engaged in the pleasures of the chase, the other earnestly seeking " the favor and blessing of God." Sometimes this contrast is seen on a larger scale. Look at the families of Noah and his sons, and the whole world. See the one floating safely on the billows of that flood which involved the other in utter ruin. Our text leads us to consider one of these striking contrasts. The ninth plague is now afflicting the land of Egypt. Thick darkness is covering the whole land, ver. 23. Universal horror is filling the minds of the Egyptians. But at this very time all the children of Israel had light in their dwellings. In this God made a miraculous and striking difference, and in this we have presented before us the contrast between the world and the Church; between the families of the wicked and the families of the pious; between the carnal and the renewed heart. Let us confine ourselves to this contrast, as existing between the world and the Church. We notice, then,

I. *Egypt, in its darkness, was a type of the world.* It was so also in other particulars. In its tyrannical dominion by the despotical Pharaoh; in its diversified idolatry; but particularly in the darkness which enshrouded it. But a question arises, *What do we mean by the world?* We mean all the intelligent responsible beings who are living without the fear of God, and strangers to his saving grace. They may greatly differ from each other. But those who constitute what in scripture is signified by the world, resemble each other in this: they are under the dominion of Satan, and not the servants of the Lord Jesus Christ. Now each such individual is a child of the world, and the whole, in their collective capacity, are in darkness.

1. *Darkness is an emblem of ignorance and error, and the world is involved in these.* In worldly matters there may be intelligence. Wise, as it regards literature and science; but with respect to God, their souls, salvation, and religion, they are in darkness—their understandings are blinded and their judgments perverted. " This darkness hath covered the earth, and gross darkness," &c.

2. *Darkness is an emblem of guilt, and the world is involved in this.* Sin is the work of darkness. Hence the apostle says, " Have no fellowship," &c. Now, the whole world is guilty before God. Every man is a transgressor. " There is not one righteous—no, not one."

3. *Darkness is an emblem of peril, and in this the world is involved.* As the world is guilty, so it is condemned. God's judgment of it is recorded. God's displeasure is announced. God's wrath is threatened. It is to be the scene of the divine vengeance. It is to be renovated by fire, 2 Peter iii. 10.

4. *Darkness is the emblem of misery, and in this the world is involved.* Now, the misery of the men of the world arises from *three things :*

(1.) From the accusations of guilt, the cause of their condemnation. As a fever it burns up their spirits, and this feeling they cannot extinguish.

(2.) From the unsatisfying nature of their portion. They want happiness, but cannot find it. They go to the briny flood which only adds to their thirst ; or they sink into wretchedness as the prodigal, and have not even husks to eat.

(3.) From gloomy fears as to the future. Bad as the portion of the world is, it is their best—their good things. But it cannot be retained. Age advances,— infirmities encompass,—death stalks forth,— the grave opens,—and then there is the unknown world, the judgment, eternity. And they have no *light*—no *hope*. Surely, then, this is enough to account for the misery of the wicked. Let us then turn our attention to the Church of God.

II. *The Israelites with light in their dwellings were a type of the Church.*

Who constitute the Church ? The spiritual seed of Abraham. Those who have left the world, and become the spiritual followers of Jesus. They are in the world as Israel in Egypt, but they are distinct and separate from it. They are not of it, even as their Lord was not of it, and like the Israelites of old they have light in their dwellings.

1. *They have the light of saving knowledge.*

They may be far inferior to the world in rank, station, wealth, and learning ; but they possess the true knowledge of God and of his Son Jesus Christ. They know Christ as the true Messiah. They know him experimentally,—they know him in his power to save. Once they were in darkness, but now are they light, &c. They have been translated, &c.

2. *They have the light of the divine approbation.*

They know they are of God. They know their love to God. Also his love to them. The word of God assures them that they are beloved of God ; the Holy Spirit bears witness, and hence their conscience testifies by its pacific voice, that "being justified by faith they have peace," &c.

3. *They have the light of holiness.*

Sin is darkness ; holiness, light. They wear the robe of light. They are obedient to the statutes of light. They walk in the paths of light, and it shineth more and more, &c. Ye are the children of the light and of the day.

4. *They have the light of a joyful hope.*

Christ in them the hope of glory. See 1 Peter i. 4 ; Titus ii. 13. Now this hope cheers and sustains the believer, and fills him with joy unspeakable.

5. *They have the light of the divine presence.*

The Lord is ever with his people. He is their sun, making their day. He guides by his glorious presence through the whole pilgrimage of life. He was thus the light of Abraham, of Jacob, and Israel in the desert. Thus by his Spirit he leads his people into all truth, and conducts them to eternal glory.

In applying this subject we behold the contrast between those who are of the world and the people of God, in several conditions of life.

(1.) See them in adversity. The wicked have an addition of darkness. No solace,— no ray to cheer them ; hence how often they sink into despair and rush into eternity. The Christian feels, but he recognizes God's hand. He bows down, bears the rod, and kisses the chastising hand, and God's blissful countenance enables him to rejoice in tribulation.

(2.) See them in sickness. No light. Painful, restless, and an overwhelming anxiety. The sick chamber is as dark as Egypt. But the righteous have light in their dwellings. The serene countenance, the pious resignation, the cheering hope, show the difference. It is all right, says the pious soul ; to live is Christ. God is my portion.

(3.) See them in death. With the wicked it is a leap in the dark—a plunge into the horrid black abyss. Oh, how terrific !— how appalling ! But the righteous have light in death—often the celestial beams of glory.

APPLICATION

1. Believers, shine in your dwellings, &c.

2. Sinners, come to the light, &c.

150
THE CHRISTIAN MINISTRY *

" And every one had four faces ; the first face was the face of a cherub, and the second face was the face of a man, and the third the face of a lion, and the fourth the face of an eagle."— *Ezek.* x. 14.

In this chapter the providence and government of God are set forth in mysterious and sublime hieroglyphics, a mode of writing particularly common to Ezekiel, and which is presented in awful grandeur in the book of the Apocalypse. The text seems to have a decided reference to the angelic hosts,—those ministers of God who do his pleasure. They are brought before us as the active instruments of the divine government, and the executors of his wondrous purposes. To resemble these should be the great desire of every Christian, that God's will may be done on earth even as it is done in heaven. But especially should this be the case with the Christian minister : his office greatly resembles that of the holy intelligences above ; he is a messenger of God to mankind, an angel of the Church, and therefore well does it become him to study the character, and emulate the holiness of cherubim and seraphim in heaven.

To show you, dear brother, the particular points of resemblance, and urge their importance, will be the design of this address. The different likenesses of these holy beings are designed to exhibit their various attributes and characteristics. Observe the first face,

I. *Was that of a cherub.*

We shall consider this as the symbol,

1. *Of exalted dignity.*

Dwelling around the throne of Deity. In his immediate presence. His especial ambassadors, &c. No office can be more exalted than that of the Christian ministry. It is that to which Jehovah appointed his own Son. One writer quaintly remarks, " God had only one Son, and he made a preacher of him." " Workers together with God," &c.

2. *Of elevated devotion.*

They are represented as holding great intimacy and close fellowship with God. They are ever praising him, serving him day and night, &c. Crying one to another, " Holy, holy," &c. How indispensable that the ministers of Christ live near to the Lord, hold close communion with the skies. Thus, to be

* For ordination series.

like Abraham, and Moses, and Samuel, imbued with the spirit of devotion.

3. *Of distinguished holiness.*

Ye that bear the vessels of the Lord, &c., as the priests of old. " Holiness unto the Lord" must be on the breastplate of the Christian minister. Not only partakers of the ordinary graces of the Spirit, but adorned with the mature fruits of holiness to the glory of God. How the apostle urged upon Timothy, " Keep thyself pure," &c. Observe,

II. *The second symbol is that of a man.*

With the sanctity of the cherub is to be united the sympathy of sanctified humanity. Jesus, that he might be a faithful and sympathetic high-priest, was made in all points like unto us. As men, Christian ministers

1. *Are to be influenced by their relationship to Jesus as head of the Church.*

They should have his meekness, humility, lowliness, desire to labor, &c. Readiness to suffer, &c. As men, they are

2. *To feel for their fellow-sinners peculiar compassion.*

They are their brethren, of one blood, spirit, and destiny. Hearts are to feel, bowels to yearn, &c. Such long for their salvation. As men,

3. *They are to know their own insufficiency and entire dependence on God's blessing.*

This treasure in earthen vessels, &c. We preach not ourselves, &c. Who is sufficient for these things, &c. Paul planteth, &c.

III. *The third emblem was the face of a lion.*

By this we are to understand the strength and magnanimity, which are necessary to the ministerial office. The Christian minister must be strong in the grace which is in Christ Jesus. He must be strong to resist evil, to stand firm in the conflict, and to conduct himself as a man of God. Whoso quails, he must not fear. Whoso flies, he must be at his post. Whoso apostatizes, he must hold fast the faith. Whoso tires, he must run to the glorious goal. He must have fortitude to brave dangers, to withstand gainsayers, to fear not the face of men ; and, if necessary, to lay down his life in the cause of Jesus. There are especial seasons, trying circumstances, and dangerous periods, when the minister cannot vindicate his official character, or fulfil his duty, unless he have the heart and face of the lion.

IV. *The fourth symbol is that of the eagle.*

By this,

1. *The true character of the minister's work is portrayed.*

He has to do with spiritual things. His business is not "of the earth, earthy," but his message, his powers, his designs, are all heavenly. He teaches not philosophy, science, economy, legislation, but the truths of the kingdom of God, the knowledge of the way of salvation. "These men are the servants of the living God," &c.

2. The symbol of the eagle may be designed also to be expressive of their *ardor and zeal.* And these are of the utmost importance to the minister of Jesus. With these his soul must burn with unabating fervency. He is to be instant, earnest, energetic, zealously affected in every good thing.

3. *His soul is to yearn with intense anxiety over perishing sinners.*

He is to devote all his powers to the exalting of his Lord, and the saving of souls. Such, then, are the symbolical features which should distinguish the ministers of Jesus Christ; and these peculiar excellences should be united. With the exalted dignity, elevated devotion, and distinguished holiness of the cherub, must be allied the lowliness, the human affection, and conscious self-insufficiency of man; and these are to be found in connection with an heroic and magnanimous spirit, and a fervent quenchless zeal in the cause of Jesus.

APPLICATION

1. Let the solemn character of the office ever be cherished, and a lively sense of its importance be maintained from day to day.

2. Let the glorious results of faithfulness in the Saviour's service animate to constancy and perseverance.

The divine word will give abundant directions, and supply ample materials for the formation of the exalted ministerial character. The Holy Spirit will impart every necessary influence and gift; and Jesus, the head of the Church, will communicate a plenitude of grace from his unbounded fulness.

151
A MINISTERIAL CHARGE

"Take heed to the ministry which thou hast received in the Lord that thou fulfil it."—*Col.* iv. 17.

OUR text refers solely to the work of the ministry. It is the apostle Paul's counsel to Archippus, that he "take heed," &c. On this occasion we shall presume that you are not a stranger to vital experimental religion. We assume it as a matter which is obvious to the members of this Church and your Christian brethren, that you are in spirit, profession, and practice, a disciple of Jesus Christ. Personal religion is of essential importance to every one, but pre-eminently so to the preacher of the gospel; otherwise his life is one scene of deception upon the Church and the world, and his addresses the mere soulless harangues of a hireling. But the profession of religion is not enough. In the pastor it should be lively, striking, decided, and influential. In the vestments of purity he is to be clad, and "Holiness to the Lord" is to be written on his breastplate, so that the light of his purity is to be manifest to all. On these momentous topics, however, we shall not now dwell, but devote all our attention to the truths expressly presented to us in the text. Consider,

I. *What duty the Christian ministry involves.*

And,

II. *The spirit in which it should be fulfilled.*

The Christian ministry presents four spheres of labor.

1. *The study.*

It is desirable that the Christian minister have such a place; that it should be a place adapted to usefulness and comfort; that it should be well ventilated, quiet, and well furnished with a choice selection of useful books. The study must be the place,

(1.) *Of reading.*

"Give thyself to reading," &c. Philosophy, science, history, poetry, general literature, may engage our occasional time. But theology is the direct course of reading which should engage your especial attention. The writings of the puritans and non-conformists present a deep rich mine of precious truth, in which you cannot dig without possessing invaluable treasure. But the holy Scriptures must be the great book of ministerial consultation. Here you have the great doctrines and truths which are to supply you with all the materials for your work. With patriarchs, prophets, and evangelists you must be on the most intimate terms. With their writings you are to be minutely conversant. Nothing can make up for a deficiency here. You must be so deeply read in biblical knowledge, that it shall impart its peculiar and divine savoriness to all your pastoral and ministerial discourses. Read much, read with distinct arrangement, and with a special object to your ministerial work. Reading must be followed by

(2.) *Meditation.*

By meditation, the food reading supplies is digested, and so incorporated as to become a part of our mental self. Meditation is urged by the apostle in connection with reading. By meditation we view subjects in all their bearings and tendencies. By meditation we avoid loading the mind with mere phantoms and useless crudities. To meditate in the law of the Lord is the duty of the private Christian; how much more necessary, therefore, is it to the Christian teacher. A good memory may store up words by reading, but meditation is essential to the extraction of the essences and the thoughts of subjects. From reading and meditation we pass on to notice,

(3.) *Composition.*

The selection and preparation of your pulpit discourses. The exact manner of doing this must greatly depend on your own peculiar characteristics of mind. As to the amount of writing, that must be left greatly to your own judgment. But in most cases some writing is essentially necessary; in many cases it should be rather extended in degree. But a few words here shall suffice. Select subjects adapted to the persons and circumstances of your congregation, especially those bearing on the great truths of religion. Never aim merely at pleasing,— seek not high things, but consult perspicuity of style, and great plainness of expression. But in all cases have both your ideas and phraseology so arranged, that without fear you may stand up to explain with clearness and ability, the topics which you have chosen. Do not go empty-handed to the hungry sheep of your pastoral care; and go not with bare disjointed thoughts or meager sketches, but laden with the good things of the gospel, having a portion of meat for all in due season. Lead the people into the rich verdant pastures of the divine word, and let not leanness be upon them through your

negligent and incompetent provision. Prepare for them the finest of the wheat, and present them with the richest clusters of the refreshing grapes of Canaan. Let your study have a large proportion of your time, and cherish for it an affection which all the attractions of society cannot shake. The next sphere of ministerial usefulness is in,

2. *The pulpit.*

Here you are to stand with the message of God, and to proclaim it to the people. The great subject of your ministerings must be Jesus Christ. You are to teach and preach Jesus Christ. Christ, in his person, offices, obedience, sufferings, death, and resurrection, and glory. Christ as the sacrifice for human guilt. As the only Saviour possessing unbounded willingness, and illimitable power. Christ, in his full, free, and everlasting gospel, and that gospel in all its doctrines, ordinances, precepts, promises, privileges, and blessings. Enter the pulpit in the spirit of prayer, and seek God's Holy Spirit to aid you in your awfully responsible duties. In preaching the gospel to immortal souls,

(1.) *Be plain.*

Both as it regards a clear style, and the adoption of familiar, not vulgar, expressions. Never adopt words of rare use; seldom interlard Greek and Latin, and never French quotations. The people cannot be edified unless they understand you, but the great majority cannot understand, unless you use great plainness of speech.

(2.) *Be earnest.*

Your message is one which demands this. You will effect little without it. A lethargic, formal preacher is a disgrace to the office, and brings insult to the gospel. If your heart glows with the love of Christ, you will preach with celestial fervor and burning zeal.

(3.) *Be faithful.*

Use not enticing words of human wisdom. Be not a trimmer, at your soul's peril. Declare the whole counsel of God. Keep no part of the truth back. Teach every man, warn every man, and let fidelity distinguish all your addresses as one who must give an account. Be faithful to your own conscience, to souls, to the Church, and to God, whose responsible servant you are. With fidelity,

(4.) *Be affectionate.*

Let love imbue your spirit, and it will breathe in your discourses. Have bowels of mercy. Cherish the tenderest sympathies. Often weep over perishing souls. Travail in anxious pangs of solicitude, till Christ is formed in your hearers.

(5.) *Be evangelical.*

Exalt Christ as the centre and glory of your system. Let him be alpha and omega. Ever seek his glory, and cause all truths to revolve around him, and be irradiated with the beams of his divine splendor. Remember—

> "'Tis all your business here below,
> To cry, Behold the Lamb!"

Threatenings and duties, ordinances and precepts, law and gospel, facts and prophecies, may all be preached evangelically. Leave the pulpit in the spirit of devotion, seeking the sanctifying blessing of God upon your labors. Your third sphere of labor is,

3. *The Church.*

Over this you have to preside, and in Christ's name and with the voice of the brethren to enforce the statutes of his kingdom. In the Church,

(1.) *Maintain discipline.*

In receiving members, in treating cases of offence, and in excluding from Church fellowship. Do not swerve from the precepts and precedents of the New Testament. Heed not mere usages, mere customs ; conform to the infallible directions of the word of God.

(2.) *Administer the ordinances.*

Faithfully, with rigid, scriptural exactness ; with due solemnity and with much prayer.

(3.) *Visit your flock.*

As often as you prudently can. With impartiality. Without ostentatious or priestly assumption. With a view to their edification. In the spirit of kindness and love. The last sphere of labor is,

4. *The world.*

You may claim, as Wesley did, the world for your parish. Wherever there is an opening for usefulness, and you have the means, labor to do good. Labor to enlarge the bonds of the Church. Seek for the extension of the gospel in your locality. Around you souls are perishing. Give your countenance and influence to the humane and benevolent institutions of the day. Plead for the poor ; befriend the destitute ; visit the wretched ; open your mouth for the dumb. Enter earnestly on the work of the religious instruction of the young. Diffuse the Scriptures. Speak for the benighted heathen. Oh! cherish an enlarged, glowing, restless spirit of liberality and exertion. In one word, be ready for every good work. Notice,

II. *The spirit in which your ministry should be fulfilled.*

With,

1. *Great circumspection.*

"Take heed." Be not rash or precipitate, but prudent. Wise as a serpent. Seek heavenly wisdom. Be vigilant, watchful. Deeply ponder your work ; intimately examine your spirit ; prove yourself.

2. *Constantly cherish a sense of your responsibility.*

Your ministry has been received from the Lord. He has put you into the office. You work for God. The steward's account will be demanded. The results are of tremendous magnitude. This will lead to lowliness, to constant prayer and continual dependence on divine grace. The text has respect,

3. *To a spirit of perseverance.*

"Fulfil it." Be not only instant in season and out of season, but endure hardness. Hold on and out to the end. The course is to extend with your life, and both must end together. Be faithful unto death. Go not, nay look not back. "Be steadfast," &c. In

CONCLUSION

1. You will have much to try you. Much to oppose you. Enemies without and fears within. It may be reviling scoffers and false brethren.

2. But you have every thing to encourage you. God is your helper. Christ is the unfailing source of your sufficiency. The Spirit in all his plenitude is promised. Angels are interested in your work. The holy and benevolent are around you to lift up your hands, and to pray down blessings upon you. And there is a glittering crown sparkling with celestial brightness before you ; then "take heed to the ministry which thou hast received in the Lord, that thou fulfil it."

SCRIPTURE TEXT INDEX

GENESIS:
    1:27 113
    4:1 116
    4:9 13
    32:24,25 121
    47:8,9 122
    49:4 36
EXODUS:
    3:2 127
    10:14 214
    10:22,23 212
    13:21 128
    20:7 23
    23:2 22
NUMBERS:
    23:10 202
DEUTERONOMY:
    5:29 77
    6:6-9 90
    11:21 66
JOSHUA:
    24:15 16
    24:15 20
JUDGES:
    5:31 205
    13:22,23 130
RUTH:
    2:11,12 131
1 SAMUEL:
    22:2 137
    30:6 135

2 SAMUEL:
    6:20 140
    9:3 138
    23:5 50
1 KINGS:
    8:27 143
    19:4 132
2 KINGS:
    6:15-17 134
    18:6,7 146
    20:1-6 147
    20:1-6 149
1 CHRONICLES:
    28:9 141
    29:15 85
2 CHRONICLES:
    32:25 150
    34:3 19
NEHEMIAH:
    9:6 94
JOB:
    23:34 57
    34:33 93
PSALMS:
    1:1-3 39
    10:4 78
    17:4 48
    34:13 33
    35:27 42
    37:1-6 96
    45:7 206

56:12,13 145
74:22 109
85:6 110
138:8 56

PROVERBS:
11:24,25 24
19:2 88

ISAIAH:
1:18 79
12:1 106
21:12 209
28:17 76
43:21 62
45:9 75
58:13,14 15
62:1 63
62:10 210

JEREMIAH:
4:14 29
8:20 11
23:28 151

EZEKIEL:
10:14 214
21:27 203
33:11 112
37:1-10 155

AMOS:
6:1 33

JONAH:
3:9 104

HABAKKUK:
2:20 68

MALACHI:
3:8 34

MATTHEW:
8:2-4 176
8:5-10 179
9:9 170
11:11 159
11:11 161
11:12 54
12:20 102
15:21-28 171
16:24 81
18:15-18 101
22:11-13 164
25:1 186
25:1 187

MARK:
5:25,&c. 135
5:36 177
12:6 72

LUKE:
1:68,69 157
8:38,39 175
9:55 28
10:36,37 189
10:40,41 167
10:42 168
10:42 169
11:21,22 194
12:5 9
12:48 152
14:21 162
15:11 180
15:11 182
15:11 183
18:10-14 190
19:10 69
19:37-40 185
22:31,32 45
23:42,43 192

JOHN:
1:46 17
5:2 173
8:12 71
13:17 91
17:21 60

ACTS:
5:29 154
17:22 37

ROMANS:
8:28 200
9:22 195
9:23 197

1 CORINTHIANS:
10:13 84

2 CORINTHIANS:
1:21 97
1:22 99
4:16 86
5:11 12
6:10 65
6:16 49

EPHESIANS:
2:11,12 40
3:12 43
4:3 59
5:14 73

PHILIPPIANS:
2:21 87
4:4 44

COLOSSIANS:
1:28 107

4:17 215
2 THESSALONIANS:
  3:15 102
1 TIMOTHY:
  1:15 158
  6:16 26
2 TIMOTHY:
  1:12 100
HEBREWS:
  10:25 82
  11:4 114
  11:5 117

11:8-10 120
11:17 119
11:24-26 125
12:16,17 124
JAMES:
  1:25 52
1 PETER:
  1:8 53
  3:15 103
  4:18 41
REVELATION:
  6:2 198

Other Sermon Outline Titles:

Briggs, S.R. and Elliot, J.H.
600 BIBLE GEMS AND OUTLINES

Jabez Burns Sermon Outline Series
149 SERMON OUTLINES
151 SERMON OUTLINES
199 SERMON OUTLINES
200 SERMON OUTLINES
201 SERMON OUTLINES
 91 SERMON OUTLINES ON TYPES
    AND METAPHORS

Marsh, F.E.
 500 BIBLE STUDY OUTLINES
1000 BIBLE STUDY OUTLINES
ILLUSTRATED BIBLE STUDY OUTLINES

John Ritchie Sermon Outline Series
500 SERMON OUTLINES ON BASIC
    BIBLE TRUTHS
500 CHILDREN'S SERMON OUTLINES
500 EVANGELISTIC SERMON OUTLINES
500 GOSPEL ILLUSTRATIONS
500 GOSPEL SERMON OUTLINES
500 SERMON OUTLINES ON THE
    CHRISTIAN LIFE

Easy-to-Use Sermon Outline Series
Edited by Charles R. Wood
EVANGELISTIC SERMON OUTLINES
REVIVAL SERMON OUTLINES
SERMON OUTLINES FOR FUNERAL
    SERVICES
SERMON OUTLINES FOR SPECIAL DAYS
    AND OCCASIONS
SERMON OUTLINES FOR TEENS
SERMON OUTLINES FROM PROVERBS
SERMON OUTLINES FROM THE SERMON
    ON THE MOUNT
SERMON OUTLINES ON THE PSALMS